CITY COLLEGE LIBRARY
1825 MAY ST.
BROWNSVILLE, TEXAS 78520

MONTEVERDI

Creator of Modern Music

Da Capo Press Music Reprint Series

MUSIC EDITOR
BEA FRIEDLAND
Ph.D., City University of New York

MONTEVERDI

Creator of Modern Music

LEO SCHRADE

DA CAPO PRESS • NEW YORK • 1979

CITY COLLEGE LIBRARY
1825 MAY ST.
BROWNSVILLE, TEXAS 78520

Library of Congress Cataloging in Publication Data

Schrade, Leo, 1903-1964.
  Monteverdi: creator or modern music.

  (Da Capo Press music reprint series)
  Reprint of the 1950 ed. published by W. W. Norton,
New York.
  Bibliography: p.
  Includes index.
  1. Monteverdi, Claudio, 1567-1643. 2. Composers—
Italy—Biography.
ML410.M77S35 1979   784'.092'4 [B]   79-12292
ISBN 0-306-79565-5

ML
410
.M77
S35
1979

This Da Capo Press edition of *Monteverdi: Creator
of Modern Music* is an unabridged republication of the
first edition published in New York in 1950. It is
reprinted by arrangement with W. W. Norton and Company, Inc.

Copyright, 1950, by W. W. Norton and Company, Inc.
Copyright Renewed 1978 by Leo Schrade.

Published by Da Capo Press, Inc.
A Subsidiary of Plenum Publishing Corporation
227 West 17th Street, New York, N.Y. 10011

All Rights Reserved

Manufactured in the United States of America

Claudio Monteverdi, from *Fiori Poetici*, 1644

MONTEVERDI

Creator of Modern Music

LEO SCHRADE

PROFESSOR OF THE HISTORY OF MUSIC
YALE UNIVERSITY

W · W · NORTON & COMPANY · INC · New York

COPYRIGHT, 1950, BY

W. W. NORTON & COMPANY, INC.

NEW YORK, N. Y.

First Edition

Printed in the United States of America
for the Publishers by Vail-Ballou Press, Inc., Binghamton, N. Y.

TO

ALBERT SCHWEITZER

as a token of deep
admiration

CONTENTS

7

ABBREVIATIONS

Adler, *HMG*	Adler, G. *Handbuch der Musikgeschichte*, 2nd ed. (1930)
AfMW	*Archiv für Musikwissenschaft*
CS	E. de Coussemaker, *Scriptorum de Musica Medii Aevi Nova Series*
DTOe	*Denkmäler der Tonkunst in Oesterreich*
Festschrift	*Festschrift Hermann Kretzschmar zum siebzigsten Geburtstage überreicht von Kollegen, Schülern, und Freunden* (Leipzig, 1918)
GBA	*Gazette des Beaux-Arts*
Kirch.Mus.Jb.	*Kirchenmusikalisches Jahrbuch*
MfM	*Monatshefte für Musikgeschichte*
M&L	*Music & Letters*
MR	*The Music Review*
RaM	*La Rassegna Musicale*
RM	*La Revue Musicale*
RMI	*Rivista Musicale Italiana*
SIMG	*Sammelbände der internationalen Musikgesellschaft*
StzMW	*Studien zur Musikwissenschaft*, Beihefte der **DTOe**
VfMW	*Vierteljahrsschrift für Musikwissenschaft*
ZfMW	*Zeitschrift für Musikwissenschaft*

ILLUSTRATIONS

PREFACE

ORACOLO DELLA MUSICA, such was the title addressed to
Monteverdi in 1640 by Benedetto Ferrari, one of his unreserved
admirers, a younger friend, and, as a musician, his devoted follower.
Monteverdi, "the prophet of music," the creator of modern music!
Indeed, the prophetic novelty of his work overthrew the art of his
ancestors to bring about the dawn of a new age. At the beginning of
the seventeenth century the new era rapidly approached its zenith,
and by 1640 the oracle's marvels were all but fulfilled.

Ferrari's lavish praise was exceeded by the actuality, for in Monteverdi's work modern music became a reality. The artistic principles he
developed within his work were to become those of our music and of
our musical understanding as well; they lived beyond the epoch that
brought them to light. Despite a long and uneven advance through
manifold complexities, music has always hewed to these principles;
even our own contemporaneous music has not abandoned them completely. In fundamental principles the art of Monteverdi has actually
more in common with the music of Haydn, Mozart, Beethoven, or
even of Brahms, than with that of Palestrina, his immediate and now
best-known precursor. And yet, more than two centuries passed before the age of Brahms, while on the other hand the young Monteverdi
shared about twenty-five years of life with the elder Palestrina. History establishes strange relations if genius guides its course, and rarely
does the logic of evolution cast any light upon the artistic phenomenon
in history. In view of the foundation of lasting principles, Monteverdi
was more than the creator of a style of historic significance. Styles
live but during their given epochs, and his specific musical idiom
lasted through the age of Bach. But the basic conceptions of composition, of harmony and melody, of expressiveness, all of which arose
with Monteverdi, transcended the ephemeral nature of style.

Monteverdi's true stature is again being recognized, for in recent
years his work has found many a new friend and admirer. If we do not

misread the signs, the new response to his music no longer comes from the small group of connoisseurs and scholars alone but from a large society of music lovers. We like to think that Monteverdi has entered our musical life to regain the place he once occupied in the musical culture of his time. His place in our own musical culture will be secured by the artistic greatness that exists irrespective of the specific idiom of any age.

The new response, however, seems, to be traceable to our own receptiveness to the music of Monteverdi. The "rebirth" of any music of the past is never truly successful unless we are prepared for it. Such preparedness undoubtedly results from a general, cultural, and social situation, rather than from a better understanding of technicalities or from purely aesthetic evaluations.

Monteverdi's operatic work is no longer an unknown quantity. That the composer of today values it is not surprising. Stravinsky's *Orpheus* reveals that there is again an affinity of minds between the artist of today and Monteverdi. But apart from any kinship among composers, Monteverdi's music drama has gained a new hold over a much larger audience. His *Orfeo* has become a standard work of the operatic repertory in France. The magnificent selection of madrigals recorded under the direction of Nadia Boulanger has had a most extraordinary influence on the favorable response of the modern listener. English concert life has frequently given the work of Monteverdi a prominent position, resulting in a rapid increase in the number of admirers and enthusiasts.

The Venetian Francesco Malipiero, Italy's renowned composer, has now completed the edition of all the works of Monteverdi. Despite the criticism that has been voiced against the scholarly accuracy of the edition, its great merits far outrank any aspects open to criticism. Should Monteverdi's work now become more widely appreciated, Malipiero's efforts will doubtless have the largest share in this newly won popularity. In this book, all musical examples are quoted from the edition of Malipiero.

Ever since Padre Martini, the eighteenth-century authority on erudite composition, scholarship has intermittently paid tribute to the prominence of Monteverdi in the history of music. The incomparable Carl von Winterfeld opened new vistas, but it was many years before historians generally followed his lead, broadening the views and exploring the historical details. From the eighties on, research has remained more or less consistently alive to the various problems of

Monteverdi's work; and the list of "specialists" now includes distinguished scholars from all countries: Emil Vogel, Hugo Leichtentritt, Louis Schneider, Henry Prunières, Francesco Malipiero, Domenico de' Paoli, Hans Redlich, and Jack Allen Westrup, the latter two being largely responsible for the recent resurgence of Monteverdi in English musical life.

The biography of Monteverdi has been dealt with by Emil Vogel in the most exemplary fashion. The fact that after his research of 1887 very little, and nothing of startling novelty, has been added to the biographical data, will always be an outstanding testimonial to the thoroughness with which he investigated his subject. As so often in the earlier history of music, the life of an artist rarely, if ever, presents itself as a complete entity. Our knowledge, in most cases, remains fragmentary, and of the fragments we know hardly any which shed light upon the intimate complexities of the artist's human nature. Rarely are we allowed more than a fleeting glance into the human aspects of the personality. All evidence is more or less directly related to artistic activity. The story of the artist's life is the story of the growth of his work. The composer's interpreter cannot attempt to present his life as a series of biological events. All known facts of the composer's life must be integrated into the artistic process. The analysis, under the strict guidance of historical thought, unfolds the aesthetic value together with the human substance of the artistic achievement. Thus, in this book, the attempt has been made to interpret the music of Monteverdi as an integral unity in which the life of genius, the problem of art, and the phenomenon of culture flow together to produce one of the most felicitous accomplishments in the history of music.

My gratitude goes to Arthur W. Dixon (Graduate School, Yale University) for his valuable help in the preparation of the manuscript, and, especially to John Derby (New York), whose admirable advice and penetrating suggestions yielded countless improvements of style; to Alvin Johnson (Yale University) for the careful preparation of the musical examples; to Miss Sylvia W. Kenney (Graduate School, Yale University) for reading proofs and preparing the index; to Miss Eva O'Meara for continual help in making all needed material available. Special thanks go to Alfred Einstein, whose most generous offer to read the whole manuscript in proof has been of great benefit. I gratefully acknowledge the interest and support given to this work by Edgar S. Furniss, Provost of Yale University.

Finally, my appreciation and thanks go to the staff of W. W. Norton & Company, whose most co-operative efforts have given the book its pleasant appearance, the author a gratifying experience.

LEO SCHRADE

Yale University, New Haven, Connecticut

PART ONE

The "Perfect Art": A Prelude to Monteverdi

CHAPTER
ONE

The Perfect Art, a Classic Ideal of Music in the Sixteenth Century

AMONG the blessings that come by chance upon mankind, the birth of an artistic genius may well be the greatest. The benefaction genius accords is as lasting as it is spontaneous, as comprehensive as it is specific. Truth undivided and wisdom abounding are the happy results when a genius creates a work of art that is in harmony with the art of life. Claudio Monteverdi was such a genius, at once prodigiously artistic and intensely human. He based his music on the secure foundation of truth of art and form, on integrity of craft and style, on the authority of law and norm. But his art also embraced the truth of human passion, experience, and tragedy, of all human existence. Monteverdi was the first and greatest among musicians in his blending of art and life.

We do not hesitate to view Monteverdi's new alliance between artistic form and human life as the most revolutionary advance in the modern history of music. Yet his innovations in purely musical techniques, structures, and idioms were no less revolutionary. Through this new union of music and man and by providing a new basis of musical composition, Monteverdi became the creator of modern music. So fundamental a change as he brought about can probably not take place without the force of a revolution. But the constellation of historical circumstances within which the artist is born determines whether this revolution shall occur with the abruptness of an outburst that sweeps everything aside, or as a slow growth, a gradual transformation which respects tradition. The vision of the artist and the nature of his genius are responsible for the revolution itself. But preparatory conditions

¹⁷

CITY COLLEGE LIBRARY
1825 MAY ST.
BROWNSVILLE, TEXAS 78520

and inner causes help to determine its character. It is these factors, perhaps more than the individual, that decide whether the revolution will be a sudden process of destruction or a well-considered metamorphosis.

Claudio Monteverdi was born in May, 1567, to Baldassare, a man of the medical profession at Cremona. At that time the musical art of the mid-sixteenth century did not forecast the coming of a revolutionary change. On the contrary, musical culture had already reached what men thought was the peak of artistic achievement. What had already been achieved in composition was regarded as the complete fulfillment of the nature of music. These compositions were the work of Northerners, and Monteverdi's birth coincided with the climactic phase of Netherlandish music. The Northern ideal of composition had held sway for many decades and now appeared to have taken the most exquisite, perfect, and classic shape. Mastery of the technique of composition was at its height, as any classic standards of style inevitably imply a matchless craft. Italians, as well as Northerners, looked upon Netherlandish polyphony as a perfect art that could not be surpassed. For it they had worked out the strongest intellectual justification. At the time of Monteverdi's birth this perfect art had also attained its widest geographical expansion. From one end of Europe to the other, in England and Germany, in Flanders and Austria, in Spain and France, in Denmark and Poland, in Hungary and Italy, one concept of musical art prevailed—the *ars perfecta* of the Netherlands.

For thirty years Monteverdi lived among the bearers of this perfect music and felt the power of this art at its height. But this music was not to be his. He was to eliminate its style and do away with the myth of its perfection, to become its greatest antagonist, to mark the beginning of a new age and become its herald. The perfect art he had studied in his youth—in fact, all music before his day—was to become archaic. The music of our time looks back to Monteverdi as its founder, and because of him we now regard all music before his day as old music.

This extraordinary success no doubt constituted a revolution. Since Monteverdi came face to face with a perfect art at its height, not at its end, this confrontation forced upon him three decades of severe struggles; it slowed down the pace of this revolution; it made him a traditionalist as well as a revolutionary, a conservative as well as an innovator, a careful builder who must weigh each stone to test its fitness for the new construction. Had Monteverdi been born twenty years later, the history of music would probably list him as an artistic Jacobin. But since for thirty years he was forced to cope with a well-established, at first apparently unshakable, artistic ideal, he became revolutionary in setting his goal, but conservative in his method of reaching it.

What was the position that Netherlandish music had attained? It had begun to spread over Europe about 1450, when Ockeghem, the founder of the school, was about thirty years of age. With its artistic achievements it created among musicians a pride in their abilities and a belief in the climactic importance of their compositions. With proud confidence the Netherlandish musicians made their appearance in the countries of Europe. They believed that after long centuries of barbarism and obscurity their work had raised music again to a high cultural level. The work of the Netherlanders made an impressive unity that prevailed in music from about 1450 to 1600. Although there were various shades of style during this period, there was such power in the unity of their musical concepts that Ockeghem and Palestrina used the same language. Despite the difference of nationality and the 175 years which separate the birth of the founder from the death of the last offspring, both spoke, as it were, the same mother tongue. This unity was such that any Netherlandish musician could always hear his musical language spoken in no matter what European country he chose as the scene of his activity.

As the various generations came and went—that of Ockeghem being the first; that of Josquin des Prés, Pierre de la Rue, Heinrich Isaac, Alexander Agricola, the second; that of Willaert and Gombert, the third; and that of Palestrina and Orlandus Lassus, the last—new contributions were made to an ideal that remained unalterable in principle. No novelty introduced by these generations affected the substance of their music. It is, perhaps, true that the uniformity of an artistic style is greatest at the time of its most vigorous expansion—here, probably, in the work of Josquin. At all events, it would naturally be greater at that stage than at the beginning, when novelty often provokes violent manifestations in the struggle between the new and the old—greater also than at the end of an epoch, when the new concepts that arise imperil the old ideal merely by their presence. Palestrina at the end of his life was no longer able to impose his style without question upon the whole of Europe, or even of Italy. His final years ran parallel with a turbulent development, the like of which the musical world had not seen for many a century. Yet Netherlandish music can be said to have maintained its essential unity unbroken until 1594, the year of the death of both Palestrina and Lassus.

Monteverdi, then, confronted an ideal of musical composition that had on its side not only the power of uniformity and international recognition but also the noble justification of old age. His struggles were also beset by other complications. He faced the intricacies of a doctrine of perfection in music that had been established in the North along with, and in support of, the Netherlands polyphony. At times, this doctrine of perfection seems to have been a more formidable opponent than the artistic style on which it was based. For when a doctrine is accepted as a creed, ideas become objects not of reason alone but of a faith that men will not easily sacrifice.

The numerous discussions of artistic perfection in the Netherlands compositions carried on by musicians in various countries may, on the surface, appear as pure theory; and we may well be reluctant to follow all the twisted paths of such theoretical thinking. But more was involved than a mere theory. The cultural achievements of the fifteenth and sixteenth centuries gave men a feeling of pride and enthusiasm and led to the belief that an altogether new epoch had dawned upon mankind. A universal movement in every province of intellectual life signaled the rebirth of man to culture and ushered in the Renaissance. In view of this new greatness and perfection, the consequence of this rebirth, men began to inquire into the beginnings of this inspiring process in order to understand more fully what had enabled mankind again to attain perfection. This search into the past served to strengthen their awareness of a culture restored to greatness. The search was common to all; artists, men of letters, musicians, shared in the quest; it was a European phenomenon. The Italian humanists who began the inquiry were joined by architects and painters, and the musicians followed suit. Thus originated the doctrine of perfection regained. Along with a fuller understanding of the new cultural beginnings came an insight into the various phases that had led to the climax of perfection. In the early years of Monteverdi's life, the doctrine of man's rebirth and the concept of a perfection that had been regained in all the arts were still firmly intrenched.

In the period between 1450 and 1600 musical leadership lay in the hands of the Netherlanders, so that it was quite natural for the Northerners to think that the restoration of musical culture was the result of their work; and they also made their contributions to the doctrine of rebirth.[1]

---

[1] This doctrine has never been discussed by historians of music. Monteverdi directly intervened in the doctrine, but in terms of opposition. The doctrine has a fascination of its own, and the reader will quickly draw the parallels between music, literature,

THE NORTHERN SCHOOL OF THOUGHT

The Netherlandish musicians, too, began to appraise the rise of their music as an event that called for a new estimate of musical development as a whole. Enthusiasm for the new achievements led to the frequent appearance of eulogies whose authors named the new style *ars nova*, a new art, and found it to be endowed with an amazing range of power. The first to outline the rise of music in this phase of culture seems to have been Johannes Tinctoris (*ca.* 1446–1511), the great theorist of the early Netherlandish school, who praised the works of the new composers. "Who does not know men such as Dunstable, Dufay, Binchois, Ockeghem, Busnois, Regis, Caron, Carlerius, Morton, Obrecht? And who would not bestow the highest praise upon these whose compositions, spread all over the universe, fill, with the sweetest sounds, the temples of the Lord, the palaces of the kings, and private homes?" [2] These words of praise are from that bold treatise in which he attempted to summarize the *Complex of the Twenty Effects of the Noble Art of Music.* Tinctoris inaugurated a new phase in the interpretation of musical history. The nineteenth of his twenty effects of music stated that "music glorifies all those that are expert in it." And whom did music glorify? Tinctoris first praised the musicians of Greek antiquity, the philosophers of music. He then turned abruptly to his own time, delimited by Dunstable at one end, by Obrecht at the other.[3] On the one hand was antiquity with its pre-eminent monuments of musical culture; on the other was the new art which the men of his day greeted with so great a feeling of elation. But there was nothing in between!

---

and visual arts. He will recognize the similarity of the ideas the musicians expressed and those he knows from the work of Leonardo Bruni, Flavio Biondo, Filippo Villani, Matteo Palmieri, Ghiberti, Alberti, Marsilio Ficino and others. The best and most recent discussion of the general problems is in Wallace K. Ferguson's *The Renaissance in Historical Thought* (Boston, 1948).

[2] In 1547, little more than half a century later, Henricus Glareanus dropped the name Dufay from the list of prominent composers. He had a more consistent view of Netherlandish music, the beginning of which he properly assigned to Ockeghem. Gifted with a keen sense of observation, he selected a more uniform group of representative musicians. No longer did he mention Tinctoris. Through Gafori, to whom Glareanus felt intellectually indebted, he nonetheless had indirect relations with the theoretical school of the "Fleming," as Tinctoris was called in Italy. Gafori had explored many a musical phenomenon with Tinctoris in the late seventies of the fifteenth century when both were at Naples. Yet by 1547 Dufay had not wholly been forgotten; he remained in the memory of men until the middle of the sixteenth century when Fra Angelico da Piccitono praised Dufay as a most excellent musician, a man "even of such excellence that in his day he held the first place and the highest degree among all other composers."

[3] CS, IV, 199f.

From the downfall of antiquity to the rise of the Netherlanders there was one huge gap—a complete lack of musical culture. It was with this juxtaposition of two widely separated cultural epochs in mind that the men of the Netherlandish school began to consider the historical development of music.

Tinctoris had more than once concerned himself with this problem of history. He devoted the entire preface of his famous treatise *Proportionale* to this question and discussed at some length the periods in which men contributed to the glory of music, and thus to their own renown. He assigned first place to the musical culture of antiquity. After it had reached the phase of fulfillment, there came "summus ille musicus Jhesus Christus" (Christ, the greatest musician). By the formative virtue of number, active in the world and in music alike, He had created the universe, as Orpheus by the same device had been the builder of cities in ancient times. In accordance with the early Christian idea of "Christ, the greatest artist," Tinctoris named Christ the greatest musician, the first in a new musical epoch of mankind. Most of the musicians Tinctoris then listed belong to Christian antiquity: Gregory, Ambrose, Augustine, Hilary, Martianus, and Boethius. Only two were musicians of the Middle Ages proper: Guido of Arezzo in the eleventh century and Johannes de Muris at the beginning of the fourteenth century; and they were theorists, not composers.

Again Tinctoris came upon that enormous gap in historical development. Without regard for any of the medieval stages in the art of composition, he skipped at once from Christian antiquity to the *ars nova*, whose "fount and origin" lay, for him, with Dunstable in England and Dufay and Binchois in Burgundy. They were immediately followed by the "moderni": Ockeghem, Busnois, Regis, and Caron.[4] Thus the art of music had reached its cultural peak twice only, and the curve of the historical process had dropped to its lowest point between antiquity and the new art.

Tinctoris made a further observation. Although he fully recognized the new rise of music, he also observed in his own time a certain decline, actual or feared, in the learned doctrine of music. As the erudite but indispensable basis of all knowledge in music and musical composition, his *Proportionale* was dedicated to the youth, to students who were anxious to study music as a "liberal and honorable" art. The student of music should become once more a student of a liberal art according to ancient conceptions. Antiquity and the new art should stand

---

4 *Ibid.*, p. 154.

side by side, and this proximity would make possible a direct rivalry between a living present and an ancient model—the old art offering the most ideal type of musicianship and the new, advancing as though driven by man's aspiration to excel the ancient culture.

When, out of his enthusiasm at the growth of musical composition, Tinctoris coined the phrase *ars nova,* the term implied a certain revolutionary spirit. This revolutionary character soon faded away, however, and even the term *ars nova* disappeared. The Netherlandish school expanded in ever wider circles, and more and more new composers achieved the distinction of leadership. With the advance of the school and the rise of new generations, the figure of Ockeghem receded, little by little, into the past, where myth added to his fame. The art of the Netherlanders became a fuller entity, and as new musicians, representative of the latest variations of the growing style, became members of the school, the emphasis upon various phases of this art shifted. Ockeghem and his work gradually disappeared from sight; Josquin des Prés came to the fore. The new situation was reflected not only by the position of Josquin's work within the total European repertory, but also by the unrivaled reputation his contemporaries bestowed upon him.

Up to the middle of the sixteenth century, Josquin maintained his place as Europe's greatest genius in music, and in the theoretical discussion of musical development he was singled out as the true representative of the style. Of those who sang his praises, Henricus Glareanus seems to have penetrated most deeply the characteristics of his music. Glareanus, the thoroughly humanistic and erudite friend of Erasmus, analyzed a great many of Josquin's compositions and from them deduced his own theoretical maxims.

Although Glareanus published his treatise, the *Dodecachordon,* about the middle of the century (1547), his theoretical observations were based upon the musical work of a generation dead for twenty years and more. He found very few living composers worthy of mention, much less of appreciation. He took into account only Netherlandish music and did not touch on the subject of secular music, which by 1547 had begun to advance with vigorous strides. He refused to consider the novelties his time produced and even looked upon his age as a period of cultural decline. "I notice that Germany perishes, once the noblest nation, now the most miserable of all; I fear intensely that, because of all her liberties and countless sects, Germany will before long be turned into a den of robbers." Glareanus was in utter despair at the sight of a land torn to pieces by religious strife. With a negative attitude toward his own time and a determined emphasis on an art already past, he was fundamentally a conservative. Indeed, he besought his contemporaries to adhere to Josquin's work, to imitate its ideal and complete perfection.

From the study of Josquin's work, Glareanus arrived at the principles of classicism in music. Josquin's work was "the perfect art to which nothing can be added, after which nothing but decline is to be expected." [5] It was to be taken as the lasting formula for all music deserving the name of classic, regardless of its period. Completeness in every formal aspect, richness of spirit, inner harmony between individual achievement, and an absolute, ideal form—these were the fundamental attributes of a classic work of art. Apparently Glareanus was the first to apply to music the idea that unless composers subordinated themselves to the established ideal nothing but decline would be the result. In consequence, he considered that music after Josquin was doomed to deteriorate from old age, since the law of nature would permit nothing else, and art necessarily obeyed natural law. At best the decline might be temporarily postponed if composers were willing to cling to the ideal as long as possible by imitation. Since "classicism" as an artistic idea was unimaginable without a definite concept of historical development, Glareanus formulated his idea of the *ars perfecta* in relation to the broad aspects of the history of music as a whole and set forth his views of historical growth in music.

In the thirteenth chapter of the third book of his *Dodecachordon*, he explains the reasons for his selections of illustrative musical works. Among them he grants preference to the "learned songs of Jodocus a Prato and other classical composers." In order that the student may learn from a variety of styles, he chooses other works also, which represent, as it were, "three different periods." The first group, of which "we shall give but a few illustrations," comprises compositions that "are old and simple and, so to speak, from the time when this art was in its youth. The first inventors of this style made themselves known about seventy years ago, I believe; as far as I can see, this first phase of music is not much older. To say quite frankly what I feel, the vocal composition in this style at times gives me wonderful delight because of its simplicity, if I take into account the soundness of the olden times and set in contrast to this the licentiousness of our music. For this composition of old allies a marvelous seriousness to a majesty that will im-

---

[5] Henricus Glareanus, *Dodecachordon* (Basel, 1547), p. 241: ars perfecta, "cui ut nihil addi potest, ita nihil ei quam Senium tandem expectandum."

press the ears of an intelligent person far more favorably than the unseemly titter and noise of those who are wanton."

In this picture of a historical development, Glareanus expressed an idea that was still current when Monteverdi made his great distinction between old and new, secular and sacred. When art is in its childhood, it is supposed to possess a striking simplicity which corresponds to the healthy vigor and intensity of that time of life. In contrast, at the time when Glareanus was living, art had attained greater variety, but men were anxious to pursue one novelty after another and exhibit the stigmata of a decadent and superrefined civilization. The luxurious *cupiditas rerum novarum*, for which Glareanus expresses his scorn in no uncertain terms, could be observed everywhere, not merely in the arts; it was even responsible for the countless religious sects that sprang up like mushrooms. Glareanus describes the past as simple, serious, and honest, and these characteristics came to be identified with "old"; the present, on the other hand, he calls noisy, decadent, shallow, foolish, confused by multiplicity. Works of art produced in times of folly must be flimsy toys. Later, as a result of Monteverdi's art, men will speak of the *stylus gravis vel antiquus*, the grave, old and sacred style, in contrast to the *stylus luxurians vel modernus*, the luxurious, modern, or secular style of music, but with no condemnation of the present, despite its "luxury."

Glareanus dated the beginning of the first, youthful, and vigorous style at about 1475.[6] This first phase of polyphonic choral music had Ockeghem as its foremost composer. Glareanus speaks of him as though his information were based on hearsay only: "Ockeghem is said to have excelled all others in genius." Yet he knew some of his works.

Then he characterized the second period. Its compositions "are such as belong to an art that grows in the state of maturing and of gaining strength, to become ripe at last; it is known that they have been sung forty years ago." In his opinion, this second generation flourished around 1500 and shortly thereafter; and its compositions were very pleasing because they already were products of the true spirit.

The last group of musicians soon followed, the best of whom was Josquin, their "princeps." His, then, is the perfect art, complete in itself. Nothing can be altered, nothing added; nothing is left to be desired. It is art at its climax about "twenty-five years ago." Josquin bequeathed to the world an absolute model of classic composition;

---

[6] Allowing for the writing of the treatise, the approximate dates may be *ca.* 1475, *ca.* 1500, and *ca.* 1520.

to be sure, his art may grow old, but men will do well to perpetuate it, for it can never be superseded.

But alas, musicians, in their anxiety to invent something new, were not content to remain on the pinnacle of perfect composition. "Unfortunately, this art now has slipped into such a state of unbridled laxity that it must call forth almost a feeling of disgust among the learned. The reasons for this are many. Especially, however, there is one reason: we are ashamed to follow the steps of our elders who rigidly observed the rules to be applied to the relationship of the modes, and in deviating from their traces we have produced a different, but distorted, composition that is by no means pleasant except that it is new. We have complained about this previously." And whenever an occasion arose, Glareanus continued to complain about novelties that disregarded the laws of an absolute art.

The completely negative attitude toward his own time that made him condemn its lack of spirit and seriousness was reflected in his judgments on musical style. Or did his musical criticism, perhaps, come first and his condemnation of the age follow? This is unlikely, if we consider the religious strife and inner tension of the age from which no one could keep himself free. In his despair at this time of religious and political discord Glareanus was not alone, although he presumably did not share Luther's wish that the day of the Last Judgment might dawn upon mankind and put an end to all the trifling achievements of human culture in which men so boldly took pride. Glareanus seems rather to have followed the view of Erasmus, who blamed Luther for having destroyed the values of the humanities, a view that even Melanchthon would not have rejected entirely. It is probable that Glareanus, through the eyes of Erasmus, saw musical studies rapidly declining as one of the liberal arts and hoped with the *Dodecachordon* to prevent the youth from completely losing sight of the *scientia musicae*. Erasmus once wrote to Pirkheimer that the humanities had perished wherever Lutherdom prevailed. As genuine a humanist as his friend Erasmus, Glareanus could not join in Luther's hostility to culture and to a life whose end was merely civilization.

Tracing the development of music in history, Glareanus recognized only everlasting antiquity on the one side and Netherlandish music on the other. Although he greatly admired the artistic values of the Gregorian chant, he did not place it securely in the main stream of the history of music. He appreciated the chant as an artistic, rather than a historical, phenomenon. He even went so far as to encourage its reform, thus understanding it, as it were, to be a "timeless" appearance. According to Glareanus, Netherlandish music was arranged in the sequence of man's ages: a phase of childhood, followed by an age of growth that led to a climactic period of prolific maturity and finally to old age.

Only five years after the *Dodecachordon*, Adrianus Petit Coclico, another of the admirers of Josquin and himself an offspring of the Netherlandish school, gave a new exposition of the history of music. In some of his ideas he was as queer as he looked, a pygmy with an antediluvian beard reaching to his knees. Listed in the registers of the University of Wittenberg as Hadrianus Petit Flemingus, Musicus, of Flanders, Coclico was about fifty-two years of age when he published his *Compendium musices* at Nuremberg in 1552. In the first part of his work he had a special chapter on the different classes of musicians, "De musicorum generibus," which gave him an opportunity to develop his views on the progress of music in history. He distinguished four classes of musicians. The oldest comprised those *qui primi musicam invenerunt* (who were among the first to invent music). It is a strange group, since it puts the most heterogeneous figures side by side: "Tubal, Amphion, Orpheus, Boetius, Guido Arenensis[!], Ockeghem[!], Jacobus Obrecht, Alexander et alii." Regardless of the quaintness and inaccuracy, what is the significance of this apparently senseless list? It seems still more senseless when we consider the names in his second group, musicians such as Dufay, Tinctoris, and Busnois, some of them older than Ockeghem, Obrecht, and Alexander Agricola in his first. One obvious explanation of this historical escapade is that Coclico no longer had accurate knowledge, either of Burgundian music, prior to that of the Netherlanders, or of the beginnings of the Flemish school proper. A second explanation, however, is found in the influence of medieval musical treatises, in which the writer was required to answer in more or less stereotyped fashion the question of the origins of music. Prehistoric, mythical, or legendary figures were indifferently listed as the inventors and originators of music. Names from pagan antiquity, from biblical history, from early Christianity, and from the Middle Ages made up the list, which was gradually expanded to bring it ever closer to the writer's own time. Since myth confers the greatest fame upon men, mention of any musician along with Orpheus, Pythagoras, Boethius, Guido of Arezzo was intended to confer the highest distinction in the hall of fame. Myth and legend were considered to have the singular power of translating an artist to regions of superhuman glory.

Only those of unique genius, creative originators in musical thought and composition, were ever granted that distinction. It was obviously such an idea, transmitted from antiquity through the Middle Ages and still held in the sixteenth century, that prompted Coclico to name Ockeghem together with Orpheus, as though he too were a legendary figure.

The second and third classes were the *musici mathematici* and the *musici poetici*. The second class, the masters of the *musica mathematica*, were utterly disqualified as composers, for Coclico had lost all understanding of the older music. He was one of the theorists who no longer recognized the doctrine of proportions as the foundation of musical structure, and so he brushed aside many great men of whom he apparently had little or no knowledge. They were lumped together as "Jo. Geislin, Tinctoris, Franchinus, Dufay, Busnoe, Caronte." In his opinion, their chief error was that they dwelt too long upon the teaching of rules and upon speculation. "They piled up immense difficulties by accumulating a multitude of signs and other things." Coclico had no appreciation of either the profound learning or the striking simplicity of the old masters whom the humanist Glareanus had praised but five years before. Everything he did not fully understand earned the abject title "mathematical," and, in his opinion, the works of the *musici mathematici* were only fit to be discarded.

There remained, however, the third class, the *musici poetici*, the "kings of music." "In the third group there are the most excellent musicians, and, so to speak, the kings of the rest; they do not cling to the teaching of the art, but combine theory and practice in the best and most learned manner. They pay attention to the virtues of songs and to the innermost disposition of compositions. They know how to ornament melodies and how to express all the emotions through them. This is the highest in music, the most elegant. The melodies of these masters are admired by everyone; they are the only ones worthy of admiration. Among these musicians Josquinus de Pres is easily the first and one whom I find every reason to prefer above all the rest. The most experienced musicians and the most skillful symphonists in this group are: Petrus de la Rue, Brumel, Henricus Isaac, Ludovicus Senffl, Adrian Willarth, Le Brun, Concilium, Morales, Lafage, Lerithier, Nicolas Gombert, Criquilon, Meyster Jan, Lupi, Lupus, Clemens non Papa, Petrus Massenus, Jacobus de Buis, and innumerable others." [7] Not only

---

[7] Petit Coclico, *Compendium musices* (Nuremberg, 1552), Prima pars, "De musicorum generibus."

did Coclico give Josquin first place in this rather large group, but he also qualified him as the master of all masters; he mentioned panegyrically Josquin's incomparable skill in teaching, although the composer interested himself only in a few real talents. Coclico also praised Josquin's scrupulous criticism of his own works and pointed to the composer's awareness that genius alone established the true value of any artistic work. This recalls the illuminating letter written to Duke Ercole of Ferrara by his art manager, who, in discussing the possibility of engaging either Isaac or Josquin, carefully weighed one against the other and attributed to Josquin's genius a uniqueness that money could not buy.

Coclico further set up a fourth class of musicians, who comprised his own generation. It appears that he was making a distinction in time, not in kind, for he characterized the fourth group as one that emerged from the school of the third class of composers: "ex tertii generis musicorum gymnasio profecti sunt." [8] Musicians of the third group had already perfected composition; they had established the *praecepta*, the ideal laws of musical form. They also knew how to penetrate to the core of the composition, how to ornament melodies: "sciunt cantilenas ornare." So did the composers of the fourth group: "ut suaviter, ornate et artificiose canant." Inviolable rules resulting from the perfect balance between theory and practice made it impossible for the fourth group to surpass the work of the third. To apply these rules consciously thus became the one task of composers of the fourth class. These younger composers could not hope to excel their teachers, but they should strive to maintain the level of their art and to preserve the classic ideals. Coclico then gave expression to conservative principles, and it is probably because of this conservatism that he placed frequent stress upon the *praecepta* as an inheritance, of which the musicians of his generation must show themselves worthy keepers. Shy of admitting that after the perfect art the curve of development must necessarily be downward unless the state of perfection could be drawn out, Coclico created this fourth, somewhat vague and colorless group of musicians, whose only characteristic was adherence to given precepts. They could never be creative originators, but were doomed to be merely continuators.

Those theorists who conceded indisputable greatness to the past but

---

[8] *Ibid.* There have been many controversies concerning the fourth group of musicians. We should recognize the emphasis Coclico placed on the *praecepta*, a continually recurring term. A distinct mastership in handling musical material according to artistic rules previously established—what does this mean, if not conservatism?

still believed in the possibility of further historical development were more liberal in their opinion of the art of their own time and escaped the static conclusions forced on the conservatives. Four years after the publication of Coclico's *Compendium musices*, Hermann Finck, another fervent adherent of the Netherlandish school, advanced the time of the latest perfection in music by a full generation. Finck's brilliant theoretical work, the *Practica musica* of 1556, was influenced by the spirit of Wittenberg, which was becoming the Protestant center of Netherlandish music. The *Practica musica* sheds much light on contemporary views of the historical development in music. The perennial question of the origin and the inventors of music gave Finck, like the other writers of his day, an opportunity to display his views. In the fifth book of his work he explained his relation to music past and present. He anxiously avoided the simple and easy estimate which so often misguides the thoughtless adherent of progress, that the latest achievement is always better than anything previous. Setting aside any personal predilection for past or present, he "impartially" compared "the more recent musicians with those of the earlier period"—the men of his own time with those of Josquin's generation. His links to the Netherlandish music were still strong, and he conceded to the two groups an "equal measure of natural gifts." But while the older composers had distinguished themselves through a larger proportion of "art and study," it was Finck's opinion that the younger men carried off the prize with "the gracefulness of their delivery." [9] "It has rightly been said" that the older generation created the art and the younger "polished it," but it would be a mistake, "which some people nowadays seem to make," to put the older generation far in the background, "for we still enjoy the outstanding accomplishments of the older." "They have laid down a foundation built upon firm principles." They also enabled their successors to take advantage of the artistic model they invented. It was but natural that the younger men should refine the art they inherited, keeping, nevertheless, always within the limitations set by the ideal. Although Finck admitted many older musicians to be worthy of praise, he still admired Josquin as the *princeps musicorum*. In him he recognized a man of the highest genius and profound erudition, a diligent inquirer into the nature of musical art, the composer who had shown modern musicians the true path.

Finck thus accepted the creative uniqueness of Josquin's work and

---

[9] The qualification of the younger men has much in common with the fourth group of Coclico.

regarded it with intense admiration, while conceding that Josquin must suffer the consequences of historical progress. He saw music advancing beyond Josquin, for originality of invention did not stand still because of the greatness of the past but was part of a continuing process. Among inventors in music, Finck included new contributors who came after Josquin, and he omitted the idea of an absolute perfection or, rather, brought the point of perfection closer to his own day. Finck attributed the latest important achievement to Gombert, whom he took to be the central figure among the composers of his day, and credited him with having shown his contemporaries how to compose [10] in a manner somewhat different from that of Josquin. To Finck, the art of music seemed still to move forward and the end could not be foreseen. Since Gombert had been successful in reaching a new peak, would all artists now come to a standstill, or would they follow a downward path? Finck believed his contemporaries were on a pinnacle, but he did not say what manner of future he visualized for music.

In discussing the Netherlandish musicians, Finck showed a growing awareness of national, or native, talent in comparison with the overpowering and ubiquitous might of the Netherlandish style. His was not so much a "nationalistic" tendency that made him "relate a few things in defense of the Germans" as a certain pride in the rise of native composers. He had no desire to deny the superiority of the Netherlandish musicians. He refuted the commonly held opinion that the Germans were completely unmusical, and disagreed with the saying, at that time on all lips, that the Germans bawl, the Italians bellow, the Spaniards howl, the Gauls sing.[11] While Finck claimed nothing more for his countrymen than a better appreciation of music, a defense such as his, made possible only by the awakening of new talent, indicated a change in the relation of native groups to the predominant, international style.

The Germans of that time never went so far as to characterize any Netherlandish composition as "outlandish" music, but the Italians, who at first praised the Netherlanders as incomparable masters of musical art, gradually moved away from the Northerners to a point where relations with them were all but severed.

At first they had not doubted that all accomplishments in music were due to the Netherlanders or, to use the Italian term, the *Oltremontani* (men of the North). All the theoretical literature in Italy was full of such unlimited recognition. It would be natural for a learned musician

---

[10] "Qui omnibus musicis ostendit viam."
[11] The saying includes the Netherlandish musicians among the Gauls.

or theorist to form his judgment according to the Northern compositions he knew, but it is significant that the cultivated layman and the general public also expressed complete admiration for the musical work of the North. Every honor was given to the *Oltremontani*, and apparently it did not occur to the Italians that these men from beyond the Alps were actually foreigners. Thus in 1506, at the time when Josquin's work began to get its firm hold over Italy, Vincenzo Quirini, the Venetian ambassador to the Burgundian court, wrote in praise of the Netherlanders that "there were three things of highest excellence": first, the finest, most exquisite linen of Holland; second, the tapestries of Brabant, most beautiful in design; and third, "the music, which certainly can be said to be perfect." [12]

While Quirini took note of the unmatched perfection of Netherlandish music, other Italians went even further and, in their eulogy of the Netherlanders, used arguments they were to reserve for their own music as soon as their relationship to the *Oltremontani* underwent a basic and complete change. They maintained that the Netherlanders had fulfilled the very nature of music with their art. Later, the Italians were to say that these same Northerners had distorted its nature because they lacked all natural gifts for music. Yet around the middle of the century Italians did not find anything that was more natural in its perfection than the music of the North. Federico Badoero, at that time the Venetian ambassador to Philip II, said in plain terms that the Netherlanders were born for music (*alla musica par che siano nati*) and that their composers were excellent.[13]

This, then, was best expressed by Lodovico Guicciardini, son of the famous Florentine historian, who during the sixties published at Antwerp a widely read description of the Netherlands. In speaking of their music he stated that the Netherlanders were "the true masters of music"; and with the climactic culture of ancient music in view, he accorded to the Northerners the restoration of music as an art; they brought it back to perfection, for one particular reason: "They owned music as a property natural to men and women, one that enabled them to sing in a natural manner, with abundant grace and melodiousness. It was through this that the Netherlanders succeeded in joining art to nature; because of this newly achieved unity, they effected that display and harmony, of voices as well as of instruments, which could be

---

[12] "La terza è la musica, la quale certamente si può dire che sia perfetta," in *Relacioni degli Ambasciatori Veneti al Senato raccolte, annotate, ed edite da Eugenio Alberi* (Florence, 1839), Series I, Vol. I, pp. 11–12.

[13] *Ibid.*, Series I, Vol. III, p. 290.

perceived throughout the courts of all Christian princes." This was the highest possible praise, coming from an Italian whose artistic feeling had been trained by the study of antiquity and whose sense of criticism had been guided by keen observation. It was the musician of the North who, in singing and composing alike, had revealed the nature of music, who, indeed, had come closest to the natural forms in his artistic accomplishment. And who were the men whom, according to Guicciardini, nature had endowed with such singular musical gifts? "In modern times there came from this nation Giovanni del Tintore di Nivelle . . . a man of extraordinary faculty, Josquino di Pres, Obrecht, Ockegem, Ricciafort, Adriano Willaert, Giovanni Mouton, Verdelot, Gomberto, Lupus Lupi, Cortois, Crecquillon, Clemente non Papa, and Cornelio Canis, all of whom have died." [14]

Not without significance is this adherence to the past at a time when Italian composers had begun to gain in reputation. By the time Guicciardini wrote his description of the Netherlands, Palestrina had reached a certain maturity of age and work, and the Venetian school, though under the artistic patronage of the Netherlandish Willaert, could count among its members many an Italian who was bringing renown to his country. Guicciardini's recognition of the uncontested predominance of Northern music in Europe is all the more astonishing in view of the way Italians were then glorifying their painters and sculptors as perfect harmonizers of art and nature.

It was shortly before the middle of the century when Italian writers began to mention their own musicians by the side of the Netherlanders. The *Oltremontani* were still ranked highest, and the names of Italians did not appear in competition with those of the Northerners but merely as docile pupils who were learning how to harvest fruits of Northern instruction. In his *Recanetum de musica aurea* of 1533, Stefano Vanneo was one of the first to add a number of Italian names to the list of leading Netherlandish composers. It was more than a score of years after the middle of the century before Italian and Netherlandish names were placed in rivalry and Italians began to think that the disciples had, after all, become as good musicians as their teachers. Italians were then given first place in lists of composers, although they still kept their work strictly within the confines of the Netherlandish style. They had in no way estranged themselves from the artistic ideal of the North-

[14] Lodovico Guicciardini, *Descrittione di tutti i Paesi Bassi* (Antwerp, 1567), p. 42. For the most recent discussion of the superior position of *Oltremontani* in Italy, see the new standard work on the history of the madrigal: Alfred Einstein, *The Italian Madrigal* (Princeton: Princeton University Press, 1949), I, 6ff.

erners, but they felt they had now acquired equal skill in a field the Netherlanders formerly had all to themselves.

In Venice, whose greatness in music Monteverdi was later to increase, there arose a peculiar situation. The Venetian school attracted many native musicians and gained the reputation of being bold in artistic experimentation and liberal in the international communication of artistic thoughts. Composers of this school even tried their hands at a reinterpretation of the Netherlandish style, but they did not abolish its fundamental principles, however bold their novelties. The Venetian school spoke more audibly than any other with a note of its own, and all who knew music immediately recognized its original character. As the century drew to its close, such Venetians as Giovanni Gabrieli expanded the inner capacities of this style to the extreme. But despite their efforts to create a specifically Venetian variant, these musicians never freed themselves from the Northern model, nor was that their intention. The school had been founded by Willaert, a Netherlander, and its last member, Giovanni Gabrieli, devoutly adhered to Willaert's ideals. The compositions of the Venetians indicate the extreme possibilities of the Northern style, but they never went beyond its limits.

ITALIAN REPRESENTATIVES

The subordination of Italian music to Netherlandish principles was advocated by the chief spokesman of the Venetian school, Gioseffo Zarlino (1517–1590). His *Istitutioni harmoniche*, the first edition of which appeared in Venice in 1558, was a glorification of the work and style of the incomparable Adrian Willaert and, through him, of Netherlandish music. Zarlino, the most distinguished theorist among Willaert's Italian students, applied his profound knowledge of musical materials to a penetrating exegesis of Netherlandish composition. The older he grew, the more he made his theory conform to that ideal which had produced a style of music that was essentially religious. As the Counter Reformation began to get a firmer hold on Italy, and especially after Cardinal Giovanni Pietro Caraffa, known for his fervent advocacy of the *riforma*, became Pope Paul IV, Zarlino inclined more and more toward the religious renewal that reform was expected to bring about. He showed this leaning not only in his theological treatise but also in his theory of music. And the religious quality embodied from the beginning in Netherlandish music now lent itself to the new hope for a revival of the original intensity. After 1555, when the Counter Reformation made itself felt for the first time, Palestrina also began to pay closer attention to the oldest, already obsolete, characteristics of the Netherlandish style, whose religious expressions were thought to have been the purest. Thus, at the moment when the long reign of the Netherlanders was nearing its end, sacred music was more than ever identified with the Netherlandish style. With a completely new meaning, Northern music had become representative of the "perfect art."

As Hermann Finck had moved the climax of this perfect art ahead by a full generation, from Josquin to Gombert, so Zarlino shifted his emphasis forward to Adrian Willaert. Zarlino, too, gave a complete outline of the history of music and set up antiquity as the standard of culture. Since the Greeks considered music "the highest and most singular doctrine" and held their musicians in the greatest esteem, inestimable reverence had been bestowed upon them. The general decline of the learned disciplines which ensued coincided, strange as it may seem, with the coming of the Christian age. Music toppled from the height where it had stood in ancient times and fell to the bottom of the abyss: "da quella somma altezza, nella quale era collocata, è caduta in infima bassezza." Music was held to be vile and abject when there were no longer any learned men to care for it. But recently a new ascent, a return to the old musical culture, had occurred, for "by the grace of the Lord our times now have Adrian Willaert, surely one of the rarest minds." This genius "explored, in the manner of a new Pythagoras, all the particulars of what is possible in music; he discovered innumerable errors which he began to eliminate; he brought music back to that degree of honor and dignity which it commanded in times past and by necessity must occupy." It was he who gave the clearest evidence that music had developed toward a new climax.

But what was to come after Willaert? Zarlino belonged to a younger generation, and although he did not put the classic art so far back as to exclude his own lifetime, Willaert lived but four years after the first publication of the *Istitutioni*. As a member of the school of Willaert, Zarlino felt obliged to maintain the classic ideal; indeed, he could do nothing else unless he chose to admit a decline after Willaert, and this he shrank from doing. Zarlino was fully aware of novelties, which he feared would imperil his ideal, but instead of recognizing that an essential decline in the classic art was taking place, he insisted that the alarming signs of deterioration were merely symptoms of superficial diseases, such as the mishandling of the choral technique or other details of the performance, and did not affect the organism of the composition. Thirty years after the *Istitutioni*, he once more and without change expressed his point of view regarding the historical development of music and the *accrescimento*, or growth, of the arts. When he published his *Sopplimenti musicali* in 1588, the signs of a new time were still more in contradiction to the "somma altezza" upon which he had placed Willaert. But Zarlino died in 1590 without abandoning his ideal of a perfect art; he did not admit the decline of his type of music or recognize the birth of a new style.[15]

Perhaps the most famous theory of the development of the arts was that expounded in Italy by Giorgio Vasari, who was a contemporary of Zarlino. Vasari discussed this theory of growth mainly in the prefaces to the various parts of his chief literary work, *Le Vite de piu eccellenti architetti, pittori, et scultori italiani*, the first edition of which—dedicated to Cosimo de' Medici—appeared in 1550. Only the edition of 1568 contained this theoretical discussion in full, in addition to other supplementary material. In accordance with the prevailing conception of history, Vasari maintained that ancient art was not only the oldest but the most perfect and had established incontestable models for all artistic forms. To him antiquity was something apart, not a period in history, one among others, but the measure of all things artistic, the expression of the very essence of beauty in art.

With the breakup of the Roman Empire, the arts entered upon their longest phase of decline. "That fall involved the complete destruction of the most excellent artists." Although much of this destruction was due to the recklessness of the barbarians who descended on Italy from the North, Vasari boldly asserted that the Christians must share the responsibility. "But the most harmful and destructive force which operated against the fine arts was the fervent zeal of the new Christian religion. . . . Every effort was made to remove and utterly extirpate the smallest things from which errors might arise." Zarlino, less audacious than Vasari, spoke merely of the barbarous epoch that started with the fall of the Empire, a fall that brought about "ruin and disorder,

---

[15] Lodovico Zacconi occupies a place of particular importance. The first part of his huge treatise, the *Prattica di Musica*, appeared in 1592. (Although the date of publication is 1596, the researches of Chrysander, Kretzschmar, and Vatielli have proved the existence of the earlier edition.) In this treatise Zacconi showed himself to be an ardent and uncompromising follower of the Netherlandish art. He laboriously differentiated between the "ancient" and the "old" composers of the various generations of the Netherlanders and thereby outlined the history of music in the same way as other theorists. (Among the "old" composers he named—in 1592!—Zarlino and Palestrina!) Later, however, he changed his point of view considerably, and in the equally ponderous second part of the *Prattica di Musica*, published thirty years later (1622), he is a different man; he has experienced nearly every phase of the breakdown of the Northern art.

through the negligence of men, the malignity of the age, or the decree of Heaven." [16]

The period when all the arts slumbered while barbarism was wide awake lasted for centuries. According to Vasari, it was the work of Cimabue that started the arts on their new ascent. As art progressed, the artists became more familiar with antiquity. The first period reached its height with Giotto. But "in the first and earliest period the three arts [painting, sculpture, and architecture] are seen to be very far from perfection, and though they possess some amount of excellence, yet this is accompanied by such imperfections that they certainly do not merit extravagant praise. . . . Having now, if I may say so, taken these three arts from the nurse, and having passed the age of childhood, there follows the second period in which a notable improvement may be remarked in everything." This second period, the youth of the arts, had men of distinction such as Brunelleschi, Masaccio, Lorenzo Ghiberti, and Donato, but it could not be considered truly perfect because of the improvements that came afterward. The masters of that time accomplished "beautiful and good" works, "but as a general rule they did not attain to the state of perfection of the third age." They "made great additions to the arts," but "they lacked freedom," necessary for perfection.

This second period was surpassed by the "golden epoch" under Pope Leo X (Giovanni Medici, son of Lorenzo the Magnificent). During his pontificate (1513–1521), art entered its manhood and produced works without equal. Michelangelo, above all, succeeded at last in controlling the material of art as completely as any ancient artist. He even excelled antiquity and became the master of all times. "The man who bears the palm of all ages, transcending and eclipsing all the rest, is the divine Michelangelo Buonarroti, who is supreme not in one art only but in all three at once. He surpasses not only all those who have, as it were, surpassed Nature, but the most famous ancients also, who undoubtedly surpassed her. . . . If by chance there were any works of the most renowned Greeks and Romans which might be brought forward for comparison, his sculptures would only gain in value and renown as their manifest superiority to those of the ancients became more apparent." Vasari also believed that the artists of his age were not rewarded for their efforts to the same extent as the Greeks—a view Zarlino shared with him. If they were equally rewarded, the men of

---

[16] These words which Vasari wrote in the preface to the first part of his *Lives* are almost literally quoted by Zarlino in the *Istitutioni*.

his age would soon prove themselves "greater and better than the ancients ever were." Vasari frequently repeated his idea that Michelangelo was the first to overcome all the obstacles that had stood for centuries between art and the achievements of antiquity. "He has displayed such art, grace and vivacity that I may say with due respect that he has surpassed the ancients, making difficulties appear easy, though they are found by those who copy them." This idea was also current among musical writers, who maintained that classic form consisted in superiority over the ancients as well as in easy control of matter and form.

So great was the praise Vasari bestowed upon Michelangelo that his own generation suffered by comparison, perhaps even more than he may have wished to imply. Theoretically, little remained for the successors of Michelangelo to do, unless they were willing to resort to complete imitation. To vie with Michelangelo, who had achieved the fullest harmony between art and nature, became indeed the aim of the next generation. This goal distinguished the fourth period, which Vasari himself represented. He accepted the perilous position in which the artists after Michelangelo found themselves. Their work must always be threatened by the possibility of decline, since none could hope to surpass their paragon.[17]

A CHANGE TO OPPOSITION

A new phase came with the Florentine musicians, who belonged to an artistic society known as the Camerata. Their leading theoretician, Vincenzo Galilei, discussed this change in his famous *Dialogo della musica antica et della moderna* of 1581. An ardent opponent of Zarlino, Galilei made the cultural aspects of ancient and modern music the central theme of a program intended to rid musical composition altogether of Netherlandish concepts, which he considered a collection of monstrosities. His argument was developed against the background of musical history as a whole. He followed Vasari closely and must have

---

[17] It seems that Vasari observed the beginning of a new phase in the latest works of Michelangelo. Historians of art have assumed that in his old age Michelangelo advanced toward the baroque; that, in fact, he became the founder of the baroque. Vasari's passage is extremely interesting. He says that "before his death he [Michelangelo] burned a great number of his designs, sketches and cartoons, in order that no one should perceive his labours and tentative efforts, that he might not appear less than perfect." . . . He was "endeavouring to realize a harmony and grace not found in Nature, saying that it was necessary to have the compasses in the eye not in the hand, because while hands perform the eye judges." *Lives*, in Everyman's Library, edited by Ernest Rhys, translated by A. B. Hinds (London, New York, 1927), IV, 171.

studied the *Lives*, for he reconstructed the history of the arts in the same manner and with the same point of view. Galilei also placed the beginnings of the art of painting in the time of Cimabue and Giotto, who "renewed" the art by bringing it closer to nature as the ancient masters had done. For that, they were worthy of praise, and if they had some deficiencies, those were excusable, since their period retained something of a primitive simplicity. The artist still suffered from the novelty of the matter he dealt with; but it was a true revival which Cimabue and Giotto had begun.[18]

As the painter had to acknowledge antiquity as his teacher, so the musician should take the art of old as his guide. Not only did the Greeks regard music as one of the liberal arts (that is, arts worthy of the free man—*degne d'huomo libero*), but they were also the masters and inventors of music (*maestri, e inventori di essa*) as well as of all other sciences. Such were the words with which Galilei began his *Dialogue*, and they were to establish the musical point of view of the seventeenth century. The Romans, indebted to the Greeks for all they knew of music, had cultivated its theatrical side for recitations in tragedies and comedies, rather than its scientific or theoretical aspects. Continually occupied with political affairs, the Romans were in part responsible for the fact that music as a liberal art later came to be forgotten. The barbarians of the North had brought about final disaster with their inundations which swept over Italy and erased all signs of culture. The destruction of ancient culture meant the end of all civilization, for man's very impulse to acquire learning was extinguished by the darkness that fell upon science. Men lived for many centuries in a "grave lethargy of ignorance," desiring no knowledge, content in their inertia. Of the art of music they knew nothing, until first Gafori, then Glareanus, and finally Zarlino, brought music out of the darkness in which it was buried and gradually led it back to its present state.

Such was the historical development of music up to the time of Vincenzo Galilei. The picture he drew harmonized with that of other writers before him, but a characteristic difference does present itself. Whereas other writers had attributed the rise of musical culture to composers of the Netherlandish school, such as Ockeghem, Josquin des Prés, Gombert, or Willaert, Vincenzo Galilei singled out the prominent theorists as innovators, men who certainly excelled in their profession but whose importance scarcely equaled that of composers in deter-

---

[18] V. Galilei, *Dialogo della musica antica et della moderna* (Florence, 1581), pp. 124, 141f.

mining the course of musical composition. However insignificant this preference for the theorists may appear on the surface, it was presumably due to Galilei's attitude toward the music which the theorists represented. In this he took a decisive step, presaging a revolution in music and intended to do more than destroy mere formulas.

Other writers, in dealing with the same problem, had declared that after centuries of a pitiful degeneracy the Netherlandish school enabled music to reach the height of the ancients. Galilei found no such achievement in the compositions of that school. Even the theorists whom he singled out as envoys of a new musical culture exhibited serious deficiencies. "To some intelligent men they did not appear to have truly restored music to its ancient state, and this could be verified by innumerable passages of ancient histories of both poets and philosophers; neither did they obtain the true and perfect notion of music; this, perhaps, may have been caused by the rudeness of the times in which they lived, the difficulty of the subject, and the scarcity of good interpreters." Yet they were praiseworthy, if for nothing else, at least for the impetus with which they moved many other men to attempt the reinstatement of music in all its old perfection.[19] Here Galilei cut himself off from the Netherlandish "past" and from all that was connected with it up to his own day. It is significant to see Galilei considering even Zarlino as a man of the past, as if Zarlino's deficiencies could be explained by the general "rudeness" of a primitive past, though he was but three years older than Galilei himself. Nothing could close the gap that Galilei opened between his own world and that of Zarlino, whom he marked as a musician of a time now obsolete. Monteverdi's day would come, when all music that exhibited Netherlandish influence would be declared antiquated and remote, whether composed around 1600 or much earlier.

But it is on larger and more momentous issues that Galilei was at variance with his contemporaries. Was it true, as many past and present writers assumed, that the Netherlandish music of their time had brought the art back to the cultural level of the ancients? In his discussion of ancient and modern music Galilei never lost sight of this fundamental question; it was the core of his comparisons. On this point he parted company with most musicians of his time; for it, he fought relentlessly. He agreed with those who believed that the downfall of the ancient

---

[19] *Ibid.*, p. 1. It is noteworthy that Galilei speaks of both the merits and deficiencies of Gafori, Glareanus, and Zarlino, in exactly the same manner and wording as, in the course of the *Dialogo,* he is to speak of Cimabue and Giotto.

world had brought upon men the catastrophe of barbarism from which they were unable to recuperate for many centuries. When at last, around the middle of the fifteenth century, men manifested a new desire to restore the arts and sciences, a new phase in history seemed to dawn.

In this movement, music had its share, and musicians, in great haste and with false hope, thought that each step would bring them closer to what they imagined the ancient ideal to be. They were anxious to work out their contrapuntal, Netherlandish style with more and more refinement. This style consisted chiefly in combining several independent melodies into a harmonious entity. "It is a matter of certainty . . . that the present manner of singing several melodies together simultaneously is not longer in use than 150 years." Counting from the year when the *Dialogue* was published, the fresh start of musical history was, therefore, around 1430. "From that time on up to the present day, all the best musicians were united in expressing their belief that music had reached the greatest peak of perfection that man can possibly imagine." So they thought; but they were grossly in error. For, Galilei went on to say, "from the death of Cipriano de Rore, a musician truly extraordinary in this manner of counterpoint, up to the present, music has proceeded by decline rather than by increase." [20]

Cipriano de Rore, distinguished also by other men than Galilei (Monteverdi was to praise him in highly respectful terms), Netherlandish by birth, had been a leading figure in sixteenth-century Italy and had died in 1565. Granted that he was a prominent musician, who had mastered his style of composition in sovereign fashion; granted he had succeeded in marking his music with the sign of excellence; granted that he was perfect in his own way: further Galilei thought he could not go. On the matter of style Galilei parted company with Cipriano. The Northern counterpoint was not in his line. The very fact that Cipriano wrote in that style severely limited his merit. If he was said to have been perfect, his perfection should be taken as relative only. One should measure his greatness in precisely such terms as a Netherlander would apply to his composition. Making this allowance, Galilei could say that Cipriano had developed his style toward a climax. As Glareanus had seen in Josquin the representative of the *ars perfecta*, as Finck had distinguished Gombert as the leading master, as Zarlino believed the summit of musical composition to have been reached by Willaert, so Galilei placed Cipriano de Rore at the peak of the development, with one essential difference: Glareanus, Finck, and Zarlino

[20] *Ibid.*, p. 80.

respected their masters as messengers of their own musical faith; Galilei assumed the aloofness of an observer who approaches his object for critical analysis. No longer should men be allowed to imagine as many peaks of perfection as there were generations of composers. Galilei made it clear that the decline had already come; the Netherlandish style had gone downhill since Cipriano's death. Other musicians might hold a different opinion, but for Galilei the decline was an indisputable fact.

For the first time, then, the development of music was viewed under aspects of historical observation. In it Galilei discovered the rise, climax, and decline of a musical style. Men's achievements come and go, as men themselves are born and die. This law of history presented itself to Galilei as a result of his opposition to the school of contrapuntists, whom he wanted to show up as distorters of the true music. Although he uncovered in musical development the law of natural growth—birth, maturity, and death—and thus provided an idea indispensable for future historiographers, he was no true historian. An observant outsider, he was not dispassionate; assuming no share in Netherlandish music, he was not indifferent; reflecting on that style from a distance, he was not disinterested. His every word, in fact, was put down *cum ira et studio*.

The hatred the contrapuntists awakened in the mind of Galilei was fanned by his belief that none of them had truly revived the ancient music. He constantly measured the so-called modern music, the *moderna prattica*, against the ancients and presented an almost endless list of reasons to prove that contemporary music had nothing in common with the *musica antica*. This bias casts its light upon every problem Galilei tackles; it alone orders the chaotic material of his *Dialogue*.[21] Galilei's tone ranges from calm and restrained judgment to aggressive invective, from appreciative respect to derisive contempt. The reader may wonder at this vacillation unless he realizes that Galilei's mind is passionately possessed by the desire to eliminate the music of the contrapuntists and to revive that of antiquity.[22] His passion often drives him into open contradictions or embarrassing misinterpretations of both Greek and Netherlandish music. We should, nonetheless, accept this passion as a human phenomenon without which his scholarship is unthinkable.

It took wondrous courage to declare war against the contrapuntists,

---

[21] Galilei's *Dialogo* has often been criticized for the lack of any organization, as recently by Fabio Fano, the editor of Galilei's compositions.

[22] A clear distinction should be made between the revival of Greek music proper and the restoration of Greek culture in music.

who had on their side the strength of experience given them by a tradition of one and a half centuries. The "declaration of war"—this is the term used by Galilei's Florentine friends—affected the majority of the most renowned composers in Italy. The adversaries Galilei challenged were by no means dull, brainless, or unlearned, as a man who had lived in their midst for sixty years must have known. Were he acting to preserve a tradition, we should readily characterize Galilei's attitude as the obstinacy of an old man impatient with the arrogance of youth, like Artusi's later condemnation of Monteverdi. But Galilei did not act to preserve the tradition; his message was addressed to the musician of the future. We must bear in mind that Galilei was a contemporary of Palestrina, in fact, five years his elder. And while, by 1580, Palestrina was becoming more and more involved in the technique of the oldest Netherlandish phase, Galilei, though speaking with respect of Palestrina, was making a determined effort to undermine this ideal of composition. One cannot belittle the significance of Galilei by pointing to the mistakes he made in his treatise, or to the disloyalty he showed his one-time teacher Zarlino, or to the contradictions between the ideal he preached and the music he actually composed. Although he was the first to compose monodies, Galilei was not dynamic enough to bring about the complete renewal of music that he foresaw.[23] As a thinker, however, he had the vision to prophesy the future of music and the courage to pull down the old that the path might be free for the new.

In his vision he saw monody as the art of the future, before which the *moderna prattica*, maintained by the Northerners and the Netherlandish Italians, had to give way. This contention was backed by the authority of the ancients, whose wealth of thought was inexhaustible enough to provide arguments for every case. Did Galilei's opponents make use of ancient sources as well? Did they consider their work as good as Greek music? Galilei plainly called this assumption an impertinence, for not even the ethical effects of ancient music were achieved by the contrapuntists. One was forced to conclude that either their music or the nature of man had considerably changed "from its first being," which the Greeks had established for both man and music. It was sheer ignorance that made the contrapuntists think they had mastered the meaning of ancient music. The Northerners, furthermore, devised rules

---

[23] The *Lamentations of Jeremiah* and the song of Dante's Count Ugolino in the monodic composition of Galilei are now lost. The extant works—madrigals, instrumental compositions, motets—do not show Galilei to be superior to composers of the school which he attacked.

and laws of composition which they made out to be sacrosanct. Galilei denied these inviolable laws (the *leggi inviolabili*) of the contrapuntists. So long as Greek music was not involved, Galilei showed himself well on the way to the discovery that no laws are eternally inviolable in art, but since he continually supported his thesis by arguments drawn from Greek music, it is clear that his discovery did not result from free and critical observation of the historical development. It was Monteverdi who in his compositions would demonstrate the changing nature of musical laws against the arguments of Artusi and all those who still had faith in the *leggi inviolabili* of the Netherlanders.

Galilei also discussed the relation between word and tone, a subject that he thought needed urgent revision. Galilei stands here on firmer ground, when he criticizes the violence done to the word by the contrapuntal style. Never should the word be degraded to the inferior and ancillary function forced upon it by the polyphonic work of the Northerners; its leading role should be re-established according to the practice of the ancients. The word must be understandable in the physical sense, so that the listener can follow the text as a whole. This is not possible in a polyphonic composition, which tears the text to pieces and calls for the simultaneous enunciation of different words. It is, therefore, monody alone that, in true kinship to ancient art, can once and for all restore the word to its old dignity.

There were still further principles governing the relationship between word and tone. The textual rhythm should be reflected in the music, if not literally, at least by a full awareness that the text has a rhythmic order of its own to be followed by the music. Finally, the meaning expressed through the word should have its musical equivalent. On this subject Galilei's ideas are in part related to the past, in part indicative of the future. The meaning of words is discovered by their importance in the sentence, and such key words imply an "emotional" element, called the *affetto* (the "affection").[24] This is to be treated as the *concetto dell'animo*, to use the term of Galilei and the men around him, for it is in the mind of the composer that the affection becomes a concept to be translated into the medium of art. The purpose of all composition is to imitate this affection; it is a constant with which the composer must always deal and which is independent of his own feeling or experience. At this point, Galilei advises the musician to beware of a frequent error, the literal imitation of the individual

---

[24] Throughout this text we shall use "affection" as the English seventeenth-century term for *affetto*.

word. In any text there are many words that signify physical objects or motions and the like. The composer will be at fault if he attempts to depict them realistically by a musical figure formed from the material image of the object. If he attempts to apply the principle of realistic imitation to every word in the text, he will shatter the unity of the work or the unity of a certain part of the composition. The continual change of affections will confuse the listener, who, carried from one realistic picture to the next, will not understand the composition as a whole, will not grasp its predominant affection. Hence Galilei demands that the composer determine which affection governs a phrase, or a sentence, or the text as a whole, and see to it that the music expresses this affection alone. However rigidly Galilei may propose this rule, he himself does not observe it without exception. There are passages in his madrigals that, as pictorial translations of individual words, betray a form of musical realism we should not expect to find in his works, though we know it to have been lavishly used in other compositions of his time.

Although the influence Galilei exerted was almost entirely limited to the society of which he was one of the spiritual founders, the Camerata Fiorentina, the merits with which the historian has to credit him go far beyond his influence on his contemporaries. The *Dialogue* is the most important as well as the most comprehensive theoretical document that originated in the Camerata, and it is probably not too much to say that Galilei fathered the Florentine version of monodic music. Monody, of course, cannot be regarded as the invention of a man or a group of men, or even as an "invention" in the ordinary sense; nor can it be explained as the result of purely theoretical considerations, for a reform of music such as the Florentines had in mind can never come from theory alone. In this, they made in all likelihood their most serious, if not fatal, mistake: they believed in the creative capacities of the theory of music. They were convinced that integrity of theoretical considerations, guided by ancient authorities, would exert a salutary effect on music. They trusted that a clarification of what was truly ancient and what was not would be enough to redeem the elementary powers inherent in musical composition. Monteverdi was to have no such confidence; he was to begin at the beginning.

Galilei's accomplishment was in the field of criticism, where he passed a severe judgment upon the music of his time and thus forced musicians to take inventory of the materials used in their compositions. Habits of long standing, though sanctified by age, were to be examined for their vigor and usefulness. When Galilei raised his voice against falsifiers of the ancient art, a new program was declared. The emulation of the ancient music, a practice familiar to all writers of the sixteenth century, was suddenly arrested and pushed in a fresh direction. Musicians had previously believed they could rest from their efforts to restore musical culture, for they had already achieved what was achievable within the scope of the Netherlandish counterpoint. Galilei came to disparage nearly all they had done; to tell them that they had never been more remote from the ideal than in their own works, that the restoration of ancient music was far from being a reality, that all had to be done over again. In his *Dialogue* Galilei dwelt at great length on such "abuses in the music of today" (*abusi della musica d'hoggi*); he wanted to demonstrate that an end should be set to the old before the new could grow.

It has always been said that the new epoch of music begins around 1600 with the foundation of the musical drama, but it is notable that Galilei pays no particular attention to it; his *Dialogue* offers no point of departure for the opera. In his compositions—the *Lamento* of Count Ugolino, by Dante, and the *Lamentations of Jeremiah*—he may have offered practical guidance to the music of the future. When, in 1582, he submitted these two works to the Duke of Mantua, he stated that he had composed them "according to the use of the ancient Greeks"—that is, in the manner of solo song, not in the polyphonic ways common among living musicians, "contrary to their bounden duty." [25] Friends and followers of Galilei saw in these two compositions the beginning of the new music. In a letter to Giovanni Battista Doni, Pietro de' Bardi (Conte di Vernio) declared of these works: So "great was their novelty that they caused much envy generally among the professors of music and were a source of delight to the true lovers of music." [26] Though of general historical significance, this was not the tendency which Galilei expected his *Dialogue* to foster. It was his intention to remove all the obstacles that barred the musician from the land of the future. Galilei fulfilled an important critical task when he demonstrated "what a difference there is between the ancient music and that which people

---

[25] See the letter in Bertolotti, "Artisti in relazione coi Gonzaga," *Atti e Memorie della R.R. Deputazione di St. Pat. per le Prov. Modenesi e Parmensi*, Ser. III, Vol. III, Part I (Modena, 1885), pp. 196f.; also: *Musici alla corte dei Gonzaga* (Milan, 1890), pp. 6of. The letter has often been reprinted; see Angelo Solerti, *Gli Albori del Melodramma*, I (Milan, 1904), 39.

[26] Angelo Solerti, *Le Origini del Melodramma* (Turin, 1903), p. 145.

commonly sing today." [27] The music that men had held to be beyond reproach had now been exposed to the light of severe criticism, and it was Galilei who took the first decisive step toward a change in sixteenth-century music.[28]

---

[27] In the letter which Galilei wrote to Guglielmo Gonzaga when he sent him his *Dialogo*. The letter is dated January 2, 1581 (1582). Cf. Bertolotti, *Atti*, p. 195: "quanta differenza sia dell'antica musica a quella che comunemente oggidi si canta."

[28] With this, the attitude of Italians toward the *Oltremontani* definitely changed to antagonism. In analogy with similar reactions, noticeable in the visual arts, the *Oltremontani* were named Goths, that is, barbarians. Netherlands musicians were now thought to be as barbarous as the Goths who destroyed the Roman Empire. (See, for instance, the letter of Pietro de' Bardi, in A. Solerti, *Le Origini*, p. 144.) Giovanni Battista Doni, the first and best historian of the Florentine Camerata, is most vociferous on the subject. He speaks of the "inundations of the Barbarians," ancient and medieval; he scoffs at the "German-Arabian" style (identical with the Gothic style; see Milizia, *Memorie degli Architetti* [Parma, 1781], I, 135). He even ridicules the names of Netherlanders: "whose very names demonstrated that they were barbarians." This mockery at Northern names came in vogue when Francesco Berni started his pasquinade, the *Poesia Bernesca*, against Pope Hadrianus V from the Netherlands. Berni, a Roman with the most malicious tongue and wit, subtle, but fatally spiteful, thought that all Netherlanders were ridiculous for the very names they have, "names so foolish as to make a dog laugh." Others, at the beginning of the seventeenth century, reported on the historical evolution of music dispassionately. The first who assumed the objectivity of a historian apparently was Marquis Vincenzo Giustiniani, a "gentleman historian." (See his "Discorso sopra la musica de' suoi tempi," in Angelo Solerti, *Le Origini*, pp. 99ff., 103ff.) Finally, Pietro della Valle (see his "Discorso della musica dell' età nostra" of 1640, in Solerti, *Le Origini*, pp. 148ff.) declared that compositions such as those of Palestrina were now held in esteem, not because they were used for practical purposes, but because they were preserved by being deposited in a museum, like the most beautiful antiques. Palestrina's work had thus become a museum piece.

CHAPTER TWO

The Position of the Ars Perfecta in Sixteenth-Century Italy

MUSIC in Italy in the second half of the sixteenth century presents a picture of the most colorful variety. The colors are, in fact, so dazzling as to confound the student. Of the uncounted thousands of compositions, only an extremely small number are accessible in modern editions [1]—a fact that is too often forgotten. It is misleading to judge the musical art of that time merely from the accomplishments of a few prominent men, but the enormous quantities of material to be examined are enough to frustrate the most tireless efforts. The further the student advances beyond the middle of the century, the more disconcerted he is apt to become. Faced with the task of setting the compositions in modern scores, the historian of sixteenth-century music must feel, most of the time, like a scribe who copies endlessly with a feeling of increasing futility.

It is necessary, however, to attempt a description of musical style in Italy at the time when Monteverdi began consciously to react to his artistic environment. It is, of course, generally accepted practice to sketch the historical background of an artist's life work, and if Monteverdi had merely made new contributions, no matter how valuable, to music as it then existed, if he had merely added another story to a structure already of staggering height, this background would provide the student of history with an understanding of the connecting

---

[1] In material the sixteenth century is one of the most prolific periods in the history of music. Critical modern editions comprise no more than one-hundredth of what actually exists. To interpret sixteenth-century music largely on the basis of secondary literature must lead to deplorable results.

phases of a gradual development. Monteverdi's work, however, almost from the outset, was in reaction against the prevailing musical style; not to continue, but to resist was his mission. He did not intend to use the impressive legacy of his elders but to oppose the influences of his environment. Monteverdi started out as a heretic, and until he had found his own idiom, he simply dissented. What was the musical style that he set out to neutralize? To answer this question, we must describe the characteristics of the musical environment, not of Cremona alone, but of the whole Italian repertory of music.

This repertory can be classified by drawing three lines across the confusing variety of musical compositions, with their stylistic diversities, their different schools and regions, their artistic personalities, native and foreign. This arrangement—somewhat simplified, to be sure—is clear enough to serve as a guide based on the various categories of composition. The first group, then, comprises sacred music, with the Mass, which was always strictly liturgical, and the motet, which was partly liturgical and partly religious in a more general sense. The second group reaches into the sphere of secular music and includes the madrigals. The last group, also secular, embraces native songs, such as the canzonetta, villanella, or villotta.

Masses and motets rank first, chronologically and quantitatively, and created the prevailing style of the epoch. It was in the medium of sacred music that Netherlandish music achieved its epochal distinction. A certain shift of emphasis took place within Netherlandish music, but in its first phase, initiated by Ockeghem, the Mass was the dominant form and stands out as the ancestor of the style. Neglecting the forms favored by his predecessors, Ockeghem composed an extraordinary number of Masses. The generation of Josquin des Prés gave rise to an increase in the number and importance of motets, which became the chief vehicle of the style in the second phase of Netherlandish music. Changes in composition first became noticeable in the motet, which was used for every kind of experiment. Josquin brought the motet into prominence with his famous *Ave Maria* and other works composed in the decisive decade from about 1495 to 1505. He achieved a transformation of the Netherlandish style by dropping the *cantus firmus* and inventing for every phrase of the text a free motif to be stated successively by each musical voice. This new style was continued by the next generation of Willaert and Gombert and lasted throughout the sixteenth century. Compositions based on a given *cantus firmus* gradually decreased in number and, with some composers, disappeared completely. Josquin's contemporaries also placed new emphasis upon the motet, though to a lesser extent than that master. His great rival Heinrich Isaac tried to maintain the Mass as the most significant form, as the relatively great number of his compositions in that category clearly proves. His extensive collection of motets, the *Choralis Constantinus*, so called perhaps because of its regional implications, does not really belong in the movement initiated by Josquin's *Ave Maria*. Even so, Isaac's motets indicate the rising importance of that form in the musical repertory. The third member of the triumvirate, Pierre de la Rue, the most outspoken in his Netherlandish manners, distributed his interests evenly between Masses and motets. His use of a *cantus firmus*, however, reveals a greater loyalty to the heritage of Ockeghem. Lack of contact with the Southern art which greatly influenced Josquin's development may partly explain this loyalty, but that is a question which cannot be answered here.

The vast contributions of Josquin's generation established the predominance of the motet and resulted in a rearrangement of the musical repertory. In purpose and performance, the motet became less restricted and better fitted to every expression of religious life. The Netherlandish school made the motet a composition for which such broad characterizations as "religious" or "sacred" must often suffice. Indeed, so manifold were its uses that in the course of time "motet" became a kind of collective name for every composition with a Latin text. At first it was used to mean a composition whose religious character was shown objectively by its place in the liturgy. As a liturgical work, the motet took the form of *De Tempore* music, allied to the church year and dedicated to the proper of the Mass and the officium. Hymns, psalms, sequences, passages of the Gospel, sentences from the Holy Scriptures—all these, when set to music, were called motets. The term motet was, furthermore, applied to a large group of compositions with Latin words. These compositions were religious in a broader sense, for they were not linked to any specific service and, as a matter of principle, were not taken into the service. For that reason their religious character was considerably less distinct. They might express some religious "feeling," but since they were not connected with any religious act as a definite part of the service, their place in the religious life of man shifted constantly. Dedicatory texts for saints, pious invocations, prayers, poems that gave expression to man's religious devotions might furnish the material for such motets. Sometimes the direct purpose for which they were composed cannot be identified. By stressing the private nature of religious devotion, these motets represented the sphere of religious activities outside the church. The indefinite function of such motets did not, of course, preclude an intensity of religious feeling, which might be present, but had no unequivocal terms of expression. Sometimes the feeling can be inferred from the particular circumstances surrounding the work. When Luther, in an hour of despair and with forebodings of death, wrote to his friend, Ludwig Senfl, the composer replied with a motet of religious consolation, *Non moriar, sed vivam*. But it is rarely that the circumstances of compositions were recorded.

The motet's great variety of purposes was not without influence on its style. It often became a medium for experimentation and thus an interesting indicator of stylistic development. In writing occasional motets the composer presumably felt less responsibility to tradition than when composing a Mass or strictly liturgical motet, which demanded that he abide by rigid, though unwritten, laws whose slightest transgression would attract criticism. In a Mass or a liturgical motet he was more exposed to the public eye, which judges by custom.

The third group of purely occasional compositions was very small in the Netherlandish school. The great festival motet in the days of Dunstable and Dufay accounted for much of the total output and was distinguished not only in number but also in quality, exhibiting the most striking structures and devices of the time. But contributions in this form by Netherlanders diminished rapidly, more in quantity than in quality. When writing such works, composers like Josquin and Isaac still maintained the extraordinary devices which give distinction to both the work and the occasion. Isaac's two motets, one dedicated to the Emperor Maximilian I, the other to Pope Leo X, are compositions whose masterly techniques were quite unusual even in a period which abounded with composers of the greatest skill.[2] The next generation of Netherlanders still composed festival motets, as is shown by the work of Willaert, Gombert, Crecquillon, Senfl and others. Gombert, who lived for many years in the suite of the Imperial court, was often called upon to provide motets for political occasions. Perhaps his most famous composition is the Mass he composed for the coronation of Charles V at Bologna in 1530. Some of his works also reflect the religious strife of which he was a close witness at the Imperial court; and he composed a motet for the Diet of the Empire at Augsburg, as did Senfl. The oc-

---

[2] *Optime divino,* for Pope Leo X, written for six voices, was published for the first time in 1520 after Isaac's death. The work, therefore, must have been composed between 1513 and 1517. For stylistic reasons, *Virgo prudentissima*, for Maximilian I, dates from the same period.

casional motet was of less interest to composers of the last generation of the sixteenth century. While Orlandus Lassus admired this kind of motet, we know little of Palestrina's activities in this form. The festival motet was no longer distinguished by the finest devices and techniques of the time; it became standardized and lost its pre-eminence.

In all three classes the motet regularly formed the largest part of the repertory, appearing with changing stress in one or the other group but always preserving its distinguished significance. The second group is stylistically the most interesting, because of its variety and a degree of individuality that the liturgical motet of the first group was slower to achieve and because it was ready to accept influences even from the secular side. The madrigal and the motet here exerted a mutual influence on each other's stylistic characteristics. Toward the end of the century this group was well on its way to becoming modernized—that is, from a stylistic point of view, secularized—so that few obstacles remained to be overcome by 1600 when composers began to transform the motet to accord with the vocabulary of the monodic style. The preceding experiments had fully prepared the motet to undergo the change into the monodic form.[3] Although our knowledge of the actual output of compositions cautions us to avoid any hasty generalization, it appears that the position of the motet during the sixteenth century casts some light on its place in the baroque age, when it had lost its previous significance and the composer complied with the tradition in various new ways. For the strictly liturgical motet, the composer sometimes preserved the Netherlandish style, by then completely outmoded; for the free religious motet, he preferably chose the modern secular style of monody; the great festival motet, however, died out and was, in purpose and artistic quality, replaced by the cantata.[4]

The third and last group of the musical repertory, comprising only secular compositions, contains on the one hand the madrigal, the most distinguished representative of all profane music, and on the other a

[3] This does not always hold true for composers who did not allow their style to be turned away from the Netherlandish motet of Palestrina's time. Angelo Berardi, for instance, who continually cites Palestrina whenever an example is to be shown, observes with no pleasure at all: "I moderni Musici vanno cercare d'allontanarsi in certo modo dallo stile antico, non per altro solo che per ritrovare una singolare espressione della parola, per maggiormente muovere gli affetti e passioni dell'animo." See *Miscellanea Musicale* (Bologna, 1689), p. 48.

[4] In Bach's work the position of the motet, which had become a funeral composition, has completely changed. The composition of motets no longer belonged to the functions of the cantor. The liturgical motets were taken from an obsolete repertory, a hundred and more years old. See Leo Schrade, "Bach: The Conflict between the Sacred and the Secular," *Journal of the History of Ideas*, VII (New York, 1946), 151ff.

body of minor, but at times greatly influential, compositions such as the villanesca, villanella, villotta, canzona, canzonetta. Before the rise of the madrigal, Italian secular music was largely confined to the frottola, barzoletta, strambotto, and related types. Many characteristics of music at the close of the century have their source in secular music, yet its status is peculiar and bound to baffle the historian. He is apt to consider Italian achievements in nearly every province of human culture as essentially profane in spirit, at least up to the middle of the century, even though from the Reformation onward the authority of the secular spirit began to wane with the growth of the new religious conscience of man. From Leon Battista Alberti almost to the time when Caraffa, the leader of the party of *riforma*, acceded to the papal throne, the world of culture was ruled by the secular, or better, the human and urbane. We have been accustomed to look upon the man of the Renaissance as the ruler of the *orbis terrarum*. This does not, however, imply that the sovereignty of the temporal sphere abolished the authority of the religious element. The mundane spirit may have affected religious intensity, but not for a moment did it discredit religion's right of existence. It merely assigned to religious expression a secondary place where it does not so readily meet the eye of the historical observer. It must be remembered that religious belief in the theological and dogmatic sense and the expression of religious thought in terms of art are two different matters, and that one does not necessarily imply the other. Religious expression in art lives under altogether different conditions from those necessary for the life of dogma. The spirit of the Renaissance is as far from atheism, or even dissent, as the art of the romantics is from true religion. Although religion must be regarded as basic in the formation of a culture, cultural epochs do not necessarily call for religious forms of expression at all times. When we look at the half-century from about 1480 to 1530, we are so dazzled by the profane brilliance of both art and man that at first, perhaps, we see solely the workings of the secular mind, and it is only on closer scrutiny that we discover traces of the religious undercurrent. The religious faculty of man has not been made void; it has not been abrogated; but since it has been driven underneath, the lasting impression of the epoch is of its mundane spirit.

A glance at the musical repertory seriously disturbs this impression, for it is predominantly religious. We imagine a period of refined urbanity and profane grandeur, yet its music expressed the most intense religious devotion. It was also the time of the revival of ancient studies and the humanism of the liberal arts, called liberal because of their power to make man's mind free. At this point, there was at least some agreement between the general situation and music, for the musical theorists of the period knew the ancient theory of music and the importance Greek writers attributed to music. But their knowledge was an accumulation of tradition rather than a direct relationship to ancient sources; and in this respect the theorists were closer to their medieval predecessors than to the venerated ideals of antiquity. The sixteenth-century theory of music was more medieval or traditional than the theories of the other arts.

Among the general notions that make up the idea of the Renaissance, not the least important is its unbreakable link with Italy; we think of Italy when we think of the Renaissance. Even discounting the calamitous effect the Reformation had on intellectual life by reason of its hostility to the humanities, we can readily agree that in artistic matters the Germans understood little of the true Renaissance and that the French were quick to make the Renaissance an academic proposition. Thus, the creation of the Renaissance style in art is almost entirely an Italian affair. But the music of that age hardly fits into such a picture, for there the Italian element is missing. In the visual arts the Italians set the pace and tone for the whole of Europe; in music they submitted to the art of the Northerners. They recognized that leadership in music was not theirs, that greatness, fame, and, in fact, all the elements that go to the forming of a style, must be attributed to the Netherlanders. Italian churches and palaces were full of Northern composers; any position of renown was occupied by them. The Italians simply recognized that they had no composers who could compete with the *Oltremontani*, who had created the style for religious compositions, such as motets and Masses.

There were, however, genuine compositions in Italy, native in origin and characteristic in style. This secular music was composed from the last quarter of the fifteenth century to about 1530, and when the Netherlanders wrote secular songs, as they did but rarely, they followed the Italian concept closely. Carnival songs, strambotti, barzolette, form the bulk of these compositions whose structures had nothing in common with the Netherlands music. Is this, then, the major contribution of music to the Italian Renaissance, and is it in these native songs that the spirit of the Renaissance chiefly manifests itself? Certainly not—and for several reasons.

Compared with the great art of motets and Masses, these native songs are inferior, quantitatively and qualitatively. Their number does not approach the quantities of music composed by the Northerners, and their position in the general repertory has little weight. In terms of artistic quality, the native songs have an unpolished, artless simplicity that is completely foreign to the leading style. Their raw, boorish character and almost shocking directness may bring out, at times, tones of extraordinary freshness, in comparison with the codified manifestations of a highly developed style, and they often seem robust and healthy, as a rustic youth. Indeed, many of these native songs had their origin in the music of rural folk, of village and peasantry, so that simplicity and neglect of art are their distinguishing marks. But by the time of the Renaissance the circumstances under which these songs appear have nothing to do with rural conditions or the life of simple folk. They have been raised into the sphere of civilization and art, and are composed by a group of professional musicians and artists in the service of the court. The simplicity they display is no longer a natural expression of men accustomed to a "natural" behavior, but an artificial product made for and by people whose satiated taste regards simplicity as a device to relieve the monotony of a stylized life. When noblemen trained in the grandiose discipline of a sovereign culture suddenly discover the charms of a farmer's life, the tone of their delight is too shrill to be genuine; it shows signs of a weariness induced by a strict and burdensome code of life. A *retournez à la nature* has been sounded more than once without ever bringing man back to "natural" conditions. Although the courtier Gontier is filled with delight at the unknown taste of coarse bread, milk, cheese, and butter, consumed in a pleasant countryside—a brook, of course, a forest, and a meadow set the scene —he will still make love to his noble lady according to all the rules of the palace. The idyl is at best a dream, and the simplicity of the native song in the Renaissance, crude as its vitality may appear, is nothing but a literary experience used by the artist to amuse the nobility. It does not herald the dawn of an age that proclaims a new relation of man to the natural world or calls forth in him a new sense of naturalness. An off-spring of low parentage, the native song has been admitted to the court, where it sounds like a "parody" of country life and its simplicities.[5] In imitating the native crudeness of the song, musicians of great skill intentionally blunder against artistic rules and make mistakes that would be ludicrous were they to appear in compositions of higher categories.

[5] For the first time, Alfred Einstein called attention to this parodistic character of the native song; see "Die Parodie in der Villanella," *ZfMW*, II (1920), 212ff.

By the time the native songs thus became "art," though of a lower rank than works in the prevailing style of the time, they had traveled a long way from their original contact with folk customs. When Baldassare Castiglione speaks of them—and he knows this type of music and its composers well—he shows them exclusively in the atmosphere of the "Nobleman's" life. To the question whether the Nobleman should display his activities to the public eye and go about among the crowd of simple people from the country at a dance or any other festivity, Castiglione gives a negative answer. But Gaspar Pallavicino relates that in his part of the country, in Lombardy, men do not have such scruples; the young folk, noble and lowly, mingle with one another, dancing, fencing, sporting. He sees no harm in this liberal behavior, for such contests do not test nobility but only physical power and dexterities wherein country people quite often match men of noble birth.[6] Lombardy appears to have been one of the regions where the artistic composition of native songs flourished. Castiglione's ideal courtier finds pleasure in listening to these songs and regards them as an extraordinary addition to his entertainments. In order that he may legitimately avoid any contact with their boorish originators, he takes the songs out of their hands and provides his own supply by imitation. He is fully aware that they are now an art which he allows to exercise an influence upon him. In speaking of the marvelous effect of music, Castiglione mentions one of the chief composers of this type of song, Marchetto Cara, along with Leonardo da Vinci, Mantegna, Raphael, Michelangelo and Giorgione, the creators of pictorial impressions,[7] thus placing a representative composer of native songs, artistically imitated for purely artistic purposes, directly by the side of artists who certainly have nothing to do with the native art of the lower classes and peasants.

Although bestowing upon the native song the rank of art, the ideal courtier seemed fully aware that this type of music was inferior to the Netherlandish art. The fact that the native song was no longer an anonymous expression of popular customs but an artificial product appeared to be the only reason for granting it the dignity of art. In style it was as far from the Netherlandish concepts as simplicity of popular expression is from subtlety of artistic accomplishment. The Netherlandish work and the native song up to 1530 existed side by side in different categories, one clearly separated from the other. There were

[6] Baldassare Castiglione, *Il libro del Cortegiano,* ed. L. Corio (Milan, n.d.), p. 94.
[7] *Ibid.,* p. 63.

a few Netherlanders who, because of their connections with Italian courts or some individual interest, tried their hands at imitating the peculiar forms of the native songs in Italy, but they would never allow any such experiment to influence the "true" art which was theirs. On the contrary, they were concerned with keeping the spheres of style clearly apart, thus maintaining rank and order in the musical repertory. The Northern composers showed only a desultory interest in the composition of native songs, probably because of the trivial effort needed for such works—songs that were pleasant entertainment but not forms in which to manifest their musicianship. They had long grown unaccustomed to occupying themselves with simple structures and had inherited an aversion to such forms from the very beginnings of their school.

It took the refined and artistically more appropriate poetry of the madrigals to attract them to secular music in Italy. They had already made French profane music conform to their contrapuntal, choral style, when they discarded poems with fixed structures, such as the rondeau, bergerette, or virelai, and chose a loose poetical form like the chanson as more appropriate. This gradual elimination of pre-established structures was quite natural, since they called for a sectional organization of the work according to groups, periods, and clear caesurae, and could hardly be reconciled with the Netherlands style, which demanded an uninterrupted, sweeping flow of contrapuntal lines and carefully avoided cuts, phrases, and all that might set off segments of the work. Naturally, also, the Northern composers dropped all forms based on refrains which strongly favored sectional organization. This process was already well advanced when Petrucci came out with his earliest editions; and by 1533 when Attaingnant began his last output of chansons, secular compositions had lost contact with fixed forms because of the immense power of the Netherlandish style. The elimination of the fixed form was complete, and isolated specimens that here and there emerge from incoherent situations do not count. We may recall that it remained for the poets of romanticism to reintroduce the forms of ballades, rondeaus, and virelais to literature; it was they who unearthed those structures from the grave where the Netherlandish musicians had buried them.

In Italy all native songs were based on pre-established structures that were difficult, even impossible, for the Netherlandish style to handle. The textual refrain and the strophic order of the poem were barriers that kept the native song from being overrun, and were the chief reason why the Netherlanders did not attempt the native forms in Italy with-out many reservations. It must arouse our astonishment that the Nether-landish generation which died out around 1520 kept away from the frottola, while less than a decade later Netherlanders set off an outburst of madrigals. The canzona has always been considered the intermediary between the frottola and the madrigal,[8] yet the assumption of this transition does not fully explain why the older Netherlanders, many of whom composed the French chanson in quantities, neglected the frottola when it was at its height. Josquin paid little attention to it; Loyset Compère made only a scanty contribution; Heinrich Isaac seemed more interested than the others, but this may be due to local conditions at Florence, where we know him to have taken part in the composition of carnival songs. An inner antagonism on the part of the Netherlanders appears to have been the decisive reason.

By 1530 the Netherlands musicians themselves had taken the initia-tive and become creators of madrigals. They seem to have started not so much from the tradition of the frottola as from their own set of ideas.[9] The "founders" of the madrigal—Verdelot, Arcadelt, and Willaert—came from the North, and the earliest madrigals probably were their reaction to the low standards of the native songs. These madrigals may also reflect their desire to please an aristocratic world which expected musical art to be genuinely expressive of its own under-standing of cultural entertainment. They most certainly represent the answer given by the Netherlanders to native talent. That the level of secular music should suddenly be raised the very instant the *Oltre-montani* lay their hands on it can otherwise scarcely be understood. Moreover, the madrigals were poetically of free structure and did not follow a pre-established scheme; consequently, they were ideally suited to the form of music the Netherlanders had brought into being.

Their composers immediately began to eliminate the structural con-trasts between the voice that carried the melody and the instruments that functioned as accompaniment. These contrasts had been marked in the secular songs previous to the madrigal. Because the Netherlanders "vocalized" the chanson in France gradually and persistently after

---

[8] Cf. Rudolf Schwartz, "Die Frottole im 15. Jahrhundert," *VfMW* (1886), pp. 427ff.; especially, Gaetano Cesari, "Le origini del madrigale cinquecentesco," *RMI*, XIX (1912), 1ff., 380, and separate (in German). Walter Rubsamen, *Literary Sources of Secular Music in Italy* (1943), pp. 7f.

[9] Alfred Einstein, in Adler, *HMG*, I, 361, points out that the development leads directly from the frottola to the villanella, while the frottola did not directly produce the madrigal.

1450, from the very start they made the madrigal primarily a vocal composition. The distinction that secular music had bestowed upon the top part as the bearer of the melody ran counter to the Netherlandish concept of expressing melody by distributing it evenly over all the parts involved. They were also deeply concerned with materializing the element of melody in their own fashion, that is to say, in a melismatic style. Apparently, this could not be done all at once by a radical solution, for some of the first madrigals composed by Netherlanders show in all parts syllabic types of melody that were not in keeping with their traditions and ideals. They interspersed quite frequently, nevertheless, short melismatic passages readily imitated by all voices. It was Willaert, his generation and his pupils, who did away with any divergence between Northern style and native concept. Willaert made the madrigal conform to the structure of Netherlandish composition and superimposed the form of the motet upon the secular composition, so that it acquired the rank and respect the Netherlanders gave to all their forms. It came to be the property of the Northerners to such an extent that it challenged the future opposition to the *Oltremontani* almost as forcefully as did the motet, and the total transformation of the madrigal became an artistic necessity, if the Italian musician was to free himself from foreign influences. The madrigal had to bear the brunt of the struggle with the Northerners about musical style as a whole; such was the price for having been made an integral part of the Netherlandish forms.

While the Netherlanders raised the madrigal in rank and created for it a style different from that of the traditional native song, they confined all genuinely native expression to the secondary sphere the frottola had once occupied. The villotta and villanella were to follow, taking the place of the previous native songs. As was the case with the frottola, the earliest collections of villotte or canzone villanesche alla napolitana are anthologies in which individuality of authorship does not appear to play an important role. It is only from the 1540's on that the individual composer makes his influence felt. From the time when Giovanni Domenico da Nola, in the form of the villanesca, and Baldassare Donato, in that of the villanella, began the publication of their most ingenious and subtle works, the collections of these native songs reflect a certain emphasis on individual authorship. Before the middle of the century some Netherlanders had already shown an interest in these types. Among those who first acquainted themselves with the villanesca was Adrian Willaert, perhaps the most open-minded of all Northern musicians in the first half of the century. Less than a decade after the first appearance of canzone villanesche, Willaert made his contributions to the species. Even so, few Netherlanders interested themselves in the miniature forms of songs, and their concern was cursory. It could not be otherwise, since the villotta and villanesca were songs based on schematic structures, fixed, sectional, connected with the dance, and as much opposed to Flemish conceptions as the frottola. Difference of form again is apparently the reason why only a few Northerners touch these songs, which were "a clownish musick to a clownish matter," to quote Thomas Morley's description of the villanella.[10] Among them were Werrekoren, in Italian sources named Matthias Fiamengo, who imitated the native villotta as he copied Jannequin in *La Bataglia Taliana (Italiana)*—descriptive of the battle of Pavia—in 1549;[11] Antonio Barges, who by the middle of the century composed a few villotte;[12] and in the fifties Giovanni Nasco, who manifested a certain interest in the villanesca, obviously as a result of his stay in Verona.[13] Of considerable interest is the first work of Orlandus Lassus. Published in the form of a strange, yet not unprecedented, anthology, it can be regarded as the fitting harvest of the extensive journeys of his youth. He placed Italian madrigals next to French chansons, motets, and villanesche.[14] Lassus here shows the characteristic reaction of a Flemish composer to native forms, although most of them never gave evidence of such prolific and profound versatility. One of the most productive of the Netherlanders, Philippe de Monte, never cultivated the villanesca, though he was greatly interested in the madrigal. Other *Oltremontani* who contributed to the native songs in the last quarter of the century were a pupil of Philippe de Monte, Giovanni de Macque, in Naples, and Giaches de Wert, with his canzonette and villanelle of 1589. Both these artists were predominantly interested in secular music, Giovanni

---

[10] Thomas Morley, *Plaine and Easie Introduction to Practicall Musicke* (1597), p. 206.

[11] Cf. *MfM* (1871, 1872); *Kirch. Mus. Jb.* (1871, 1873); *SIMG*, VI (Elsa Bienenfeld).

[12] Barges published interesting ricercari in typically Netherlandish style.

[13] See a catalogue of his works in Don G. Turrini, "De Vlaamsche Componist Giovanni Nasco te Verona," *Tijdschrift der Vereeniging voor Nederlandsche Muziekgeschiedenis*, Deel XV, 2e Stuk (Amsterdam, 1937), pp. 84ff. Cf. also the interesting notes concerning Magister Johannes Nascus de Flandria, in Giovanni d'Alessi, "Maestri e Cantori Fiamminghi," *ibid.*, Deel XV, 3e Stuk (1938), pp. 159ff. See G. Turrini, "Il Maestro fiammingo Giovanni Nasco a Verona," *Note d'Archivio* (Rome, 1937), Nos. 4-6.

[14] It is only in the earliest collection that we find the mixture of villotte and motets in the repertory (1535); the frottole collections have this mixture also as an exception (1526).

de Macque perhaps exclusively so, unless nearly all his motets are lost.[15]
Giaches de Wert, the predecessor of Monteverdi in Mantua, had an
enormous output of secular compositions—eleven books of about 350
madrigals, including the canzonette, with which the volume of his
published sacred compositions can hardly compare. But in his function
as maestro di cappella at the Ducal Chapel, Santa Barbara ("Jaches
Wert musici suavissimi ac chori illustriss. et excellentiss. Ducis Mantuae
Magistri musices"), he must have composed more sacred works than
were printed. Perhaps in this there is an indication of the future, for
we find an ever increasing number of composers who, although chiefly
choir leaders at cathedrals or princely chapels, stressed secular music
in their publications. It is as though the productions of their official
functions could no longer satisfy all their artistic intentions. This was
definitely true of Monteverdi.

Although these Netherlanders, and a few others, turned to secular
music and the native forms, native talent played a much larger part in
its development. In any list of the repertory the names of Northerners
almost disappear amidst the impressive group of Italians. The repertory
of madrigals is full of *Oltremontani,* but they rarely appear in the list of
composers of native songs. In the evaluation of the repertory as a
whole, this is of decisive importance for the future. Whoever sets out
to oppose Northern art in the field of secular songs will be free from
foreign influences and will find something he can regard as an unequivocally genuine expression of Italian concepts in music. Here he
will not have to reckon with a musical form that was Netherlandish
even when composed by Italians. Here he may tap musical resources
powerful enough to shake the Netherlandish style to its foundation.
Monteverdi discovered the possibilities inherent in the native song, and
when in 1584 he appears as a composer of canzonette, he is already on
his way to oppose the *Oltremontani.*

ANTHOLOGIES

The musical repertory, with its various species or categories of composition and their individual styles, forms an inner harmony, an in-
dissoluble unity. Each category of composition compels the composer
to respect its form before he can venture to manifest his own individu-

---

[15] That motets must have been lost is obvious. The communal library of Thorn
possesses an organ tablature which contains motets of Macque arranged for organ;
the identification is, however, not incontestable as long as the original motets are
missing.

ality. A composition cannot be discussed according to general characteristics of style thought to be "in the air"; it must be studied within the category of which it is an example. A composer who writes a motet does not form its style merely by applying generalities upon which music as a whole is based; these are too uncertain and have little force. He is obliged to consider the path along which the motet has traveled, and his strongest responsibility is toward the category. This has determined the endurance and vitality of the style into whose fixed limits the composer must fit his own individual concepts. To be sure, this process causes a relatively slow stylistic development, but a category reaches its peak only once in the period of its predominance.

When Monteverdi began his career as a composer, we should expect him to have modeled his first motets on those of the last phase of the Netherlandish school, which was closest to him and of which he must have had the strongest impression. The last phase of the motet style seems to have begun in Venice within the large school of Willaert: first in the work of Willaert himself, and then in compositions by Andrea Gabrieli and Cipriano de Rore, the latter—like Willaert—an *Oltremontano*. The first signs of this phase occurred during the 1540's, though the older form was continued for a long time. In this decade Venetian printers once more printed Northern compositions—works by Gombert, Willaert, Clemens non Papa, Crecquillon, Verdelot, Morales, and many other musicians of minor significance. Girolamo Scotto, who was fairly conservative with regard to the choral music of his time despite his interest in instrumental music, published large collections of motets and Masses throughout the decade. He was anxious to make the most prominent Netherlanders widely known in Italy, and some of his collections of the forties reappeared about the time of Monteverdi's birth. Scotto's competitor in Venice, the printer and composer Antonio Gardane, followed suit in bringing out the music of the North. His *Flos florum*, a collection of twenty-six motets, mostly psalms, published in 1545, is as genuine a picture of Netherlands art as can be expected; he gave preference to Arcadelt, Gombert, Lerethier, Lupus, Verdelot; and not a single work in his selection is by an Italian. In the last years of the decade Gardane also drew on works that Scotto had previously published, as the collection of *cantus firmus* Masses of 1547 proves. So far as the motet and the Mass are concerned, Gardane continued for a long time to include the older generation of the Netherlanders.

Gardane opened the fifties with his famous collection of psalms, divided into two choirs, the *cori spezzati*, composed chiefly by Willaert, but also by a few other Northerners. The enormous compilations of motets in the fifties in Antwerp by Susato, Phalèse, and Waelrant, have their equivalent on a smaller scale in Scotto's *Motetti del Laberinto*, with special emphasis on the work of Clemens non Papa and Crecquillon. Altogether the fifties show an incredibly large output of motets, while Italian collections of Netherlandish Masses decline from the place they held during the previous decade. Antwerp, Nuremberg, and Venice seem to have worked closely together, and the repertories of anthologies printed in those cities have many features in common. The printers had a lively exchange and made up their anthologies on the basis of common interests, so that these collections offer illuminating cross sections of the musical repertory of the time. It is significant that the voluminous anthology *Novum et insigne opus musicum*, which the alert and careful printers, Berg and Neuber of Nuremberg, published in three parts in 1558–59 with 224 motets "of the most famous symphonists, old and new," contains no more than two works of two Italians, Costanzo Festa and Vincenzo Ruffo, both devoted to the Netherlandish ways of writing. No less important is the *Thesaurus Musicus*, in five books of 229 motets, published in the year 1564, also by Berg and Neuber. They presented here a group of famous musicians from Josquin to Orlandus Lassus and a very large group of minor composers with no more than local importance, yet the Italians were still neglected. Gardane seems to have been stimulated by this extraordinary survey to show in his own publication the art of motet composition at its finest, and also at its average level. The selection was made by Pietro Joanelli, who at his own expense, edited the works in the office of Gardane in 1568 [16] and dedicated the anthology to Emperor Maximilian II, whose musicians he liberally included. Old and new were combined in this volume, and even Josquin was represented by a composition. Among almost 250 motets, there are only two by Andrea Gabrieli, the Italian composer of the Willaert school in Venice. Once again in one of the more comprehensive anthologies containing works of composers whose average talent seemed important enough to the editor to be made known in the South, Italian talent was still neglected. The Venetian printer would not have thought of printing in five large volumes this *Novus Thesaurus*, if he expected only disapproval and negative returns. On the contrary, there must have been a fairly strong demand for such a work,

---

[16] *Novus Thesaurus:* "Petri Ioanelli Bergomensis de Gandino, summo studio ac labore collectae, eiusque expensis impressae."

otherwise Claudio da Correggio would hardly have reprinted the *Mutetarum divinitatis Liber primus*, originally a Milan publication of 1543. The *New Treasure* of 1568 could easily have been in use when Monteverdi started his musical activities under Ingegneri in the cathedral of Cremona.

The anthologies published during the seventies in Italy contain no sacred compositions but stress all forms of secular music—the madrigal and the various types of the villanella or canzona. The Netherlanders have a prominent position in nearly all the collections of madrigals, as in *La Eletta di tutta la Musica intitolata Corona de diversi* of two volumes; yet the Italians also hold their own. In collections that contain native songs, however, Italian musicians have the whole repertory to themselves, as may be seen in the *Corona* with villanelle napolitane (the first book, 1570–71, the second and third books, 1571),[17] or in the anthology which Giovanni de Antiquis edited in 1574 with various contributions of his own, all in the form of the Neapolitan villanella. There were also continual reprints of earlier collections for which there was still considerable call—anthologies of madrigals in which Netherlanders and Italians kept a nearly even balance.

It is impossible to say why the seventies, and even the eighties, did not yield any collection of sacred music. The reason may be that the fairly large output since 1550 had already satisfied all needs. The *Theatrum musicum*, edited in 1580, is centered on the motets of Orlandus Lassus but takes up the works of older composers, such as Clemens non Papa or Manchicourt, as well as those of younger composers like Cipriano de Rore and Philippe de Monte. However, it does not seem to be an Italian publication.[18] A great many anthologies which contain madrigals and canzonette do not change the picture materially, except that they include works by younger men such as Luca Marenzio, Ingegneri, Vincenzo Ruffo, and Claudio Merulo. But the Netherlanders still keep their place in the repertory of the madrigals. Some collections of the eighties have almost deceptive titles; they are called *Harmonia Celeste*, or *Musica Divina*, or *Symphonia Angelica*, or *Musica Spirituale*, making use of terms ordinarily reserved for sacred music.

---

[17] The date 1570 for the publication of Book I of the *Corona* is not certain; we have only the reprint of 1572. Books II and III are not real anthologies since they contain only works of Girolamo Scotto, the printer, with the two exceptions by Giovanni Bassani in Book III.

[18] Cf. Robert Eitner in *MfM*, V and VI. The print appeared in both volumes without name of location or printer. According to its content it is more likely than not to have been edited in a Northern country, perhaps Germany.

This may well be due to the influence of the Counter Reformation. Books were also published containing compositions of native forms in the style of the Neapolitan canzonetta, with Italian texts of religious character: as, for instance, the *Diletto Spirituale* of Simone Verovio (1586) or the *Canzonette Spirituali de diversi a tre voci* (I, 1585). Most collections of secular music made in the eighties are "spiritual," either in title alone or in the individual texts of the compositions. In that decade also appeared a collection of parodies in which originally secular Italian madrigals were provided with new sacred texts. Finally, in the eighties the large collection of 165 *Laude Spirituali,* in four books, all anonymous, was published by Alessandro Gardano in Rome. The third book was significantly dedicated to Cardinal Frederico Borromeo, a man who as advisor to the Pope had taken a leading part in the religious revival of the Counter Reformation.

In the sphere of sacred music, a growing religious intensity marked the rather sparse collections of the eighties. While printers or editors from 1550 on had, in most cases, selected the music according to style and individual reputation, there was now a noticeable emphasis on liturgical principles. The individual composer and modern or fashionable styles were neglected in favor of religious factors, such as the liturgical order of the service in which the compositions were to be sung. Angelo Gardano, of Venice, for example, selected thirty motets to be used in the church of Santa Barbara for all major double feasts, with complete disregard of authorship. This may be the truest form of liturgical observance, since the objective quality of the service makes the individuality of the artist unimportant. Although no general collection followed Gardano's arrangement, the procedure of listing works according to the services of the church year was taken up by other publishers.

All in all, the eighties presented themselves as a decade of decisive importance. The increased representation of Italian composers in collections outside Italy reflected clearly a rising interest in them in Northern musical centers, where previously Flemish men alone had been heard. This interest was largely due to the enormous output of madrigals after 1550, of which fully half were the work of native Italian talent. The Northern publishers now became acquainted with the names of Italian musicians and gave them a new hearing. Hubert Waelrant, a keen and farsighted publisher, may be taken as a fine example of this lively interest in the development of Italian music, the advanced stage of which he represents chiefly in madrigals by Giovanni Ferretti, Luca

Marenzio, Vincenzo Ruffo, Gastoldi, Orazio Vecchi, and Ingegneri. He also includes a number of minor Italian composers and cites Netherlanders only in passing.[19]

It is quite comprehensible that interest in Italian composers was also reflected in collections of religious music. We notice the change in the *Harmoniae miscellae cantionum sacrarum, ab exquisitissimis aetatis nostrae musicis* (never before printed in Germany), a collection edited by Leonhard Lechner and published by Gerlach in Nuremberg in 1583. For the first time in an anthology of sacred music Italians equal the Northerners in number: Alfonso Ferrabosco, Andrea Gabrieli, Gioseffe Guami, Ingegneri, Annibale Padoano, Costanzo Porta and Palestrina stand by the side of Lechner, Gosswin, Lassus, Philippe de Monte, and Cipriano de Rore. Gerlach apparently kept a close watch on musical events in Italy, for two years later, in 1585, he made a further advance of an almost revolutionary nature. It was previously unheard of for a publisher in the North to proclaim the excellence of Italian musicians and make himself the agent of their fame, but Gerlach's editor, Friedrich Lindner, selected the motets, dedicated to the most prominent feasts of the church year, from compositions "of the most famous musicians of Italy . . . some of them published before in Venice separately, others entirely new . . . and now edited for the benefit of German schools and churches." In this small collection of forty-one motets, the Italians obtained the first place, although the Northerners were not ruled out completely. Lindner even called attention to minor musicians among the Italians, though Claudio Merulo and Palestrina gave the anthology its special character. From that time on, publishers who planned to give as complete a cross section of sacred music as of madrigals attributed fresh significance to Italian composers of motets. Of course, not every anthology reflected this aspect. When Giulio Bonaiuncta edited Masses for publication in Milan in 1588, his anthology represented chiefly Orlandus Lassus and Adrien Hauvil and contained only one Mass by an Italian, Antonio Piccioli, a man of no more than local importance. But the sphere of influence the Italians had gained for themselves was rapidly growing. Friedrich Lindner and Gerlach used the relationship between North and South as a principle according to which they chose their collections. In their volume of Masses in 1590, they placed Palestrina and Guami next to Northern

---

[19] It is the collection *Symphonia Angelica di diversi Eccellentissimi Musici* (Antwerp, 1585), published in the house of Pierre Phalèse, containing fifty-eight madrigals. Waelrant did not publish the work himself; he collected the madrigals and added also five of his own. The anthologies of 1583 have the same character.

composers. In their *Corollarium cantionum sacrarum* of that same year, about two-thirds of the motets were by Italians, among whom Palestrina, Ingegneri, and Andrea Gabrieli were treated with special distinction. They even included so young a composer as Giovanni Gabrieli, whose works had been published before 1590 only with those of Andrea, his uncle. Lindner and Gerlach continued their publication of Italians in 1591 with an anthology of Magnificat compositions, put in order for liturgical use according to the eight ecclesiastical modes.

At the beginning of the nineties eight new anthologies of sacred music were published in Italy. Most important for the characteristics of the repertory is the *Musica per concerti ecclesiastici di diversi autori*, which Vincenti published in 1590. Here for the first time an anthology of sacred compositions consists of Italian works only, chiefly parts of the ordinary of the Mass. The collection was intended to represent the Venetian school, but its very nature shows that the *Oltremontani* were no longer needed to make up a sacred repertory. Though he was the father of the Venetian school, Willaert had been dropped. The same development is seen in an edition published in Rome in 1592. The anthology *Psalmi, Motecta, Magnificat, et Antiphona 'Salve Regina' Diversorum Autorum* has Felice Anerio, Palestrina, Ruggiero Giovanelli, Giovanni Maria Nanini, Paolo Quagliati—that is, the entire Palestrina school, excepting Luca Marenzio, who is represented with only one composition. This shift toward native composers does not imply an original native style of composition, for the sacred music of Italian musicians still adhered to its Netherlandish prototype. It merely shows that a definite preference was granted the Italians, now considered the equals of the Netherlanders whose idiom they had imitated long enough to become masters in their own right.

A similar pattern was followed by Northern publishers. The *Treasure of Litanies*, which Adam Berg published in Munich in three volumes (1596), has nearly the same arrangement as the Northern anthologies of the eighties, and in the second book Palestrina leads all other composers. Even the foremost printer in the center of the Flemish output, Phalèse, in Antwerp, could not escape the ever growing influence of the Italians. He had the "phonascus" of Notre Dame in Antwerp, Matthias Pottier, who is known only through a Mass for five voices, edit the *Selectissimarum Missarum Flores, ex praestantissimis nostrae aetatis authoribus . . . collecti* (1599) in which all the Masses were by Italians, with the exception of two by Orlandus Lassus and one by Pottier himself.

At the end of the century, the contributions of Italians were so numerous as to allow the arrangement of a repertory for the North according to the characteristics of a special school of composition in Italy. Two such anthologies have already been mentioned. Another famous anthology which belongs to this group is the *Sacrae symphoniae diversorum excellentissimorum authorum*, whose first volume came out under the editorship of Kaspar Hasler in 1598, followed by a second in 1600. No doubt, the relations of Kaspar's brother Hans Leo Hasler with Venice were a good reason for showing the Venetian school at its best in fourteen works of Giovanni Gabrieli and twelve compositions of Claudio Merulo. The compositions were also obviously selected according to the style of writing, so that Northern composers who wrote in the Venetian manner were included. A similar arrangement is followed in the *Motets and Psalms*, which Vincenti published in 1599 with a dedication to Cesare Schieti, canon in Urbino and also a composer. Although the composers have been chosen from the Roman school, Palestrina himself being represented, the style shows a definite leaning toward the Venetian idiom and gives further evidence that the Italian dialects of the musical language, still basically Netherlandish, have acquired enough strength to regulate certain sections of the repertory.

The numerous anthologies reflect popular taste and demand, though they do not always indicate the latest developments in musical style and, in many cases, exhibit a conservative tendency. This is quite natural, since any new phase of style is initiated by the individual composer and presented first in books containing his compositions exclusively, and from such collections novelties are later chosen for the anthologies. At times, however, it is surprising to see how quick the editors or printers were to include any new trend in their anthologies.

A survey of all the anthologies published in the two decades from the middle of the sixteenth century to the birth of Monteverdi offers an instructive picture. Although the numbers in the groups are merely approximations, we believe that the basic relationship between the groups is nearly correct, and that new findings would not alter the situation essentially.[20] We have seen that the Mass, the most distinguished of all liturgical compositions, was not favored by collectors of anthologies, so that not more than fifty Masses of various composers were published in collections in the years 1550 to 1570. If we except the work of Palestrina, the Mass occupied the same relative position in the output

---

[20] In this survey, the anthologies of French chansons have been disregarded.

of individual composers and no longer played any decisive part in forming new phases of style. During the fifties and sixties a few composers adapted the style of the Mass to that of motet, so that it was kept abreast of advances in composition, but others drew upon the past instead of composing Masses in a more modern style. The decline in original composition for the Mass influenced Monteverdi's attitude toward compositions for religious services, and it is of historical interest to see that it had taken place by the time he was born.

This decline of the Mass was offset by the superior position of motets of all kinds, including the strictly liturgical, the generally religious, psalms, and compositions linked to certain occasions, mostly dedicatory in character. The total output of motets in anthologies amounts to about twenty-five hundred,[21] and exceeds every other category of composition. The motet occupied the foremost place in the repertory and set the style that was followed in nearly all other compositions. It was regarded as the noblest medium in which to express the ideals of composition of the time. Counting all forms of Italian secular music and motets together, the repertory in the anthologies presents approximately thirty-five hundred compositions of this sort or about 72 per cent of the total. When Monteverdi began his musical career, the motet was the most significant composition in rank and the most important in style.

Secular music is represented in the anthologies by a little more than one thousand works, including madrigals as well as such native songs as the villanella and canzonetta. About a fifth of this secular music is in the form of native songs; the rest are madrigals, a large part of them written either by Flemish musicians or in Flemish style. Thus, these collections contain about eight hundred madrigals and approximately two hundred villanelle and canzonette. Since native songs were seldom composed by Netherlanders, this part of the repertory has a specifically Italian quality. They occupy, however, a very modest place in the total of thirty-five hundred works, amounting to less than 6 per cent of the total, while the madrigals comprise 22 per cent. When one makes due allowance for madrigals composed by Flemish composers and adds this quota to the motets, where they are clearly in the majority, one gets a fair idea of their continued preponderance in repertory and style.

These percentages are probably about the same for the repertory of individual composers, some of whom composed nothing but motets and

---

[21] These are round figures without any claim to absolute correctness. Bibliographical materials as well as transcriptions have been used for the estimate.

liturgical music, while still others wrote only native songs, and a few contributed, with universal capacity and flexibility, to all the forms. Palestrina concentrated on the Mass and therefore cannot be judged by the relatively few madrigals he composed, which, though by no means without interest, are historically irrelevant. Orlandus Lassus demonstrated the importance of the motet by the vast number he composed, but we must not overlook the large body of his secular music, for though Palestrina can be comprehended without his secular music, Lassus cannot. Although individual composers gave distinct preference to various forms of secular music, there had been no reaction against the Netherlanders at the time when Monteverdi was born. Neither the repertory nor the style bears out any such assumption, for as long as sacred music maintained its superiority, no opposition could achieve success. The Northern style, based on religious concepts, had to be overthrown before style and category of composition could attain a fresh and integral unity.

Doubtless, the most fascinating of the Italian composers is Luca Marenzio, who before Monteverdi, or almost simultaneously, made secular music his supreme form of artistic expression. The list of his works shows not only the unparalleled fame he enjoyed in his own time and thereafter, as evidenced by numerous reprints, but exhibits secular music at its greatest breadth. Amidst an endless list of madrigals, villanelle, canzonette, the book of forty-two motets for the feasts of the church year, published in 1585 for the first time, makes a strange appearance and produces an almost confusing effect. Though this book shared in Marenzio's high reputation—for three more reprints were issued—its existence is difficult, if not impossible, to explain. He also wrote a few other sacred compositions: a Magnificat, a Mass, and several other motets, preserved in anthologies and manuscripts. Since the printed motets of 1585 are all for four voices, while those in manuscript are for five, six, and eight voices, it may be suggested that the compositions in the manuscripts have been selected from previous printings now no longer in existence. Even so, these motets are somewhat abnormal in Marenzio's work, and it is hard to account for the appearance of a motet book based on strictly liturgical factors. One possible explanation is the influence of the Roman school and the religious tendencies awakened by the Counter Reformation; but the motets are so completely alien to Marenzio's artistic goal, which lies in the sphere of secular music, that they appear "aimless" and rootless.

Many of Marenzio's madrigals are marked by the Northern style;

many of his secular songs, however, are remote from the influence of the North, for he placed great stress on native forms from the very first, and the villanelle not only constituted a large section of his secular music but also influenced his style in general. Marenzio began with the form of the madrigal that was most highly appreciated: that for five voices. After publishing four books of these madrigals and some additional spiritual madrigals, he turned to native songs, villanelle and canzonette, of which he published seven books within three years. It is as though he had discovered new musical values opposed to those of the North. Marenzio led the madrigal to its climactic height within the capacities of the sixteenth-century idiom, which he expanded to the utmost without ever breaking with its basic concepts. In this respect he remained the fulfiller of secular music in terms of the sixteenth century. With him the old ended, but the new did not begin. Marenzio did not set out to eliminate the art of his age; he is its final representative in secular music. It may well be that had he lived longer he, too, would have taken a leading part in founding the new style, since he was an observer of the events that led to the Florentine opera. With his vigorous concentration on secular expressions in music, Marenzio broke a path along which Monteverdi could proceed, and his work was a necessary prelude to the new music.

Among those who showed Monteverdi his way from his early days on, Vincenzo Ruffo, Cipriano de Rore, and Marc' Antonio Ingegneri take the first place. None of these composers anticipated the exclusiveness with which Marenzio worked in the field of secular music. The list of their compositions is another illustration of the character of the repertory. Cipriano de Rore made a decided shift toward secular music, approximately two-thirds of his output being given over to madrigals. For a man born in the North and working under the guidance of Willaert, this is quite unusual, but Cipriano, perhaps more than any other composer, endowed the madrigal with all the technical refinements of Flemish music. The rest of his output is divided between Masses and motets, which show fully his Northern origin and schooling. They are "conservative" in the sense that Cipriano never allowed the strength and character of the Flemish style to be diminished. The Mass *Vivat Felix Hercules*, dedicated to Ercole II of Ferrara, was apparently composed after a model of Josquin des Prés, but his later Masses increase the fullness of sound by extending the number of parts to seven. His famous *Passion*, printed in 1557, has—at least in the Turba choruses—the style of the Flemish motet. Any religious form was subject to Northern concepts, as is clearly the case in his motets proper, where Cipriano followed the initiative of Adrian Willaert in building up a Venetian dialect. The first books of his motets, however, are composed in the purest Flemish fashion, and among them are a few compositions that represent a rare species, the secular motet with Latin text. Cipriano set a few lines of Virgil's *Aeneid* as well as an ode of Horace to music. Best known and most widely discussed was the ode *Calami sonum ferentes,* a work that—composed before 1555—marked an epoch in the treatment of chromaticism within the scope of the Northern style. Among the secular motets the dedicatory type is represented in *Labore primus Hercules.* Despite Cipriano's flexibility and his eagerness to add new tones to the old ideal, he did not corrupt the style, but maintained the pure Netherlandish concept in his last motets with as much determination and clarity as in his first. We think especially of the grandiose motet *Infelix ego omnium auxilio destitutus,* which he must have composed in his last years.[22] It is a double motet, that is, one with two texts, the first alto singing the initial words of Psalm 56, *miserere mei,* throughout the composition, for which the psalm tone is used as *cantus firmus,* nine times repeated in the *prima pars* of the motet, fourteen times in the *secunda pars,* while at the end all voices take up the exclamation simultaneously. The model for this structure is Josquin's miraculous *Miserere mei* of around 1500, which fathered many imitations. In Cipriano the full strength of the Netherlandish form appears, influencing the whole life of a composer whom we too often remember only for his madrigals, forgetting his motets and Masses. As Zarlino designated Willaert the father of all sixteenth-century music, so younger men regarded Cipriano as the leader in musical art. Ingegneri wrote in 1586 to Octavio, Duke of Parma, that Cipriano had advanced the art of music so greatly as to be an example forever and the master of all in perfect composition. Ingegneri's opinion, at least in part, was later shared by Monteverdi.

Vincenzo Ruffo, of the same generation, had many features in common with Cipriano, especially in the field of madrigals. Ruffo kept pace with the novelties Cipriano introduced; both worked toward the same

---

[22] The motet has been published posthumously by Gardano (Venice, 1595), in *Sacrae cantiones quae dicuntur Motecta.* (The portrait of Cipriano names the composer as "Flemish.") *Infelix ego,* No. 32, appears as a certain climax at the end of the collection, which contains thirty-four motets. See the modern edition of this work in Josef Musiol, *Cyprian de Rore, ein Meister der venezianischen Schule* (Breslau, 1933), p. 80 and Example 34. Musiol did not recognize the relation of the *cantus firmus* to the psalm; neither did he notice the relation of the work to Josquin's model.

end; both were advanced; and Ruffo even anticipated many a later phase of the madrigalesque style. Yet while Cipriano's repertory reflected the composer's concern with the promotion of the madrigal to a more distinguished position in the repertory, Ruffo's works were evenly distributed between sacred and secular music. Exactly half of his works were madrigals, the other half were motets and Masses. In his compositions of sacred music, Ruffo did not deviate from the Northern precepts and even attributed great significance to the liturgical element that the motets and Masses should represent. In so doing, he made use of the Flemish style to strengthen the religious qualities of his music. It is interesting to see him arrange collections of motets in strict observance of the liturgical order, in which various psalms are dedicated to the officium of the ecclesiastical hours. It is also striking to find that some of his religious works were influenced by the Counter Reformation, which, musically speaking, adopted the Flemish style for church music of a religious character. In the eighties Ruffo published a collection of Masses, which was expressly "purged" of any inadequacy or error, "according to the formula of the Council of Trent." The eighties were probably the period when the Counter Reformation exercised its greatest effect on music, and it was then that Marenzio edited his book of motets and published his "spiritual" madrigals. Ruffo's work is a perfect example of the experience of many a composer of the time: he gives full recognition to what was regarded as the necessary superiority of the motet, while retaining a strong interest in the madrigal.

Marc' Antonio Ingegneri was considerably younger than either Ruffo or Cipriano and closer to the generation of Luca Marenzio. He stood precisely midway between Ruffo, whose pupil he was, and Monteverdi, whose teacher he was to be. Ingegneri favored secular music only to the extent of composing madrigals, most of which show no trace of the influence either of the villanella or the canzonetta. The majority of his madrigals are less advanced than those of Ruffo and Cipriano, to say nothing of Marenzio; he leans toward as pure a Netherlandish style as possible.[23] Ingegneri's works exhibit a decided prefer-

---

[23] In her dissertation, *Marc' Antonio Ingegneri als Madrigalkomponist* (Berlin, 1936), Ellinor Dohrn explained the relationship between word and tone as though it were a phenomenon of the madrigal alone and thus always a sign of "modern" style. The type found in Ingegneri's works holds true for the motets also, not only of Ingegneri himself, but also of the older Netherlandish-Italian composers. Peter Wagner, *Geschichte der Messe* (Leipzig, 1913), p. 402, had observed "the concise treatment of the text" to be a peculiarity of the northern Italian musicians, and not only of Ruffo or Ingegneri. The chapter on the influence of Ingegneri on Monteverdi has not been included in the dissertation. E. Dohrn apparently assumed the influence to have been very strong.

ence for sacred music in the form of the motet, with Masses and motets making up almost two-thirds of his compositions, and his example proves that we must not take it for granted that a musician who was closer to the end of the century would necessarily devote himself to secular composition. Ingegneri belongs to a group of composers, Costanzo Porta among them, who continued to express their firm belief in the Northern ideal of the predominance of the motet. The famous Responsories of Ingegneri have been erroneously attributed to Palestrina on bibliographical grounds, but there is a certain stylistic support for the error.[24] Both were vigorous representatives of the Netherlandish ideal. Instead of yielding to modern tendencies, Ingegneri strengthened the position of the Flemish style in Italy by cultivating once more its finest qualities. Between this conservation and the new concepts of Monteverdi there would seem to be no bridge.

---

[24] As is well known, these Responsories appear in the complete edition of Palestrina's works.

The Struggle with the Past

CHAPTER THREE

Beginnings in Cremona

IN 1567, the year of Monteverdi's birth, or perhaps a year later, Marc' Antonio Ingegneri, of Verona, was appointed cantor at the cathedral of Cremona, and in due course was made prefect of music and maestro di cappella.[1] Since the cathedral was the focus of musical activity, Ingegneri must have been chiefly responsible for Cremona's rapid rise as a center of musical culture. The city had given birth to musicians of renown before Ingegneri received his appointment: Costanzo Porta, Tiburzio Massaini, Benedetto Pallavicino, all were famous in their own country and abroad, but they perfected their art elsewhere. All of them were considerably younger than Ingegneri, and since they left Cremona at an early age, it is difficult to imagine what tradition they might have established and how Ingegneri might have continued it.[2] We know no prominent composers who chose Cremona for its glorious tradition, and nearly all records of Cremona's musical greatness date from the time of Ingegneri. There was before him, of course, a certain Cremonese tradition in music, but its level was ap-

---

[1] Ellinor Dohrn, *op. cit.*, p. 12, takes the year 1568 as the limit for Ingegneri's change from Verona to Cremona. Gaetano Cesari, *La Musica in Cremona nella seconda metà del secolo XVI e i primordi dell' arte Monteverdiana*, in *Istituzioni e Monumenti Dell'-Arte Musicale Italiana*, Vol. VI (Milan, 1939), p. x, accepts the date. Despite thorough investigation of the documents, the biographical dates of Ingegneri remain obscure; very little has been discovered. The most recent publication of G. Cesari does not give any clear picture of the musical activities at Cremona, except for organ music at the time of Ingegneri, for which more documents are available than for other musical activities.

[2] *Ibid.*, p. LVII: "Ingegneri, il quale proseguiva allora in Cremona la bella tradizione artistica di Costanzo Porta, Tiburzio Massaino e Benedetto Pallavicino." Obviously Cesari takes the birth of these men in Cremona as reason to attribute the foundation of an artistic tradition to them, although they were much too young.

parently no higher than that of many another place. We connect the name of Costanzo Porta with Venice and the school of Adrian Willaert, with cities where he played a leading part, such as Padua or Osimo, but not with Cremona. When Alessandro Lami di Federico, a nobleman of Cremona, sang the praise of the city's music in his poem *Sogno non men piacevole che morale* of 1572, he attributed its world-wide fame to Ingegneri and did not mention Porta or Massaino, but, instead, Barera (Barella), Cherubetti, Maineri, Morsolino, Zermignari—all men of purely local significance, and now only names. Of Maineri and his compositions we know nothing, yet he was probably celebrated in his day as organist at the cathedral of Milan. After Ingegneri, however, Cremona ranked high as a city which made notable and original contributions to music.

Musical life there was organized around the cathedral, and musical training was in the hands of the church musician, who fortunately received vigorous support from his superiors. Choral compositions made up the repertory, and the church choir was the only organization adequate to the needs of the style in all Italian cities where Flemish choral singing had taken root. Such an organization naturally trained more people than one which was based on solo performance and devoted, consequently, to the development of virtuosi and the needs of a small minority. Choral technique required a high average of musical talent, and there has rarely been a period when group singing was so widespread and reached such heights. Any large city was certain to have well-trained choirs of great merit, which provided the best imaginable grounds for a steady growth of music. A first-rate composer could make excellent use of this highly developed instrument, and such an impetus was undoubtedly given to Cremona's musical life when Ingegneri became its chief musician.

This choral training was the background for Monteverdi's musical education. Although there is no record of his being a chorister in the cathedral, such a beginning can be taken for granted. Composition was taught, as well as choral technique, and Monteverdi would become familiar with the choral music used by Ingegneri both for church services and on lay occasions. Almost nothing is known of the civic festivals upon which music cast an extraordinary splendor, and little is known of musical activities in the palaces of Cremona's noble families. Lack of documents, however, does not imply a lack of such activities, and there is no reason to believe that music was less enjoyed by the nobility of Cremona than by the Italian nobility of other cities, where madrigals were sung and compositions for solo instruments, such as the lute, were played in the palaces, and motets were sung or played when religious needs or artistic interests called for them. That the young Monteverdi shared in many such activities can be taken as a matter of course.

Cremona was widely celebrated in another field of music: the manufacture of musical instruments, especially of violins. All lovers of music have heard of the Amati, the Guarneri, the Stradivari, who spread the city's glory throughout the world. Amati began his work before Ingegneri came to Cremona, and throughout the sixteenth century the city's reputation for the production of excellent instruments was widespread. There were also instrument makers by the name of Monteverdi, who may indeed have been relatives of the composer.[3] At any rate, we know that Monteverdi got his first appointment in Mantua as a violist, and that it was probably Ingegneri who taught him that skill.

The *Libri di Provvisione della Fabrica del Duomo* of Cremona, investigated by Luigi Lucchini, notes that Ingegneri "was a violinist of distinction and . . . had the privilege of having trained our greatly famous Claudio Monteverdi in the school of counterpoint. . . . Under the direction of the able Marc' Antonio Ingegneri the musical 'cappella' began, around 1593, to be supported by a company of players in the manner of an orchestra." [4] Toward the end of his life, and perhaps shortly after his appointment in 1581 as maestro di cappella, Ingegneri, called a player of the violino di grido, produced a collaboration between the cappella of the cathedral and a company of instrumentalists. Consisting of the musicians of the city, this company may well have been organized according to guild rules. All the larger cities had their own musicians, the *compagnia di suonatori,* and the musician's guild, originally a medieval organization, lasted till the end of the baroque age. Between the choral institute of the cathedral and the civic musicians of the town there were occasional disputes concerning the maintenance of privileges. Some such quarrel between the administration and singers of the cappella at St. Mark's and the *Compagnia di suonatori,* or Guild of Minstrels and Players, caused a sensation when Monteverdi was maestro at St. Mark's. This dispute had all the earmarks of a contest

---

[3] Concerning Domenico Monteverdi, see Stefano Davari, "Notizie biografiche del distinto Maestro di Musica Claudio Monteverdi," in *Atti della R. Accademia Virgiliana* (Mantua, 1885), p. 79.

[4] *Libri di provvisione,* V, fol. 93. Cf. Luigi Lucchini, *Cenni storici su i più celebri musicisti cremonesi* (Casalmaggiore, 1887), p. 13. The date 1593 is, of course, erroneous, since Ingegneri died July 1, 1592. Lucchini must have misread the manuscript. Cf. E. Dohrn, *op. cit.,* p. 14, n.27. Gaetano Cesari was unable to correct the date.

between free labor—the singers of St. Mark's—and the organized union —the guild, which exerted pressure on the singers to join it.[5] In Cremona, however, singers and players seem to have worked together without friction, and Ingegneri was praised for making possible a new co-operation between the two musical organizations.

The cathedral choir, the town company, and the activities in the noble families made up the musical life in which Monteverdi shared, and it has always been assumed that he also took academic studies at the University of Cremona. Monteverdi's family was of some distinction, and his father is said to have given much care to the education of his children. It is more than likely that the man who was to vie with the musical artists of antiquity, who was to conceive of the liberal arts as the basis of his work, who was to distinguish himself by profundity of thought and breadth of knowledge, took advantage of the opportunities furnished by the university.[6] Only one other musician of the time— Heinrich Schütz—rivals Monteverdi in mastery of the humanities, and both understood that the art of music should be based on the humanities. We know that Schütz went to a university, and it is probable that Monteverdi was also a university man.

The University of Cremona was neither as old nor as distinguished as many other Italian institutions of higher learning, and the days of its prime were probably in the fifteenth century, when it was founded. Thanks to the imperial leanings of the Condottiere Gabrino Fondulo, the ruler of Cremona, and in gratitude for many signs of his loyalty, the Emperor Sigismund II drew up the brief of foundation for a university to be erected in Cremona. In this edict of May 8, 1415, he decreed that "the general study of theology, of jurisprudence, both canonic and civic, also of medicine, of philosophy, natural and moral, and of the liberal arts be set up and be observed forever after." The university was to have the same privilege, liberty, immunity, special license, and favor (*indultum*) enjoyed by the *studia generalia* at Paris and Bologna.[7] Since the liberal arts were included, the subject of music may have been taught as a part of mathematics, but we do not know what,

---

[5] See the interesting references to this quarrel in Henry Prunières, *Claudio Monteverdi* (New York, 1926), pp. 106f. and notes 100f.

[6] Prunières, *op. cit.*, p. 5, suggests that Monteverdi studied at the university.

[7] See Antonio Campo, *Cremona fedelissima Cita et nobilissima colonia* . . . (Milan, 1645), pp. 110ff. "Ut in eadem civitate Cremonen. Studium generale Sacrae Theologiae, utriusque Juris, videlicet tàm Canonici, quàm Ciuiles, necnon Medicinae, Philosophiae naturalis, et moralis, ac artium liberalium, erigatur, et ex nunc in antea perpetuis temporibus obseruetur."

if any, course of study was adopted.[8] Though the best days of the university had passed by the time Monteverdi was old enough to attend its courses, he presumably laid the groundwork for those studies that occupied him for the rest of his life and gave inspiration to his art.

The first work Monteverdi published—a collection of motets—came out in 1582. By that time the output of his teacher Ingegneri was considerable: two books of madrigals for four voices, three books for five voices, a book of Masses, a book of motets for five voices, and presumably many compositions not available in print. The hymns and psalms of the vespers, for instance, were published posthumously and may date back to the eighties. It was at this time, from Monteverdi's birth through the eighties, that the influence of the Counter Reformation made itself felt in the musical life of Cremona. It engendered an atmosphere with which Monteverdi must have become familiar and which seems to have affected his first works. Ingegneri himself was closely associated with men who played a leading part in the intensification of all aspects and expressions of religious life and dedicated part of his sacred work to this end. The Counter Reformation was thus a decisive factor in the early life of Monteverdi.

Marc' Antonio Ingegneri dedicated his first book of motets for five voices (1576), as well as three more collections of Masses and motets, to Nicolo Sfondrato, Bishop of Cremona since 1560, who was made a cardinal in 1583 and elected Pope Gregory XIV in 1590. As Bishop of Cremona, Sfondrato fought vigorously for the ideals of the Counter Reformation. His attempts to restore a truly religious conduct in the affairs of church and clergy were instigated by Carlo Borromeo, the Archbishop of Milan. Borromeo became the chief adviser of Pius IV in all matters of reform at the Council of Trent and was co-author of the *Catechismus Romanus*. Since Sfondrato was an ardent admirer and patron of music and musicians, he was among those in the Council who took the initiative in discussions concerning the renewal of church music. Moreover, he saw to it that the principles formulated by the Council were put in practice by the musicians who composed for church services. Ingegneri came into close contact with Sfondrato in Cremona, and this led to an intimate friendship. Sfondrato certainly encouraged Ingegneri to work for the ideals of the Counter Reformation; and the

[8] On the study of music at Italian universities, see Paul Oskar Kristeller, "Music and Learning in the Early Italian Renaissance," *Journal of Renaissance and Baroque Music*, I (1947), 255ff.

publication of four books of sacred compositions, three of them dedicated to the patron himself, was obviously in response to his inspiration.[9]

The ideas Sfondrato must have discussed with Ingegneri were not entirely new to the composer, who may have made a direct acquaintance with the new principles of church music in Verona, where he worked under Vincenzo Ruffo. It was to the chapter of the cathedral of Verona that Ingegneri dedicated his first book of Masses in 1573. Ruffo collaborated as closely with Carlo Borromeo as Ingegneri with Sfondrato, and after 1563 he was maestro di cappella at the cathedral of Milan, where Borromeo became archbishop. Ruffo's collection of psalms, as well as his Masses, was revised according to the formula of the Council of Trent. "My intention in both the Masses and the psalms is to show how one can introduce into the divine offices a form of music, grave, sweet, and devout, and such a one as to be totally adequate to the spirit of the Sacred Council of Trent, which does not permit music to be sung in the churches of the Lord that has an impure or lascivious character." [10] Thus Ruffo and Borromeo in Milan, Ingegneri and Sfondrato in Cremona, took decisive steps toward realizing what appeared to the leaders of church reform to be the true nature of religious music. The dedication that prefaced the famous Responses of the Holy Week, once attributed to Palestrina, shows that Ingegneri had an intense interest in the goal of the Counter Reformation. This preface is addressed to the Abbot Marc' Antonio Amidano, who at some time before 1588 held a meeting of learned and pious men to whom he explained the nature of hymns, antiphons, and responses. Ingegneri must have attended that meeting, for his Responses were intended to embody the religious intensity of which the Abbot spoke, and to materialize those tones of angelic origin which, in the words of Amidano, religious ecstasy enables man to perceive.

The influence of the Counter Reformation resulted in a renewed interest in Netherlandish polyphony and furnished this style with new strength and new artistic justification. In the eighties Ingegneri advocated the purest form of the style for the sake of restoring religious qualities to music and supported his plea by writing Masses for four and five voices. Most of his motets follow the same ideal, and the most

---

[9] For the relationship between Ingegneri and Sfondrato, see E. Dohrn, *op. cit.*, pp. 16ff. and G. Cesari, *Istituzioni*, p. xxviii.

[10] Preface to the Psalms of Ruffo (1574); quoted by F. X. Haberl, in *Kirch. Mus. Jb.* (1892), p. 92. Haberl assumes that Ingegneri obtained the ideas concerning a reform of church music from Ruffo. Sfondrato was probably more influential in this respect.

"modern" phase he would concede to the motet was its Venetian version, which had brought about a considerable increase of parts and a growth of volume in sound effects. So far as the fundamental structure of his religious works is concerned, Ingegneri always clung to the Netherlandish elements, which he and many other Italians regarded as the most genuine musical expression of religious values.

How does Monteverdi's work fit into the movement of which his teacher made himself a spokesman? Does he contribute to what Ingegneri and Sfondrato had set up as the ideal of composition in the religious form? Monteverdi's first work is the collection of twenty-three "little motets" for three voices, published by Gardano in Venice in 1582 and dedicated to Stefano Caninio Valcarengo.[11] From his texts, we should assume that Monteverdi began his musical work in full harmony with the ideas that flourished in Cremona during the eighties. The texts are of a religious nature, selected from the Bible, and provide external evidence for classifying the compositions as the continuation of Ingegneri's plans concerning church music. One could take them to be the result of his musical studies in the school of counterpoint at the cathedral.[12] But a closer examination shows the historical significance of the work to be less simple and less clear, and there are certain features which strike the attentive observer as peculiar: first, the unusual brevity of all the compositions, which is stressed by the name given them—*cantiunculae;* second, the use of the *tricinium,* a combination of only three voices; third, though of lesser importance, the omission of the customary reference to religious significance and purpose in the dedication.

The use of a three-part form is startling. The motet had long since attained the fullness afforded by the combination of five parts and for the sake of greater fullness, the number of voices was often further increased. In fact, the *tricinium* seems to have become something of an anachronism. It originally had been a form favored by the Netherlandish composers, who used it for independent motets and for sections inserted in the Mass. The *bicinium* was also favored by Northern musicians, and both were more characteristic of Netherlandish music of the first half of the sixteenth century than of the period after 1550. As a category of sacred music, the *tricinium* gradually died out and was used only by musicians who insisted on the preservation of the Netherland-

---

[11] The first modern edition was published around 1910 by Terrabagio. Despite this edition, all biographies have neglected the early work of Monteverdi, which was thought to be lost. The *Sacrae Cantiunculae* are now available in the editions of Malipiero and G. Cesari.

[12] G. Cesari, *Istituzioni,* p. LV.

ish style. After the middle of the century, most anthologies of *tricinia* were published in the Northern centers of Netherlandish music. In 1569 Phalèse, of Antwerp, published three books of motets in the form of *tricinia*, and their repertory characterizes the situation as a whole.[13] Almost all the composers belong to the generation of 1490 to 1500— Clemens non Papa, Morales, Crecquillon, Costanzo Festa, and Willaert. The youngest is Orlandus Lassus, who contributed only two of the sixty-two compositions contained in the three books. The origins of Lassus' motet composition were Flemish, and it was natural that he should still contribute to the category, as he also did in his 1575 edition of motets for three voices. But Palestrina, one of the most ardent followers of the Netherlandish style, did not compose motets as *tricinia*, except in his possible contribution to the collection of *Laudi spirituali*, where the use of three voices was in keeping with tradition. In Italy, some interest in the category seems to have survived thanks to the influence of Willaert, who alone appears to have had a genuine liking for the *tricinium*. The motet gradually discarded the form of the *tricinium* after 1550, except in a certain few sections of the Mass.

Three-part composition also occurred in the field of secular music. Many collections of madrigals and chansons published after the middle of the century contain *tricinia*, but wherever the madrigal appears as *tricinium* after 1550, the composers—Gero, Willaert, Festa, Animuccia —are among the oldest. In the second half of the century the favorite combination was that of five voices, four and six parts being also in use. Gardano and Scotto brought out various collections of three-part madrigals during the sixties: in 1561, works of Arcadelt, Giachet Berchem, Donato, Gero, Giovanni Nasco, Willaert and Ruffo;[14] in 1562, *Il primo libro delle Muse*; in 1566, the *Musica libro primo*, with Arcadelt, Berchem, Donato, Festa, Gero, and Willaert. But these compositions no longer embodied the ideal most favored during the sixties.

There remain the villanella and canzonetta written for three parts, the canzonetta also appearing in four parts. For these forms of what may be called the native song, the *tricinium* was a medium not only in keeping with tradition but entirely genuine and "contemporaneous," even in the second half of the century. For the villanella and the canzonetta, the *tricinium* must have been the most satisfactory expression.

Was Monteverdi's choice of the *tricinium* for his first motets an at-

---

[13] *Selectissimarum sacrarum cantionum* (*quas vulgo moteta vocant*) *flores, trium vocum: ex optimis ac praestantissimis quibusque diuinae Musices authoribus excerptarum* . . . (Louvain, 1569).

[14] *Madregali a tre voci de diversi eccellentissimi autori* . . . (Venice, 1561).

tempt to revive a species already obsolete and dying out, or a result of the influence of secular music? The answer to this question is of extreme importance in any consideration of the beginnings of Monteverdi's art. If he chose the *tricinium* in order to keep up an antiquated form, he must have done so because he believed in Netherlandish art as a whole. If he selected it in order to carry over types of native song into the motet, he must have opposed the Netherlandish music from the very start. Only a careful investigation of the style of Monteverdi's *Cantiunculae* will reveal the full story.

CHAPTER FOUR

The Style of the Cantiunculae

THE brevity of the *Cantiunculae* arouses suspicion as to the religious connotations of certain cuts made by Monteverdi, and his treatment of the texts is decidedly individualistic. These motets are sacred compositions in the truest sense: they are composed for definite liturgies, and most of them belong to the officium. Monteverdi's selection shows that certain parts of the services of the church year have been given preference. He obviously preferred texts that were lyrical and expressive, and singled out those that refer to the stark events of religious history. Many of the compositions are dedicated to the liturgy of saints and, most significantly, martyrs. The officia of SS. Stephan, Andreas, Lucia, Helena,[1] Peter, and Thomas are represented. This emphasis on martyrology was encouraged by the Counter Reformation in all the arts and letters as fostering a new, intense devotion. From an artistic point of view, these stories of passionate martyrdom allowed the composer increased musical expressiveness.

Several texts of the story of Christ's life, as given in various services of the year, were chosen by Monteverdi, notably those centering on the Passion, which strike the same note as the stories of the martyrs. The Christmas text has a narrative form—the report of Christ's birth given by the angel to the shepherds—taken from the Gospel of Luke and used for the antiphon to the lauds on December 25. The same subject is treated in *Hodie Christus natus est*, the antiphon to the Magnificat at the vespers of the same day. Both texts have an emotional inten-

---

[1] There was no special officium of St. Helena. Monteverdi used *Veni, sponsa Christi*, the antiphon to the Magnificat, in both vespers of the *Commune Virginum. Veni, sponsa Christi* is also the antiphon for the first vespers on the Feast of St. Mary, in Apparitione B. Mariae Virginis Immaculatae, on February 11.

sity, especially the second, which consists of joyful exclamations befitting the nature of the feast. The second group of the Christ motets comprises works which treat several incidents of the Passion or are prayers to the Holy Cross. With the exception of *O Magnum Pietatis*, the antiphon to the first vespers in the officium to the Feast of the Inventio S. Crucis (May 3), and the sequence *Lauda Sion Salvatorem* to be sung In Festo Corporis Christi, all the Christ motets fall in the weeks around Easter. Passages from the Gospels, from the Psalms, or from Ecclesiastes make up the liturgical texts, nearly all of them expressive of Christ's martyrdom. Two motets stress the adoption of Christ's doctrine as the basis for the foundation of the church. The St. Peter motet, *Tu es pastor*, can be added to this group, although it also belongs among the motets for the saints. Only three compositions are dedicated to the Virgin Mary: one whose text is the medieval poem *Ave, Maria, gratiae plena*, the other two with texts from the highly poetical Song of Solomon, all of them to be sung in the canonical hours.[2]

With the exception of two texts, all the compositions employ passages from the Scriptures, and one of the two exceptions may be a paraphrase of a Bible text. Most of the liturgical works use antiphons of the officium, four take up the texts of responsories, and one the passage of a lesson.[3] Paraphrases of Gospel texts are not infrequent. In view of the strict observance of the liturgical place to be assigned to the motets, we should not hesitate to assume that Monteverdi's compositions were intended to express the religious intensity of the Counter Reformation. Yet we find that Monteverdi had treated some of the biblical texts freely, in a manner that did not conform to the principles of the Counter Reformation. The leaders of the reform were severe in their insistence that musicians should not change the texts from the approved version. Often composers did no more than purify their texts from such deviations in order to comply with the demands of the office that granted the imprimatur. Monteverdi, however, had his own ways of arranging the passages he chose from the Scriptures. He made frequent cuts—a practice not uncommon with other composers, as some texts were too long to be used in their entirety. But it was not common practice to cut, as Monteverdi did, the twenty-four verses of the *Lauda Sion* to three lines!

---

[2] The motet *Surge propera* has been assigned to the "Feast of St. Mary" without any further indication by G. Cesari, *Istituzioni*, p. civ. Monteverdi's version of *Quam pulchra es* does not literally conform to the official text.

[3] The second part of the St. Peter motet is not the antiphon to the first vespers, but the responsory (without verse) of the first nocturn after the third lesson in the matin.

In arranging his texts, Monteverdi made various deviations from the established versions, the most harmless of which is repetition, often with a change of word order. The fifth motet has the following text in the tenor: "Ubi duo vel tres congregati fuerint in medio eorum sum, in nomine meo, dicit Dominus, in nomine meo, in nomine meo, dicit Dominus, dicit Dominus, Alleluja (six times)." The text is drawn from Matthew XVIII. 20: "Ubi enim sunt duo vel tres congregati in nomine meo, ibi sum in medio eorum." The grammatical order of the gospels naturally made the proper sense, but Monteverdi shifted the accents: he severed the "in nomine meo" from its context, stressed its importance by repetition, and concentrated on the climax—the ending of the composition with the added exclamation "Alleluja!" Monteverdi wanted the artistic climax to appear at the end, and attached so much importance to this effect that he frequently changed the text, even at the expense of grammar. Words or passages of important emotional content are usually repeated, even in the middle of the composition. If no other climactic device is available, Monteverdi adds "Alleluja" as a repetitive exclamation, even though it may not be found in the liturgical formula. Most of the motets end with this additional "Alleluja!"

Another way of adapting the material is by combining texts drawn from different sources. This procedure has precedent in the liturgical books, where the texts for the services of the year often combine passages from different books of the Bible. One of Monteverdi's motets illustrates this procedure. The response of the nocturn used on Friday of the week after Easter has the official text: "Surgens Jesus, Dominus noster, stans in medio discipulorum suorum, dixit: Pax vobis, alleluja; gavisi sunt discipuli viro Domino, alleluja." This is a combination of a sentence of Luke (xxiv. 36) with one of John (xx. 20).[4] Except for the repetition of the "Alleluja," Monteverdi did not change the text. The composer also must have freely combined passages on his own account, unless he availed himself of arrangements made by others. The motet No. 20 has two additions that cannot be accounted for: the exclamations "O bone Jesu" and "O Adonai." For the rest, the text combines the fourth verse of Psalm 12, with slight deviations, a sentence of Luke (xxiii. 46), and the sixth verse of Psalm 30. In each of these lines, however, the version is not literal and must be taken as a free, nonliturgical arrangement, although the motet has its definite place in

---

[4] Luke xxiv. 36: "Dum autem haec loquuntur, stetit Jesus in medio eorum, et dicit eius: Pax vobis." John xx. 20: "Gavisi sunt ergo discipuli, viso Domino." Monteverdi's combination of the texts does not contain "slight variants" of the official version as G. Cesari, Istituzioni, p. cvi, assumes; it is the responsory without change.

the liturgy. A peculiar, but characteristic, combination is presented in the motet *Quam pulchra es et quam decora*. The text is a mixture of four lines taken from the Song of Solomon, each of which has an entirely different context in the original.

The second part of the motet *O Magnum pietatis opus* offers an interesting arrangement. It contains the story of Christ's death: "Eli clamans, (Eli clamans) Spiritum Patri commendavit, latus ejus lancea miles perforavit, terra tunc contremuit et sol obscuravit." For this text, all four versions of the Gospel have been used: Matthew xxvii. 46, 50; Luke xxiii. 45, 46; Mark xv. 34, 37; and John xix. 34.[5]

This free and easy treatment of official texts suggests that Monteverdi did not intend his *Cantiunculae* as contributions to the musical plans of the Counter Reformation, since the authorities would certainly have objected to the liberties he took with the Scriptures. Though religious in their function as settings for the services, the motets are entirely lacking in the intensity considered suitable to the purposes of the Counter Reformation. Monteverdi's choice of texts, his ways of combining passages, of underlining the important phrases, of distributing the accents, are the result of artistic considerations, not religious devotion. The *Cantiunculae* are not part of the movement through which Sfondrato and Ingegneri gained distinction for Cremona; in fact, it appears almost certain that Monteverdi did not compose these works for Cremona at all. The motet that is related to the officium of St. Helena and another composition set to a text used in the Ambrosian liturgy suggest that Monteverdi may have composed the *Cantiunculae* for a specific diocese or monastery or parochial church. This may account for the use of only three voices, in order not to overtax the local musical resources. At any rate, a careful appraisal of the texts reveals no link between this first collection of motets and the goal of the Counter Reformation. But is Monteverdi as far from the Netherlandish style as he is from the ideals of the religious movement?

In several ways the *Cantiunculae* are the work of a beginner; they have a certain stiffness and some technical deficiencies, but not because of the lack of skill one is prepared to find in youthful compositions.

---

[5] Matthew xxvii. 46: "Et circa horam nonam clamavit Jesus voce magna, dicens: Eli, Eli, lamma sabacthani?" . . . 50: "Jesus autem iterum clamans voce magna, emisit spiritum." Luke xxiii. 46: "Et clamans voce magna Jesus ait: Pater in manus tuas commendo spiritum meum. Et haec dicens exspiravit." Mark xv. 34: "Et hora nona exclamavit Jesus voce magna, dicens: Eloi, eloi, lamma sabacthani?" . . . 37: "Jesus autem emissa voce magna exspiravit." John xix. 34: "Sed unus militum lancea latus eius aperuit." Luke xxiii. 45: "Et obscuratus est sol, et velum templi scissum est medium."

We should not expect the fresh vitality of youth in any product of the aged sixteenth-century music, but there is something that may be attributed to the adolescence of the works—a monotony as distinct as it is striking. This is not a monotony of sound—for the works were not intended to be performed one after the other in the manner of a concert program—but a monotony of method, resulting from a concentration on only one or two problems of composition. A narrowness of view and a lack of musical knowledge forced Monteverdi to draw continually on the one technique he had studiously acquired. But in quite a different sense he was also a beginner: he began to obscure the categories of composition. He did not develop the motet out of its own tradition, but allowed the intervention of other elements. It is a definite indication that a certain musical category has entered a phase of insecurity, when tradition no longer protects it from arbitrary change, for soon the category itself will be questioned. At a superficial glance we would not hesitate to assign the *Cantiunculae* to the Netherlandish style of motets, but on closer examination we are likely to revoke our judgment completely. Their musical character is revealed, naturally, by the structural disposition of the material as a whole, but most of all by the treatment of melody and rhythm.

An analysis of the *Cantiunculae* reveals a serious disturbance of balance. Alien elements appear to yield with reluctance to the artistic process of unification. There is a fluency which never comes to a halt, never allows the inner periods to become noticeable, never permits the strong cadences and sharp caesurae to organize the composition, and this is in accordance with the Netherlandish concept of musical form. There is also something of the uninterrupted melodic flow which is essential to the nature of Netherlandish melody. Nevertheless, these characteristics appear to be somewhat superficial, for the melody lacks the bold curves that encompass an ample range and it does not have the drive which makes Netherlandish melody irresistible. Netherlandish melody is essentially melismatic, but Monteverdi gives his melody an essentially syllabic shape.[6] Here begins the conflict between the elements that make up the structure of his melody. Monteverdi's melody is based on declamation derived from the natural qualities of the syllables. This procedure has many implications for melody and rhythm alike. All long or accentuated syllables are regularly given a higher rhythmical

---

[6] The melismatic style of melody has more or less large groups of tones set to a syllable, whereas the syllabic style shows only one tone to a syllable. The melisma may combine tones from three upward to any number; Netherlandish melismata with twenty tones to a group are not rare.

value, and since the relation between long and short values varies in all cases, stereotyped formulas are easily avoided.

Ex. 1

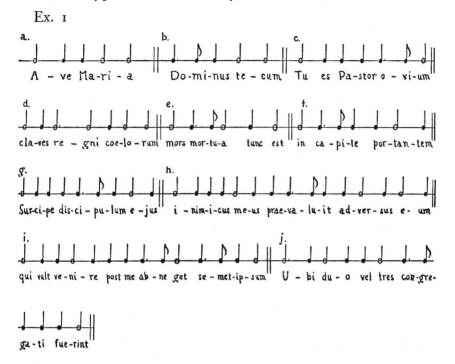

Thus the musical rhythm follows harmoniously the accentuation of the text. Since the text is prose, without regularity of meter or any organized succession of rhythmical qualities, the musical rhythm is never crystallized into a pattern, and the rhythmical formula never becomes stereotyped or repetitious. But we can easily imagine that such treatment of a text with a metrical or rhythmic regularity would automatically result in repetitive patterns.

Musical rhythm produced in imitative relation to the text is not an attribute of the Northern school. At times declamation was used deliberately and energetically, especially by Josquin, and some Venetian composers under the guidance of Adrian Willaert had introduced declamatory elements in their melodies. Motets by Andrea Gabrieli continued a practice that may have originated with Willaert himself, and Orlandus Lassus treated declamation still more seriously, making it a specific mark of his style. Although these predecessors may well have inspired Monteverdi, none of them acknowledged the principle of imitation as the main source of musical rhythm. That this imitation

brought forth so many varieties was by accident rather than from artistic intention. Imitative, declamatory, and principally syllabic rhythm
was used by Monteverdi in his first compositions. Syllabic declamation,
though kept up on principle, did not exclude the use of the melisma,
which assumed two forms: a simple ligature combining two tones [7]
or a full group of tones varying in numbers. Monteverdi used the
melisma for two purposes. One was to distinguish an individual word
and underline its significance. In this use, the melisma varies in length,
depending on musical necessities.

Ex. 2

The examples show that Monteverdi used the melisma whenever
the meaning of a word naturally suggested it, or when the importance
of a word made it musically prominent. The word "Alleluja" has, of
course, a special place in this category. The Netherlanders were familiar with this kind of melisma, particularly in the last generation of
the school, and it was from them that Monteverdi learned its use. One
form of this melisma is the realistic imitation of a word through tones
which take on the character of a material gesture to convey the meaning of the word symbolically. Thus, a succession of ascending tones,
rising either according to the scale or by an interval, may represent the
word "Surge." The Netherlanders made use of this form of realism,
and Monteverdi at times adopted it in his *Cantiunculae.*

Ex. 3,1   XIV, 8

Ex. 3,2

It is significant, however, that this type of realistic gesture was less
frequently used by Monteverdi than by Northern composers, probably
because he realized that the realistic melodic motif, with a procedure
of its own, did not conform to syllabic declamation.

---

[7] The only ligature used is the so-called *ligatura cum opposita proprietate.*

Of greater importance is Monteverdi's second use of the melisma when the regular declamation requires a relatively large rhythmic value to mark an accentuated or long syllable. When Monteverdi puts both forms side by side, the pure declamation does not ordinarily come first, with the melisma as an increase and intensification, but the melismatic version is used first and then reduced to the declamatory type.

Ex. 4

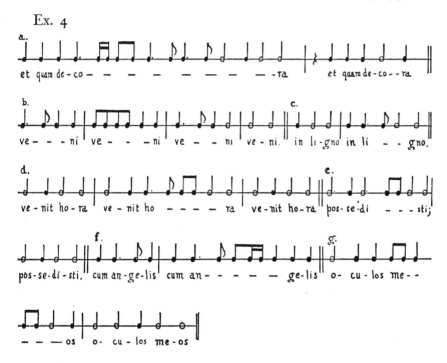

At times two different melismatic versions are set over against two declamatory forms and made to alternate symmetrically, with the melisma taking the place of a long rhythmic value. When both forms occur in the same composition, the artistic implications are considerable and reveal a concept of melody in terms of motifs that dissociates Monteverdi from the Northerners. When a melodic phrase of Monteverdi's can be reduced to a primary form, the melisma proves to be superimposed upon a simple form of the original phrase. The Netherlandish composer, however, took the melisma as the essential part of his melody, for his melodic thinking was always in terms of the melisma. He never started with a basic and simple phrase of which any and all ornate variations must be regarded as offspring. Such a concept would produce a clearly defined motif above the uninterrupted melismatic stream of melody, and this is precisely what takes place in Monteverdi's melody. He handles the motif, set to a text phrase, as a melodic entity, which has its own force and tends to organize the melodic course, not for the sake of producing endless melodic lines, but to achieve clarity by means of the well-designed contours of the individual phrases. This force which organizes the melody, though still irresolute and somewhat indistinct, is strong enough to make itself felt in certain sections of Monteverdi's work. The power of a melodic motif may be such as to produce its immediate sequel, regardless of the text; that it to say, because of its tendency to complete itself, one melodic type may be used for two different successive phrases of the text.

Ex. 5   XIV, 12

ac - - ci - pe   spi-ri-tum me-um   et ne sta-tu-as il- - - lis hoc pec-ca-tum

Motif *a* is productive in that the logic of its motion calls forth a variation of its own, *b*. Thus the motif has independence, follows its own law of progression, is sufficiently strong to cover two phrases of the text, and shows the evolution of a melody for its own sake. This is possible only when the composer allows a group of tones to be crystallized into a motif which proceeds according to its own power. That Monteverdi thinks of melody as composed of short, concise motifs rather than as a flow of melismata without phrases or caesurae is most strikingly shown by the motet of the Song of Songs—*Quam pulchra es*.[8]

---

[8] The melody is analyzed according to the motifs *a-d*; the same, or varied, form of these motifs is marked *a¹-d¹*. The letter *a* refers to the last phrase within *c²*, treated as sequence.

Dr. Alfred Einstein kindly called my attention to a most interesting find made by Mr. Arnold Hartman (Columbia University, New York), to whom I am indebted for the information. Mr. Hartman discovered that for *Quam pulchra es* Monteverdi made liberal use of Costanzo Festa's three-part motet on the same text. The motet of Festa is contained in Gardane's *Motetta trium vocum ab pluribus authoribus composita*, of 1543, which has been used for the modern editions by Burney, *History of Music*, and in *Monumenta Polyphoniae Italicae*, Vol. II, "Constantius Festa, Sacrae Cantiones," ed. by Ed. Dagnino (Rome, 1936), pp. 15ff. Dagnino also included the four-part motet *Quam pulchra es* by Festa from the collection of motets Antiqui published in 1521; between the two compositions of Festa there is an obvious relationship.

It seems certain that Monteverdi followed the sixteenth-century custom of using models to produce "parodies," and surely any young musician was advised to parody models as a study of composition. For the first part of *Quam pulchra es*, the quotations from Festa are more or less literal, but always characteristically changed or shortened; for the second part, they are few and almost entirely free. At all events, the changes Monteverdi made are extraordinary and conclusive as to his inability to be truly Netherlandish. For he changed the declamation, the cadences, the motifs, the accentuation, the rhythms, the phrasing, the harmony; and what he cut out from his model is as revealing as the change of the material he used.

Ex. 6 XIV, 13

A further simplification gives the following picture:

Ex. 7

The order of Monteverdi's melody is ruled by a symmetry that only motifs can provide. Even if Monteverdi embellishes the phrases with melismata like those of Costanzo Festa, the frame of the melody is built according to rigid principles of phrasing and accentuation, and the melismata merely adorn the melody, without serving any such structural purpose as in the motet of Festa. The three melodic phrases set to "et quam decora," have nothing to do with the text but grow out of the plan to complete the melody by way of symmetries. When the requirements of symmetry are fulfilled, the melody is complete, and the text has to be repeated as many times as the melody requires. When the composition proceeds to "quam pulchra es," the first motif reappears (in the original a^1 rhythmically reduced), and the section progresses in such a manner as to materialize the structure of couplets $A: A^1$, which the model actually suggests. Above all, each of the motifs or phrases Monteverdi parodies is, in fact, "purified" from the Netherlandish aspects of the model.

Firm melodic outline, clarity in phrasing, a balanced relation between the constituent sections, logical correspondence of antecedent and consequent, and precise groups of rhythmic accents—all these are characteristic of songlike structures and occur in the melody of Monteverdi's motets. Contrary to Northern procedure, Monteverdi applied a preestablished structure to his melody and allowed the tones to be grouped in melodic patterns. At times he even went so far as to have the melodic and the rhythmic pattern coincide.

Ex. 8 XIV, 15

These phrases show the tendency to complete themselves melodically in such a way that the entire melody is made up of complete and clear entities held together by a concise rhythmic pattern. The accents of the text are translated into terms of a musical rhythm that imitates the accentuation of "Ave Maria." The result is the pattern: ♩♩♩|♩♩♩|, which appears several times in its proper form. All deviations from it are devices to cover up the stereotyped appearance of the pattern or to meet needs arising from the combination of the three voices—in other words, from the problem of harmony. Nevertheless, on account of the pattern, the rhythm exercises a compelling effect that makes itself felt throughout the work. The polyphonic structure that Monteverdi chose for his *Cantiunculae* does not allow such patterns to be stated evenly and simultaneously in all the parts. But each voice, taken individually, exhibits a regularity that is the result of a prevalent rhythmic form. Of course, the melismata, characteristic of the Netherlandish style, tend to interfere with the establishment of a fixed pattern, since

(Innsbruck, Ferdinandeum)

1 Claudio Monteverdi

2 *Orfeo: Aria Possente spirito*

the Northern composers eschewed rhythmic patterns and cultivated irrational forms of rhythm.

The predominance of a motif that influences the growth of the melody as a whole is perhaps best demonstrated in the Christmas motet *Hodie Christus natus est* (No. 12). The initial melodic phrase is presented as a unit:

Ex. 9 XIV, 26

The two sections *a* and *b*, treated as the basic constituents of the melody, are responsible for all that follows. The twenty-one motifs which make up the melody can be derived from the initial "theme." Monteverdi cuts it in two, handles the sections separately, inserts the motif to "Hodie" (*a*) in alternating fashion, either unchanged and merely shifted to another pitch, or in its inverted form, which in turn gives rise to a new motif for another text, while section *b* always produces "variations" of the original form; *a* and *b*, first a unit, are alternating with each other.

Ex. 10 [9]

A comparable situation can be found in *Salve, crux preciosa* (No. 17) and in *O Domine Jesu Christe* (No. 13*b*),[10] although the derivation of the melodic material from an initial "theme" is not so clear as in *Hodie natus est*. The latter motet shows how the composer operates with two brief motifs, of which one is the inverted form of the other:

---

[9] The numbers refer to the sections of the melody, of which there are twenty-one.
[10] *O Domine Jesu Christe* is the *secunda pars* of the motet No. 13 with the same *incipit* of the text. There are also "thematic" relations between *prima* and *secunda pars* —for instance, on "deprecor te."

Ex. 11 XIV, 32

Frequently Monteverdi links the melodic phrase and the text closely together in such manner as to have one and the same text call for the same melodic motif. This occurs either in literal form, or as a melodic sequence, or together with a slight variation.

Ex. 12

The variation of a melodic type whose original form is often difficult to establish can be seen by comparing three melismatic specimens of one motif, whose melisma Monteverdi gradually reduces without ever giving it in unornamented form.

Ex. 13 XIV, 36

This displays the technique of melodic variation in which the least varied form appears last and shows how Monteverdi relies on the sharp outlines of a motif in order to develop melody. Without them, this technique would be impossible.

Some melodic and rhythmic formulas may present themselves to the hasty critic as genuinely Netherlandish, especially when the motifs are pieced together to form typical Northern lines without end and, seemingly, without organization. A highly interesting and instructive example may be closely examined.

Ex. 14   XIV, 15

If we disregard the text, we should not hesitate to consider the phrase Northern, for it has all the distinguishing marks of Netherlandish melodies: the marginal tones of tetrachords (f-c, d-a) are the points of limit for the range of the melody; each tetrachord is passed through by the descending scale (f-e-d-c; d-c-b-a); the melody does not rest on its lowest point but swings immediately to its other end, the junction made by the characteristic skip of the octave. But every connoisseur of such melodies will be disturbed in the second half of the phrase (*b*), where there occurs an element of interference, strange if presented by a Netherlander, though comprehensible as a form used by Monteverdi. The entire phrase is brought forth in such a way as to make section *b* follow as a well-balanced response to the first (*a*), so that melodic completeness is established and one section harmonizes with the other. From the Netherlandish point of view, however, period *b* contains a confusing factor, for the center of gravity appears to be "wrongly" placed. Monteverdi puts it on c (*), and a Netherlander would not have done so. The melodic phrase swings into motion by a syncopation. As soon as the lowest point in the melody is reached, the Northern composer maintains the force that the syncopation grants. In order to avoid any break in the melody, he would have anticipated the center of gravity by placing it in the skip of the octave, or he might perhaps have located the concentration on d″, never on c″, as Monteverdi has done. A genuinely Netherlandish version of the phrase would go as follows:

Ex. 15

The next motif is equally interesting and important, as it shows that Monteverdi is not in full accord with the model he tries to imitate.[11]

Ex. 16 XIV, 15

et be-ne-dic- - - - - - tus fruc-tus ven - - - tris   tu-is Je-sus tu- -is Je- - - -sus

The order of the melody seems to be in the Netherlandish manner, especially the flow of the rhythm, the "swinging." The succession of half notes gives a regular motion, and, as a counteraction, a continual syncopation appears. But a Netherlander would have been forced into this swinging of constant interferences by his understanding of rhythmic movement. With Monteverdi, this motion is mechanical, for it results, not from the needs of melodic progression, but from the syllabic declamation, and the syncopation in period *b* is caused by the qualities of the syllables. Monteverdi's declamation does not have the characteristic Northern swinging movement that produces an uninterrupted stream of melodic lines that force singer and listener alike into their spell. In this case, it is the text that produces the melodic motion, and there are many other such examples in Monteverdi's *Cantiunculae*.

What is it, then, that conveys the impression that these early compositions originated under the influence of Northern music? If the melody is formed according to motifs and a syllabic declamation, which at times even allows the rhythm to take the shape of patterns, there would seem to be no traces of the Northern style. This is where the historical contradictions of Monteverdi's motets become manifest. He used two methods of composition, both drawn from the Northern school, and applied them so forcefully that they cause all the inner contradictions. The first of these—the method of piecing the melody into a whole—has already been discussed. The second concerns the fact that almost all the *Cantiunculae* have canons, canonic technique, or imitation between the voices.

Monteverdi invented phrases with such clear outlines and caesurae that he must have had enormous difficulties in realizing a melodic unity. In order to avoid the full consequences of the tendency of caesurae to divide the melody into sharply defined periods, he joined his brief, syllabic motifs to one another without breaks, or any sort of stop, and

---

[11] The phrase is connected with the preceding melody without break or rest.

thus produced long lines, not as melismata, but as persistently syllabic declamation. When a cut is unavoidable by reason of a cadence, Monteverdi has recourse to a typically Netherlandish technique. He bridges the gap by prolonging the rhythmic value of one or the other tone to be carried into the phrase to come; or, when we expect a lengthy rest, he makes the last accentuated note of the cadence intentionally short and continues immediately with a long rhythmic value, thus producing syncopation: ♩|♩ ' ♩♩| instead of ♩|♩ ♪ ♩|♩ . This was a favorite device of the Northerners to secure continuity. Monteverdi knew its effect and wisely applied it to his melody, but it remained, as it were, an external application, for the precise, short motif of declamatory character functioned as the creative element. Hence, we have the paradox that Monteverdi's melody has the full size and length of a Netherlandish melisma and is as "endless" as a Northern melody; yet it is not organically a melisma but is syllabically organized according to patterns, motifs, periods, and symmetries, very much in the manner of a song. It is not surprising that Monteverdi did not succeed in his attempt to combine these contradictory elements. Songlike organization and the melody of the Netherlandish motet are historical incongruities.

The second device—the canonic and imitative technique—is one to which the Northerners devoted their musical mastership and enormous skill. In nearly all his motets Monteverdi piously observed the technique of canon and imitation for the structure of his compositions. Indeed, a beginner probably could not expect to be heard unless he gave evidence of having mastered the Netherlandish manner of polyphonic writing, particularly in the traditional field of the motet. Monteverdi's use of this technique had an extraordinary result in that it covered up many contradictions that the individual voice by itself would make obvious. The asymmetrical entrances of the voices made all the melodic lines uneven in length, so that the endings of the phrases were as irregular as the entrances. This was of considerable assistance in obscuring the caesurae and periods that appear in Monteverdi's melody.

Despite the extraordinary regularity with which Monteverdi carried out the canonic technique, his compositions have a far less convincing structure than their Netherlandish models. The organization Monteverdi imposes upon the melody, the use of motifs, the conciseness of phrases, the procedure according to patterns, the correspondence of phrases—all these express the concept that melody should accord with the structure of a song. Such a structure, however, requires one melodically prominent part to which all other parts should be subordinate. Netherlandish melody, designed for polyphonic interweaving and formed with all the other parts in view, made use of a "relative" melody. Song structure, on the other hand, demanded that one part should stand out as an "absolute" melody. No matter how Monteverdi tried to obscure his songlike concept of melody, he did not fully succeed, for in applying the Northern technique of imitation to this type of melody, he was combining incongruous elements. He made use of that technique since it afforded the "endlessness" of Northern composition, but his solution was exceedingly artificial. The impression of formal inconsistency in his *Cantiunculae* comes from this inner discrepancy and not from an unskillful handling of the technique of imitation. But the stereotyped application of the technique, as though it were nothing but a mechanical device, shows the artificiality of the procedure. In Monteverdi's work all the features expressive of the Northern style are artificial. The long, "unorganized," endless line of melody is the result of piecing motifs or phrases together without a break, and the imitative structure is not a natural outgrowth of the melody. Monteverdi had no genuine understanding of the Netherlandish form; he was not born with that sense of the Northern melody which was still found in Palestrina. In later years he admitted as much. When he consciously tried to imitate the Northern style in certain Masses, he had to confess that it took considerable intellectual effort to force his mind and musical nature into a style in which he actually felt himself a stranger. When he composed his *Cantiunculae*, the sacred motets, it was necessary for him to follow the traditional Northern style as his model, yet he was at variance with the Netherlanders from the very beginning. The natural qualities of his musical gift directed him toward forms other than the motet and away from the tradition. The *Cantiunculae* must later have appeared to him as faulty youthful works, to be pardoned for their immaturity, but fundamentally unsatisfactory. They awakened him, however, to new necessities, to the beginnings of his struggle with the past.

It has been said that Monteverdi acquired the technique of counterpoint needed for these first motets in the school established by Ingegneri. Yet Ingegneri could hardly have called forth the particular form of melody which appeared in the *Cantiunculae*, since his motets adhere to Northern melodic concepts. He still had a natural understanding of melismatic melodies, and the procedure of piecing syllabic motifs together is nowhere found in his motets or Masses. On the other hand, it was only by an extreme effort that Monteverdi could produce any-thing comparable to Netherlandish melody.[12] The category of the motet necessarily linked his first compositions to the Northerners'; otherwise their structure would have been entirely different. For the form of Monteverdi's melody came from the categories of secular music with its songlike structures. This he realized after the *Cantiunculae*. His struggle with the past was to be a struggle with the musical art of the North, not because he condemned that art in any theoretical manner, but because he could no longer reconcile his nature to it.

MADRIGALI SPIRITUALI

From now on Monteverdi was to work systematically toward a definite end, and every phase of his development is a step in this process. His development is progressive in the truest sense, in that one step logi-cally follows another, so that we observe with fascination a process that seems to bear the marks of a powerful mind trained to think in terms of artistic necessities.

Monteverdi started with a certain belief in the religious qualities of music that led him to accept the musical forms of Northern origin. When he came to realize that his talents were not suited to such forms, he dropped them. But in a time that was permeated with the ideas of a religious renewal and in a place where men of fervor were devoting their efforts to the advancement of religion, a complete turning away from religious subjects would have been unsuitable. And so Monteverdi retained certain religious aspects in his work, while giving free rein to the secular form.

The work that follows the *Cantiunculae*, the collection of *Madrigali Spirituali*, is a typical product of the Counter Reformation in that the substantially secular nature of its music is found in an enforced alliance with the prevailing religious tendencies. We know only too well that the numerous spiritual madrigals of the period differ musically from ordinary madrigals only in that the Italian texts, instead of being pro-fane, are intentionally made to appear devout. Such a compromise was apparently acceptable by the standards of the time. But was it also ac-ceptable by artistic standards? Monteverdi did not seem to think so. After completing his *Madrigali Spirituali*, he dropped the category al-together.

---

[12] Stylistically, the melody of Monteverdi cannot be judged under the aspects of its modal character. He writes melodies according to the modes and the system of solmization. This, however, is not the essential factor in the disposition of the melody as a whole.

The collection of *Madrigali Spirituali* for four voices, published in 1583,[13] contains twenty-one compositions, ten of which have the customary *seconda parte*. It is unfortunate that the bass part alone has been preserved, the three other voices being lost. From a purely artistic point of view, the loss may not be significant, since the compositions may not have gone far beyond the technical standards of the *Cantiunculae*. From the point of view of his logical development, however, the loss is severe, for the *Madrigali Spirituali* surely represent important steps toward a melodic and rhythmical expression closer to the nature of his gifts. Francesco Saverio Quadrio, the eighteenth-century historian of Italian literature, surprisingly mentions the spiritual madrigals, but has nothing to tell about them.[14] Their stylistic character, therefore, cannot be established, but the choice of four voices may have had some implications. Publishing his first book around 1570 [15] and a second book in 1579, Ingegneri had preceded Monteverdi with secular madrigals for four voices by more than a decade. It may well be that Monteverdi worked under the influence of such compositions.[16] About 1580, however, the madrigal for four voices declined rapidly in importance, and even during the seventies the five-part madrigal was beginning to be favored. Ingegneri himself did not continue the series of four-part madrigals after the second book. At the time when Monteverdi published his *Madrigali Spirituali* they were already slightly antiquated. Perhaps Monteverdi was trying to maintain a link with tradition, for he was never an abrupt revolutionary, who broke with the past suddenly and completely, but always proceeded slowly and systematically. Though the *Madrigali Spirituali* still come within the religious sphere, the composer was now ready to oppose the Northern heritage still dominant in Italian music.

This opposition is evident in Monteverdi's next works. Again his

---

[13] The bass part has been published in facsimile by G. Francesco Malipiero in *Opere* (Asolo, 1926–42), Vol. XVI.

[14] Quadrio does not "describe" the madrigals as has often been stated. Francesco Saverio Quadrio, *Della Storia e della Ragione d'ogni poesia*, Vol. II, Book II (Milan, 1742—only the first volume is published in Bologna, 1739), p. 324: "Claudio Monteverde, Maestro di Cappella di San Marco in Venezia, pose in Musica, e pubblicò un Volume di Madrigali Spirituali a 4. Voci, la qual Opera fu stampata in Brescia nel 1583." It is not even clear if Quadrio had really seen the work. In Tomo VII (Milan, 1752), p. 176, he added to the list of Monteverdi's works mention of the seventh and eighth books of madrigals; of the latter he stated that Petrarch's sonnet *Vago augelletto* appeared at the end of the book, which is not correct. Here too, it is uncertain whether he had seen the publications.

[15] The year of the first edition is not established, since all copies have been lost. Only the later editions from 1578 on are preserved. Cf. E. Dohrn, *op. cit.*, p. 12.

[16] The influence of Ingegneri on Monteverdi's later madrigals is negligible.

course sprang logically from the phase represented by the *Madrigali Spirituali*. What the *Cantiunculae* had merely indicated was about to be realized in the canzonetta, whose capacities Monteverdi now tested. If, indeed, he had begun to visualize opposition to the *Oltremontani* as necessary to overcome their manner of writing—and we believe he did—the shift to the canzonetta was the logical step forward. It was also the most momentous decision the young man could have made. For now he was to experience the full power of a rhythm that strives for steady patterns and to make use of the clarity and distinctness which the motif can give to melodic organization. His musical disposition and the characteristics of the canzonetta must have met halfway. What had previously been possible only obscurely and indirectly was realized in perfect harmony. Monteverdi made the all-important discovery that the tradition of Italian music already possessed in the canzonetta a form which was bound to effect opposition to the *Oltremontani*. The native canzonetta had properties entirely foreign to the Northern ideal, which merely needed to be used as part of a planned opposition to make the disintegration of the Northern style an artistic reality. But first Monteverdi was to be the student and explorer, one who set out to fathom the innate characteristics and potentialities of the native song in the form of the canzonetta. This development was to have far-reaching consequences.

CHAPTER
FIVE

Monteverdi's Canzonette

THE *Canzonette à tre voci* were published in 1584 by the Venetian printers Giacomo Vincenti and Ricciardo Amadino. In these compositions Monteverdi was using a category traditionally different from everything Northern. The canzonetta was the third art form evolved by native talent in Italy. The first of these, the frottola, was followed by the villanella, which was from the outset "a protest against the madrigal." [1] For this reason, the tone of the villanella was a novelty, although there was nothing really new about the character of the text, which was straightforward, sometimes uncouth and obscene; at all events it was rustic, and in most cases intentionally simple, boorish, and unpolished. The same simplicity and "popularity" were artfully employed in the music. The villanella was gradually superseded but not eliminated by the canzonetta, which added a more courtly tone to text and music. At times the canzonetta was musically more pretentious, and the number of voices was occasionally increased from four to six. This increase in volume brought the canzonetta closer to the stylistic techniques of the madrigal, which in turn was somewhat influenced by the fashionable canzonetta. The number of canzonette had been constantly on the increase since the seventies, and in the year 1584, when Monteverdi published his canzonette, no fewer than 170 compositions in that form were brought out. By the time Giovanni Gastoldi published his first collection of dance canzonette in the early nineties, the output was well past the first thousand, not counting the many

---

[1] A. Einstein, "Die mehrstimmige weltliche Musik von 1450–1600," in Adler, *HMG* (1930), I, 371.

collections in which particularly effective and successful compositions were reprinted.

The art of the canzonetta had come from the South, particularly from Naples, where Giovanni Domenico da Nola was its most prominent exponent. The canzonetta of Domenico rapidly spread over all Italy and called forth fresh energies among the musicians of northern Italy. By 1570 there were a number of cities where musicians, Southerners and Northerners alike, cultivated the new native songs. From Milan, a center of this activity, there were two routes along which the influence of these songs spread: one, south of the Alps, leading through Verona, Padua, Venice, and Treviso, to Capodistria; the other, north of the Apennines, leading to Mantua, Viadana, Reggio, Correggio, Modena, Ferrara, Bologna, Imola, and, on the eastern coast, Ravenna and Sinigaglia. Of these centers, Venice, Milan, Modena, and Bologna were probably the most important. In Venice, interest in the native song was traditional; Willaert had made distinguished contributions and stimulated the greatest of his Italian pupils, Andrea Gabrieli, to continue in that vein. Since Venice had become the publishing center for such songs, Venetian musicians had a comprehensive and immediate knowledge of their various forms. The interest of Milanese composers was at least equal to that of the Venetians, but many musicians there seem to have concentrated exclusively on the canzonetta. Cesare Borgo, Gasparo Costa, and Giuseppe Caimo were among those who specialized in that form. Bologna was perhaps next in importance, while Modena achieved its great distinction in the composition of canzonette chiefly through the work of Orazio Vecchi, whose compositions made the name of the city familiar all over Europe. Vecchi was not the first in Modena to concentrate on this kind of composition; his predecessor, Salvador Essenga, is also said to have been his teacher.

Except for a few leading figures, the musicians who took part in the advance of the native song did not compose in the musical forms of the great style, such as the motet. In this respect, the situation characteristic of the frottola around 1500 repeated itself with the canzonetta in 1570. A large group of musicians is known to have composed nothing but native songs, though their works in other forms may have disappeared in the course of time. Apparently they paid no attention to the Mass or the motet, not even to the madrigal, whose character should have satisfied their craving for secular music. It cannot now be determined whether this concentration was solely due to their narrow talents and one-sided nature. Since the native song was stereotyped in character and developed along traditional lines, the intention of the composer was to maintain the traditional tone, and this could be done by a musician of minor talent perhaps as skillfully as by a composer of first rank. If he were closer to the tradition, the mediocre talent might even have an advantage over the genius. This may be the reason why we have so many entirely colorless and unknown composers of native songs, who make their appearance in anthologies of songs with less than a handful of compositions. But if a genius chose the category, the result was nearly always notable, not so much for the greatness that he achieved, since no real profundity was possible in the category, as for the reasons that made him use it.

Such was the case with the canzonette of Monteverdi. He used a type which was new, in his development, to comply with a fashionable trend, and also to acquire knowledge of a musical structure whose nature was utterly opposed to the Netherlandish style. His acquaintance with this branch of composition marked the beginning of the end of sixteenth-century concepts.

The texts Monteverdi chose have the structure of the villanella rather than that of the canzonetta, whose Anacreontic character was becoming the fashion toward the end of the century. The couplet in *rime basciate* (*a-a*) is preceded or followed by verses differently rhymed, and at times a refrain concludes the stanza.[2] The length of the lines also conforms to the scheme of the villanella, for they are in meters of seven or eleven syllables. As the structure of the poems, whose authors were usually unknown,[3] corresponds to the villanella, so does the nature of Monteverdi's music, which is closer to the older type than to the later Anacreontic canzonetta which, though light in character, is more ambitious poetically and more artistic musically. In other words, Monteverdi maintained the villanella's original significance, its opposition to, and derision of, the highly artistic madrigal. August Wilhelm Ambros has described the villanella most vividly as a form which has only "a reflected simplicity," and is the result of "an escape from the fragrant, distinguished, noble atmosphere of the madrigal into lower regions where people can occasionally relax themselves without renouncing their inborn and well-bred manners of nobility." And so

---

[2] The refrain must not be literal; slight variations often occur especially for the last appearance of the refrain.

[3] Occasionally the name of a poet is mentioned. Aluvise Castellino, for instance, who published *Il primo libro delle villotte* in Venice in 1541, is the poet and the composer of his villotte. The stanza of the villotta has a certain resemblance to that of the villanella.

"these songs are much like a gentleman who leaves his marble palace in order to rush into the crowd of the masques at St. Mark's disguised as Chiozotte or Barcajuol. The cut of gown and cap is genuine, but the material is velvet and silk." [4]

This seems to be precisely the character Monteverdi assumed when he made use of the canzonetta tradition at a time when the villanella had already begun to lose its deliberately satirical quality. He may not always have hit the target, but he most certainly aimed at satire. Perhaps the student of his work will discover that his music reflects a satirical intention even more clearly than do the words. The texts do not use witticism directly or extensively to ridicule the higher poetry of the madrigal, nor do they abound in obvious allusions to the language of that cultivated species. Their method is to exaggerate the usual tone of the amorous madrigal by overindulging in sentimentality and by detailing repetitiously the torments caused by unrequited love. Their satirical intention is revealed by the stereotyped sentimentality and the use of exaggerated expressions, which expose the feeling as false. The poet treats his subject artificially: he does not feel what he presents as a lyrical expression but parodies a poetical form that was highly esteemed in its proper noble setting. Since the idiom of the madrigal was made up of greatly refined and stylized expressions that were practically formulas and since the nobleman's behavior was also regulated by the strictest rules of fashion, a slight overaccentuation of these stylized forms could easily produce a travesty. Another way in which the texts achieved an effect of caricature was by the combination of incompatible elements. If a simple, unpretentious form like the villanella is made the vehicle of learned allusions to ancient mythology, the effect can hardly be serious. An excellent example is Number 12 of Monteverdi's texts, which depends entirely on this contrast between form and content and has little genuine wit. In *Quando sperai del mio servir mercede* (No. 10) the use of an old theme excludes any personal experience or individual feeling and at the same time reveals the witty ingenuity of the poet in his treatment of a familiar subject. The poet tells the story without expecting the listeners to take it as his own. The eager lover, having most carefully prepared the field of action, finds himself suddenly deprived of the fruits the other fellow comes to pluck; and when he bursts into the extravagantly clamorous refrain "E il frutto, ohimè, di mie fatiche ha colto," the effect is broadly comic. The listeners are not expected to pity the unhappy lover but to think his stupidity

---

[4] August Wilhelm Ambros, *Geschichte der Musik*, III (1868), 510f.

rightly served. In only one of the texts is gross indecency assumed to be witty: in *Godi pur del bel sen, felice pulce* (No. 16), which treats the well-known theme of the flea that has unspeakable privileges in its ever *pizzicando* approach to the girl. But the villanella should occasionally be base if it is to be true to the nature of the category, and the wit does not lie so much in the indecent story as in the shocking contrast of a base subject appearing in refined society. Being a "cosa bassa," as Vincentino declared, the villanella strolled like a clumsy stranger into the high sphere of nobility, where it startled a society that did not dislike being shocked.

The musical character of Monteverdi's canzonette confirms this picture. The student will observe an undeniable lack of originality, or better, of individuality in the musical form of each composition. This has a double significance: First, it shows Monteverdi to be responsive to a musical category which precludes an ingenious individualism whose capricious turns might undermine its nature. Second, it proves his subtle understanding of the villanella, which was never suited to grandiloquent feats of artistic composition. The canzonette of Monteverdi are more or less alike in their basic structure and their characteristic simplicity. Since the villanella was a "cosa bassa," the learned theorists seldom paid attention to its music or to the forms of its ancestors. Whenever it was discussed, the simplicity of its structure, particularly apparent in a villanella for three parts, was always pointed out. Cerone, who in *El Melopeo* devoted a chapter to the composing of frottole, strambotti, and canzonette, is emphatic in his statement that these "folklike and vulgar melodies" (*cantares aldeanos y grosseros*) should be accompanied by the simplest chords. He derives their harmonic make-up from the nature of the fauxbourdon, where singing in parallel thirds and sixths, or tenths, or even fifths, was customary.[5] Three or four such successions of fifths should not be taken as faulty or unusual. Zacconi has an additional explanation of this singing in parallels: he declares them to be habitual when people attempt to seize upon the melody while singing in parts.[6] This parallelism in the harmonies of the canzonetta and its ancestors is, at all events, regarded as a folkish, nonartistic form which belongs in the sphere of *usus*, rather than of *ars*.[7]

---

[5] Domenico Pietro Cerone, *El Melopeo* (Naples, 1609), p. 693: "como es haziendo cantar las partes con cantares unisonadas à modo de fabordon. Aqui se concede et cantar immediatamente con dos, tres, ò quatro Quintas."

[6] Zacconi: "per rendere il canto simile al canto musicale."

[7] These medieval terms *ars* and *usus* may here be accepted in order to distinguish artistic compositions from those that originated without any contact with art and artistic problems.

We must add that in the course of the sixteenth century this utterly simple succession of parallel chords as harmonic accompaniment is not a natural outgrowth of folk music, but is artificially brought in to arouse feelings of rusticity, in conformity with the tendency toward travesty found in the text.[8] Monteverdi's canzonette embody this concept of harmony in the almost monotonous simplicity of their chordal form, with its characteristic parallel thirds and sixths. This combination of tones in the manner of the fauxbourdon is the frame that holds all the harmonic problems together. In fact, few other problems of harmony are allowed to arise, and when Monteverdi breaks through the frame of the fauxbourdon, he does so for special reasons which will presently be mentioned.

Within this concept of harmony, he also made use of the parallelism of perfect fifths, and Cerone observed two, three, and even four such fifths in succession. The purest type in the villanella is this:

Ex. 17

The composer who uses such harmonies cannot possibly be thought to have violated the artistic rule that perfect fifths, or perfect consonance for that matter, should not follow in succession. He is merely following an old custom, firmly established outside the sphere of art and still found today under certain local conditions.[9] The appearance of these parallels in sixteenth-century composition cannot be regarded as a violation of artistic rules, for it has as little to do with rules as with art. It is as though a compact group of musical habits had shifted into a new province, where they did not retain their original meaning but were used as a sort of musical allusion to what they had once expressed in their former environment. They never become "art"; and so there can be no neglect of rules, no violation of the laws of art. Although Monteverdi never used this parallelism of fifths to the extent of making it the major feature of a full composition or even of a large section, he nonetheless brought it into play. These long rows of successive fifths, set without hesitation in the clearest possible manner, represented of course the purest type of nonartistic usages which appeared in the

---

[8] By far the best interpretation of the meaning of such techniques has been given by A. Einstein in ZfMW, II (1920), 220ff.

[9] See the example quoted in footnote 10.

villanella, where they were supposed to be particularly effective in evoking uncivil, rustic, and folkish manners. Giovanni Domenico da Nola and many other practitioners overworked this mannerism, but Monteverdi did not allow it to govern the work as a whole. In one instance he invoked the nature of the parallelism most effectively by making the succession of fifths seem the result of a traditionally learned device. He applied the canon, in unison and octave, a time-honored product of learned composition employed by the Netherlandish school in all its possible varieties and artistic complications. This combining of an elaborately artistic device—the canon—with a primitive and nonartistic device—the parallelism of fifths—gave an effect of pronounced travesty.

Ex. 18 [10]   x, 15

It is quite possible that Monteverdi even intended something of a covert mockery of the *Oltremontani*. At any rate, just as the passage "Corro volando" of the canzonetta *Corse a la morte* contains contradictory musical techniques which prevent its being taken seriously, so the text also reveals an incongruity. The commonplace love affair of a lad is told in terms of learned comparisons. Narcissus, Helen of Troy, and Ganymede appear, but the simple lover speaks with an ordinary vocabulary and in flat imagery. The heavy classical comparisons do not fit, and the result is ridicule of a platitude. This incongruity was underlined musically by Monteverdi. A learned composer using elaborate techniques would have set a *fuga* (*fugare*-canon) to words such as "run" or "fly" (*correre, volare*), so Monteverdi proceeds in the passage "Corro volando" to apply the canon device as *fuga* on the ground of words that

---

[10] There is an interesting example of the very same type (principle of canon and parallels in fifths) mentioned by Felix Mendelssohn in a letter he wrote to Carl Friedrich Zelter, dated Secheron, September 13, 1822. Mendelssohn speaks of an experience which he had in the Berner Oberland in Switzerland; there he heard girls singing in horrible parallels of fifths which he quickly corrected because he thought them to be a mistake.

suggest its use. Parallelism of fifths is the profound result! Nothing could show more eloquently the nature of the category.

In general, however, Monteverdi's use of parallel fifths, though fairly frequent, was confined to two in a row. A special procedure of his, often repeated, is perhaps also expressive of hidden ridicule, of travesty and contradiction. He appears to be intentionally avoiding parallel fifths by his voice-leading. But only on paper. The actual sound of the passage plainly and unequivocally brings out the straight parallels. One example may stand for many:

Ex. 19 x

The impression that no rules have been violated may be achieved, in theory, by as many variations as there are cases. Since the listener, however, is more than ordinarily conscious of the voice-leading in a three-part composition, the impression conveyed by the actual sound is capable of considerably less variation.

The matter of parallelism between fifths may by itself be of little significance. But if we compare the *Canzonette* with the *Cantiunculae*, also written for three voices, it is immediately clear that Monteverdi abides by the rules of counterpoint in the motet but not in the canzonetta. This parallelism is one feature of a harmonic concept derived from such primitive types as the fauxbourdon, and it is important to note that their vertical, chordal structure was the basic principle of the harmony in Monteverdi's canzonetta.

In addition to this harmonic verticalism, which was in sharp contrast to Netherlandish ideas, the rhythmic and melodic forms allowed a brilliantly effective opposition to the North. Here the traditional characteristics of the canzonetta corresponded to Monteverdi's own nature. There were no contradictions such as those he painstakingly but unsuccessfully attempted to resolve in the *Cantiunculae*. Here the objective medium and the subjective disposition were in perfect agreement.

As a native song, the canzonetta was linked with the dance and dancelike rhythms. It goes without saying that the dance demands a strict adherence to rhythmic groups and repetitive patterns that does not exist in the canzonetta. Nevertheless, the canzonetta has a grouping and a rhythmic feeling that tend to crystallize into a clear and definite pattern. The melody of the canzonetta is generally syllabic, its rhythm based on a line containing an odd number of syllables (7, 9, 11, and 13). Since the stanza of the canzonetta allowed these various combinations, the rhythmic group might show a corresponding number of variations. But Monteverdi did not always avail himself of this opportunity to modify the structural basis of his music. He often seems to have preferred symmetry to variety and frequently subordinated the rhythmic order of the words to melodic considerations by repeating the words of the line or tacking a repetition onto the end of a line. He thus regulated the lines and balanced the melodic phrases, using this device often enough to establish it as a recognized procedure whenever he wanted the melody to swing into the natural cadence of a phrase.

On the other hand, a great variety of rhythmic groups was achieved by a continual change in the basic rhythmic units, made possible by the flexible relation between the long and short values and the accentuated declamation, so that the verses changed their rhythmic grouping as often as the composer altered the basic unit. A selection picked at random from the *Canzonette* indicates the great variety of musical groups possible in a line of seven syllables:

Ex. 20

The possibilities are, in fact, infinite. If the composer changes the basic units for long and short values ($\quarternote$ = long; $\eighthnote$ = short; or $\eighthnote$ and $\sixteenthnote$ respectively, etc.), he produces a new rhythmic group for each verse, although the number of syllables remains the same. If this procedure is carried out consistently throughout the stanza, there will be no repetition of any rhythmic group. This makes the canzonetta appear more artistic and moves it further away from the dance, whose nature insists that the patterns be repeated. In composing the canzonetta, Monteverdi wanted to use the potentialities of the dance form, but he was more eager to achieve clarity of rhythmic organization than to interpret the dance literally.

Monteverdi revealed in another way that for him the canzonetta was still close to the actual dance. His canzonette were regularly organized in two sections, each of which was repeated. In a few of his compositions the second section has a triple rhythm. Out of twenty-one canzonette in the collection only three (Nos. 2, 4, 9) have the triple section,[11] while one (No. 16), *Godi pur del bel sen,* puts the first section in triplets. This appearance of triple rhythm clearly relates the section to the so-called *proportio* or *Nachtanz*—that is, to that secondary part of an actual dance which turns the tonal material into the triple proportion. This was the arrangement used in instrumental dances throughout the sixteenth century, and its particular effectiveness came from the presentation of material, first in duple rhythm and then in triplets. Vocal compositions whose musical structure and social purpose were related to the dance occasionally took over this sectional grouping, and the closer they were to the dance, the clearer was this arrangement.

Monteverdi stressed the dance with the *proportio* as his point of departure by making the refrain or a refrain-like part of the canzonetta appear in the characteristic triple rhythm. All three of his compositions in that manner end with a refrain that remains more or less literal in all the stanzas. *Canzonette d'amore* (No. 2) has the refrain "Le man bacciando a la mia bella Clori." [12] *Raggi, dov'è il mio bene* (No. 4) ends with a refrain of two lines: "Ch'io me n'andrò cantando." [13] *Su su su che'l giorno* (No. 9) brings the refrain "Che fan cantando a la bell' Alba honore." [14] In two of these refrains, the poet explicitly calls for a song,

---

[11] The "triple" rhythm corresponds to the older form of *tempus imperfectum cum prolatione majore.*

[12] The third stanza, however, ends with "In sen vivendo alla mia bella Clori."

[13] The refrain is literal at the beginning and has changes toward the end. Only the first line of the refrain is in triple rhythm; the second line is again in duple rhythm.

[14] The last lines of all five stanzas have variations: 2. "Fan mormorando a la bell'Alba honore." 3. "Che fan partendo a la bell'Alba honore." 4. "Facciam cantando riverenza a l'Alba." 5. "A far cantando honor a la sua Dea."

as though a group of bystanders were being requested to join in singing the refrain. This direct reference in refrains to singing, and at times to dancing, is characteristic of songs that have their origin in the dance, and such refrains were often put into a dancelike rhythm of triplets. It is not likely that Monteverdi implied any actual dancing when he rendered the refrain in such a way.

Monteverdi used several methods to give the refrain special distinction. When the beginning of the stanza had its structure broken up by successive entrances of the voices and loosened by the use of figurative material, the refrain would pull the parts together in compact harmonies and omit all figuration. This at once clarified the rhythmic organization. The broken form of the first part did not allow the rhythm to fall into patterns, and the figuration in particular gave the rhythm a somewhat artificial cast. In the refrain, however, all the parts went closely together, and the omission of figurative material produced a simplicity of syllabic progression, so that the rhythmic motion became as clear and intense as the rhythm of a dance. *Raggi dov'è il mio bene* reveals Monteverdi's intention clearly. Despite its brevity, characteristic of all canzonette, this composition combines three contrasting structural elements, each concentrated within a narrow space. It begins with a figurative melisma on "raggi," obviously invented in madrigalesque imitation of the meaning of the word. This melisma is at once taken up by the two other parts, and the whole first section runs into a harmonic cadence of firm texture. The refrain of two verses follows. While its first verse is rhythmically differentiated by the striking triplets, the second verse, "Questi son gl'occhi che mi dan la vita," falls into the rhythmic pattern:

$$\flat\flat\flat\flat \mid \flat.\flat\flat\flat \mid \flat\flat\flat \parallel \flat\flat\flat\flat \mid \flat.\flat\flat\flat \mid \flat\flat\flat \parallel \circ \parallel$$

imposed upon all three parts, which proceed simultaneously in simple chords. This directness of rhythmic and harmonic impact is in conformity with the nature of the dance.

The reverse procedure is rare—where the first section is in compact harmonies and the second is in a looser, more figurative style. *Il mio martir tengo* (No. 6) might perhaps be an example. Here the refrain "Nessun cred'il mio mal" pretentiously assumes "canonic" structure. The rhythmic pattern has an even motion ($\flat\flat\flat \mid \flat\flat\flat$), and the voices enter successively in canonic fashion, so that the whole refrain maintains an uninterrupted motion in equal quarters. The continuity of the rhythm creates a certain quality of the dance, in spite of the learned aspects of the structure. These "learned" devices are employed merely as allusions and hardly affect the simplicity of the compositions.

In Monteverdi's approach to the canzonetta, a new organization of rhythm was a primary artistic problem. Since the canzonetta was a recognized literary form, its musical setting should likewise be artistic. The use of varied rhythms, related to the verses, served to express some of these artistic tendencies and led Monteverdi away from the straightforward dance song. Here we come upon a rather puzzling question. The texts he chose resembled the villanella closely in structure, and the musical form of the villanella was distinguished by an unimpaired directness of the rhythmic order and was, therefore, more intimately related to the dance song than was the canzonetta. If Monteverdi was primarily concerned with rhythm, why did he not at once avail himself of the villanella which offered him a better chance to realize his intentions? Or are his compositions canzonette merely in name and not in fact? [15] The answer seems to be that the villanella had no very high rank in the world of art and that the technical problems it posed were practically nonexistent. The canzonetta ranked higher and, though also a light genre, could serve artistic needs while preserving some of the purposes of a dance song, such as the villanella. It was from the madrigal that the canzonetta obtained certain idioms of a more refined nature: melodic phrases, chiefly figurative and melismatic, that were realistically expressive of the connotations of words (e.g., *cantare, fiamme, raggi, ridere, foco,* etc.); the imitative outline of voice entrances, usually at the beginning of the lines without strict adherence to the device of imitation; and variety of rhythmic and melodic motifs. All these madrigalesque idioms were incorporated in the canzonette of Monteverdi, despite his leaning toward the style of the villanella. Thus it seems that Monteverdi wanted to take fullest advantage of both forms by preserving the artistic quality of the canzonetta along with some of the outstanding characteristics of that "cosa bassa," the villanella.

In Monteverdi's choice of the canzonetta as the medium for a new artistic expression, the element of melody was just as important as the rhythmic implications of the native dance song. Monteverdi's *Sacrae Cantiunculae* had been neither successful nor satisfactory, though they had had a beneficial effect in making the composer recognize that the temper of his melodic gifts was opposed to Northern melody. In the canzonette, however, he met a form of melody that agreed with his inclination toward a clear organization achieved through fairly short

---

[15] In *Opere,* XVI, 542, Malipiero published Monteverdi's *Ahi che si parti,* a villanella, for three voices, also only in name; the date of composition of this villanella, taken from a manuscript of the Biblioteca Estense, Modena, is impossible to establish; it may have been composed in the period of the canzonette or of the early scherzi.

phrases. The canzonetta melody was organized in short periods which ordinarily coincided with the line, with each phrase set to a line composing an entity. To secure the completeness of a phrase, the melodic cadence, either half-conclusive (that is, "open") or final, was given full control over the organism of the melody. The enormous organizing power of the melodic cadence gave the melody its structural forms. In this, the melody of the canzonetta resembled the dance songs, whose short melodic periods were similarly organized by cadences. The all-important role of the cadence in regulating the melodic flow was all the more striking because of the brevity of the composition. If, in a stanza consisting of four or five lines, the melodic phrase of each line ended with a more or less complete cadence, the rapid succession of cadences was a primary effect.

The cadence, indeed, has something of an elemental force, of an objective power, which might well dominate a composer's will. Often the first tones of the melodic phrase hold the potentiality of the cadence, and only an artificial intervention can prevent the immediate release of that potentiality. Such an intervention can easily be recognized. The cadence is delayed by extending the phrase for the sake of balance, by repeating the same cadence in all the parts successively, or by swinging around the cadential tones. This last procedure is followed only when there is the risk of getting phrases too short for the melody. For, in general, the conciseness of groups and the precision in aiming at the cadential tones, among which the intervals of the fifth and fourth are most frequent, contribute to the ideal canzonetta melody. All these features appear in Monteverdi's work. The potency of the cadence is the organizing factor throughout; in fact, there are melodies that seem to consist of nothing but cadences. One example may illustrate many cases: *Giù li a quel petto giace* (No. 17).

Ex. 21   X, 20

The composer exploits the power of the cadence because he is sure that structural clarity in the melodic groups will be the reward. Clarity is essential to the canzonetta melody—a clarity that is the result of handling simple matters in a simple manner. Also, the grouping of the tones within the phrase is simple enough. The cadential tones, such as fifth, fourth, and octave, determine the range, and seldom does a single phrase go through the whole range of an octave. This occurs only for special purposes, such as the imitation of the meaning of words like "raggi" or "sole."

Ex. 22   x, 6

Ex. 23   x, 15

Only once before in the history of music—in the first half of the fifteenth century—did musicians allow the melodic cadence to play the leading role in organizing the melody. Significantly, this occurred in a category which cultivated subtle, but clear, shapes of melody: the solo song, such as the rondeau, with instrumental accompaniment. There are rondeau melodies of Gilles Binchois or Guillaume Dufay in which each phrase brings one stylized, conventional cadence after the other. The result is a matchless clarity of organization. This art of exploiting melodic cadence for the benefit of the structure was completely obliterated in the polyphony of the Netherlanders, whose melody followed a totally different ideal. But the native dance songs retained the conception, though in a form considerably less refined, quite without subtlety, and rather crude. Monteverdi's discovery of the potentialities of the melodic cadence came, of course, through the native forms.

Finally, the canzonetta imparted to Monteverdi the conception of a structure antagonistic to the Northern school of his early training. As a matter of fact, the characteristics of melody and rhythm were so closely allied to the elements of formal structure that all the factors worked together. The procedure of lucidly arranging the melodic groups, of setting up well-designed rhythmic patterns, was further aided by the activity of harmony. Melodic and harmonic cadences usually coincided, and the structure of the whole became perspicuous through the clearly defined periods. This clarity affected the organization of the canzonetta as a whole. As has been mentioned, all the compositions were bisectional, each section being repeated. At times the first section covered nearly the full stanza, and only one line remained for the second. In such cases, the musical composition would have been thrown entirely out of balance, and the lack of proportion would have had a peculiarly painful effect in so small a form as the canzonetta. Monteverdi, therefore, lengthened the second section by repeating the line as many times as was needed to restore the balance with the first section, so that all the canzonette in the collection have sections in perfect balance.

The harmonic characteristics of the canzonetta affected Monteverdi's thinking in terms of musical form still more deeply and more decisively. The canzonetta—or the villanella, for that matter—offered him an opportunity to grasp musical form as a phenomenon governed by the interaction of the melody and the harmonic bass. One element—the melody—was entirely concentrated within the highest voice; the other element—the harmonic function—was exclusively assigned to the lowest part. The contrasting relation of the melody and the harmony implied a certain tension between the constituent elements of structure, since each had its own sphere of activity, and constituted a major problem. Not all of his canzonette were devoted to a solution of this problem, and not every canzonetta in which the problem occurred carried it through the whole of the composition. Monteverdi often locked the parts tightly together and, in consequence of the fauxbourdon, moved them in a parallelism that had a disorientating effect upon the melody. In such parallel motion, it no longer mattered where the melody was located. While the part of the soprano (descant) might prevail to a certain degree, its claim upon the melody could not become exclusive. Because of the parallelism, the descant had to share the melody with the bass and the tenor. Even in such compositions, the cadences usually prompted a change in the situation. The bass moved out of the limitations of the parallel motion and took over the independent procedures of the harmonic function—that is, it set up the basic tones of the chords and took the steps needed to produce the harmonic cadence. This procedure on the part of the bass simultaneously impelled the upper parts to contrasting activities of their own: the descant moved into the melodic cadence, while the middle tenor usually followed the melodic independence of the descant. This, then, was the definitive arrangement: the functions were distributed according to the musical elements of harmony in the bass and of melody in the upper parts of the composition. To be sure, the cadence allowed this dualistic structure to be established only on a rather small scale, but the frequency of cadential periods in the canzonetta increased the importance of the structure. Monteverdi also used this arrangement outside the cadence, in larger sections of the work, and therefore in a more significant manner. It was the cadential situation, nevertheless, that gave rise to his dualistic conception of musical structure.

Within the scope of this dualism Monteverdi formulated a procedure that was to become basic in the structure of his later works and—through him—in the structural vocabulary of the baroque era. As a matter of fact, the procedure is only an expansion of the cadential arrangement, but because of its historic importance, it deserves detailed description. The chief part, and, as it were, the "productive" one, is usually the bass, which appears in a standardized or stereotyped form. The limits of its range are fixed by harmonically decisive tones, such as the tonic, the dominant, and the subdominant. These tones are reached gradually, usually stepwise, by passing through the scale, ordinarily in slow motion, at all events in a simple, even rhythm. As an example, the canzonetta *Tu ridi sempre* (No. 13) may be cited. It is a work notable for the use of this device, though not by reason of any absolute aesthetic values. The bass of this canzonetta is as follows:

Ex. 24   X, 16

Per dar-mi pe- ne e gua-i Per dar-mi pe- ne e gua- - - i

The bass proceeds here from the dominant (to use modern terminology) to the tonic (F), to the dominant again, with a final return to the tonic; that is, the bass swings between these poles with no "melodic" expressiveness and in no relation to the text; all its tones, rhythmically emphatic, serve harmonic purposes exclusively. It is also noteworthy that the bass does not have the initial line; it takes the second line, repeated twice. This procedure, too, is significant in relation to methods that Monteverdi later used extensively; it has a certain bearing upon the *basso ostinato*, which will be discussed in due time. Finally, the bass is not necessarily the first part to enter; in this canzonetta, it comes second. This belated entrance is the more surprising since the bass is, in fact, the productive part of the composition. Here the second factor of the structural device occurs. Both the upper parts form a duet and a unit. The melody, however, is derivative. The bass sheds, as it were, the melody for the upper part. That is to say, while the bass moves slowly and regularly from one harmonic tone to the other, the upper parts present as their melody a figuration of the basic tones, derived directly from the bass. To illustrate from the same canzonetta:

Ex. 25   x, 16

As Monteverdi progressed, he worked out this device until he established it as a norm of baroque musical structure. The purely harmonic bass with a stereotyped formula will determine the figuration of the upper parts and will retain its creative power even when it comes in last. There will be compositions where the appearance of the bass will be preceded by a fairly long passage whose material has already profited from the formula of the bass. Since the basic motif is stereotyped, the figuration derived from it will have the same characteristics. The descant of the canzonetta *Tu ridi* is worth quoting once again as a stereotyped, conventional formula:

Ex. 26   x, 16

Such stuff is to become part of Monteverdi's idiomatic vocabulary. The composer is to rely more and more on conventional materials gained through figuration. It seems to belong to the nature of the device that the basic motif shall make its appearance in the upper parts at some time in the course of the composition, and then it is given unadorned, without figuration. This canzonetta has the motif directly following the figuration because of the brevity of the composition. Since its structure is compressed into the narrowest possible space, this little composition is a most ingenious work, whose importance can hardly be overrated in view of its far-reaching consequences.

In his use of the canzonetta, by exploiting the elements of the native song, Monteverdi definitely won new ground. His new structural conceptions affected all three essential elements of composition: melody, rhythm, and harmony. In handling these fundamental materials he acquainted himself with new organizations of form which had nothing in common with the Northern music. The canzonetta was a guide, a revelation that told him of the existence of different conceptions of art. With the knowledge and the technique gained through the canzonetta, he could attempt to overthrow the past, to dethrone the art of the North. But was it imaginable that such a truly ambitious effort could be made through the medium of so unpretentious a form as the canzonetta? Even if Monteverdi had been most enthusiastic about the clarity achieved by the native songs, he could not have mistaken the rank of the canzonetta in the hierarchy of musical compositions and must have realized that it stood outside the highest circle of artistic forms. In the sphere of profane music, only the madrigal qualified as a high-ranking category. Monteverdi now abandoned the canzonetta and shifted his artistic activity once and for all to categories of higher rank. The canzonetta, however, had determined the course he would take in his struggle with the past. It had clarified his views and established his position in the music of the time. The new epoch was about to begin.

The Madrigal: The New Artistic Medium

AFTER the publication of the *Sacrae Cantiunculae* in 1582, the *Madrigali spirituali* in 1583, and the *Canzonette* in 1584, Monteverdi needed time for thought and careful preparation. In turning to the madrigal he was about to become a rival not only of the Northern polyphonists but also of the most renowned madrigalists. This was not a task to be accomplished lightly or impulsively, and it took him nearly four years to complete his first collection of twenty-one madrigals for five voices.[1] In 1587 the Venetian printer Angelo Gardano published the *Primo Libro* of the *Madrigali a cinque voci di Claudio Monteverde Cremonese, Discepolo Sigr. Marc' Antonio Ingegneri*.

Monteverdi's decision to compose profane music must have estranged him from his master, Ingegneri, at least in his official capacity. Nevertheless, he called himself the pupil of Ingegneri, and there is no reason to doubt his sincerity in so doing. As he abandoned his interest in religious music, Monteverdi now came closer to circles whose cultural climate was secular. Although we know little about the role of music in Cremona, it is safe to assume that the aristocracy there was as sensitive to the amenities of social music as it was elsewhere in Italy. One noble house which opened its doors to all who were devoted to the genius of music was that of Count Marco Verità. He attracted many musicians of renown by his magnanimous patronage and had many compositions dedicated to him. It was this Count Marco to whom Monteverdi dedicated his "fiori di Primavera," the first madrigals, the flowers of

---

[1] There are twenty-one individual compositions, but one, *Fumia la Pastorella*, consists of three *parti* which belong together; the final madrigal *Ardo si ma non t'amo* has a "risposta" *Ardi e gela* and a "contrarisposta" *Arsi e alsi*.

his artistic spring. He must have found the Count a benevolent connoisseur whose cultured taste enabled him to recognize the genius of the young composer, for twice in the dedication [2] Monteverdi referred to courtesies (*tante cortesie*) graciously shown him and to favors received from the nobleman (*favori c'ho ricevuti da lei*).

Monteverdi had now wedded his art to the profane forms of music. Why, if he had neglected the guidance of his teacher, did he still call himself Ingegneri's pupil? Irrespective of politeness or utilitarian advantage, the statement was objectively possible. His adherence to Ingegneri's style would, at all events theoretically, hold true in sacred polyphony, and in the field of profane music Ingegneri had never been his master. In view of the first book of madrigals, he has sometimes been reproached for having been a "faithless disciple" of Ingegneri.[3] Actually he was no disciple at all, and his compositions of 1587 have no roots in the madrigals of Ingegneri. Marenzio's influence, well-established by 1587, was presumably greater, though none too strong. Marenzio had already composed one book of madrigals for four parts, three books for six parts, and five books for five parts, the latter being the most important for Monteverdi, since style and number of parts were naturally interrelated. In later years Monteverdi pointed to Cipriano de Rore as his real teacher in the art of the madrigal. Since that admission was made in connection with a polemic dispute, in which the name of Cipriano was cited in order to give greater authority to the stylistic features under discussion, its importance must not be exaggerated. As a matter of fact, Cipriano's style does not appear to have had any remarkable influence on Monteverdi's first madrigals. Far more important than the influence of any one composer was the artistic problem to which these madrigals were designed as a solution. This problem was the unification of the characteristics of a five-part madrigal with the achievements gained through the native song. Marenzio had already imparted stylistic elements of the canzonetta to the many-voiced madrigal, yet Monteverdi had to discover his own solution. Such mixtures of styles involve conflicts between the different categories, which each individual composer must resolve in his own way. In his solution to this problem, the startling logic of Monteverdi's advance revealed itself, and the significance of his previous work with the canzonetta became clear.

[2] The dedication is reprinted in G. Franceso Malipiero, *Claudio Monteverdi* (Milan, 1929), p. 68.

[3] In H. Prunières, *Claudio Monteverdi*, p. 7, and oftener in the literature on Monteverdi.

Monteverdi's canzonette, though appropriate and delightful in their way, were not eminently artistic works,[4] nor were they intended to express great individuality. It was in the madrigals that Monteverdi showed for the first time the hand of a master and established himself among the leading madrigalists. His previous compositions scarcely betrayed the scope and depth of his genius, which was probably only revealed in social intercourse with his friends and patrons, such as Pietro Ambrosini, the recipient of the *Canzonette*, or the Cremonese lover of music, Alessandro Fraganesco, to whom the *Madrigali spirituali* were dedicated, or now Count Marco Verità, who, with the madrigals in his hands, held the first real token of the composer's promise.

In his choice of poems, Monteverdi seems to have followed no particular plan. Later he was careful to select texts that agreed with his own purposes and ideals. But in the first book no special preference for any poet can be detected, nor is any bent toward a particular type of madrigalesque poetry discernible. There are, however, two groups of madrigals which form cycles in the middle and at the end of the collection. *Fumia la Pastorella* with *Almo divino raggio* (*seconda parte*) and *All'hora i pastori tutti* (*terza parte*) make up the first cycle by Antonio Allegretti, one of the minor poets in the second half of the century. The second cycle concludes the collection and may have added significance both because of its place and the poet whose texts Monteverdi chose— Torquato Tasso. This cycle begins with a famous madrigal that challenged the artistic imagination of many composers, *Ardo si ma non t'amo*, by Giambattista Guarini. Two years before, Giulio Gigli of Imola had collected no less than twenty-eight musical renderings of this poem by various composers and, with Adam Berg in Munich, had published them as an anthology called *Sdegnosi Ardori*. Guarini's madrigal also served as a challenge to the poets, and Torquato Tasso parodied it in his *Ardi e gela a tua voglia* and *Arsi ed alsi a mia voglia*, one being the "risposta," the other the "contrarisposta." [5] Monteverdi combined the three. Guarini is also represented by another madrigal, *Baci soavi e cari*, which Monteverdi gave one of the finest settings in the collection. Among the poets of Monteverdi's choice is G. B. Strozzi, who appears with *Questa ordì il laccio*.

Monteverdi chose the poems because they represented poetic material

---

[4] It seems that students of Monteverdi's work have always overrated the canzonette from an individualistic point of view. It is true they are charming little pieces, but so were hundreds of others of that time. To manifest artistic uniqueness was not their purpose.

[5] See the discussion of the relationship of these poems to one another in Angelo Solerti's edition of Tasso's works, "Le Rime di Torquato Tasso," in *Collezione di opere inedite o rare* (Bologna, 1898), II, 453ff. *Arsi ed alsi* is attributed to Tasso.

with which the madrigalists of the time were thoroughly familiar and which they often set to music. When Monteverdi selected Guarini's *Ardo si ma non t'amo*, it was because of the fame of the poem rather than the challenge of its content. He followed his fellow-composers in adding his skill to the madrigalesque repertory of the time, and his choice of poems was not made on the basis of any individual relationship between the poet and the composer. In this first book, Monteverdi was not so much concerned with a choice of poems as with raising his medium to a level where he could challenge Northern art, by comparing the madrigal with the characteristics of the native song.

The canzonetta affected the madrigal in two ways: in individual elements, such as the organization of melody, phrasing, diction; and in the over-all aspects of structure. A glance through the five-part madrigals shows that Monteverdi used a grouping of parts peculiar to the native song. The parts are: canto, alto, tenore, basso, and quinto. The quinto is like the old vox vagans, a voice whose range is not stable but shifts around, "wanders" (*vagare*), and joins now a high voice, now a middle part, now the bass. The range of the quinto thus changes with every madrigal. Out of these voices Monteverdi formed a duet in high or middle range and gave this duet the support of a voice that functioned as harmonic bass. He repeated this combination in the same composition by altering the range. Thus a duet of low voices might imitate a preceding duet in the high voices. This was the way in which the three-voiced canzonetta influenced the grouping of the madrigal. The trio, that is, the duet with harmonic bass, intervenes in order to regulate the groups of the composition, so strongly that at times only for very short passages are all five voices simultaneously active. The imitative replies in the form of trios that follow each other with various combinations of voices have been said to show the stylistic influence of the so-called *chori spezzati*, of separate choirs as choral units, cultivated by the Venetian composers since Willaert. But these surely had nothing in common with Monteverdi's early madrigals, whose form is shaped in accordance with the three-voiced canzonetta. The beginning of *Se nel partir da voi* could be part of any canzonetta that Monteverdi had previously composed:

Ex. 27 I, 36

The first madrigal *Ch'io ami la mia vita* appears to be a composition of almost programmatic significance, chosen to indicate the artistic tendency, the stylistic program, of the entire book. In every feature it shows the powerful influences of the canzonetta. *First:* It illustrates the grouping of material into a duet of upper parts and a harmonic bass, and the opening shows this type of trio at its purest. *Second:* Clarity of organization is achieved by allowing cadence, melodic and harmonic, to play the same role as in the native song, where the music is brought to a cadence, total or inconclusive, at the end of each line. Rhythmic irregularities, anticipations of motifs, successive entrances of voices, or all these devices together are used to connect the lines and keep the composition from falling apart into little units, yet the clarity of the period is never obscured. *Third:* An attempt is made to give the bass the form of a motif capable of holding together the structure of the work. Monteverdi has the bass enter last, and its sections separated by long rests. With the exception of one small phrase, the bass is built upon a bisectional motif that is repeated in spite of the change of text. This repetition serves the purpose of a *basso ostinato* as an element of structural unification. The example deserves proper illustration. (The phrases are here written one below the other, whether the motif is the same or varied.)

Ex. 28 I, I

This is an attempt, and no more, to use a basic motif as a structural entity, regardless of any connection with the text. This repetitive function of a motif is a step toward the *basso ostinato*—that is, toward one of the most powerful structures of the coming age. This procedure, however, has nothing to do with the canzonetta, while the conciseness

3 Letter of Monteverdi, February 2, 1634, addressed to an unknown person in Rome

4 The Parlor of the Nunnery, Venice; Presentation of Masque with Music

5 Palazzo Mocenigo, the Salon Where *Il Combattimento di Tancredi e Clorinda* Was Performed

of the motif may be regarded as a result of the native song. *Fourth:* The madrigal is divided in three sections, the last being a complete and literal repetition of the second (a ||: b :||). Sections *a* and *b* are as closely connected as the material for the individual verses, yet they are clearly recognizable as sections. The repetition of the second part at the end is a structural arrangement taken over by the madrigal from the canzonetta. The madrigal often contained repetition of individual phrases, motifs, or single words, but repetition of a full section was a feature borrowed from the native song. A special form of this repetition was tried out several times by Monteverdi. Instead of repeating the section to the letter, he exchanges voices. Nothing is materially altered, except for a change in tone color perceptible only to sensitive ears. These madrigals, however, are all rendered soloistically, and therefore even such slight alterations are effective.

This structure of sectional repetition (*a:bb*) is an important stylistic factor in Monteverdi's madrigals and gives rise to one of the leading forms in the opera and the cantata of seventeenth-century Italy. The sectional aria, structurally organized through the repetition of its second part, later to be marked by "dal segno al fine," is a direct derivative from such a madrigal as Monteverdi's *Ch'io ami la mia vita* and is therefore an indirect descendant of the canzonetta. From the time of Monteverdi on, and chiefly in the second half of the seventeenth century, this type of aria structure became so popular as to be called the "seicento aria." In view of this eminence, it is but appropriate to give Monteverdi's madrigal its due.

Other devices that were to be of increasing importance in Monteverdi's creative work are also anticipated in this book. The madrigal *Filli cara e amata* shows an ingenious arrangement. Phyllis is to answer the immortal question of whether her beautiful lips will belong to her lover: "Questa tua bella bocca, non é mia?" (Thy sweet lips, are they not mine?) As the question is naturally the core of the matter, it requires emphatic treatment. Hence Monteverdi provided for the words "non é mia?" an exclamatory motif with simple sustained tones, which also fulfills a harmonic function:

Ex. 29   I, 21

To heighten the impression of the motif, the upper voices in a duet are at the same time declaiming more softly the first part of the question, "Questa tua bella bocca?"

Ex. 30 I, 21

This is a simple trio passage, with the melodic declamation in the upper duet and the harmonic support in the bass. The harmonic function is, in fact, so strong that at first we are scarcely aware of the significance of the phrase as a motif. However, when it recurs in immediate repetition, together with the declamatory passage rendered by a different combination of voices, its importance becomes clear, especially since an equally sustained motif to "non é mia" is set against it in countermotion:

Ex. 31 I, 21

This basic motif appears with different texts throughout the composition, both with slight variation and in literal repetition.

Ex. 32 I, 22

This device of inventing a special motif for the artistically and emotionally central material and using it as the basis for the composition as a whole was employed by young Monteverdi only on a relatively small scale, and its meaning becomes apparent only in his later compositions with their intricate structure. He invents simple or rather ordinary motifs even for the most expressive phrases of the text—which is surprising in a composer capable of writing melodies of extraordinary and noble beauty. The simplicity of the motifs, however, serves harmonic purposes and contributes to the structural organization by reflecting the importance of a phrase in the text. When we hear the initial trio in *Filli cara e amata*, we are never conscious that behind it lies the discipline of intellectual logic. The effect in this and similar madrigals is of an engaging and highly sensuous euphony—apparently written only for their appeal to the senses. The more mature Monteverdi grew, the more successful he became in disguising such artistic devices by alluring effects of sound. The rationalistic element was ever present, but wholly hidden. A similar situation existed in the early part of the fourteenth century, when the rigid scheme of a rational organization was concealed by a sweetness of sound that seemed to preclude any intellectual approach. Monteverdi re-established this relationship between the senses and reason in his first madrigals.

When he intended to unfold the emotional implications of the text for expressive purposes only, Monteverdi used less original techniques, closer to the tradition of madrigal composition and to the idioms of his time. Such words as "pain" (*dolore*) and "death" (*morte*) almost always call forth certain chromaticisms. Since the poems are of an amorous nature, using stylized expressions for unfulfilled love, which causes pain and brings a longing for death, the chromaticisms are a recurrent feature. Other words of extraordinary tension and objects which convey emotional associations are chromatically expressed, especially "heart" (*cor*), as the seat of all emotions. All these forms are commonly classified as madrigalisms. The specific chromatic procedures of Monteverdi's first madrigals reflect his study of Cipriano de Rore, but without the most elaborate constructions. Their intimate relation to the canzonetta limit Monteverdi's madrigals to a concise, but vital, brevity.

Decorative melisma is as much a part of the madrigalesque vocabulary as chromaticism. Words such as "flower" or "laughter" are often expressed in groups of tones of more or less extensive length. Such melismata are at times carried in successive imitation from one part to the other, and this interplay loosens somewhat the direct contact with the individual word that originated the melismatic figure and brings a structural element into the foreground. Not all the melismata, however, are expressive of the connotation of words; some seem from the very start to have been invented with structural purposes in view; others remain ambiguous—as, for instance, in *Questa ordì il laccio* where the words "fiori," and "erba" occur, but the melisma is set to "il tese":

Ex. 33 I, 46

This melisma culminates in a definitive cadence reached in the straight line of a diatonic run through the scale. The phrase is impelled to complete itself in the cadence. Something of a favorite with Monteverdi, such a formula was also used in previous canzonette, as a similar motif in *Raggi dov' è il mio bene* may show:

Ex. 34 x, 6

Words that refer to dancing, singing, or the attendant gaiety are here and there expressed by the rhythm. To imitate the dance, a passage of the madrigal may change its basic meter from duple to triple time, and all the voices may simultaneously swing into dance rhythm. An example is given in *Usciam Ninfe homai*, or in *Fumia la Pastorella*.

Although Monteverdi used these and other madrigalisms in a rather impersonal, though skillful, manner, one of these idioms seems to have more individuality—a special expression of the torments of love in which the tones gradually die away. A passage of lively declamation may precede, and then, at an emotional phrase, in particular with the word "morire," the motion slows down and the voices proceed with hesitation; they decline, fade away, linger on, and lose rhythmic determination; and the passage dies away with a languid sigh. This expression of melancholy, of the pain of sorrow and death, realistic in principle, is poetically most convincing, and it is a striking mark of Monteverdi's art. The first madrigal gives such a form to the words "il cor afflitto," and there are other remarkable examples, such as the passage "Ch'io mi sento a morire" in the madrigal *La vaga Pastorella*, where the lover begs his shepherdess not to flee or else he must die. What we discover in these youthful works is probably not a perfect artistic expression, but one undoubtedly as genuine and individual as any in the later works of the great tragedian that Monteverdi was to become.

The group of three madrigals with which the collection ends is of particular interest. Students of Monteverdi have severely criticized these compositions for their complete lack of originality and because of the composer's failure to render the dialogue of the lovers dramatic.[6] These criticisms are rather beside the point. It is true that Monteverdi's first book showed that he had not yet discovered how to give an adequate form to dialogue or to direct speech, a task he set for himself later. But this last group of madrigals is by no means inferior to the rest from a technical point of view, and the problem Monteverdi wanted to solve was an entirely different one. The relation of the texts to each other is not that of a true dialogue, but of a parody. Tasso's poem parodied Guarini's madrigal, and Monteverdi translated the parody into musical terms by patterning one composition on the other. When he composed *Ardi e gela* as Tasso's "risposta" to Guarini's *Ardo si ma non t'amo*, he used the musical material of the first madrigal. The bass of *Ardi e gela* is, in fact, a variation of the first madrigal, while in all parts both have the same ending, with only slight variation. The next parody *Arsi e alsi*, the "contrarisposta," has many features in common with the two preceding compositions, as is most strikingly shown in the initial themes:

Ex. 35 I, 61

Ex. 36 I, 67

It is this technique of parody that Monteverdi accepted as a problem to be solved, and it is by no means a minor problem. Parody had been extensively used by all Northern composers and also by the older generation of madrigalists. Monteverdi tried it out here in a medium that was a mixture of madrigal and canzonetta, and this appears to be the significance of the last three madrigals.

One more collection of madrigals was completed before Monteverdi left Cremona, and was published in Venice in 1590. It was dedicated to

---

[6] Leichtentritt, Prunières, Schneider, and Redlich have made this criticism.

a nobleman of Milan, Giacomo Ricardi, President of the Senate and a patron of music. This second book, with which Monteverdi's Cremonese period concluded, showed the musician well advanced beyond his previous work. The problem of how to incorporate the form and characteristics of the canzonetta into the madrigal had been given a solution he could well regard as definite, and the study of native songs had borne fruit. The second book gave evidence that he was now attempting to raise the formal conceptions of the madrigal to new eminence and using the canzonetta only to give color to subtleties of detail. No longer did the canzonetta control the form of the madrigal as a whole. This relation between madrigal and canzonetta was to last for many years. The native song continued to play a secondary role until Monteverdi, in a fresh approach, found new resources in the wealth of material it had to offer.

The Madrigals of 1590

IN THE three years between the publication of the first and second
books of madrigals, Monteverdi rapidly matured in discipline, logic,
and creative originality. In spite of the differences between the two
books, there is no break in the logical continuity. The differences are
not the result of revolutionary changes, but the product of an orderly
mind that presents each book of madrigals as a uniform entity.

The most striking change is in the choice of texts. In the first book
Monteverdi yielded to the fashion of the time as to what was befitting
a madrigalist and did not permit the texts to pose problems of their own,
concentrating all his thoughts on the music. In the new madrigals, as a
result of his greater artistic freedom and assurance, the choice of texts
took on added significance.

The second book of madrigals contained works by several new poets:
two by Girolamo Casoni, two by Filippo Alberti, one by Ercole Bentivoglio. There is again one poem by Guarini, and the concluding work
is by Pietro Bembo.[1] The appearance of Bembo came as an anachronism.
By the time Monteverdi began his work, the days were over when
Petrarch's *Canzoniere* filled every collection of madrigals, and Bembo's
poems in the style of a classical purist were favored by madrigalists.
Petrarch was not represented in Monteverdi's earlier books, and Bembo
very rarely—once in the second book, and once again in the third.
The poetry of the age had discarded Bembo's severe classicism based on
the imitation of ancient rhetorics, his elegant, formal verbiage and his
ideal of beauty for beauty's sake.

---

[1] Rudolf Schwartz, "Zu den Texten der ersten fünf Bücher der Madrigale Monteverdis," in *Festschrift* (Leipzig, 1918), p. 148.
135

In the place of Petrarch and Bembo was the new glory of Torquato Tasso. His lyrics were chosen by Monteverdi for the place of honor in the second book, and ten of its twenty-one madrigals were by him. Monteverdi's choice thus established a personal relationship to a certain poet and a certain kind of poetry. It was an avowal that poet and musician were dedicated to the same ideas and influenced by the same spirit. This does not imply that such a relation had never existed before, but it existed here in Monteverdi's work for the first time, and he maintained it in his later collections of madrigals. The musician turned to the poet who seemed to him the truest incarnation of the spirit of the age, of its human desires and artistic ambitions, and gave Tasso's *Non si levava ancor* the place of distinction at the beginning of his second book.

How does this agree with Tasso's own views on madrigal writing? In 1584, at the time when Tasso wrote most of his dialogues, he completed his "La Cavalletta ovvero de la poesia toscana." In this dialogue he criticized the madrigal writing of his day with surprising directness and practically suggested that he would have nothing to do with the new tendencies. "In the course of degeneration the music of the madrigal has become soft and effeminate; and we shall beg of the Messrs. Striggio, Jacches [de Wert], Luzzasco, and any other master of the excellent art of music, to bring it back to that gravity, in deviating from which it has partly lost its balance. But about this it is better to be silent than to argue." [2] The gravity of old, the restraint and disciplined seriousness that the best of the past always seems to have, must now be revived.

A strange demand, indeed, to come from Tasso! But perhaps the time at which he made the statement helps to explain his opinion. This dialogue was written in Tasso's darkest period, when, after roaming restlessly around northern Italy, he returned to Ferrara in 1579, as though drawn by a sinister fate that must take its predestined course. Shortly after his return, he was confined in the Insane Asylum of St. Anna for several years. Not until 1586 was he freed by the intervention of young Vincenzo Gonzaga, then heir apparent of Mantua, whose service Monteverdi was soon to enter. During this period, the *Gerusalemme liberata* was published without his supervision; his lyrics were revised by Ferrara's court poet, Guarini; and Tasso himself, maddened by the unseemly treatment of his poetical work, suffered from repent-

---

[2] See Tasso's dialogue "La Cavalletta ovvero della poesia toscana," in T. Tasso, *Dialoghi* (ed. by Alessandro Tortoreto), p. 221.

ant scruples, from hallucinations, and from the persecution of the Inquisition. It may well have been under the strain of haunting thoughts that he made himself the judge of frivolity and demanded that gravity be restored to the music of the madrigal—that *gravitas* which was the prevailing mood of the Counter Reformation. But his lyrics were unaffected by this critical attitude, and a musician could admire Tasso's poetry without agreeing with his pessimistic views on the subject of madrigals. When Monteverdi, still in Cremona, chose Tasso as his poet, he certainly did not heed the demands of the Counter Reformation, whose ideals he had abjured in his youth. He was drawn to Tasso's lyrics by the character of their poetry.

In Tasso's lyrics the element of music had come to new life. The fancy of the poet was fed by his emotions, and he spoke in images designed to call forth similar emotions. Not the clear vision that appeals to reason and to human knowledge, not the definite objects that make up the abundance of the human world, but fleeting feelings and indistinct emotions were his subject matter. The uncertainties of his emotions corresponded to the uncertainties of human life. Life in an aging society had become fraught with risk and tragedy, and the tone most suitable for poetic expression was one of melancholy. The world presented a melancholy scene, however colorful, for though ambitions and desires were strong and unrestrained, their fulfillment remained uncertain. An example of this is from Tasso's *Gerusalemme liberata* (XII, 66): "In queste voci languide risuona/Un non sò che di flebile, e soave" (A sound, I do not know, of sweetness and of grief/A ringing echo in these languid rhymes). The rhymes were stylized, like the emotion, the languor, the lachrymose melancholy that made the listener weep with the poet. The floating musical rhythms and the vague images expressing broad human emotions had a strong appeal for the musician. The stylized artistic melancholy was the idiom of the time, which the composer also spoke, not because he had gone through the same personal experiences, but because he shared the poet's belief in the artistic expression of the lyrical affections.

Monteverdi at once spoke Tasso's idiom as a master of the technical structure needed to convey the affection, the prevailing feeling of the poems. The placing of Tasso's *Non si levava ancor* at the beginning indicated the "program" of the second book from the poetical point of view, and the musical form given this madrigal was undoubtedly also meant to be programmatic and to set the structure, expression, and style for the book as a whole.

The traditional madrigal had no comprehensive structural unit that governed the subordinate elements. The "motifs" or "subjects" were invented for the text of each line and imitated successively by all the parts in polyphonic fashion. Some of the madrigalists, especially Cipriano de Rore and Giaches de Wert of Mantua, were successful in establishing greater unity by the repetition of one or another structural section, thus paving the way for new, over-all organization.[3] Monteverdi started from this point to invent such structures and a new contrapuntal style. His inventions were by no means unique, but as a "program" the principle was new. Monteverdi must have felt much like Forestieri, the chief interlocutor in Tasso's dialogue "La Cavalletta," who said, "The rule is bent and departed from in accordance with the occasion; and this deviation from the rule is at the discretion of the artist."[4] The goal of the first madrigal was a structure deliberately linked to the occasion.

The poem of Tasso is used for two madrigals that belong together. After a narrative part that sets the scene for the two lovers, there follows the amorous dialogue; and it is there, with the words "E dicea l'una sospirand' all'hora," that Monteverdi begins the second part of the madrigal. It is significant that he differentiates stylistically between the description and the dialogue.[5] This arrangement, made in accordance with dramatic considerations, shows Monteverdi's advance beyond the madrigals of his first book. The idea of such a dramatization was not original. Marenzio, Giaches de Wert, and others had provided models that, in all likelihood, stimulated Monteverdi. Although the two madrigals *Non si levava* and *E dicea* are compositions to be sung together, each of them is a musical entity, and in spite of stylistic or structural differentiation, the dramatic contrast between the narrative and the direct speech is not realized within the continuity of one complete entity. The dramatization is thus not the result of an inner conflict, but is merely an external contrast based on the division of the material, each section of which is musically complete. The harmonic situation, however, pulls the two sections together, as the second

---

[3] Tasso's dialogue "La Cavalletta" contains an interesting account of style, structure, and especially of formal repetitions in the madrigal from the poetical point of view.

[4] *Ibid.*, p. 204: . . . "che la regola sua si torca e si pieghi secondo l'occasioni; il qual piegamento è il giudicio dell' artefice, o almeno egli non è senza il giudicio."

[5] In his analysis of this madrigal, H. R. Leichtentritt, *SIMG*, XI, 261f., referred to the division, while Redlich, *Claudio Monteverdi* (Berlin, 1932), pp. 52f., called attention to the stylistic differentiation of the two sections, one being contrapuntally composed, the other homophonically.

re-establishes the initial "key," to complete the circle: d-G // g-d.

On the other hand, Monteverdi rounds off the *prima parte* in such self-sufficient completeness that it can be fully understood without recourse to the *seconda parte*. The first part of the madrigal is built upon repetition, in which the whole initial section recurs at the end with slight variation and to a different text. The characteristically rising first theme with its descending counterpoint is probably designed to accompany the line: "Not yet has the first ray of daylight risen." [6] But when toward the end the same material appears again with a wholly different text, the connection of the first theme with the first line is deprived of all its force, and the purely structural consideration of the music takes precedence. Indeed, the repetitive arrangement as such makes it obvious that clarity and completeness of structural form are Monteverdi's first concern. The repetition is certainly derived from similar arrangements in the canzonetta-like madrigals of the first book, but is used to perform new functions. For undoubtedly the composer is here carrying the principle of *da capo* repetition into the madrigal,[7] where it naturally strengthens the impression of roundness and finality. The composer thus reveals his conception that a repetitive cyclic order is preferable to an interminable co-ordination of the sections. He also attempts to evaluate sections as primary and subordinate, just as in handling the different voices of a native song, the uppermost part, from a melodic point of view, and the organic bass, from the harmonic point of view, are given a privileged position in contrast to the subordinate middle parts. This gradation of the elements used in composition is basic in the rise of new conceptions of form, and Monteverdi carries this process a step forward in the madrigals of his second book.

Non si levava ancor may serve as an example of Monteverdi's intentions in another respect—the invention of "thematic" material. It bears the mark of a personal style. Three factors determine the peculiar form of the theme: a possible relation of the melody to the connotation of the text; the shaping of the melody as a stereotyped formula; and the exploitation of the structural possibilities of the material. The tenor and the quinto, which in this madrigal has the range of a second soprano, have the following themes:

---

[6] So Redlich, *op. cit.*, p. 53, who believes that the theme's "Provenienz aus der Stofflichkeit des Gedichts ohne weiteres klar ersichtlich wird."

[7] Leichtentritt, *op. cit.*, p. 261, pointed to the *da capo* structure of the madrigal but related this arrangement to the motet. More likely is its relationship to the canzonetta and those madrigals in which Monteverdi had previously tried out the principle.

Ex. 37 II, 1

As has been pointed out, the subject sung by the tenor may have the realistic purpose of bringing out the meaning of the text. But the particular form of the subject—a gradual rise and passage through the scale with a strong tendency to reach the melodic cadence—has been used by Monteverdi before in different contexts and always in a characteristic manner. This would seem to imply that Monteverdi is aiming at a formula in order to obtain the objectivity of a stylized expression. The part of the quinto functions as the counterpoint. It issues in full contrast to the tenor subject and moves against the tenor in prolonged values, descending stepwise as the tenor rises. Such an arrangement becomes the basis of a structure in which two subjects of equal importance are used, both appearing simultaneously.

Although the main function of the theme of the quinto is to give the subject melodic character, its form testifies to its structural nature. The line of tones descending stepwise in slow and even rhythm is a figure Monteverdi is beginning to use as an organic bass. There are various such basses in the madrigals of this collection.

A passage in the range of a fifth in *Non sono in queste rive*, with anticipation by the canto seven measures before, is shown here:

Ex. 38 II, 37

A more characteristic example is presented in *Mentre io miravo fiso:*

Ex. 39 II, 61

And finally, in an equally brilliant madrigal, *Ecco mormorar l'onde:*

Ex. 40 II, 73

L'au - ra e tua mes - sag- ge- ra, e tu de L'au - ra

None of these basses results from imitation of the text, and they are not invented for the sake of melody. The more stereotyped, objective and nonmelodic such a bass is, the greater its structural strength and capacity; it draws the upper parts or any combination of them into its sway, and their form is also stereotyped. With the exception of *Non si levava ancor*, all the examples shown have the duet in lively motion above the bass, the figuration being typical. The parts of the duet are coupled in parallel motion of thirds or sixths, and since the duet follows the bass, the descent is a general one, perhaps more ingeniously rendered in *Ecco mormorar l'onde*.

The duet with a harmonic bass remains an essential factor in the structure of nearly all the madrigals. Monteverdi has increased its artistic possibilities and has used it with elaborate finesse. Clear but simple groups of sectional divisions, set off by themselves, no longer appear, unless there is special reason to employ them. Monteverdi has developed a subtle technique of rapidly changing the parts that make up the duet. Small, precise, figurative motifs are given to the duet, and all the voices successively share in these motifs, as the parts assigned to the duet continually change in the five-voiced madrigal. The varieties are even greater when a distinction is made between primary and secondary parts. The duet and the bass are given pre-eminence. However, the duet may not appear in pure form; it may be accompanied by one or more subsidiary parts, but always in such a way that it remains the leading group. With these devices Monteverdi probes all possible combinations, and not only achieves a highly effective structural variety but also exploits the potentialities of tone color which the rapidly changing combinations afford. The madrigals of the second book give the first evidence of Monteverdi's keen sense of vocal effects produced with tone color in view. The procedure is similar to that of an "orchestration" where shades of color are put in for the sake of special effects. Monteverdi often uses the dark colors, the low regions of the tonal system, to reflect somber emotions of sorrow and tragedy. By altering the structural components of the duet, by continually recasting the combinations bound to motifs, by imitating the motifs now in light and high, now in low and dark, now in middle and mezzotint colors, Monteverdi reveals that his structural genius has reached maturity.

The slowly descending bass, whose characteristics have been pointed out in various examples, has two further aspects that influence the structural form of the composition—one involving the derivation of the material in the duet from the bass, the other the variation of the bass itself. *Mentre io miravo fiso* demonstrates both in a brilliant fashion. After stating the descending line in even rhythmic values with the text "Facendo mille scherz' e mille giri," the bass proceeds to the following passage:

Ex. 41   II, 62

And twelve measures later the bass, still holding fast to its original "theme," gives a new variation:

Ex. 42   II, 63 [8]

In these passages, there is noticeable a certain unity of material, a musical force that embraces different texts and gives evidence of the productivity of the original material. Motif *a*, derived from the descending steps of the bass, is exactly the same as motif *b*, used for the duet; and the long line of the bass, slowly descending, and the derivatory motif in the duet sound together. Thus the productive power of the bass sets off a varied duplication (*c*) and imposes simultaneously a derivatory small motif upon the other parts. The result is a unity that is entirely due to the over-all importance of the bass.

In nearly all cases, the bass has fully absorbed the harmonic function. It continually swings around the basic tones of prime, fifth, fourth, and octave and, with these intervals, indicates the points of harmonic sup-

---

[8] See the bass in the madrigal *Bevea Fillide mia;* the "theme" of the last verse, "Che dolcement' anch' ei mi bacia il core," is identical with the theme quoted above.

port. This clearly shows that all the melodic characteristics and purposes of contrapuntal polyphony have gradually disappeared. The bass has lost the position as a melody assimilated to the other parts, which it had in the polyphonic structure, and its harmonic function has now become the strongest. There are madrigals in which the bass consists of nothing but harmonic phrases made up of supporting tones. Such basses are stereotyped and lack the individuality that comes from a more melodic treatment. In certain madrigals of the second book, which are particularly illustrative of Monteverdi's extraordinary gifts, he invents basses that are stereotyped and impersonal, and that may be used for a variety of purposes, but which still preserve a certain amount of expressiveness. To illustrate this situation, three phrases may be taken from the bass of *Dolcissimi legami,* a madrigal of the highest artistic qualities:

Ex. 43   II, 20

All three phrases are so standardized, so impersonal, that their expressive implications seem wholly irrelevant. Their impersonal objectivity is so great that they could easily be attributed to any composer of the baroque age, which shows how basic Monteverdi's material was to the period he initiated. Despite the objectivity, all three phrases are obviously related to the meaning of the text, or of special words. They are, first, the "scherzi," that have caused the figurative melisma (*a*); second, the accentuated rhythms (*b*); third, the "catene" (the chains), which are realistically portrayed by the peculiar, sequential steps of the bass (*c*). Is there not an irreconcilable contradiction in expressing a unique situation, which would seem to call for a characteristic phrase, by a stereotyped phrase, which would seem the form least fitted for such an expression? But such is the mystery of genius that the contradiction does not become apparent artistically. On the contrary, Monteverdi will more and more use such stereotyped phrases, each of them directly invented from the material in the text.

If the bass is given over to harmonic functions, thereby losing its character as an independent melody within a polyphonic structure, is it possible to speak of a contrapuntal style in these madrigals? Counterpoint normally implies that each part must have a certain melodic independence, in any event, a distinctly melodic voice-leading. Monteverdi is beginning to look for a counterpoint that will combine the harmonic function of the bass and the melodic independence of the other parts. The madrigals of the second book show that his findings are not always mature and definitive, but each discovery will contribute to the foundations of modern counterpoint. It is the distinctly harmonic bass that begins to guide the form of the motifs to be used contrapuntally. The tones of the bass indicate certain harmonies, and the motifs of the upper voices are determined accordingly and bear the marks of chordal invention. When such motifs are used for the simultaneous "accompaniment" of the bass, the chordal form of the upper parts is quite natural and needs no special explanation. This form is of particular interest, however, when the upper parts, combined as a duet, spring from the harmonic tones of the bass and strive to maintain themselves as a counterpoint against the bass. Perhaps the best example is found in *Ecco mormorar l'onde*, which seems to be the most modern madrigal of the collection. With the verse that begins "E sovra i verdi," the bass (here the lowest part, the alto) starts a purely harmonic line that cannot possibly have any relation to the text:

Ex. 44   II, 69

This form speaks for itself with regard to the harmonic outline. Above this bass is a duet of two soprani, canto, and quinto; and the duet largely operates with chordal material drawn from the character of the bass, except for the figurative passages on "cantare" and "rider," surely intended to be expressive of the text:

Ex. 45   II, 69

Innumerable are the motifs built upon the material of the chord as indicated in the bass, but handled in the polyphonic manner of imitation. The motifs are fairly short, and the successive entrances of the parts follow each other rapidly; yet the imitation of one and the same motif is seldom carried out through all the parts. Since the motif is chordal in outline, it is the impression of harmony that prevails. Hence only the "method" is polyphonic; it uses the horizontal approach, but without making the motifs independent melodic lines. This method, abstract as it appears to be, therefore does not affect the harmonic core of the motif. The short motifs, the unsystematic incomplete imitation, and, above all, the invention of the motif out of the harmony will remain part of the character of baroque counterpoint. The beginning of *Non giacinti o narcisi*, which in canzonetta fashion has the *da capo* repetition in varied form, is indicative of the contrapuntal motif. The whole madrigal, with the exception of a brief middle section, builds itself up by way of a polyphonic technique that operates with short, very precise material set up for imitation without ever making a complete round through all the parts. Indeed, this madrigal can well be regarded as a model of Monteverdi's treatment of motifs which consist of no more than half a dozen tones.

The new counterpoint has an additional feature of importance—the freedom from strict or predictable regulations. The solutions the composer presents do not suggest any rules. The freedom may be only incompletely achieved in these madrigals of 1590, but it surely lies within the range of the composer's vision as an ideal. The composition may begin with the statement of the first motif by one voice and continue with new motifs for the following verses. Thereafter the process of imitation on the basis of the first motif may take its course, while the second motif is contrapuntally set against it. Of this, *Non mi è grave* gives a characteristic illustration. Such a procedure means that the appearance of the motifs can in no way be foretold. His method—if method there is—springs from the inspiration that a special poem has called forth. He may or may not work with the motif immediately after it has been stated; he may or may not delay the structural imitation which at all events comes unexpectedly; he may imitate a motif, now in two voices, now in four; he may repeat another motif twice in the same voice. Of such unpredictable varieties there are many, and from none can a rule be deduced. This great flexibility, which allows the composer a seemingly unlimited freedom, is another result of the invention of motifs with harmonic implications in view. Because of this, most of the motifs closely resemble each other, and if for a certain length of time the harmonic situation remains basically the same, which in fact is intended, the motifs will easily fit into the picture wherever they are inserted. To overwork the argument: so close is the resemblance of the motifs on the basis of the fixed harmony that they might be even interchangeable.

The madrigalesque counterpoint, whenever it had novel features, brought about a certain simplification compared with the old polyphony. Simplified though it was, this new counterpoint did not merely cut out whatever appeared difficult, learned, and according to the manner of the old polyphony. With a somewhat hesitating gesture, Monteverdi reached out for the new artistic "license" that discovered a point of departure for the new contrapuntal style. The new technique rested principally on considerations of harmony; the old technique was essentially the product of melodic thinking in terms of complete horizontal lines.

Although the first decisive advance in this new direction had been made, Monteverdi did not present his thoughts systematically, or radically, or even completely. The madrigals of 1590 did not present a picture in one color, with one theme. Old elements lingered on to no small degree, while the new features, though often distinct, were not always prominent. Monteverdi's concentration on Tasso in this collection of madrigals indicated a certain advance over the first book and was more than a preference given to a poet for reasons of poetry only. All the poems of Tasso in this volume show Monteverdi's musical composition at its most advanced stage from a stylistic point of view, and none of them is artistically inferior. Any new conception usually occurs in a work based on a poem of Tasso, and the features of the madrigals in the first book that are basic to the new style can be linked with the Tasso madrigals of the second book.

Nothing that Monteverdi's artistic mind had previously absorbed was lost in this more advanced phase. The refrains, favored in the canzonetta, were used again and more elaborately worked out as *da capo* repetition. The short motifs had previously been tried out under the influence of the canzonetta. The rhythmical patterns, among which the canzonetta formula ♩♪♪♩♩|♩♩ ⅞ | grew to be typical, retained their striking precision. The organizing force of the cadence kept its full effect upon the structure, but Monteverdi now made use of his skillful work with motifs to cover up the cadences and interlock the phrases.

There were even intimations of the harmonic polyphony in the earlier madrigals.

The Tasso composition announced the modernistic trend. Even *Donna nel mio ritorno*, whose motifs, especially at the beginning, with their slow rhythmic motion might suggest an older form of the madrigal, is in fact representative of this modernism, for it has a purely harmonic counterpoint and, above all, a continuous use of cadential effects. There are long passages in the madrigal in which one cadence follows the other without splitting the composition into little groups.[9]

The last madrigal seems to be a total recantation of all that Monteverdi had presented as "modernism." This composition, *Cantai un tempo*, has the characteristics of the old, polyphonic style in all its purity. Nothing modern, none of Monteverdi's own stylistic idioms, disturbs the picture. All students of Monteverdi agree upon the antiquity of the style.[10] What was the reason for closing with a composition that was in contradiction to his plans for the foundation of a new style? The poem was by Bembo, a representative of an older epoch that had little to say to Monteverdi's generation. The younger men had not lost a feeling for the greatness of their elders, but they were striving for other tones, new words, and new expressions. Monteverdi was aware that Bembo and the spirit of his poetry belonged to the past, and it was this feeling for the past as a part of history that began to take shape in his mind. When he turned to the poetry of Bembo, he knew that he was keeping something alive that had already been marked by death. For the first time in the work of Monteverdi this awareness of the past made itself felt as an artistic matter. Monteverdi had logically and systematically apprehended the polyphonic style of the old madrigal and was

---

[9] Leichtentritt, *op. cit.*, p. 263, referred to the "ältere Madrigaltechnik," an opinion accepted by Redlich, *op. cit.*, p. 56. The arrangement by cadences as well as the harmonic counterpoint seem to speak against it. The melodic contours have no resemblance to the polyphonic line of older madrigals; they show the characteristic influence of harmonic considerations. The madrigal *S'andasse amor a caccia* (Tasso) has been related to the style of the French chanson by Leichtentritt, *op. cit.*, p. 264; A. Tessier, "Les deux styles de Monteverde," *RM*, Vol. III (1922), p. 242, nn. 3, 4; Prunières, *Claudio Monteverdi*, p. 13; Redlich, *op. cit.*, pp. 57f. There does not seem to be any particular reason for this. The lively declamatory motifs and other characteristics of the brilliant work can be better explained through the Italian canzonetta. We like to point to the interesting beginning of the composition—it has a canonic entrance of the voices. The tradition of setting a "caccia" in canon had not entirely died out as this and other works of the sixteenth century show.

[10] Leichtentritt, Prunières, Malipiero, and Redlich appropriately characterized the madrigal as a "copy of style" and considered it a "farewell gesture" to an age that was past.

capable of writing in the language of the past, but he had to assume the style consciously and for a definite purpose; it was not naturally his own. There is an important difference between an influence of the past that penetrates the work without the full awareness of the composer, and the imitation of the past as a conscious act, and this difference is clearly reflected in Monteverdi's madrigals. In some of the compositions of the second book there are details that obviously must be taken as reminders of the style of the older generation, the artistic fathers of Monteverdi. There is, also, this perfectly uniform madrigal in the old style, presented as an imitation. In one case, we have Monteverdi, the heir of the past; in the other, Monteverdi, the historical observer. Thus, Tasso's *Non si levava ancor*, the initial composition of the second book, announced the program of a new style, and Bembo's *Cantai un tempo*, the final work, reminded the listener of what the artistic program of the past had been.

When many years later the new style was all completed, Monteverdi showed the artistic ideal of old in still another way. In 1627 he republished Arcadelt's first book of madrigals for four voices, which had appeared in 1539. The composer of the new age could, thus, pay homage to the master of the old madrigal whose idiom, though foreign and historical, might be worthy of admiration.

PART THREE

Rise to Fame:
The Foundation of the New

CHAPTER EIGHT

Music in Mantua

THE GONZAGAS

FROM the dedication of the second book of madrigals to Giacomo Ricardi, a gentleman of Milan, we learn that Monteverdi had been in that city and had appeared there as a player of the viola. Apparently he had given a good account of himself, for he felt that the favors he had enjoyed could be repaid only by affectionate reverence and "atti armonici" (compositions). By the time he had composed these new madrigals, he was obviously beginning to look around for conditions that would allow his talent to come into its own in the service of a renowned patron of music. Cremona offered him little opportunity, since the only outstanding position there was occupied by his teacher, Ingegneri. Relations between Cremona and Milan were close, and it was natural for Monteverdi to try his fortunes in the larger and more important center, but nothing came of the attempt, and he returned home to complete the madrigals and prepare them for publication.

It was not long, however, before an opportunity arose that held great prospects for a musician of Monteverdi's caliber. He was appointed "singer and player of the viola" at the court of the Gonzagas and went to Mantua in 1590. Despite his youth—he was twenty-three—this was a respectable position, though not one of the first rank. It is worthy of note that in the same year he was elected a member of the Congregazione ed Accademia di Santa Cecilia in Rome, a rather astonishing sign of recognition.[1]

---

[1] The list of the members is quoted by Alberto Cametti, "Girolamo Frescobaldi in Roma. 1604-1643," *RMI*, Vol. XV (1908), p. 702, n.1.

At this time the house of Gonzaga seemed to be at the height of its glory. During the long reign of Guglielmo Gonzaga, Mantua had enjoyed great prosperity, and its wealth had grown immensely. Despite the extravagant luxury of this court, the Duke administered the economic resources of the Mantuan lands exceedingly well. Much of its wealth and commercial fame had been contributed by the cloth weavers, who constituted the most powerful guild since the fourteenth century. Their wares had the highest reputation at home and abroad, and, unlike his son, under whom the weavers were to suffer much, Guglielmo knew how to encourage this flourishing commerce. Related to some of the great houses in Italy—the Medici in Florence and the Este in Ferrara—and married to Eleonora, daughter of the Emperor Ferdinand, Guglielmo had been influential at the papal court since the days of Cardinal Ercole of Gonzaga, who in 1561 presided at the Council of Trent, and had become one of the most powerful princes in all Italy. In an age when public display was the indispensable accompaniment and symbol of princely might and glory, the Duke enjoyed exhibiting the brilliance of his court on fitting occasions, and the chroniclers had many opportunities to describe the dazzling scenes at special celebrations, such as the official visits of princes or state marriages. Guglielmo also spent extraordinary sums to satisfy his passion for architecture and derived particular satisfaction from the erection of the Chiesa Regio Ducale di S. Barbara, his favorite church, which was built upon his initiative. The building of his palace at Goito took no minor part among Guglielmo's artistic projects and surely a major share of his budget. During his reign Mantua had a considerable reputation as a center of the arts. Works of art had been collected by the house of Gonzaga for over a century, especially by the famous Isabella d'Este da Gonzaga, and her successors were tireless in adding to the collection and in employing artists to work for them. The Mantuan collection had become so highly renowned that in the dark days to come dealers and agents of princes from all over Europe awaited with eagerness the final blow that would disperse the Mantuan wealth and art. Guglielmo, it is true, could not rival the artistic splendors of one of his predecessors, Federigo, who had employed Giulio Romano as court painter and architect, but he continued in suitable style the traditional patronage of his house. A fondness for music and musicians was equally traditional with the Gonzagas and apparently grew stronger with the generations, reaching its height about the time Monteverdi went to Mantua. Duke Guglielmo had called musicians of extraordinary fame to his court, among them Giaches de Wert, who had the reputation of being one of the best composers in Italy.

At Guglielmo's death in 1586, only four years before Monteverdi's arrival, the dukedom appeared stronger than ever and its government was regarded as exemplary among the sixteenth-century principalities of Italy. The wisdom of the Duke had raised him to the place of a respected adviser among the princes. His work in the administration of justice and his revision of the criminal laws had brought him the esteem of other sovereigns and the love and admiration of his subjects, who looked up to him as to a paterfamilias. In his minute description of the Duke's funeral procession, the chronicler Federico Follino reported that the people who lined the streets burst into lamentations over the loss of their sovereign, and we may well believe their tears were sincere. "Thus departed Serenissimo Guglielmo Gonzaga, a man of admirable judgment, of the keenest intellect, of the most vivacious memory; endowed with infinite prudence and goodness, and so well versed in the liberal arts that few, if any, were his equals in the world of his day; but above all, he spent so much time and effort in the study of theology and of music that we can truthfully say: in these he rose to the same level with, or even surpassed, anyone else."[2] The death of Guglielmo closed a glorious period of Mantuan history. His son Vincenzo, the fourth Duke of Mantua and the second of Monferrato, was to make full use of the wealth his father had accumulated; but like many sons of strong princes, he added much to the glory and display, but nothing to the power, of the state.

Follino also described Vincenzo's coronation, which took place on September 22, 1587. The ceremonies betrayed the new duke's unrestrained liking for luxury and pomp. The gathering of high dignitaries from the various parts of Italy was most impressive. The gowns they wore displayed a dazzling abundance of colors and jewels, of gold and satin, but Vincenzo's ceremonial dress far outshone the others. The interior of the cathedral of San Pietro, where the coronation was held, was decorated with drapes of cloth of gold, silk, taffeta, satin, velvet and brocade. Musicians were present in large numbers, divided into choirs of singers and bands of trombones and cornets.[3] The coronation

---

[2] Don Federico Follino, *Descrittione dell' infirmità, morte, et funerali dell Sereniss. Sig. Il Sig. Guglielmo Gonzaga, Ill. Duca di Mantova, e di Monferrato I.* (Mantua, 1587), p. 5.

[3] Don Federico Follino, *Descrittione delle solenni cerimonie fatte nella coronatione del Sereniss. Sig. Il Sig. Vincenzo Gonzaga. IlIl Duca di Mantoua, e di Monferrata II. &c.* (Mantua, 1587), fol. A4. The "Concerti" mentioned here are the choral groups of instruments and voices.

Mass, said by the Bishop of Mantua, had a solemnity befitting the occasion. Of particular significance was the ceremony of the kissing of the Gospel, the kiss of Peace, and the incensation. After the Gospel had been read, the Missal was brought to the Duke and the members of his family to be kissed where it was opened at the page of the Gospel of the day. Since the incensation involved all the dignitaries, the ceremony lasted a long time and was musically accompanied by "the concerti which were usually performed during the Offertory on more solemn days." [4] The music for the coronation Mass was altogether "most perfect and to this effect composed by the very excellent musician and Maestro di Cappella of His Highness, Mr. Giaches de Wert, a man most famous in the world because of the excellence of his compositions." The performance included "concerti for organ, voices, cornets, and trombones." [5] After these concerti had all been played, the ceremony was over and the court moved to the door of the cathedral, where Vincenzo, sitting on a luxuriously garnished "Sedia Imperiale," received the oath of allegiance taken upon the Gospel. He promised that he would always guard the welfare of his people and exercise justice in all integrity. As a token of his good will and generosity, he at once and forever abolished half of the taxation on wine. "A harmonious concerto of trombones began to be played, placed on an elevation of marble, just above the door of the church toward the piazza, and at the same time there was an outburst of cannon, of drums, small and large, of cries of joy, even of horses neighing, and of so many bells that in such a noise truly the onlookers could not understand their own words." [6] This spontaneous benevolence—probably ill-advised—was characteristic of the Duke. His taste for magnificence and his real magnanimity might have made him a prince of princes had they been blended with wisdom and discipline.[7] But he lacked both wisdom and restraint.

Vincenzo's character was a contradictory mixture of noble and repellent traits. He enjoyed the benefits of the meritorious government

---

[4] *Ibid.*, fol. A 4[1]: "& a far questa così lunga cerimonia, aiutorono i concerti che si sogliono fare a quellhora dell'Offertorio nelli dì più solenni."

[5] *Ibid.*, fol. B: "Finita la Messa, la quale fu di Musica perfettissima, composta per questo effetto, dall' eccellentiss. Musico & Mastro di Cappella di S.A. il Sig. Giaches Vuert, huomo per l'eccellenza dell' opre [*sic*] sue, assai famoso al Mondo: & spediti i concerti d'organo, voci, cornette, e tromboni, si cominciarono tutti ad incaminare per una sbarra, che correua al longo alla Chiesa, sino alla porta: & era guardata dalli Arcieri, perche la moltitudine del popolo iui concorsa non l'occupasse."

[6] *Ibid.*, fol. B 3.

[7] See L. P. Volta, *Compendio Cronologico della Storia di Mantova*, under the year 1587.

of his father, and the wealth he inherited put him in a position to be as generous as was suitable to the dignity of his station. The wealth of Mantua was not of his making, and he did not add to it or secure its permanence; in fact, his craving for splendid display and lavish entertainment largely undid the work of his father. His indiscriminate generosity and his lascivious dissipations were notorious while he was still a youth. The scandal of his divorce from his first wife, Margherita Farnese, the daughter of the Duke of Parma, whom he had married in 1581, gave reason for alarm at his dissolute life and was the cause of strained relations between Mantua and Parma. His father hoped to detach Vincenzo from the path of license by marrying him to Eleonora Medici, but his hope was vain.

Endowed with handsome features and impressive stature, liked by his friends and his people, Vincenzo had excellent traits that his chroniclers have duly praised. His magnanimity and sympathy were undeniable. He freed Tasso from ignoble confinement in Ferrara, though an ambition to glorify the Mantuan court by the presence of this illustrious poet may have been his main incentive. Many persons of distinction were attracted to him, not always for material advantages, for even when Vincenzo was exceedingly slow in giving them their due, they preserved an unswerving loyalty to the Duke and to the house of Gonzaga. Rubens, who ten years after Monteverdi's arrival was for some years the official court painter, often expressed his devoted feelings in letters to Vincenzo, and Monteverdi himself was perhaps the best witness to a bond of loyalty which held over the years through all trials. Almost all the letters the composer wrote while in service at Mantua contain bitter complaints that the court was always considerably behind in its payments, though well in advance in its demands for artistic productions. The letters reveal that Monteverdi had many other reasons for irritation and did not enjoy his stay at Mantua, where he suffered from the oppressive humidity arising from the lakes and held it responsible for his fevers and continual headaches. Nevertheless, he remained attached to Vincenzo for many years after he left the Mantuan service.

There is no doubt that Vincenzo had qualities which attracted all those who worked for him. One of his letters shows a wisdom scarcely to be expected of one devoted solely to dissipation. This letter, dated 1608, was sent from Paris to Annibal Chieppio, the ducal secretary, with whom Monteverdi also had some correspondence. Chieppio, an able administrator and a man of great honesty, had been exposed to slander and malice. "My dearest Chieppio," wrote the Duke, "I have received your letter, in response to which I want to write you two words only. Pay no attention to what the people say; let them say what they please; people speak evil of all the world, even of Christ. Maintain your conscience pure, as I am convinced you do, and then let everyone gossip to his liking. That is all I have to say to you at this time for your consolation." [8]

Vincenzo's patronage of Rubens and of François Porbus, the other Mantuan court painter who had come from Flanders, reflected the old passion of the Gonzagas for the arts. Vincenzo was most eager to add to his collection of paintings, but he also craved curiosities and was attracted to the extraordinary as much as to the genuine in art. On his frequent journeys to Hungary, Germany, Holland, France, he was on the lookout for artists, to be sure, but also for artisans and craftsmen known for odd skills. He no longer had that instinctive taste which is the sign of generally high standards of culture, and his craving for novelties undermined his taste and, certainly, his funds.

The Italian poets were also honored by Vincenzo's patronage. Tasso dedicated a canzone to the Duke on the occasion of his coronation,[9] and Guarini, Tasso's great rival, whose poetry was soon to absorb Monteverdi, dedicated his pastorals to Vincenzo. Ottavio Rinuccini, the foremost poet in Florence at the court of the Medici, had frequent discussions with the Duke on matters poetical and musical, and Monteverdi was to benefit from these close relations when he later used Rinuccini's lyrics and dramas for his work. Chiabrera dedicated odes to the Duke, and his poetry also offered Monteverdi material worthy of being set to music. Vincenzo's literary interests thus created an atmosphere in which musicians and poets worked together in an ideal unity, so that both arts could serve a common purpose.

Guarini and Rinuccini, Marco da Gagliano [10] and Monteverdi, Rubens, Porbus, and Viani, all took part in the harmony that Vincenzo conducted. In that harmony, Vincenzo gave first place to the theater and to music in general, to singers in particular, and most of all to

---

[8] From the "Lettere originali dei Gonzaga" in the Archives of Mantua quoted by Armand Baschet, "Pierre-Paul Rubens, Peintre de Vincent Ier de Gonzague, Duc de Mantoue (1600–1608)," in *GBA*, Vol. 20 (Paris, 1866), p. 427.

[9] *Canzone nella coronatione del serenissimo Sig. Don Vincenzo Gonzaga. Duca di Mantova et Monferrato &c. del Sig. Torquato Tasso* (Mantua, 1587). The canzone, consisting of ninety-three lines, has no particular poetical quality, but is rather conventional sixteenth-century poetry.

[10] Vincenzo expressed his interest in the madrigals and motets of Marco da Gagliano.

women singers. His fondness for theatrical representations and for actresses was apparently a real mania, and the troupes he engaged were the most welcome guests at his court. The Duke was anxious to have other princes witness these costly entertainments, and did not tire of writing letters of recommendation to kings and princes in behalf of his comedians. Thus we can easily understand the proverbial reference to the Duke's comedians. These displays required a proper setting, and Vincenzo had Antonio Maria Viani, his architect, build a new theater. Viani, a Cremonese like Monteverdi, had also done work at the Appartamento di Corte and at the new palace, the "Villa," in Maderno on Lake Garda. This new theater was used to splendid effect at an event that was to be of the greatest importance in Monteverdi's creative life: the marriage of Vincenzo's son Francesco to Margherita of Savoy in 1608.

Vincenzo's theatrical activities had another important effect: they prepared the way for the appearance of the musical drama, the opera. Monteverdi was to give Mantua opera only a few years after its first creation in Florence. Intermediate as well as incidental music had certainly been used for theatrical performances long before the first opera was produced in Mantua, but though the insertion of music into the spoken drama is generally regarded as a precursor of the opera, this occurred everywhere, and there was nothing specifically Mantuan in such usage. It was the unlimited enthusiasm for the theater that gave a special flavor to activities at the court. The Duke's fondness for the theater must have produced connoisseurs of acting and drama, and quickened the responsiveness of the Mantuans to all manifestations of the art of the theater, so that when the music drama first appeared, it redoubled an already existing enthusiasm.

Interest in the new music drama must have been awakened in Vincenzo when, in 1589, he visited Florence on the occasion of the marriage of Ferdinand of Medici to Christine of Lorraine. Vincenzo was related to the Medici by his second marriage, to Eleonora, a niece of Ferdinand. The Duke of Mantua displayed all imaginable pomp and magnificence when he appeared in Florence, and it is reported that he spent no less than 100,000 ducats. What he could have added to the splendor that Ferdinand himself had provided for the marriage almost surpasses human imagination. For we are told that Florence no longer looked like her own self, but seemed a city out of a fairy tale, with scenery and scaffolds erected for great pageants, tournaments, sea battles, and the storming of a Turkish fortress. A full month passed in the presentation of one spectacle after another, each more impressive than the last.

One of the most sensational and most favored productions was the performance of Ottavio Rinuccini's intermezzo *Il Combattimento d'Apolline col serpente*. This has been regarded as the cradle of the opera, though in itself, of course, it was not a music drama. All the intermezzi had basically musical subject matter, and included in the ballet of the planets was a representation of the music of the spheres. More important than the production, which could not have been entirely a novelty to Vincenzo, was the participation in it of the men who were to collaborate in the music drama during the last decade of the century—Count Bardi, Caccini, Peri, Emilio del Cavalieri. Some of the musicians took parts on the stage—Peri, for instance, and Marenzio. The famous madrigalist Alessandro Striggio had an active share in the performance as one of the instrumentalists. The Grand Duke Ferdinand had commissioned his architect, Bernardo Buontalenti, to build the stage and scenery. "The *Intermedii* were of a special kind in view of the almost supernaturally artistic presentations and machinery, an invention of the excellent architect Bernardo Buontalenti, who also was responsible for the decoration of the Great Hall." [11] Great singers were heard in the performance, especially the glorious Vittoria Archilei, who enchanted the listeners—among whom, we have no doubt, Duke Vincenzo was one of the most rapturous. Besides Archilei, the singers Luca and Margherita Caccini participated in the singing and dancing. The great success of the intermezzi called for several repetitions.

Among the artists, such as Rinuccini and Count Bardi, the subject of the music drama may well have come up for discussion. It had been a favorite one ever since Bardi and Vincenzo Galilei began a dispute about the revision of the musical style. Even if Duke Vincenzo did not talk with the artists, it would have been strange if one who was continually on the lookout for artistic novelties and employed agents to search for them had been apathetic on such an occasion. His later contacts with Florentine artists, the commissions he gave Rinuccini, the musicians he drew from Florence to his residence, all prove that Vincenzo was an attentive listener. So it may be assumed that he returned to Mantua with new ideas to enliven still further the theatrical and musical activities of his court. Unfortunately, in the same year, 1589, his own

---

[11] See Bastiano de Rossi's fascinating description: *Descrizione dell apparato e degl'Intermedi fatti per la commedia rappresentata in Firenze* (1589).

Teatro di Corte, located in the beautiful Reggia, burned down and brought a temporary halt to his plans.

The new musical possibilities of the theater had given fresh vigor to Vincenzo's passion for singers. When the time came, he seized upon the music drama, with its new style of virtuoso singing, as a most appropriate vehicle for royal display. The style that evolved from the music drama was to be called the *stile rappresentativo* because of its use in stage presentations of musical and dramatic material. It was Vincenzo who discovered the possibility of adapting such a style to courtly purposes of his own. The drama and comedy—indeed, all of the arts —had been put to good use for court display, but the music drama might well become the most glorious presentation of all. Inherent in the relations between art and the nobility was the fact that art was less esteemed for its aesthetic value than as a symbol of princely power and position. The new art of singing, the virtuoso star, employed and fondled by the prince, dramatic music proper—all were but additions to the luster of the court. But the brilliant singers and the elaborate musical machinery would be purposeless without the important contribution of the composer, whose genius would create the setting for the new ideal. Monteverdi was to supply the genius, but it was to be many years before he was called upon to do so. At the time of his appointment to Mantua, Vincenzo had just witnessed the magnificent Florentine spectacles, and there was no indication that Monteverdi would be asked to contribute his services in the field of dramatic music.

THE COMPOSERS IN MANTUA

When Monteverdi came to Mantua in the double capacity of singer and instrumentalist, he must have been deeply impressed by the brilliance of the court life and cultural activities. The city's prosperity, material and cultural, had the appearance of lasting vitality, though there were indications of an unhealthy growth that would eventually produce disaster. During Vincenzo's reign these indications were to grow very numerous indeed, but in 1590 all seemed well, even promising. Musical activities in Mantua were at least as lively and cultivated as those in the other arts. Though the churches of the city, especially the cathedral of S. Pietro, were partly responsible for the vitality of musical culture in Mantua, they did not approach the standards at the court. The music at S. Barbara, the Cappella Ducale, surpassed that of the other churches, since the musicians, singers, and instrumentalists were always the best the court could provide.

The most prominent figure at the time of Monteverdi's arrival was still Giaches de Wert. He had resigned his post as maestro di cappella of S. Barbara but remained the leading musician of the court. He was called upon to compose the festival Mass for the coronation of Vincenzo and half a year before the event notified the ducal secretary that he hoped to be able "in music to sing the praise of both the Saint and His Highness," indicating that the Mass was to be dedicated to St. Barbara and Vincenzo.[12] His fame rested largely upon his numerous madrigals, of which he published eleven books. Although his longest period of service was in the reign of Guglielmo, who favored religious music, he must have been held in special esteem by Vincenzo, who undoubtedly preferred profane compositions. In 1584, when still "Prince of Mantua," Vincenzo learned that Giaches de Wert had set to music Tasso's *Qual musico gentil ch'al canto snodi*, and requested a copy, adding that the composer should include any new madrigal he might have composed; in short, "the greater the number of your compositions that are sent me, the more shall I be obliged to show gratitude at our convenience." [13]

Are we to assume that on his return from the wedding of Ferdinand in Florence, Vincenzo was resolved to bring the music drama to Mantua? There is a curious note in a letter of Muzio Manfredi, dated November 20, 1591, and written to "Giaches Duuert," in which mention is made of the "representation of the Pastoral [*Poema boschereccio*] that Manfredi had sent to the Duke, and for which music should be composed." [14] Was it composed in a monodic form, or in a set of madrigals? Unfortunately, we know no more about the matter; but it seems to show that the Mantuan efforts to attain dramatic music were about as old as the discussions in Florence. We also know nothing of the reaction of Giaches de Wert to the request. That he was capable of a "dramatic" rendering of a musical composition he had amply proved in his latest madrigals. Indeed, it was the modern, dramatic style of his madrigals that attracted Monteverdi.[15]

The successor of Giaches de Wert as maestro di cappella at the ducal church was Gian Giacomo Gastoldi. From his youth he had been a singer in Mantua, and in 1582 he was promoted to this leading posi-

[12] See A. Bertolotti, *Musici alla Corte dei Gonzaga in Mantova dal secolo XV al XVIII* (Milan, 1890), p. 46.

[13] See the letter, *ibid.*, p. 45.

[14] *Ibid.*, p. 46.

[15] I wish to express my gratitude to Dr. Alfred Einstein (Smith College, Northampton, Mass.), who generously permitted me to study his copies of madrigals by Giaches de Wert.

tion. His post involved official duties as a composer of religious music, and his output of sacred compositions was large, though not comprehensive from a liturgical point of view. His Masses were not numerous and his motets were few, but his psalm compositions for the vespers, collections for four, five, six and eight voices, and for the whole year, had an extraordinary success and were reprinted far into the seventeenth century. Gastoldi's world-wide fame, however, was based on his balletti. The native song was his chosen medium and harmonized best with his temperament. The list of his works shows a balance between sacred and profane music, and the discrepancy between his natural interests and his official functions caused no conflict in Gastoldi. Although the appointments of musicians *da camera* (of the court), and *da chiesa* (of the church), were made separately, their activities frequently overlapped. Moreover, the style of the *musica da camera* affected that of the *musica da chiesa*. Gastoldi, who went about the performance of his duties in church and at court without concerning himself with the possible complications of his position, swung the balance definitely in favor of the native song.

Monteverdi was quick to recognize Gastoldi's special gifts. He had already had his attention drawn to the idiomatic qualities of the native song, and his study of Gastoldi's profane compositions strengthened his sense of rhythm. The dance rhythms that underlie Gastoldi's balletti proceed in regular patterns of great simplicity that run through the whole composition. The chosen pattern is repeated verse by verse, often without the slightest variation, and frequently governs the entire composition. The balletto more than any other category retained a close relation with the dance. Indeed, in compositions whose rhythm is reduced to one pattern, we may safely assume that the dance is still an active force. Gastoldi ingeniously tapped the resources of powerful, rhythmic organizations and taught his contemporaries the proper use of accentuated rhythms. Monteverdi studiously observed these contributions of Gastoldi, and they influenced his understanding of rhythmic expressions more profoundly and lastingly than any other source.[16]

Benedetto Pallavicino, the musician next in prominence to Gastoldi, was, like Monteverdi, a native of Cremona and had served the Duke since 1582. He became maestro di cappella when Giaches de Wert

---

[16] Prunières and others have advanced the theory that these pattern-like, rhythmic organizations were drawn by Monteverdi from the French metrical compositions of the Royal Academy. In view of the early canzonette, the Italian native song is the more natural and historically correct source. We shall discuss the theory at length together with the analysis of the compositions.

died, and held this post until Monteverdi succeeded him. His work resembled that of Giaches de Wert, but was of somewhat less artistic and aesthetic value. His religious compositions were about as important as the comparable works of Giaches, and in his eight books of madrigals he followed the path of his predecessor. His madrigals were for from four to six voices, with five-part compositions predominating. Neither as bold nor as experimental as Giaches, he was still an artist of considerable merit, but his place is not among the great. His lack of originality and dependence on tradition may explain why Monteverdi took no special interest in his work. Consciously or unconsciously, Monteverdi seems to have made a differentiation with regard to the qualities of the Mantuan composers. When in 1601 Pallavicino's post became vacant Monteverdi submitted to the Duke, in the first letter of his that we have, his request to be appointed "maestro de la camera et de la chiesa sopra la musica." In this letter he referred to the "famose sig. Striggio," to the "eccellente sig. Giaches," to the "eccellente sig. Franceschino," but also to the "soffitiente messer Benedetto Pallavicino." [17] We may be mistaken in reading something derogatory into his qualification of Pallavicino as a "capable" (*sufficiente*) musician; nevertheless, between "fame" and "excellence" on the one side and "talent" on the other there seems to be a distinction that is clear enough in any language. If Monteverdi really meant to differentiate in a subtle manner, the only element of surprise is that the remark was made in such an official document. The "Franceschino," mentioned in Monteverdi's letter is Francesco Rovigo, who, according to Mantuan documents, was a protégé of the dukes of Mantua from 1570 on, when he was sent to Venice to study organ under the famous Claudio Merulo. Later, he got a year's leave of absence for study in Germany, after which he must have promised to return and resume his service at the court of Mantua.[18] Apparently, he abused the grant, for the Duke had to remind him of his promise. Rovigo occupied the position of organist at the court church of S. Barbara, as his death certificate of 1597 informs us. Monteverdi thought highly of him during seven years of collaboration and mentioned him in the letter of 1601 as one of his predecessors as maestro di musica.

Two other leading musicians in Mantua were Lodovico Grossi da Viadana and Salomone Rossi, or "Ebreo," as he called himself. Both attracted Monteverdi's attention a few years after he had begun to

---

[17] Letter No. 1, ed. Malipiero, *Claudio Monteverdi*, p. 128.
[18] See Bertolotti, *Musici alla Corte* . . . , p. 57.

work at the court. Lodovico came to Mantua in 1594 from Viadana, one of the Mantuan possessions. He was not connected with the court, but became maestro di cappella at the cathedral of S. Pietro. Of a strong, pious nature, he appears to have entered the order of the Franciscans shortly after he took over his duties at S. Pietro. In that capacity he remained nearly as long as Monteverdi worked in Mantua. Were Grossi's relations to Monteverdi of more than incidental significance in the latter's development, as is the assumption of nearly all historians? Grossi is commonly regarded as one of the precursors of modern musicianship because of his share in the origins of the figured bass, although he was not its inventor. However, if we take an inner conflict with the choral polyphony of the sixteenth century as essential to the new style of modern music, we shall hesitate to count Grossi among those who led the opposition. He hastened to comply with the secular character of the coming age, as his canzonette and two books of madrigals prove, but his profane music has little or no importance in comparison with his sacred compositions. This emphasis on religious music was not forced on him by his official functions but grew out of the goal he set for himself and for music in general: music should serve "ad majorem gloriam Dei." Most of Grossi's compositions were created to serve a liturgical purpose. This holds true especially of his motets, whose place within the order of the liturgies of the year he wished to secure. This intimate relation to a religious service raises his sacred work above the level of merely personal piety and gives these compositions objectivity. In a profane age, the attempt to build up an impressive liturgical work must have cost the composer strenuous effort. There is no doubt that he drew on the sacred polyphony of the Netherlands, and it may well be that the ideals of the Counter Reformation gave him the enthusiasm necessary to carry out so difficult a task. An early collection of his works, the vesper psalms, published in 1595, was composed expressly "iuxta ritum sacrosanctae atque orthodoxae ecclesiae romanae." That is a standard formula used by composers who served the ideals of the Counter Reformation. It is no accident that Grossi's work was soon taken up by Northern (Flemish) printers and published in anthologies of sacred music with that of Northern composers of the sixteenth century, in one case even with a Mass of Clemens non Papa. Nor is it an accident that Grossi's work received its most enthusiastic reception in the North—a reception not confined to his famous *Cento Concerti Ecclesiastici* of 1602 but also accorded to a large body of his liturgical music. His religious purpose and his habit

of thinking in liturgical terms prevented him from opposing the Northern musicians. He could not possibly renounce the art of the past without proposing a new end for his music. In view of these considerations,
there is obviously no bridge between Grossi and Monteverdi.

Grossi was only three years older than Monteverdi and belonged
to the generation whose work would cover a third of the new century.
It was not, therefore, a difference in age that separated them, nor even
the difference between the sacred and secular purposes of music, but
a difference in artistic style. And yet, do we not think of the *Cento
Concerti Ecclesiastici* as the work with which Grossi stepped forward
into the new age? It is true that the principle of the concerto as a contrast between soloistic voices and *basso continuo* accompaniment by
the organ was applied by Grossi in his collection of 1602. But his reasons
for these innovations were decidedly negative. He had observed serious defects in the musical performances given by the choral organizations connected with the cathedrals. There were not enough singers in
the choirs, to say nothing of their lack of training! He had heard the
most ludicrous performances of sixteenth-century choral polyphony,
which required a well-trained and profusely equipped choir such as
no longer existed in most churches. Since he could not hope to restore
choral institutions to their former glory, Grossi set out to offer a remedy
in the composition itself. He would compose motets to fit any situation,
no matter how modest the available equipment. He composed concerti
for one, two or three parts, and shifted the "many-voiced" sonority
into the harmonic accompaniment of the organ. This, clearly, was not
the conception of the structure of the modern composition but the
totally negative approach of a soloistic art, of monody with an accompaniment. It was designed, not with an eye to the future, but in the
hope of saving all that could be salvaged in the music of the past. A
close analysis of Grossi's concerti shows that his melodic writing has
nothing in common with the new form but bears all the earmarks of
the older Northern composition. There are passages whose lively motion at first glance suggests a modern treatment, but they are not an
organic part of the melody, only "ornamentations" for special words
in the text (*Alleluja, radium, velociter, gloria,* etc.), such as can be
found even in compositions by Andrea Gabrieli. The contours of
Grossi's melody are exactly those of polyphonic works of the sixteenth
century and are constructed with full awareness of the function of
the voice within the whole polyphony But his melody can only sketch
the general contours and must renounce the polyphonic relativity of

many voices, so that it is convincing neither as a modern soloistic melody nor as an old polyphonic type. Monteverdi and Grossi differed in their fundamental ideas, even though Monteverdi adopted one or two features of Grossi's music in his sacred compositions.

Monteverdi's relations with Salomone Rossi were much closer, for Rossi was a thoroughly modern spirit and even collaborated with Monteverdi in later years. Rossi can hardly be regarded as an essential influence in Monteverdi's artistic growth, but he was certainly an important musical figure at the Mantuan court and probably a more gifted composer than either Lodovico Grossi or Benedetto Pallavicino. A Mantuan by birth, Rossi belonged to the historically famous Jewish community of the city, in which his family apparently enjoyed particular distinction and esteem.[19] His extraordinary musical gifts must have been recognized at a fairly early age, and he was drawn to the court, perhaps at the time of Vincenzo's succession. Like Monteverdi, Rossi was both a singer and an instrumentalist—a violinist—and was still listed as an instrumentalist in 1622. We do not know where he received his musical training, possibly at the synagogue in Mantua, since he published a unique work, the psalms and canticles in Hebrew, at Venice in 1623.[20] The volume was introduced by Leo di Modena (or Juda da Modena), who explained the use of the choral psalms in the Hebrew service. The work is a great rarity and shows Rossi's intention to harmonize the religious music of the synagogue with the artistic style of the period.[21]

For the most part, however, Rossi was in sympathy with the profane spirit that prevailed at the court. His canzonette and madrigals—including his fifth book of madrigals for five voices, published as late as 1622—were all a direct outgrowth of the sixteenth-century tradition in secular music, and it was only after Monteverdi had left Mantua, and surely under his influence, that Rossi finally turned away from that tradition. In his *Madrigaletti* of 1628, on which his claim to fame rests, he gave his version of Monteverdi's trio cantata, the vocal equivalent of the trio sonata. Rossi's originality is great and the artistic value of his instrumental compositions high, but so far as the stylistic behavior of the standard combination of parts is concerned, the typically baroque

---

[19] See Ed. Birnbaum, *Jüdische Musiker am Hofe zu Mantua von 1542–1628* (Vienna, 1893). Bertolotti, *Musici alla Corte* . . . , lists him among the "musici straordinari" as recipient of a court stipend in 1587 and 1622.

[20] The modern edition in score, published by S. Naumburg and Vincent d'Indy (Paris, 1877), gives 1620 as date of the original.

[21] Dr. Edith Kiwi (Jerusalem) has prepared an interesting study of this work.

form of the trio sonata did not originate in instrumental music and is a direct derivative from the vocal solo duet with accompaniment. In Monteverdi's five-part madrigal the basic structure of the trio cantata had already been anticipated. With his keenly creative mind, Rossi was the first to carry over to instrumental music the principles of Monteverdi's vocal composition. This by no means diminishes his historical merits, which suffice to make him stand out on the threshold of the new age, but Monteverdi overshadowed the figures around him and made them appear smaller than they actually were. We have here considerably anticipated the course of time, since Rossi's successful attempt to adapt the achievements of the new vocal style to instrumental forms did not occur much before 1610, that is, at the end of Monteverdi's stay in Mantua.

We have named the leading Mantuan musicians who were associated with Monteverdi and exchanged ideas in frequent communications, each with something of particular value to contribute. Many other musicians, listed in the records of the Mantuan Archives, are but names to the historian; and the lists are probably not complete, failing to record all the musicians who came and went after special performances. What these lists and names do convey, however incompletely, is something of the colorfulness that surely gave the musical life at the court its distinction, so that we can understand why Monteverdi was attracted to Mantua when he received his first appointment.

The demands upon the musicians, singers, and instrumentalists were great. The regular services in the Court Chapel of S. Barbara required a great deal of work, and we may be sure that at least on Sundays there was a solemnity of performance befitting the artistic tastes of the Duke. The heaviest burden of these services was undoubtedly carried by the singers, but the participation of instrumentalists in church music increased with the new style and the new age. On the profane side, the duties of the musicians at court were still greater. Vocal and instrumental music made a regular appearance, and on special occasions, such as receptions, feasts, entertainments for visiting guests, both contributed to the magnificence of a stately show. At all dances and balls the instrumentalists provided the music as a matter of course. To satisfy the demand for artistic recitals that would display the skills of performer and composer and allow an appreciation of the harmonies composed for familiar poetry, other gatherings of the court, the *camera*, were arranged. Vincenzo also managed to have frequent opportunities to hear his brilliant singers at weekly soirees on Fridays in the brilliant

Hall of Mirrors. There madrigals with or without instrumental accompaniment could be heard; there the virtuosi presented themselves for the admiration of connoisseurs; and there each new composition met its first critical audience. Every occasion required its own music, novelties were in continual demand, and the composer often had difficulty in keeping up. This ever changing renewal of the musical repertory is the true mark of vitality in musical activities, as the work of the composer lives for the occasion, and the frequent occasions offer a perpetual challenge to the musician. Works of particular artistic worth, enthusiastically acclaimed by the audience, were naturally called for repeatedly, but the essential element in this musical repertory was a continual renewal, an uninterrupted growth. No wonder that Monteverdi once complained to the Duke that he had no time left for the studies he was expected to pursue in order to gratify His Highness' taste. The large output of new compositions made frequent rehearsals necessary. Monteverdi did not approve of presenting unrehearsed compositions, even when he had the services of virtuosi, and at one time he reported that rehearsals of singers and instrumentalists were taking place every day.

CHAPTER NINE

Monteverdi in the Household of the Court—
The Journeys to Hungary and Flanders—
The French Influence

M ONTEVERDI'S position in Mantua was not one of great responsibility. Although appointed as a violist and singer, he was
presumably expected to contribute compositions. He had made a name
for himself as a madrigalist, and Vincenzo was the last person to overlook any talent in those with whom he surrounded himself. That
Monteverdi was called upon as a composer from the very start seems to
be confirmed by the publication on June 17, 1592, of his third book of
madrigals, which he dedicated to Duke Vincenzo. His compositions
were in the nature of voluntary contributions, since his position did
not include the obligation to compose. For a good many years Monteverdi's official position did not change, and his salary remained de-
plorably low. His letters are full of justified complaints that grow more
and more bitter every year. This inexcusable neglect did not necessarily reflect the Duke's appreciation of Monteverdi's gifts. Vincenzo
was never quick to pay his musicians and artists their due, though he
was always ready to make enthusiastic use of their gifts.

Among the court instrumentalists was one Giacomo Cattaneo, whose
daughter Claudia was also a musician, a singer in the court household.
Some time before 1595 Claudio Monteverdi and Claudia Cattaneo were
married with the consent of the Duke. Claudia continued as a singer of
the court, thus adding to the small income of the young couple. Shortly

after his marriage, in 1595, Monteverdi was one of the musicians who accompanied Duke Vincenzo on a campaign against the Turks. No such expedition could be undertaken without an impressive suite, and a good part of the ducal household went along with Vincenzo. In 1593 the breakdown of peace negotiations between Turkey and Hungary led to a sudden renewal of war, and in 1595 Rudolph II, in his capacity as Emperor and King of Hungary, called together an army of allies against the infidels under Sultan Mohammed III. The Sultan captured Erlan and defeated the Imperial army at Keresztes in 1596, but Mohammed's heart was not in the war and he left his troops to return to a life of leisure. Thus the defeat did not lead to the serious consequences it might easily have had. Vincenzo is reported to have exhibited the typical Gonzaga valor and skill in battle in Hungary. The campaign brought about a brilliant gathering of princes, and the extended intervals between battles were pleasantly filled with entertainments. Among the musicians who went on the adventurous journey were G. B. Marinoni and Serafino Terzi, bass singers, Monteverdi, and Teodoro Bacchino, a "cantore castratto." Monteverdi makes no reference in his letters to his experiences, but we know that he incurred debts for his campaign expenses on this journey, and on a second soon to follow. While Monteverdi was away from Mantua, Claudia lived in Cremona with his father, Baldassare.

The second journey was a more peaceful affair. In a letter dated March 22, 1599, Vincenzo wrote his cousin, the Duke of Nevers, that he was planning a trip to Flanders in order to visit the baths at Spa. It did not take long to complete the preparations, and early in June Vincenzo set out with his suite. The party passed through Trent on June 7, proceeded to Innsbruck, where they arrived a week later, and on July 2 they were in Basel. From there they followed the northern route, by way of Nancy, to Spa, where they stayed for a month. On August 11 they departed for Liége, and on August 21 they were in Antwerp, where Vincenzo took full advantage of the opportunities offered by the presence of many painters; he seems to have visited the studio of Otto van Veen, with whom Peter Paul Rubens studied. Either in Antwerp or in Brussels he met Rubens and apparently engaged him on the spot, for a year later he inquired of Francesco Marini in Brussels whether the painter "whom I engaged there for my service has already left; if not, Mr. Marini should encourage him to depart as soon as possible." [1] Vincenzo's party went to Brussels on August 26 and remained there

---

[1] See Baschet, *GBA*, Vol. 20, p. 407.

for about four weeks. On September 20 they began the journey home, and on October 15 arrived in Mantua.

Monteverdi had been away for a little more than four months, and most of the time was spent in traveling. Only in Spa and Brussels was the stay prolonged, and in both places a full program of festivities must have kept everyone busy. The musician probably had little time for his own studies and explorations, but we can imagine that he might have visited some of the famous music printers in Antwerp and had other artistic experiences. Indeed, this has been affirmed, with particular emphasis, by his brother. Six years younger than Claudio, Giulio Cesare had also been appointed at the Mantuan court as a musician and composer. In the famous *Dichiaratione,* a summary of Monteverdi's artistic program, appended to the 1607 edition of Claudio's *Scherzi musicali à tre voci,* Giulio Cesare declared that his brother brought home an artistically significant harvest from Spa in 1599. "Especially with regard to the *canto alla francese* in this modern form which, now set to words of motets, now to those of madrigals, now to those of canzonette and arias, one continually observes in the printed publications of the last three or four years, who had brought it back to Italy before he came from the baths of Spa in 1599? Who, before him, had begun to set it to texts in Latin as well as in our vernacular tongue? Did he not now make these scherzi?" [2]

This passage has been the most controversial in the literature of Monteverdi. Precisely what was it that Monteverdi brought home to Italy as a new artistic experience? It was once confirmed that the French chanson in the fashion of the sixteenth century was the fruit of his journey to Flanders, but this idea has been discarded, since it makes no sense historically. The French chanson was already well known in Italy, and no Italian in 1607 would have dared to present it as a novelty to his countrymen. Prunières was the first to decry this assumption, stressing Giulio Cesare's reference to the modern form of the *canto alla francese* as known only for a few years past, from 1601 or 1602 on.[3] The same observation was made by A. Heuss, who also

[2] Since this passage has often been translated inaccurately or too freely, we quote the original: . . . "haverebbe non pochi argomenti in suo favore, mio fratello, in particolare per il canto alla francese in questo modo moderno che per le stampe da tre o quattro anni in qua si va mirando, hor sotto a parole de motetti, hor de madregali, hor di canzonette, e d'arie, chi fu il primo di lui che lo riportasse in Italia di quando venne da li bagni di Spà, l'anno 1599, e chi incomminciò a porlo sotto ad orationi lattine e a vulgari nella nostra lingua, prima di lui? non fece questi scherzi all'hora?" (Malipiero, *Monteverdi,* pp. 82f.).
[3] The *Dichiaratione della Lettera Stampata nel Quinto Libro de suoi Madrigali* was apparently written in 1605, but published in 1607; for Giulio Cesare begins his declara-

singled out the words "questo moderno modo," and found that the folklike character of the scherzi, the use of the instrumental ritornelli, and the instrumental style reflected French influence.[4] Louis Schneider, the Monteverdi biographer, scarcely went beyond a bare reference to the *Dichiaratione*.[5] The more serious attempt to arrive at a correct interpretation was that of Prunières.[6] He went further than any other historian and maintained that Monteverdi discovered in Spa the music of Baïf's Academy, whose composers created the *musique mesurée à l'Antique*, in imitation of ancient meters. Claude Le Jeune, Thibault de Courville, Jacques Mauduit, and Du Caurroy were among the chief of these composers. Since collections of their work had already been published in Belgium, Prunières suggested that the three volumes of music by Le Jeune and Du Caurroy were studied by Monteverdi while he was in Spa. He believed that Monteverdi was "doubtless little interested in Baïf's classical researches,"[7] or in the theories of the French verse, but that "he was certainly struck by the elegant rhythmic formulae of certain chansonettes mesurées and was inspired by them in his *Scherzi musicali*." On the other hand, Prunières stated that Monteverdi did not "attempt to compose airs to Italian poetry written in antique meters, although a good deal of it existed. In common with a large number of French musicians, he preferred to take rhymed stanzas and to deduce from the general rhythm of the verse a metrical formula to which he adapted the melody."[8] He supposed that Monteverdi in his compositions previous to the *Scherzi musicali* had cultivated ele-

---

tion: "A few months ago there appeared in print a letter of my brother Claudio Monteverdi." This is, of course, the *Lettera ai Studiosi*, added to the fifth book of madrigals of 1605 as Monteverdi's reply to Artusi's attack. The reference, quoted in the passage, to a period "three or four years past" must, therefore, be related to 1605, not 1607. Since Giulio Cesare at the beginning of the *Dichiaratione* mentions the pamphlet, now lost, which Artusi published against Monteverdi under the pseudonym "Antonio Braccini da Todi," it is clear that this pamphlet must have been published in 1605, not 1606 or 1607 as has been suggested. These dates are not without bearing upon the theory concerning the *canto alla francese*.

[4] Alfred Heuss, "Die Instrumentalstücke des Orfeo," in *SIMG*, IV (1902–1903), 178ff.

[5] L. Schneider, *Claudio Monteverdi* (Paris, 1921), pp. 58ff. Schneider's French translation is frequently incorrect.

[6] Especially in his biography of Monteverdi, pp. 15ff., 46ff. See also Henry Prunières, "Monteverdi and French Music," in *The Sackbut* (London, 1922), and "Monteverdi e la Musica Francese del suo tempo," in *RaM*, II (1929), 483ff. The essays are more or less literal translations of the chapter in Prunières' book on Monteverdi.

[7] Prunières, *Claudio Monteverdi*, p. 16; see, however, p. 47: "Monteverdi, who was most profoundly influenced by humanistic ideas, and who was at the time seeking in Plato and the Greek philosophers a solution to the problems which he could not solve with the sole assistance of the theorists of musical art, could not fail to be interested in the French researches."

[8] *Ibid.*, pp. 48f.

ments of melody and harmony but "had somewhat neglected rhythm," and that the French music in ancient meters awakened in him new rhythmic intensities. Prunières extended the French influence still further and maintained that Monteverdi also studied the airs de cour and vaudevilles in Flanders in order to adapt their qualities to Italian composition, and that the relation between the instrumental ritornello and the vocal part in the *Scherzi musicali*, as well as their simple harmonic structure without dissonances, is derived from French influence. Finally, he pointed out that a special arrangement found in a few compositions of Monteverdi must have been carried over from France to the Italian music. The nature of the arrangement was this: In soloistic performance, one voice brings the statement of the melodic phrase for one line; the statement is repeated but harmonized by a full choir in tutti form; the next line has the new melodic phrase, first in solo, then in full harmonization by the choir; and so on, line by line, solo and tutti alternating. From all this, it seems that Monteverdi learned various techniques, and the problem of their exact nature is worth further study.

We know that in the early days of the Academy in Paris around 1570, under Baïf and Courville, the methods and characteristics of measured music were among the most jealously guarded secrets. At performances no one in the audience was allowed to make copies of the music, which was played from manuscripts which no one was permitted to touch. And so the first collections which made "measured" music accessible to all appeared in the eighties after the Academy had died. In 1586 Jacques Mauduit published his *Chansonettes Mesurées*; and eight years later Le Roy and Ballard brought out the *Airs, mis en musique à 4 & 5* by Claude Le Jeune. All the other works of Le Jeune in measured form appeared in the next century: *Le Printemps* in 1603, the second book of the *Airs* in 1608, and the French psalms "en vers mesurez" in 1606. In Antwerp the printer Christopher Plantin published the *Livre de Melanges de C. Le Jeune* in 1585. Two years before Monteverdi's visit Phalèse in Antwerp had printed the anthology *Le Rossignol Musical des Chansons de diverses et excellens autheurs de nostre temps* (1597), which contained, among compositions of Philippe de Monte, Sweelinck, Alfonso Ferrabosco and others, six works by Le Jeune and one by Du Caurroy. But none of the compositions in these collections, quoted by Prunières as Monteverdi's source, had anything to do with the principles of the academic *musique mesurée*. Monteverdi may have called at the printing office of Phalèse and have seen *Le Livre de Melanges* and

Le Rossignol Musical; but even so, he could not have approached the measured music of the French Academy through them. To familiarize himself with that style of music, he would have had to study the collections of the eighties. He may have seen them, in Spa or in Brussels; there is no evidence for or against such a hypothesis.

If the novelty of style, "questo moderno modo," was really the measured music of the Academicians, would Giulio Cesare have said that the novelty had made its way in the publications (*per le stampe*) of the last three or four years only? We cannot make the dates agree, nor do we believe that the music of the French Academy was such a novelty to Monteverdi that he decided to bring it to Italy. There are two main reasons for this conclusion. First: The measured music, composed in close accordance with the principles of the old Academy of 1570, was no longer a "modern" manner of composing when Giulio Cesare wrote the defense of his brother. Historically, it was on the way out by 1610 and had no international influence, because it was too artificial and too closely linked with French verse. The later reprints of French psalm compositions were called for, not because of the *musique mesurée,* but for religious reasons. The French *musique mesurée* was of importance only within the circle where it originated and had no effect on the international musical situation.[9]

The second reason is that the rhythmic order of Monteverdi's *Scherzi musicali* is not derived from the text as are the rhythms of the French music, where the rigid schemes regulating the relation between long and short values are not primarily musical and the rhythm as a whole is without a beat. If the text is in the same meter, line by line, the musical rhythm is similarly consistent throughout the composition. Monteverdi also maintains a consistency of rhythm in his scherzi, but this consistency comes from a rhythmic musical pattern organized by a regular beat. His patterns are outgrowths of the dance song; they are the basic dance rhythms of Italian native songs and are close to the patterns of Gastoldi's *Balletti* and the rhythms Orazio Vecchi chose for some of his native songs. They are also related to Monteverdi's previous studies of the qualities of the native song, carried out in his canzonette. The scherzo *Giovinetta Ritrosetta* is based on the following rhythmic pattern:

[9] See D. P. Walker, "The Aims of Baïf's Académie de poésie et de musique," in *Journal of Renaissance and Baroque Music,* I (1946), 91ff. For the latest and most comprehensive study of the French Academy see the magnificent work of Frances A. Yates, *The French Academies of the Sixteenth Century* (University of London: The Warburg Institute, 1947).

Ex. 46   x, 51

These rhythms, deeply rooted in the tradition of Italian dance songs, regulate the beat with their repetitions, and the bass, with its equalized motion, strengthens the forceful pattern. They are typical of the scherzi of Monteverdi, and do not resemble those of the French *musique mesurée*. Exactly the same rhythmic order, with the same pattern in the upper duet and the same motion in the bass, occurs in Monteverdi's *Amorosa pupilletta,* and a number of other scherzi.

To support his thesis that the meters of the French chansonette mesurée and Monteverdi's rhythms in the scherzi are identical, Prunières placed an example from Claude Le Jeune's *Le Printemps* (1603!) and Monteverdi's *Damigella tutta bella* side by side.[10] At first glance the rhythms seem to be alike:

Ex. 47

The resemblance is only superficial; in essence, the two examples are totally different. Le Jeune arrives at the rhythm by strict adherence to the short and long syllables of the text. Monteverdi, however, chooses one of the favorite native dance patterns, in which the continual shift, measure by measure, from ¾ to ⅝ is typical. Monteverdi's rhythm is fundamentally musical, but the French composer must follow the qualities and quantities of the text, if his composition is to be acceptable to the Academy.[11]

An analysis of the *Scherzi musicali* shows clearly that Monteverdi's

---

[10] See Prunières in *RaM*, II, 484, 488.

[11] See D. P. Walker, "The Influence of Musique mesurée à l'antique, Particularly on the Airs de Cour of the Early Seventeenth Century," in *Musica Disciplina*, II (1948), 148f. Walker rejects Prunières' thesis. The characteristic rhythm of 6/8 and 3/4 in the ritornello of *Orfeo* has correctly been explained by Peter Epstein, "Zur Rhythmisierung eines Ritornells von Monteverdi," in *AfMW*, VIII (1926-1927), 416ff.

rhythmic thinking was in no way influenced by the principles which guided the French composer of the Academy. It cannot have been the rhythmic organization that Giulio Cesare had in mind when he praised his brother for bringing the modern type of the *canto alla francese* to Italy.

But what did he have in mind? In the first place, Giulio Cesare speaks of the *canto*, not the *canzona alla francese*. It is significant that the Italians, when speaking of the French chanson as form or category, rarely, if ever, used the word *canto* as the equivalent in their language; they invariably spoke of the canzona. Giulio Cesare may, therefore, have been referring to a special manner of singing, to a performance rather than to any particular musical category. Indeed, this becomes certain if we take another part of his statement into consideration. All interpreters of the passage have disregarded Giulio Cesare's remark that the modern form of the *canto alla francese* can be found in music set to motets, madrigals, canzonette, arias. This clearly rules out any category whatever, including the chanson and the chansonette mesurée. *Canto alla francese*, therefore, has reference to a manner of performance, perhaps to a particular structural arrangement connected with the performance, but not to a specific category. In referring to his later compositions, where he admitted the influence of French music, Monteverdi never used the term *canzona, chanson, canzonetta,* or *chansonette alla francese*,[12] for he did not imply any category but a manner of performance, and hence used the phrase *cantare alla francese,* or *canto alla francese*. Since he himself applied the term to religious compositions as well as to profane, to the motet and the madrigal alike, there can no longer be any doubt about the implications of Giulio Cesare's remarks.[13]

In the eighth book, the *Madrigali Guerrieri et Amorosi*, Monteverdi included two five-part madrigals, *Dolcissimo uscignolo* and *Chi vol haver felice*. The first of these has the explanatory remark that it is to be *cantato a voce piena, alla francese,* with the additional indication in the soprano part as *solo* and *canto in tuono*. This latter term means

[12] Manfred F. Bukofzer, *Music in the Baroque Era* (New York: W. W. Norton, 1947), p. 39, states that Monteverdi came in contact with the *vers mesuré* "during his stay in France." Monteverdi stayed in Flanders; he passed through Lorraine only on his speedy trip from Basel to Spa. Monteverdi's "preface" to the *Scherzi*—he did not write any—does not contain the reference to French music; it appears only in the *Dichiaratione* of his brother. Furthermore, the designation *canzonetta alla francese* is not to be found in Monteverdi's works at all.

[13] In his review of Prunières' book A. Pirro, in *RM*, V (Paris, June, 1924), 274ff., is considerably more reserved in the interpretation of the passage in Giulio Cesare's *Dichiaratione*.

singing with full voice and is, therefore, identical with *cantare a voce piena*. The second madrigal has only the prescription *cantato a voce piena, alla francese*. Both compositions, though published as late as 1638, suggest a considerably earlier date. Monteverdi also presented a motet *alla francese*. It is the third version of *Confitebor tibi Domine*, a psalm paraphrase, published in the late collection *Selva Morale* of 1640. The title of this version is *Confitebor terzo alla francese*, and like the preceding versions it is composed for five voices with thorough bass. The composition can be accompanied by a quartet of viole da braccio, except for the first soprano, which must be sung *a voce sola*. This is necessary because the singing is in the French manner, as in the two madrigals. This *Confitebor* surprisingly uses musical material of particular interest and is, at least in part, a parody. Monteverdi took this material from the madrigal *Chi vol haver felice*, as may be seen in the solo passages of the beginning:

Ex. 48   VIII, 280

Although some deviations occur in the course of the motet, the use of the madrigal as a model remains clear. The deviations were necessary because the text of the psalm paraphrase was considerably longer than that of the madrigal.

All three works have another feature in common: in each of them the musical material of a verse or text phrase is first presented solo in the highest part of the composition and then repeated in full chorus, with the phrase retained in the upper part but harmonized by the other voices. The composition proceeds with alternations of solo statement and harmonized repetition, though not always in a fixed pattern. The principle of alternation, however, is common to all compositions *alla francese* and may perhaps also be seen in Monteverdi's treatment of two lines in his grandiose psalm motet *Dixit Dominus*, for six voices and six instruments, with ritornelli to be played ad libitum. The lines are

"Virgam virtutis tuae," and "Juravit Dominus." The motet, published in 1610, differs in every other respect from works in the pure French fashion.

Prunières pointed to this arrangement as one that Monteverdi took over from the French composers and quoted an example from Pierre Guédron, the "Superintendent of music" under the French kings Henry IV and Louis XIII.[14]

Ex. 49

Pierre Guédron's *Airs de Cour* for four and five parts appeared from 1602 on. Since Monteverdi transplanted the technique literally, he was doubtless familiar with this form of the air de cour, of which Guédron is by no means the only representative. These French airs were popular after Monteverdi's return from Flanders, and Duke Vincenzo himself expressed an interest in them. I. B. de la Clyelle wrote the Duke from Paris on November 25, 1611, that at his request he had found and sent to Vincenzo "les airs en musique derniers imprimeez du Sr. Q. Guedon ministre de la chambre de Roy." [15] This is, of course, Pierre Guédron.

The specifically French form of alternating structure implies a repetition of the solo melody, harmonized by the choir. Mere alternation of solo and tutti passages was known in Italy and widely practiced there, as in Monteverdi's first *Confitebor*, composed for three solo parts and five choral voices, *in ripieni*. In his presentation of three stylistically varying versions of the *Confitebor*, Monteverdi clearly indicated that only the third was *alla francese*.

At this point a problem arises concerning the *Scherzi musicali*. In the original text, the connection between the *canto alla francese* and the scherzi is not as clear as has always been assumed. Giulio Cesare

---

[14] Prunières in *RaM*, II, 491.
[15] Bertolotti, *Musici alla Corte* . . . , p. 93.

praised his brother as an artist and cited the introduction of the *canto alla francese* into Italian music. As further praise, he asked the rhetorical question: "And did he not now compose these *Scherzi?*" This does not necessarily link the scherzo with the canto. Be this as it may, some of the scherzi have a feature that seems related to the special structural arrangement we have mentioned. All of the scherzi, written for three voices, have instrumental ritornelli, to be played in the two upper parts by two "violini da braccio," in the bass part by a chitarrone or clavicembalo or "another similar instrument." At the beginning, the ritornello must be played twice, then the three voices sing the first stanza; the second stanza may be sung by a soprano solo and accompaniment (in the same manner as the *Confitebor terzo alla francese* with the soprano *a voce sola*, and the four viole da braccio accompanying), but the last stanza must again be sung by all three voices. After every stanza the instrumental ritornello is to be repeated. Quite apart from performing the scherzo solo and tutti, a few of these little compositions link the ritornello and the stanza closely together on the basis of common musical material. The closest link exists in the scherzi *Dolci miei sospiri* and *Giovinetta ritrosetta*. Other scherzi anticipate the material of the stanza only in the second section of the ritornello or in one of the instrumental parts; still others give the material of ritornello and stanza in free variation; and in a number of scherzi there is no relationship at all. Wherever the instrumental ritornello anticipates by quotation the music of the stanza, a French influence is possible. Moreover, the function of the ritornello before and between the stanzas may be taken as an influence of the airs de cour; but of this we are not at all sure.

CHAPTER TEN

The Mantuan Madrigals

BY 1592 Monteverdi, as we have seen, had collected a new set of madrigals for publication. They appeared in Venice in that year, with a dedication to his patron, Vincenzo of Gonzaga, and without any reference to his being a disciple of Ingegneri. In the dedication Monteverdi offered his services as a composer to the Duke, pointing out significantly that though his viola playing had opened "the fortunate door to service" at Mantua, it was merely the flower of his musicianship, and that composition was the true fruit.

The madrigals of the third book, though more mature, more concentrated, and emotionally deeper, present no stylistic changes. A change, however, is noticeable in the choice of texts: Giambattista Guarini begins to replace Torquato Tasso. No lyrical poems by Tasso appear, but another work of his now holds Monteverdi's interest: the *Gerusalemme liberata*. From the sixteenth canto the composer chose three stanzas (58, 59, and 63), which he grouped together in a succession of three madrigals; and from the twelfth canto he selected three stanzas (77, 78, 79), for another group of three madrigals. The central subject of the twelfth canto is the ill-fated fight between Tancred and Clorinda that ends in Clorinda's tragic death. Left alone with his despair, Tancred bursts forth in lament over the wretchedness of his future life pursued by the furies of his fate: "Vivrò fra i miei tormenti e le mie cure, Mie giuste furie, forsennato, errante" (I shall live with my torments and toils, amidst my furies well deserved, a man maddened and unsettled). The sixteenth canto centers around a no less intense situation: the impassioned scene in which Rinaldo abandons Armida, who implores him to stay. When all her pleading fails, in her wrath she utters a curse (58, 59) and is left alone, "deserto e muto," to pitiful despair (63). These passages present climactic scenes, embodying passionate and tragic emotions. Here are no gentle tones of enchanting lyricism, but dramatic pathos, expressed in the language of tragedy and human suffering. It is to this Tasso that Monteverdi feels himself akin.

From Guarini, Monteverdi selected eight poems, one of them, *O primavera gioventù,* from the opening of the third act of his *Pastor fido,* a pastoral drama that had just been published in 1590. Guarini's lyricism is more baroque than that of Tasso and therefore closer to seventeenth-century poetry, although in more than one respect Guarini followed Tasso in his lyrics and especially in his *Pastor fido,* which can hardly be imagined without Tasso's *Aminta.* But after Tasso lyrical expression becomes more artificial and indirect. Images, metaphors, rhetorical phrases, stand between the poet and the world. They increase in number and are perhaps more resounding; they have an appearance of greater refinement and are certainly more subtle; but they speak more of the world and less of the poet. In that sense, directness of poetical expression has diminished. The greater refinement, however, is relative, not absolute, for the added subtleties are ornate, minute, even redundant sinuosities. The images are elaborated with a redundancy that is the result of the poet's indulgence in fluency and sonority. His personal feelings are more detailed and less involved in his poems than his highly emotional verses might lead the reader to suppose. Masterly locutions, employed to describe a single object, feeling, or situation, often for the sheer sound of the words, add to the musical character of the poetry. Guarini's poems offered most limitless opportunities to musicians, who used them repeatedly.

Another effect of the ever varied locutions was to place the emphasis on appearance. Appearance in man, in human feelings and human relations, in things material and fancies immaterial was exalted above reality. This stress on appearance in the conduct of life, as well as in artistic expression, was based on a code that regulated every action and expression. Guarini once criticized the philosophy of courtly life, which confounded appearance and reality. He said he had thought that princes were more humane the more they lived in abundance, since he believed humaneness to be the noble fruit of cultural wealth. But he found the contrary to be true. In appearance, the nobility speak politely; in reality, their acts of politeness are rare. In appearance, they seem gentle and affable; in reality, they are haughty and fierce. Things usually considered virtues—speaking the truth, acting righteously, loving sincerely, being truly pious, having inviolable faith, leading a blameless life—all these they hold to be signs of a base mind and a mean spirit. They cheat, lie, steal, and enrich themselves at the expense of others. They have no merit, no valor, and no reverence for age, rank, or law; they have no restraint and no respect for love or for life. To them, nothing is sacred or beyond the reach of their greed and lust. They are people of appearance alone (*Gente sol d'apparenza*).

Few men have taken to task the rulers of their time with so much bitterness and severity, but Guarini himself was a servant to such masters all his life. He knew their thought and conduct, for he had observed them at court after court in Italy and abroad. Experience had taught him that though they appeared to be all subtle, sweet refinement, in reality they were rotten to the core. Yet, did he himself behave so differently? Was not his musical and ornate verse itself an appearance confined to the glittering surface of reality? Though Guarini might condemn the shrill discords of life in public and in private, he added his own poetry to the fascinating appearances of the world. He was no less addicted to the fine art of representation than were the princes whom he censured; and if he "humanized" poetry, if he sang of human emotions in musical phrases, we do not test his sincerity against his personal feelings, which, in fact, he most skillfully veiled. Human emotions, publicly displayed as part of man's behavior toward the world, were the subjects that called forth his resounding flow of words, that made his poems serve appearance.

This objective, yet highly emotional, presentation of human passions drew Monteverdi to Guarini and accelerated the composer's approach to the baroque age. In this respect, the third book of madrigals opened a new vista. Both the dramatic scenes of Tasso and the passionate lyricism of Guarini guided him toward the future. Although his subjects presented new aspects, Monteverdi continued to use his tried and tested style, merely increasing the number of his devices. The madrigalesque style allowed him a still further advance and a more masterly control in expressing his new vision of certain characteristics in poetry in a manner of composing whose flexibility he had already probed.

In the first two collections, the initial madrigal indicated the stylistic program, but we can discover no such indication in the first madrigal of the third book. The work is not even especially distinguished in comparison with others in the collection. For there are some of such excellence as to suggest (for the first time in Monteverdi's career) a mastery that transcends the limitations of his era. His settings of Guarini's *O primavera* and *Perfidissimo volto* or of Tasso's cycles give promise of a greatness amounting to musical immortality.

In these madrigals Monteverdi's greater artistry manifests itself in a skillful adaptation of the canzonetta style to his personal uses for expressive purposes in relation to the text. In a sense, he thus obscures the stylistic features that belong to the category, but it is the canzonetta style that imparts to his compositions a precision and brevity of phrase now totally transformed so that it becomes the basis for a contrapuntal technique which was not originally a part of the style. The phrase now becomes a motif for a section of the madrigal in which the motif functions as the basic material of the counterpoint. At times, Monteverdi uses two motifs simultaneously, handling them according to the rules of a double counterpoint, a technique he had used in a few compositions of the second book. Some madrigals are supplied with no more than three or four such motifs of central significance. The contrapuntal function of the motif is asserted not only in the imitation by single voices but also in an imitation by full groups of voices, especially in the duet form with a bass part, which has been previously described. When a group in the form of a trio appears successively in low, middle, and high ranges, there result from this peculiar "polyphony" color effects which have also been observed in some madrigals of the second book. Monteverdi worked out these madrigals more elaborately and artistically in accordance with a counterpoint that remained as free and unsystematic, as unpredictable and original, as before. This technique helped the composer to knit together shorter passages as well as larger sections of the madrigal, and this was no small gain, since the melodic cadences, as frequent as ever, have a tendency to split up the composition. It is the skillful counterpoint that keeps the sections from falling apart.

Monteverdi's preoccupation with the possibilities of the motif brought out some idiosyncrasies. In compositions where he wanted to stress the emotional element, the first motif is stated soloistically in full, without accompaniment by any other part, and in a declamatory manner:

Ex. 50 III

O pri-ma-ve-ra gio-ven-tù de l'an-no   Perfi-di- - - si-mo vol-to

As though by imitation, the motif is taken up immediately by a whole group of voices, by a trio for instance, and in harmonization. This procedure sets off the initial motif in such a way as to enhance the importance the composer attributes to it, not so much for the structural function he expects it to perform as for the emotional quality he intends it to convey. And when the special form of the motif is invented in close relation to the text, the solo performance has a poignancy that is to become characteristic of Monteverdi's musical expression:

Ex. 51   III

The two Tasso examples show that, in keeping with the text, Monteverdi works out in the motif a declamatory pathos which gives the individual interval extraordinary expressiveness. Another feature that becomes more and more a mark of his personal style appears in motifs that have a monotonous declamation of considerable length on one tone only. These motifs always have a direct relation to the text and may be one of the fruits of Monteverdi's study of canzonetta melody. They give the effect of simple recitation and can be as poignant as motifs with the most passionate exclamations:

Ex. 52,1   III

In a descending line: *Poi ch' ella* (*terza parte*), Tasso:

Ex. 52,2

Ma dove o lasso (*seconda parte*):

Ex. 52,3

and Ex. 52,4

It is noteworthy that most of these declamatory motifs occur in the two Tasso cycles. Can we assume that these motifs are related to the dramatic character of the scenes? The composer has not yet fully clarified his intentions, but there is no doubt that the motifs have an expressive purpose and that in these madrigals Monteverdi was ahead of his time. *Ma dove o lasso,* with its haunting melancholy, reveals his dramatic gifts, and *Stracciami pur il core* by Guarini is perhaps the most artistic and skillful composition in the whole collection.[1]

In the third book of madrigals Monteverdi has equaled, and sometimes excelled, the best madrigalists; here he is the equal even of Luca Marenzio, whose genius, though with different aims and different ways of expression, had set high artistic standards for the madrigal. Though the scanty material rewards he received show that the court of Mantua in general and Vincenzo in particular paid no immediate attention to the startling rise of the young genius, Monteverdi's work had begun to attract the attention of the artistic world. Besides the many editions of the third book which became necessary in the course of time, his compositions began to appear in other countries as among the best Italian productions in the field of madrigalesque composition. The rich anthology, *Fiori del Giardino di diversi eccelentissimi autori,* which the German printer Paul Kaufmann published in Nuremberg in 1597, offers an interesting survey. Monteverdi with seven works and Luca Marenzio with the same number are the leaders in the repertory of fifty-eight compositions by such composers as Gastoldi, Benedetto Pallavicino, Andrea and Giovanni Gabrieli, Claudio Merulo, Massaino, G. M. Nanini, Francesco Rovigo, Orazio Vecchi, and Giaches de Wert. In the estimation of foreign observers, Monteverdi now shares in the fame which others had enjoyed for some time.

Some madrigals from the third book were later chosen for appreciative discussion by Doni, who referred to them, particularly to *Rincanti in pace,* in his *Annotazioni sopra il compendio de' generi.* Monteverdi's position also exposed him to attentions of an unfriendly nature.

---

[1] In connection with *Stracciami pur il core,* Redlich, *Claudio Monteverdi,* pp. 69f., has quoted the technical analysis of this madrigal by P. Martini, *Saggio fondamentale* (1775), II, 180ff. Redlich has justly called attention to Martini's extraordinary analyses of Monteverdi's madrigals.

Certain madrigals in the third book aroused the suspicion of the older generation, whose ideals were formed in accordance with the Northern music. It is significant that when, about 1600, Artusi made himself the spokesman of this critical faction, Monteverdi was the target, not Marenzio, nor Gesualdo da Venosa, nor any other madrigalists, no matter how radical. Why was he singled out as the victim of Artusi's vicious polemic? The compositions under attack were not in themselves of far-reaching importance or profound interest. The attack is indirect proof that Monteverdi had set out to oppose the Northern school and to make his madrigal the medium for undermining the music of the past. Monteverdi was indeed the pacemaker among musicians, and however narrow-minded Artusi might have been, he was still keen enough to take him as a target worthy of his aim.

THE END OF THE CENTURY: THE FOURTH BOOK

Up to 1592, Monteverdi's works had been published in regular succession, but after the third book, there is a sudden halt. His next publication, the fourth book of madrigals for five voices, does not appear until eleven years later, in 1603. We know that Monteverdi was occupied with the composition of these madrigals for a good many years, and some of them must have been made public in manuscript. Nevertheless, this gap—the longest of his artistic career—remains largely unaccountable. At twenty-five Monteverdi was in the prime of his youth, and though not in a particularly distinguished position, he was living at one of the most musical courts in Italy. He had advanced logically, systematically, with undiminished energy, and clearly knew where he was going. Then came this sudden stop. Was he overburdened with duties that took all his time and strength? In the inferior position he occupied for many years, and without the responsibilities of leadership, this could hardly be true. Indeed, when he writes to the Duke in 1601, applying for the position as "maestro de la camera e de la chiesa," he mentions his devoted service but does not say that he has been overburdened with work. This complaint, however, was to become frequent in later years.

We have already mentioned three events of personal importance that occurred during this period. His marriage with Claudia Cattaneo took place around 1595 or shortly before. In that same year he accompanied Vincenzo on the campaign against the Turks and was away from Mantua until about the middle of 1596. His second journey, to Flanders, lasted from the beginning of June to the middle of October, 1599. Altogether, his two journeys may account for the loss of a full year of productive time.

In his aggressive pamphlet, published in 1600, Artusi quoted from three madrigals, two of which appear in the fourth book of 1603 and one in the fifth book of 1605. This obviously implies that by 1599 Artusi knew *Anima mia perdona* and its second part, *Che se tu se'il cor mio*, as well as *Cruda Amarilli*, the opening madrigal of the fifth book, so that Monteverdi must have worked on those madrigals by about 1598. On the other hand, the madrigals of the third book must have been completed late in 1591, since the printed dedication is dated June, 1592. This leaves a gap of six or seven years in which no composition is recorded. At best, the gap can be narrowed down to an interval of five years. Monteverdi dedicated his fourth book to the Accademia degli Intrepidi,[2] which was founded shortly after the death of Duke Alfonso II d'Este. In this dedication Monteverdi says he originally planned to submit the madrigals to Alfonso II, but that because of the death of the Duke in 1597 nothing came of it. He now dedicates these madrigals to the academicians, saying that they are familiar with many of them, but that some have been newly composed. Duke Vincenzo of Mantua is reported to have been the "principal" of the Accademia for some time.[3] The composition of some madrigals that now stand in the fourth book can thus be dated back to 1597. But whatever his activity in composition, there was no effort on Monteverdi's part to publish during these eleven years, and it would seem that he must have had some reason to refrain from the publication of the works.

Did Monteverdi enter upon a new and critical phase of his artistic development after his first real masterpiece, the third book of madrigals? There are, as we shall see, certain stylistic novelties in the madrigals of the fourth book, but they are hardly radical enough to have required so much time and thought. One might be inclined to discard this rather vexing puzzle as purely academic, were it not that Monteverdi's artistic actions were never the product of unreflective impulse or unaccountable accident. There are no new religious compositions to fill the gap, for the earliest collection of sacred music after the youthful *Cantiunculae* comes as late as 1610, and there was no reason for Monteverdi to compose religious works before 1601. It is true that Monteverdi, in his letter of application to Vincenzo, refers to his ability to write motets

---

[2] Malipiero omitted the dedication of the fourth book.

[3] Emil Vogel, "Claudio Monteverdi," in *VfMW*, Vol. III (1887), p. 339, n. 3.

and Masses in the finest taste, but there cannot have been many of them. There is no doubt that up to the turn of the century Monteverdi's artistic interests were exclusively absorbed by madrigalesque, profane composition.

Taking everything into account, the only possible explanation seems to be that Monteverdi had changed his ideas about publication. Up to 1592 he published his compositions as soon as they were completed, naturally making a careful selection, for we can be sure that he did not publish all his compositions. But after 1592, a new self-criticism born of his maturity must have suggested a different method, a fresh approach. The twenty madrigals of the fourth book are an amazingly small output for such a long period as eleven years, and he must have discarded many compositions that he did not regard as worthy of publication. His practice of circulating his compositions before they were printed apparently meant that he wanted them to have a critical hearing in order to gather the reactions of artists and connoisseurs. His previous collections presumably contained the greater part of his output, and those of the years 1582, 1583, 1584, 1587, 1590, 1592 offer an extensive and even selection. Speedy publication was necessary to satisfy the ambition with which he strove for distinction. Now that he had become sure of himself and certain of acclaim he could afford to wait, to discard, to emphasize quality rather than quantity. How many compositions he discarded, of what sort, and for what reasons, we shall never know. But the self-criticism awakened in him during the period from 1592 to 1603 makes it clear that he has entered on another phase of his career. This critical attitude will remain with him. From now on his process of composition will be slower and more concentrated, and there will be intervals between his publications.

Meanwhile, during these very years, events of sensational importance were taking place outside Mantua. As the end product of extensive, theoretical discussions and researches, the Florentine members of the Camerata produced the first music drama, *Dafne*, a pastoral drama by Rinuccini with music by Jacopo Peri. The first private performance was given in the house of Corsi, one of the leading spirits in the Camerata, and it was perhaps in 1597 that the first opera came to life.[4] According to Rinuccini, the performance aroused "incredible pleasure among the few who heard the work." If Peri is correct in his report, *Dafne* was repeatedly given at the Carnivals of the following years.

[4] See for the discussion of the date A. Loewenberg, *Annals of Opera* (1943), *sub anno*.

Since the music of the opera is lost except for a few fragments,[5] Rinuccini's *Euridice*, with the music of both Peri and Caccini, offers the
first complete example of Florentine monody in a dramatic setting.

The occasion of its performance was an extraordinary event—the
marriage by proxy of Henry IV, King of France, with Maria de'Medici,
celebrated in Florence in 1600. Once again, Duke Vincenzo represented
the Gonzagas at the festivities, and again he doubtless took keen interest in the elaborate pageants, the musical performances, and the
brilliant artists. That he was capable of a purely artistic appreciation of
the Florentine style of monody may be doubted, but he probably would
have agreed with Rinuccini, who called *Dafne* "the simple proof of
what the song (*canto*) of our age was capable of" within the music
drama. The festivities were so dazzling that Vincenzo, with his natural
disposition for impressive shows, must have been stirred to ambitious
competition by the new medium of the music drama. We have pointed
out that from the events of 1589 in Florence he had probably brought
home a good many new ideas, and the events of 1600, when the music
drama became a reality, must have excited him even more. It has been
suggested that Vincenzo may have had Monteverdi in his suite in
Florence.[6] Monteverdi himself never mentioned such a visit, nor did
his name occur in any of the Florentine documents. Though his presence in Florence does not seem likely, it is certain that there was close
communication between Mantua and Florence after the events of 1600,
and that even before 1600 Monteverdi had a fairly clear idea of Florentine monody. What the members of the Camerata had been doing was
no particular secret. The singer Francesco Rasi had appeared in both
cities,[7] and both Rinuccini and Caccini had close contacts with Mantua.
Artistic developments such as those in Florence were more likely to be
publicized as sensations than to be veiled in secrecy.

Despite the necessary assumption that Monteverdi had all the information he needed, despite the fact that fruitful contacts with Florence
existed, Monteverdi did not react in any way to what happened in the
Florentine circles. This lack of response is rather surprising on the part
of a musician who was regarded as one of the leaders of the modernists.
The explanation must be that the Florentine style of monody had little

[5] See the facsimile in A. Wotquenne, *Catalogue de la Bibliothèque du Conservatoire
de Bruxelles*, Annexe I (1901), p. 46. For a valuable discussion of the fragments see F.
Ghisi, *Alla fonti della monodia* (Milan, 1940).

[6] Prunières, *Claudio Monteverdi*, p. 22.

[7] Concerning Rasi and the great singers in Florence and Mantua, see the important
work of A. Ademollo, *La Bella Adriana* (Città di Castello, 1888), *passim*. The account
of the sources makes fascinating reading.

to offer him. It was not alone because he was immeasurably greater than any and all of the Florentine musicians, otherwise he would have been inspired to compete with and excel the Florentines. His indifference would seem to prove that he saw his art as radically different from that of the Florentines. For Monteverdi, music, not theory, was the beginning and the end, though he too had a definite philosophy which gave substance and direction to his art. He had come to see the need for transforming the musical heritage by establishing new artistic standards as high as those of the past. Such a transformation could be successful only if carried out as an exclusively musical project. No protest, no polemics against the older generation would advance the new art one step, and the violence with which the Florentines set themselves against the techniques of counterpoint might result in the sacrifice of many artistic skills. When Monteverdi instructed his brother Giulio Cesare to draw up the *Dichiaratione* as a manifesto of his own artistic growth and ideals, he made it absolutely clear that he did not want to destroy, and never had destroyed, anything of essential value in the art of music. Except for mentioning Peri and Caccini in passing, there was no word in the *Dichiaratione* about the Florentines in support of his own new ideals. When he sought justification, he took it from the past. To him, the problems of the new composition never involved the question of how to destroy counterpoint. The Florentines had shown how easy that was. The question was how to create a new counterpoint. Not until he had found an answer to this question did he turn to the style of pure monody, and when he did so he made use of the elaborate techniques he had worked out for the new style as a whole. In this light Monteverdi's silence concerning the Florentine Camerata becomes comprehensible, as does his continued adherence to the madrigal. When the new century opened, Monteverdi was still composing five-part madrigals because he could still contribute to the old medium.

In the fourth book of madrigals Guarini still occupies the place of distinction, but Tasso's poetry is completely missing. Of the twenty madrigals in the book, nine are by Guarini, and again the pastoral drama *Il Pastor fido* holds Monteverdi's interest. The initial madrigal, *Ah dolce partita*, is from the third scene of the third act, and from the same act the monologue of Amarilli provides the poetical text for *Anima mia perdona*, with *Che se tu se'il cor mio* as the *seconda parte*. The rest of the Guarini poems are lyrics. Two great favorites with the sixteenth-century madrigalists are included: *Io mi son giovinetta* and *Quel augellin che canta*, both by Boccaccio. Monteverdi's selection of Ottavio

Rinuccini's *Sfogava con le stelle* is of special interest because of the link with Florence, and musical analysis reveals its even greater significance, for in this piece Monteverdi finds his answer to dramatic music.

The fourth book is impressive both for originality of form and variety of style. The madrigals based on texts of Guarini are foremost in the realization of the new style, and the collection as a whole exhibits all its fundamental elements: dramatic narration; exclamatory motifs of passion and pain; the expressive grouping of melodies and harmonies, of "soloistic" motifs and of "choral" passages; the new counterpoint; the concentration of the essentials of composition in two parts, melody and bass; the use of stereotyped figuration; the sequences, melodic and harmonic; the boldest harmonies or dissonances for the sake of expression; the intensive, humanized quality; and, above all, the unification of the technical structure and expression. In the hands of great composers, the madrigal of the sixteenth century had strength and expressiveness, but the means of expression were stylized and generalized to such an extent that a group of madrigals on a similar subject sounded very much alike. Monteverdi individualized the composition by providing new stylistic elements for each work. This change of style was intended to do full justice to all the implications of the subject matter and was the work of a born dramatist who devised a flexible form that was responsive to changing situations. Monteverdi himself clarified this aspect of his philosophy of art in a brief but profound statement made in the fifth book and quoted again in the *Dichiaratione* by Giulio Cesare: "And believe me, the modern composer builds upon the foundations of truth; this my brother told me recently, because he knew that, by virtue of the command the text holds over music, modern composition does not observe and cannot observe, the rules of the First Practice." The artistic form and the rules of composition stand on the basis of truth; truth dictates new laws of art, different from the rules embodied in the so-called First Practice of the sixteenth century. The modern composer must be faithful to the subject matter, to the text, to the innermost connotations of the poetry, and, above all, to the truths of human nature. Monteverdi, with the gift of genius, heard and saw more than others in the poetry he rendered musically, and by penetrating to the heart of his subject matter, became a discoverer of truth.

In this new conception the subject prescribes the form. As the poem progresses with its changing emotions and situations, the form responds and is molded by the composer's genius into a complete unity. This flexibility of musical form is perhaps best illustrated in the madrigal *Sfogava con le stelle* of the fourth book. The poem, with its moving simplicity and emotional directness, is the lament of a lover who in the middle of the night under the starry sky bewails the pains of his unrequited love. He implores the stars, the beautiful images of his idol, to show his beloved the ardor of his love as they show him her rare beauty; with their golden glitter they should make her sympathetic, as they have made him loving. In two lines the scene is set, and the direct speech of the lover begins. To distinguish by formal means between the initial narration, of which the lover is the subject, and his emotional implorings, Monteverdi ingeniously invented a startling novelty in madrigalesque composition. The madrigal begins with a psalmodizing narration. All parts, in harmony of five voices, recite "Sfogava con le stelle," and the phrase ends in the canto with a figure typical of Monteverdi's cadences:

Ex. 53   IV, 15

Such is the form of religious psalmody; in recitation the harmony is repeated as many times as the text has syllables:

Ex. 54   IV, 18

Each phrase is followed by harmonies in a loose, but altogether homophonic, rhythm, somewhat in the manner of a recitative. The phrases "Sotto notturno" and "E dicea" are set in psalmodic recitation. The initial section proceeds in deliberate, measured harmonies that seem to conform to the narrative outline of a scene. When the direct speech begins, with "O imagini stelle," the style is suddenly changed. The canto offers a contrasting motif, rising and, in typical Monteverdian manner, simply passing through the octave, in accentuated rhythms that reflect the tense emotion. The motif is immediately imitated by quinto and alto, and then the upper voices repeat the phrase raised by one tone:

Ex. 55   IV, 15

Against this motif the bass moves in countermotion downward diatonically through the octave and in even tone values. The motif of the basso is polyphonically treated as the tenore imitates it:

Ex. 56   IV, 15

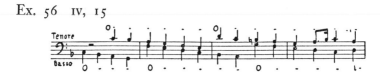

Thus the three upper voices and the two lower parts are contrapuntally set against each other. Short as this polyphonic passage is, it has the basic characteristics of Monteverdi's new counterpoint. It originates out of only two contrasted elements: the upper part that functions as the vehicle of the melody and the lower part that affords harmonic support. In placing these two fundamental elements against each other in artistic elaboration, each takes the form of a complex group of voices related to each other as "counterpoints," whereas in the past the counterpoint had consisted of individual melodic lines. The complexities of such groups are the elements of the new polyphony.

To heighten the intensity of the implorings, the phrase "O imagini belle" is once more repeated, but in the same harmonized recitation that was used for the narrative part. Here the psalmody has the dramatic effect of a prayer whose symbolic meaning is as perceptible as if it were conveyed by the physical gesture of praying. The new lines of the lover's prayer to the stars are given new motifs, each of them treated individually: "De l'idol mio" with a short, swift canzonetta motif; "Si com'a me mostrate," in almost narrative, simple chords. From "Mentre così splendete" on, the style of a trio with two melodic upper parts and one harmonic bass (soloistic duet with *basso continuo*) is consistently maintained with a change in the groups: ·

Ex. 57 IV, 17

The final appeal is again recited in a psalmodizing prayer, and in order to heighten the appeal, Monteverdi repeats the recitation three times with a climactic grouping of the harmonies. The harmonic cadences of the phrases fall on "Pietosa." To convey the emotional connotation, sharp dissonances are introduced and are continued in the final motif for "come me gat' amante," whose contrapuntal treatment is responsible for the accumulation of dissonances. For the sake of truthfulness to the subject, Monteverdi relentlessly carries through his counterpoint.

Monteverdi did not again make as bold an attempt to dramatize the musical form, but he used other methods to convey the characteristics of the subject matter. Declamation more and more controls the melody, a declamation that both conforms to the accentuation of the text and fulfills an expressive function. The declamatory motif to "Un vivace morire che da vita al dolore" combines two inspirations drawn from "vivace" and "dolore," in the first madrigal of the collection. A lively declamation at the beginning of the phrase retards at the end, in order to express the meaning of the text appropriately:

Ex. 58 IV, 4

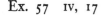

The way in which the faultless declamation of the natural rhythm of the words here coincides with the melodic expressiveness is characteristic of the melody throughout the fourth book. In this respect the madrigal *Si ch'io vorrei morire* is one of the most perfect examples of melodic and harmonic declamation. Nearly every phrase reflects the masterly blending of declamatory form and expressive purpose. The madrigal begins with a declamation in full harmony, in which all five voices at once take part. The melodic phrase placed in the canto has a form which is to become typical of Monteverdi and of the declamatory style:

Ex. 59   IV, 78

Si ch'io vor- rei   mo- ri- re   ch'io vor- rei   mo- ri- re

The expressive declamation is again shown in the motif to "Ahi car' e dolce lingua";

Ex. 60   IV, 79

Ahi   ca- r'e dol- ce   lin- gua

With this phrase begins a structural process that is used so frequently as to become a feature of Monteverdi's style. This declamatory phrase, which no longer lends itself to the strict procedure of the old melodic, linear imitation, is repeated in sequences: each time the phrase is raised one tone through the whole octave, and each time the phrase is stated by another voice. The technique has all the appearances of polyphony; in one mounting surge the participation of the various voices heightens the extraordinary dramatic effect.

Ex. 61   IV, 79

At the height of the tension, on "di dolces' in questo sen m'estingua," Monteverdi, with his ever growing sense for new structural proportions, turns from the climax to begin a slow descent, also in sequences, of harmonies that give the structural symmetry a new expressive effect by contrast to the preceding declamatory rise:

Ex. 62 IV, 80

The phrase "Ahi vita mia,"

Ex. 63 IV, 80

whose declamation and expression are perfectly balanced, begins a new section of the madrigal; the harmonic structure is fully indicated by the descant and the bass while the third part merely fills in. This phrase is directly worked into the next, with the same structure of harmony. Then follows a new process of sequential groups which reveal Monteverdi's genius for combining structural factors with expressive intentions. The passage of the first sequence begins with "Deh stringetemi":

Ex. 64 IV, 81

These syncopated melodic lines are followed by a repetition of the full harmonies on "A questo bianco seno." The symmetrical balance is established by a return to the sequential lines, now adding a new voice and ascending through an octave. "A questo bianco" is once more repeated, this time in trio fashion. Canto and alto follow with the descending sequences to "Deh stringetemi," which they have given before, and the additional bass indicates the descent by its harmonic tones. In order that the musical form may complete itself, Monteverdi with harmonically rising sequences takes up the suggestion of the text "Ahi bocca, ahi baci, ahi lingua, torn'a dire" and returns to the beginning of the madrigal *Si ch'io vorrei morire* with a regular musical *da capo*.

This madrigal showed for the first time that new structural elements could establish a full harmony between a purely musical evolution of the form and the development of the expressive intention. All the new devices of proportions, of balanced contrasts, and of tension and release have their strong foundation in a strict musical logic. This is not to belittle the significance of the text in the process of musical thinking, for Monteverdi's chief argument against his critic, Artusi, was that he neglected the text and considered the music alone. Artusi did not realize that the new musical logic, being highly individualistic, could not be defined in the old terms of standard devices, and Monteverdi was unable to make clear to him the flexibility and ever changing standards of his logic, except by stressing the need for observing the expressive demands of the text. For Monteverdi never indulged in purely descriptive tone painting, but always endeavored to find the proper harmony between the descriptive passage and the superior principles of the form, which must be comprehensible in its own right.

In Guarini's *A un giro sol de' begl' occhi*, a most instructive example, though not the best madrigal of the fourth book, every phrase is invented in close relation to the text, and the musical motifs attached to a line or a word are usually descriptive. The motifs on "giro," "mar," and "vento," all suggestive of motion, are "pictorially" rendered. The first descriptive motif has a stereotyped figuration:

Ex. 65   IV, 49

This conventionalized figuration seems invariably to call for a stereotyped structure as well: the trio arrangement with two upper voices moving along in chains of thirds or sixths together with a harmonic bass part. Monteverdi carries this structure consistently through the first part of the madrigal. The form of the bass upon which the upper parts harmonically depend reveals that structural considerations are primary.

Ex. 66 IV, 49

Ri- de l'a- ria d'in- tor- no Ri- de l'a- ria d'in- tor- no d'in- tor- no

There is nothing "descriptive" in this bass, which holds the upper parts firmly in its harmonic grip.

Such a stereotyped motif as appeared on "A un giro" is not necessarily used with the same word or with the same connotation. It occurs frequently in both melismatic and syllabic forms. We quote the syllabic form, the phrase on "Alma ch'è tutta foco e tutta sangue" from the madrigal *Luci serene e chiare*:

Ex. 67 IV, 37

Al - ma chè tut-ta fo- co e tut-ta san- gue

Such figurative material as this has been taken to be "instrumental," if not in actual performance, at least in character. All such motifs in dotted rhythms and melodic formulas, like those in the quoted examples, are said to be instrumental because they seem to have a "mechanical" make-up, more easily reproduced by an instrument than by the voice. The "mechanical" aspect is indeed there; it is even the composer's aim, for he is operating with stereotyped material; yet these motifs originated as vocal ornamentation, mostly improvised. Monteverdi did not use them as ornamentation or improvisation but gave them structural functions, yet vocal they remain, regardless of the difficulties we may find in singing them. Seventeenth-century instrumental music was to use material borrowed from the vocal medium at a time when the baroque style was employing the same musical idiom in all media.

The madrigal *Anima mia perdona* was the composition of the fourth book which Artusi selected for attack. His choice—if he had other madrigals of this book to choose from—is understandable. The composition belongs with *Si ch'io vorrei morire*, since both aim boldly at new structural conceptions and new laws of composition. Artusi, of course, had no eye for the far-reaching attempts of Monteverdi and could not see in them the birth of a new musical structure. What he did see was the treatment of dissonance in composition, and to this he could apply the terminology of the old techniques. He should have been much more alarmed at Monteverdi's audacity in altering the formal basis of composition—a change that implied far graver violations of the old composition and had more serious consequences. That Artusi was narrow and rancorous, irritated and malicious, may be regretted for the sake of the discussion as a whole, but it is quite true that Monteverdi did present dissonances at the conclusion of both madrigals that a man of Artusi's type and background could not possibly bear. Artusi took the dissonances as absolute entities, judged them by themselves, and neglected the text. Not understanding Monteverdi's use of such material, he identified it with total "imperfection," maintained that it was typical of "modern" music, and brought out his pamphlet, *Artusi, or on the Imperfections of Modern Music.*

The conception of form which Monteverdi wanted to materialize in the madrigal *Anima mia perdona* was that of harmonized declamation. In most of his compositions in the fourth book he carefully avoided letting the cadences, harmonic and melodic, split the composition into small groups, but in this work he did not want the sweep of a comprehensive structure that would pull all the other elements together into a unit. Here he chose to let the principle of recitation in harmonized melody, of expressive declamation, govern the work. The recitation was to proceed phrase by phrase, and each individual group was to be an entity. The grouping is directly related to the declamatory recitative; indeed, the term "recitative" is applicable to some of the groups. The beginning of the madrigal introduces a characteristic form of such harmonized recitative, in which the harmony is actually present, though it could have been expressed by a figured bass, functioning as a *basso continuo.*

Ex. 68   IV, 26

No less characteristic of this new declamatory style is a motif like that set for "Nei dettie nel sembiante Riggida tua nemica," which has a recitation on one tone over an extended period. Reciting phrases or motifs with exclamatory effects soon become formulas that appear in almost every madrigal. One such formula may be quoted from three madrigals.

Ex. 69 IV

This formula becomes part of the idiom of the expressive recitative.

The declamatory madrigals of the fourth book were Monteverdi's first answer to the problems of dramatic composition in recitative style. In contrast to the Florentine monody of modest artistic capacities, he arrived at the *stile recitativo* by totally different methods and with original solutions. Even his preliminary solutions were more enduring and more modern than the sensational monody of the Florentines. In gradually building up the artistic material of the dramatic recitation within the madrigal form, in adding stone by stone to a construction whose outlines he early foresaw, Monteverdi proved himself a more prudent architect and a better artist.

The fourth book concludes with a composition, *Piagne e sospira*, which is remarkable for its startling structure. For the form of the initial theme, Monteverdi drew upon typically sixteenth-century madrigalisms. The form of the theme, associated with the connotation of the text, is chromatic:

Ex. 70 IV, 96

In both its parts—the chromatic "weeping" and the "sigh"—the theme is "descriptive," and for both these illustrations of the text there were many models. The first statement of the chromatic theme by the tenor is unaccompanied; then the alto takes it up a fifth higher. This arrangement suggests that the structure will be "fugal" in the style of the sixteenth-century melodic polyphony. The suggestion is deceptive, because Monteverdi's polyphony has become harmonic. The alto and the canto, which enters first, complete the chromatic statement and turn the supposedly polyphonic behavior into a harmonic procedure.

Ex. 71 IV, 96

The theme is not carried through all the voices. A harmonic accompaniment with a new motif in the tenor alters the picture. Monteverdi has his own harmonic "polyphony," which becomes the medium of the baroque age, and later of modern music. The invention of the theme is unoriginal and traditional, but the composition as a whole is a manifestation of the modern spirit. Monteverdi apparently attempted in this extraordinary work to unite almost incompatible elements—a melodic theme that required a treatment as fugal subject, and the principle of the trio structure:

Ex. 72   IV, 96

and furthermore the declamatory recitative:

Ex. 73   IV, 97

Even the separate grouping is combined with the chordal recitation at the end. Monteverdi undoubtedly set himself a difficult task, and the importance he attributed to the work is reflected in its place of distinction at the end of the collection. Whether he accomplished his task successfully and, from an aesthetic point of view, altogether satisfactorily is another matter.[8] Whatever the definitive value of the composition, it has distinct importance in the formation of modern music.

THE FIFTH BOOK

Prima e Seconda Prattica

The fifth book of madrigals, published in 1605, is at once an end and a beginning, "the parting line of the waters," as it has been called.[9] All historians have recognized its significance in Monteverdi's development and in the evolution of the new style. It is an end because all

---

[8] Redlich, *Claudio Monteverdi*, p. 100, asserts that in its entirety the composition is not satisfactory.

[9] *Ibid.*, p. 100.

Monteverdi's contributions since his first madrigals for five voices are brought to a synoptical conclusion along the lines of the fourth book. It is a beginning because new experiments are included, in which the range of the madrigal is expanded and for the first time the supremacy of the five-voiced madrigal is threatened. With unswerving persistence Monteverdi had adhered to that form because it seemed to assure high artistic standards, but now that he had succeeded in his effort to create new musical structures, the need for one particular medium ceased to exist.

The chief novelty of the fifth book is in the harmony. In his previous madrigals Monteverdi had consistently endeavored to clarify the functions of the bass in the structure of the work: it should impose a vertical conception of harmony and also organize and support the general structure. He had succeeded in working out these functions and in establishing the bass as the counteragent of the melody. Consequently, between the pressures of the melody and the harmony, the functions of the middle parts were completely modified. The obligatory *basso continuo*, added to six madrigals of the fifth book, is merely the logical conclusion of his previous studies in basic harmony. He allowed the *basso continuo* to be elective in the first thirteen madrigals of the collection.[10] The optional use of the *basso continuo* has no direct bearing on the form of the work and is a matter of performance as *basso seguente*, but the *basso continuo* of the last six madrigals has a harmonic and structural function that Monteverdi had set out to achieve in his preliminary works. The introduction of the *basso continuo* in the fifth book is not an abrupt, revolutionary novelty, but rather the last step on a long and somewhat curving path toward this definite goal. Here, too, the end of one journey is the beginning of another, for the *continuo* madrigals will serve as models for future works.

The fifth book is again dedicated to the Duke of Mantua, and this dedication, as we have noted, gives evidence that many of the madrigals were completed and circulated among musicians before they were printed. Among those who saw them was Giovanni Maria Artusi, one of the most bigoted spokesmen for the contrapuntal style. The first

---

[10] That was possible because of the character of the *basso seguente* which followed the vocal bass, and this was largely the case in the first thirteen madrigals. A *basso seguente* was added by Phalèse in Antwerp when, in a Monteverdi vogue, he edited the Northern edition of the madrigal books in 1615; the *basso continuo* was added to the third and fourth books. Bukofzer, *op. cit.*, p. 35, mentions only that the fourth book got the additional *basso continuo*, that it was published in 1613 and revised by Monteverdi himself. There is no edition of the fourth book of 1613; and Monteverdi did not add the *basso continuo* to the books previous to the fifth in any of the editions.

work of the fifth book, *Cruda Amarilli*, was especially irritating to him, and he attacked Monteverdi in his notorious treatise, *L'Artusi, ovvero delle imperfettioni della moderna musica, Ragionamenti due*, of 1600. His attack centered around the age-old problem of dissonance, with Artusi maintaining the inviolability of the Netherlandish rules for its use. Monteverdi had already denied this in his work and had made it clear that his art belonged to a different world. Since each man spoke a language that was unintelligible to the other, their arguments could have no common ground, but the controversy undoubtedly caused a stir in the artistic world. Monteverdi's reply, which demonstrated his noble nature, took the form of a letter addressed to the "Studiosi Lettori" of the fifth book. "Do not wonder that I gave these madrigals to the printer without first answering those attacks that Artusi has launched against a few little parts of the compositions. Being in the service of His Highness of Mantua, I do not have the time necessary for an elaborate argument. Nevertheless I have written a reply in order to make clear that I do not compose my works at random. As soon as the reply is completed [literally 'rewritten'], I shall publish it under the title *Second Practice, or On the Perfection of Modern Music*. Those who do not believe that there is any other practice than that taught by Zarlino will perhaps be amazed at such a title. But they may rest assured that with regard to consonances and dissonances there is still another consideration, different from the usual and established, which by reason of its full agreement with sense and reason is the defense of the modern composition. This I wanted to tell you, lest the term *Second Practice* be received abusively by others, and also in order that sagacious men may take into consideration other aspects of harmony and believe that the modern composer builds his work upon the foundation of Truth." Here for the first time Monteverdi openly admitted that the art of the sixteenth century and modern composition had parted company.

As Artusi's aggressiveness continued—he published three more pamphlets against Monteverdi—the composer's brief statement needed to be elucidated in order to justify his position in the eyes of his contemporaries. Since the burden of his official duties kept Monteverdi from engaging further in the discussion, his brother Giulio Cesare, the editor of the *Scherzi musicali* of 1607, undertook to fill the gap. His *Dichiaratione della Lettera Stampata nel Quinto Libro de suoi Madrigali*, though in no way intended as a substitute for the treatise Monteverdi planned to write, shed new light on the implications of the *Se-*

conda Prattica. Analyzing the preface of the fifth book sentence by sentence, Giulio Cesare gave explanations that may not have persuaded Artusi but were greatly desired by all those who were beginning to think in terms of Monteverdi's music. The chief characteristic of his music was the changed relationship between word and tone, indicated by the phrase that became the motto of the *Seconda Prattica:* "l'oratione sia padrona del armonia e non serva" (the word, the text, with all its values and qualities, should be the master, not the servant, of the musical harmony). Since the text comprises the "most important and principal part of music," it must also be the basis of criticism. This unequivocal formulation of the new law of the *Seconda Prattica* may be misleading in one respect. Does it follow from this statement that the musical elements must submit themselves to the text in slavish dependence? Does the composer not recognize that there is also a purely musical evolution of form and structure? His close attention to the significance of the text and even to the connotations of individual words did not keep Monteverdi from working out superior musical structures. He was always in search of appropriate ways to harmonize the demands of text and musical form, and though he neglected to stress the evolution of musical form, the reference to the new *cantilena* may have included such an idea.

Monteverdi had justified the *Seconda Prattica* by a passage from Plato's *Republic,* which Giulio Cesare quoted as "non ipsa oratio Rithmum et Harmoniam sequitur." Surely the theoreticians of the sixteenth century knew that Plato had said that the word should not yield precedence to the other two elements, rhythm and melody, but they did not find in the passage the meaning Monteverdi gave it. He believed he had discovered a new truth, that his idea was what Plato had really meant. But this discovery of new meanings in a well-known source was like that of Montaigne: "Ce n'est non plus selon Platon que selon moy, puis que luy et moy l'entendons et voyons de mesme." [11]

On the basis of Plato's statement that had been misinterpreted or overlooked by others, Monteverdi distinguished his *Seconda Prattica* from the *Prima Prattica* wherein the exact opposite was maintained as a principle—that harmony controls the text: "cioè che considera l'armonia non comandata, ma comandante, e non serva ma signora del oratione." To clarify his brother's point of view, Giulio Cesare gave a list of com-

---

[11] In the famous essay on the education of children (*Essays,* I, 25). "And it is no more according to Plato's opinion, than to mine, since both he and I understand and see alike." (Translation by John Florio.)

posers who represented the First Practice. All are Netherlanders, since Monteverdi identified the *Prima Prattica* with the Netherlandish style. Ockeghem is mentioned, followed in nearly exact chronological order by Josquin des Prés, Pierre de la Rue, Jean Mouton, Crecquillon, Gombert, and Clemens non Papa. The last perfection of the style was considered to have been reached by Adrian Willaert in the field of artistic activities, and by Gioseffo Zarlino in the field of theoretical discussion.

The representatives which Giulio Cesare grouped in the category of the *Seconda Prattica* display less uniformity. In addition to Cipriano de Rore, who is named as an innovator of the first rank, there appear Ingegneri, Marenzio, Giaches de Wert, Luzzasco, Peri, Caccini—men whose works have no common denominator, not even with respect to the relation between word and tone. In idea and characterization, however, the two camps are separated from one another, and Monteverdi clearly distinguished the first school as old, and his own composition as modern. In contrast with the excited language of Artusi, the calmness and certainty of Monteverdi is striking. He is almost aloof, and certainly objective, when he clarifies what he means by both practices, the old and the modern. As Giulio Cesare says, "They were both honored by my brother, revered, and praised." [12]

For many years we hear no more about the *Seconda Prattica;* theoretical discussion was put aside for activities of greater import. In fact, Monteverdi never did complete the treatise he set out to compose in his earlier years, though it probably never ceased to occupy his mind. When Monteverdi was sixty-six years old a learned ecclesiastic asked him about it. We do not know the name of this person, a resident of Rome; neither do we have the three letters, which it seems he wrote. It has been suggested that he was Giovanni Battista Doni,[13] because Monteverdi said that when he visited Rome he looked forward to seeing and hearing his "most noble instrument," which may have been the famous "lira Barberina," Doni's invention. When on October 22, 1633, Monteverdi answered the Roman scholar, he again stated that he

---

[12] Published in Malipiero, *Claudio Monteverdi*, pp. 72f.

[13] Henry Prunières, *Claudio Monteverdi*, p. 198 and note 168. Prunières thinks that in his capacity as secretary of the Holy College at the court of Pope Urban VIII, Doni "must have held some ecclesiastical office" that would explain the title "reverendissimo" which Monteverdi used in his reply. This is, however, not conclusive, and Malipiero, *Claudio Monteverdi*, p. 291, denied that Doni was an ecclesiastic. While Malipiero has no other suggestion, Prunières also mentions Paolo Giordano Orsini, Duke of Bracciano, as the possible recipient of the letter. In previous years Monteverdi had some correspondence with the Duke. But we cannot find that Orsini was in Rome in 1633 or 1634.

was working at the treatise whose first design was at least in part connected with Artusi, "un certo Theorico di prima practica." In
addition to giving the story of its origin and the reasons which
had kept him from carrying out his intentions, Monteverdi informed his correspondent that his treatise, named *Melodia, ovvero
seconda pratica musicale*, would be divided into three books according
to the three elements of melody; in the first book he would discuss the
oratione, the significance and the qualities of the word; in the second he
would deal with harmony; in the third he would treat the problems of
rhythm. And he said he hoped that the musical world would appreciate
his discussion of problems whose solution might help future composers
to escape a predicament he himself had experienced. When he wrote
the *Lament of Arianna*, there was no book available to explain the
natural method of imitation nor any work, except Plato, that shed light
on the proper functions of an imitator in art. To lighten the difficulties
of a composer who attempts to apply the principle of imitation to
musical composition, Monteverdi intended to write his treatise for the
musicians of the Second Practice.[14]

It is certainly to be regretted that the treatise was not finished by
the man who was one of the most learned musicians of his age, as well
as a profound thinker. An elaborate discussion of the two phenomena
in musical composition, melody and rhythm, generally neglected by
the theorists, would have been unique not only for Monteverdi's period
but for all time. But the creation of the work of art was his first concern; he was not interested in a problem for the sake of its theoretical
solution, nor even for the sake of the theory of music as a discipline in
its own right. "It is my intention to show, through the medium of our
practice, what I was able to adopt from the spirit of the ancient philosophers to the advantage of the good art." [15] This was his explicit reply
to those who made the search for the characteristics of Greek music
their prime concern and who by their attempts to revive ancient music
would have abandoned the principles on which the music of the present
has developed. Monteverdi's interest was focused on the completion
and intensification of the new style of which he was the founder, and
all his efforts were concentrated on the creation of the musical language
of seventeenth-century Europe. No wonder that the reminder of Doni
(or whoever may have written the letters in the thirties) struck him as
a discord. For he had continually worked to explain the properties of

---

[14] Letter No. 118; published in Malipiero, *Monteverdi*, pp. 293f.
[15] Letter No. 119, to the same person, dated Venice, February 2, 1634; *ibid.*, pp. 295f.

the Second Practice directly through his music and had renounced the theoretical exposition which he once believed he would be able to accomplish.

Monteverdi now looked back on the music of the sixteenth century as something that belonged to the past. This knowledge was the result of his own artistic achievements and not of theoretical observations, and it gave him a calm security that permeated his every mention of the First Practice. He never raised his voice to the piercing tones of the pure theorists. The passion aroused in him by the issue had found an outlet in his compositions. Because he had succeeded in formulating the language of the new style, he was justified in regarding the Northern polyphonic style as obsolete. The *Seconda Prattica* was intended not only for the contemporary art of his day but also for the music of the future.

Through his music Monteverdi established the meaning of "style" as a historical phenomenon. The term "style" or *stylus* was known, of course, to writers on sixteenth-century art, who applied it to the materials of composition, regardless of the epoch. Style meant the way in which the principles of "arte, modulatione, diletto, tessitura, contrapunto, inventione, buona dispositione" were handled, and time and circumstance were not taken into account as factors in the formation of a style. When Monteverdi made the *Prima Prattica* obsolete, Netherlandish counterpoint became a historical style, according to our ideas.

The composer could now avail himself of a historical idiom, if and when he saw fit. Monteverdi had defined the *musica antica* as essentially religious and characterized by an impersonal, slow, dignified gravity. This gravity was identified with religious expression in music and appeared to be possible only within the medium of the Northerners. Since Monteverdi had shown that his new style was the outgrowth of an essentially secular concept, the composer of religious music was the victim of a conflict which continued throughout the baroque age. In writing religious music, he had to fall back on a style of the past, at the risk of appearing obsolete, and imitate the Netherlanders in full consciousness that he was using a historical style. Monteverdi composed à la Gombert, à la Palestrina, and many others did the same. Thus the composer was at variance with his own time or if he composed in accordance with the Second Practice, his music lacked a religious quality. In the field of sacred composition the musician faced the alternative of being antiquated and religious or modern and profane.

Monteverdi's influence extended even into the field of the theory of music. As musicians came to be more style conscious, they became more detached from the past in their theoretical observations and multiplied the number of subtle stylistic distinctions. Monteverdi's ideas soon reached the North and Germany, where the art of the Netherlanders had been uncontested. Heinrich Schütz, the great intermediary between North and South, brought them to his country after his second stay in Venice with Monteverdi. One of the few German musicians who understood the depth and scope of the Second Practice, Schütz exhibited the new style at its most august and presumably formulated the new concepts of musical composition into a doctrine which he handed down to his numerous pupils. A version of the Schütz doctrine has been preserved by his disciple Christoph Bernhard, in which the heritage of Monteverdi is manifest. Complete awareness of the essentials of style led to clear-cut categories, and accordingly Bernhard divided counterpoint into a *contrapunctus gravis* and a *contrapunctus luxurians*, identical with the *stylus antiquus* and *modernus*, or the *Prima* and *Seconda Prattica*. The gravity of the old style is evident in its slow motion, its strict observance of harmonic rules, and sparing use of dissonance. The *contrapunctus gravis* consists of not-too-fast notes, of a limited number of dissonances, and is concerned with the harmony rather than with the text. Since it was used by the older composers, it was called *stylus antiquus*, and sometimes "*a cappella Ecclesiasticus*, since it is befitting to the church rather than to any other place; also the Pope gives preference to it in his Chapel and other churches." In it, "Harmonia Orationis Domina est." Monteverdi's phrase reappears here in translation. The *contrapunctus luxurians*, on the other hand, "consists of fairly fast notes with extraordinary skips appropriate to stir the affections; it has a greater variety of dissonances and more *figurae Melopoëticae*, which others call *Licentiae*; it also possesses the element of melody, of a good aria, and this fits the text better than the manner of the grave style." In it, "Oratio Harmoniae Domina absolutissima." [16] To illustrate the gravity of the style Bernhard quotes examples mostly from the works of Palestrina. In conformity with the deeply religious implications of the style, Schütz wrote Bernhard in his last years that he should compose a work in the old style of Palestrina to be sung at his deathbed.

The fifth book, indeed, served as a dividing line between the ages of the First and Second Practices. Monteverdi now stood out as the great-

---

[16] *Die Kompositionslehre Heinrich Schützens in der Fassung seines Schülers Christoph Bernhard* (Leipzig, 1926).

est musical genius of Europe, a genius rare in his own or any other time. Seldom has an artist accomplished both the complete transformation of the traditional music and the equally complete foundation of the new art. He made his contemporaries conscious of style and gave them new resources of musical expression by his transformation of the three main elements of musical composition—harmony, melody, and rhythm. He was the true originator of modern music.

Though Artusi and his followers belittled the achievements of Monteverdi, most of the reactions to the new collection of madrigals were enthusiastic. The name of Monteverdi gained an international reputation as his earlier works continued to be published in foreign countries. Besides the edition in Nuremberg, a Danish printer provided a selection for his country in 1605, the year in which the fifth book of madrigals appeared. In Italy alone there were eight editions of the fifth book by 1620, and Phalèse in Antwerp included it in his publications of Monteverdi's works. The first enthusiastic response to Monteverdi's novelties had naturally been inside Italy. The edition of 1605 included a poem—of mediocre quality, to be sure—in praise of the composer, though such glorifications were quite customary in those days and not necessarily a sign of fame. In this poem by Padre Cherubino Ferrari, Monteverdi was greeted as a true musician of Paradise: "Quest'è un Musico ver del Paradiso." More indicative of the composer's growing importance was a series of publications brought out by Aquilino Coppini, from Milan. He published a selection of Monteverdi's madrigals in 1607, not with the original profane poems but with new religious texts in Latin: *Musica tolta da i Madrigali di Claudio Monteverde, et d'altri autori à 5 & à 6 voci, e fatta spirituale da Aquilino Coppini.* The dedication was to no less a figure than Cardinal Federico Borromeo, the nephew of St. Borromeo, a leader in the Counter Reformation. Under the influence of that movement it had become customary to "spiritualize" originally profane works, and the desire to acquaint religious institutions with the highest artistic achievements without giving offense may have been one of the reasons for making Monteverdi's madrigals available in such a "spiritualized" form. That Coppini's selections met with a favorable response is shown by his further publications. In 1608 he published a second selection of Monteverdi's madrigals spiritualized, in 1609 a third anthology, and in 1611 a reprint of the first book.

Coppini introduced his second book with an interesting preface, which has extraordinary words of praise for Monteverdi: "The *musica rappresentativa* of the fifth book of madrigals of Claudio Monteverdi, ruled by the natural expression of the human voice in moving the affections (*nel movere gli affetti*) produces the sweetest effects upon the hearing and in so doing becomes the most pleasant tyrant of human minds. The music is, therefore, well worthy of being sung and listened to, and not just in rustic country and among shepherds,[17] but during the receptions of the most noble ones, and at royal courts; and this music can also serve for many as an infallible norm and model (*infallibile norma & idea*) to compose madrigals and canzone harmonically in accordance with the best laws." [18] Thus for the first time Monteverdi's music was declared the norm of composition—rare approval for a new style that was still in the making. Of particular interest in Coppini's brief statement is the effect he attributed to Monteverdi's music: it becomes the tyrant over human minds (*de gli animi piacevolissima tiranna*). This was due to its power of moving the human passions, or affections. *Il movere gli affetti* was by no means a new term, for sixteenth-century theorists had extensively discussed the phenomenon. The music of the baroque age, however, was to proclaim the moving of the listener's passions as the composer's goal. The fact that in this brief appraisal the two most important characteristics of the new art—the norm of the structure and the purpose—are singled out makes Coppini's preface a remarkable document. A third statement that catches the reader's eye is where Coppini calls the madrigals of the fifth book *musica rappresentativa*. Since the rise of the Florentine music drama, this term had been reserved for music performed dramatically on the stage. Coppini's use of it raises an interesting question. Did he suggest that the madrigals were made dramatic simply by "moving the affections?" That they had any direct relation to the theatrical stage is difficult to believe, although Monteverdi himself later designated any composition set for stage production as belonging to the "representative" species (*in genere rappresentativo*), even if the work was not a music drama proper. Coppini, in all likelihood, was thinking of the dramatic effects inherent in the compositions, the effects that Monteverdi had rendered so convincingly by translating affections into gestures. In that sense, his music might well be called "representational."

---

[17] It is interesting to see Coppini refer to the cattle herds, *le mandre;* he obviously has in mind the etymological derivation of *madrigale* from *mandriali, mandra*.

[18] Document No. 4 in the appendix to Vogel's essay; see *VfMW*, III, 428.

The Compositions of the Fifth Book

A well-conceived plan of composition is more evident in this book than in any previous collection, for Monteverdi devoted it almost exclusively to one poet; of the nineteen madrigals which the book contains, sixteen are based on poems by Guarini. This time it was the dramatic *Pastor fido* that most attracted Monteverdi; no fewer than eleven of the madrigals were taken from it, and *Cruda Amarilli*, from the second scene of the first act, was placed at the beginning of the book to indicate its programmatic tenor. Monteverdi also grouped large cycles together more extensively than before; thus, a group of five madrigals is followed immediately by another of three. The first consists of passages from the fourth act of the *Pastor fido;* the second gives a selection from the third act. This pastoral drama also furnished poems for three separate madrigals. In his setting of these selections, Monteverdi proved himself a dramatist of great sensitivity and once more showed that he never did anything at random. The fact that these cycles of the fifth book offer large sections from a drama that had actually been produced in theatrical form may have been the reason why Coppini called the book as a whole *musica rappresentativa*. In that case, we should have to assume that these passages were actually sung on the stage when the drama was produced. But in view of the fact that there is no consecutive order and that only selected passages are given, even in the cycles, such use on the stage is difficult to imagine. After the appearance of the *Pastor fido*, the composition of settings for the poetical material of the drama became fashionable, but the use of dramatic texts does not imply that the music was given a stage production. It was dramatic only in a rather general sense, and presumably Coppini's *musica rappresentativa* had that connotation.[19] *Cruda Amarilli*, which set the style of the book, both textually and musically, has been ever since the days of Artusi's criticism the most widely renowned composition of Monteverdi.

Monteverdi's artistic plan, or program, did not change from the fourth book to the fifth. The many-voiced declamation, either in all parts or in a selected group of parts, and the new polyphony are still the outstanding problems to be solved, not by new techniques based on new principles but by old techniques worked out with greater subtlety and logic. In matters of harmony and in the counterpoint of

---

[19] Rudolf Schwartz, *Festschrift*, p. 148, seems to suggest a contact between the actual *musica rappresentativa* and the dramatic text of the *Pastor fido*.

harmonic groups, the logic of Monteverdi is stricter than ever. The structural functions of the bass seem strengthened. Despite occasional complex structures, a simple declamation in which all voices take part, note against note, is astonishingly frequent. In this connection, we must distinguish between the narration that sets the stage for the action and the dialogue between the dramatis personae, usually lovers. For this latter form of speech the reciting declamation is used more and more frequently. An excellent example is found in *Che dar più vi poss'io*. Although this madrigal has not met with much appreciation in modern literature of Monteverdi, it has historical significance as an illustration of the phase of the composer's development which ended in dramatic monody.[20] It presents the declamation in various forms, chiefly in many-voiced simple harmonization, in which the upper voice functions melodically as expressive declamation. At the beginning this declamation is in the canto, which actually governs the procedure; it is melodic because its balanced organization groups two phrases together as a unit, and it contains typical mannerisms that Monteverdi worked out for his dramatic declamation.

Ex. 74   v, 51

Che dar più vi pos- s'i - o   Ca- ro   Ca- - ro mio ben pren - de - te

This declamatory melody is accompanied by simple harmonies; later, Monteverdi changes the procedure and places the declamatory motif in the soloistic tenor. This motif, though simple, has the effect of a physical gesture and lends itself to the use of sequences.

Ex. 75   v, 51

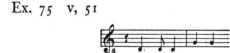

ec- co- vi il co- re

The soloistic statement is followed by a choral response on "prendete"; rising sequences then predominate up to the prominent phrase in which the lover offers his heart as a pledge of his loyalty and love. This phrase, "cor pegno della mia fede e del mio amore," is given in "psalmody" as free declamation on one chord for one measure only.

---

[20] Leichtentritt, *SIMG*, XI, 288, does not attribute artistic value to the composition, while Redlich, *op. cit.*, pp. 115f., finds that it contains many "building stones" of the *stile nuovo*.

Throughout the rest of the madrigal there alternate: a soloistic recitation, accompanied by a group of voices; a duet, as counterpoint; and a simple harmonic recitation in which four or all five voices participate. This arrangement centers the whole madrigal around the "recitative."

Compositions such as this give clear evidence that Monteverdi, uninfluenced by the Florentine theorists, had found his own artistic solution for the dramatic recitation long before he turned to the drama itself. Exactly the same style appears, for the most part, in the two large cycles of the *Pastor fido*, which also have not met with great favor among students of Monteverdi. It has been suggested [21] that the boundaries of the madrigal have here been crossed, and that since the madrigal is a specifically lyrical category, the epic and dramatic elements of the text interfere with its natural character. But we must not forget that it was the intention of the composer to transform the madrigal, and that when he chose the texts for the narrative part that unfolds the dramatic action, he was fully aware of what they implied in relation to the composition as a whole. He attempted to bring out the epic and dramatic character in the forms of his recitation, using once again declamation in full harmonies, in which the two leading elements are the canto as the declamatory part and the bass as the harmonic voice. In such passages, the *basso continuo* as figured bass is fully realized, so that the composition might well have been written as a monody with figured bass. In other respects canto and bass are structurally coupled, frequently in the form of imitation: one of the two parts will begin with a motif to be imitated by the other, while the middle voices do not necessarily take part in the imitation of the motif. In this relation between the upper and lower parts, the bass obtains from the canto as much in mobility as the canto gains in harmonic firmness from the bass. The heart of the matter is that Monteverdi worked out the *stile recitativo* within the madrigal form in such a way as to retain a high artistic quality in the individual parts. The Florentine composers who tried to write monody on theoretical principles without any intermediary phase, could not set the bass in motion, so that it appeared as a bare skeleton made up of a few harmonies, and, lacking any interlocking, structural relationship to the canto, was stiff and monotonous. Monteverdi completely avoided this fault in his recitative. How fundamental and comprehensive was the relation between canto and bass in his madrigals can be illustrated by innumerable examples. We may

---

[21] Leichtentritt, *op. cit.*, p. 288.

take a phrase from *Dorinda, ah diró*, the *terza parte* in the first Guarini cycle:

Ex. 76   v, 24

All the essentials of the passage are contained in these two parts from which the three middle voices are harmonically derived. Had Monteverdi used a figured bass, the harmonization would scarcely differ from the written form as it stands. The fully harmonized declamation is not the only type of dramatic "recitative," which is also given in small groupings of voices, instead of being arranged in compact chords. The recitative may appear in rapid syllabic declamation or in slow, emphatic motion with prolonged rhythmic values, the choice depending on the emotional connotations of the text.

Ex. 77   v, 24, 25

The phrasing in these madrigals is marked by definite cadences and falls into a succession of separate groups similar to those found in compositions of the fourth book. Monteverdi presumably felt that there was an inner connection between this grouping of separate phrases and the declamatory recitation.

His style of declamation also includes the use of a motif with repetitions and sequences rather than variations. A characteristic example is found in the second part of the Guarini cycle, in *Ma se con la pietà*. In full harmonization there is a recitation of the lines "Non mi negar a l'ultimo sospiro un tuo solo sospir." While the tenor continues to repeat the lines, which now form the harmonic basis, the two upper voices give, above it, the new motif of "beata morte."

Ex. 78   v, 21

After the first sequential rise, the short, exclamatory motif of "beata morte" provides the material for the work. The tenor continues with the line "Un tuo solo sospir," while the two upper voices sing a new line, "Se l'adolcissi tu." The three low voices, as a harmonic background, then repeat once more the line "Non mi negar," while the soprano alone contributes a short declamation of "beata morte," each time in sequential rise. This motif is extended over three voices in successive responses, until with climactic finality all five voices state the motif in chordal fashion. This is the method Monteverdi most frequently employs when working with a motif. He gives a highly effective, dramatic conclusion to this madrigal, which ends with the lines "Voce cortese e pia Va in pace anima mia." The music to the last lines reflects the dying out of sound; the three low voices present the motif, which is then repeated by the two upper parts, so that the five-part madrigal ends in the most unusual manner with only two voices. Motif, dramatic expression, tone color, and tone volume are linked together to form a unity.

Monteverdi excels in discovering new means of expression, suited to the narrative. Even the simplest, almost commonplace, mode may be given haunting effects, as in the beginning of Guarini's *Era l'anima mia*. The tone color in itself has a dramatic effect, although the recitation, in keeping with the narrative character of the poem, is carried by the three low voices for four measures on one chord only. "Close to the last

hour was my heart, exhausted, like the dying soul that wastes away"—
thus begins the poem, and to keep the music faithful to the text, Monteverdi chooses the simplest recitation, which with the dark tone color
gives an effect of poignancy. The simpler Monteverdi's art becomes, the
more it gains in convincing directness, even when he draws upon forms
that have been used a thousand times. He has structurally perfected
the possibilities of grouping voices in low and high ranges to provide
tone color for expressive and dramatic purposes.

The desire to endow the recitative with expressive power led to
typical formulas, as many of the famous madrigals in the fifth book
show. The opening of *O Mirtillo*, which for harmonic reasons enraged
Artusi, who called it "impertinentia d'un prinzipio," is in *stile recitativo*,
with all the qualities of emotional intensity that the text suggests. It has
rightly been compared with the exclamation in Arianna's *Lamento:*

Ex. 79   v, 5

The rest of the canto has so many features typical of a melodic line
in modern declamation that it could have occurred in any of the dramatic recitatives. This line has a life, a motion of its own, and is counterbalanced only by the bass:

Ex. 80   v, 5

The last six madrigals are the culmination of Monteverdi's various
achievements. It is only in these last compositions that through a *basso
continuo* the constituent elements are entirely on their own.[22] Melody

---

[22] The *basso continuo* is for the most part still a *basso seguente*.

and harmony, which are assigned one to the bass, the other to the upper parts, now have all the freedom they had been seeking in the unaccompanied madrigal. The harmonization now becomes a functional accompaniment subordinated to the melody. To heighten the contrast of functions, the accompanying harmony, as *basso continuo*, becomes principally instrumental, while the melody is rendered vocally. Four of the *continuo* madrigals have five vocal parts in addition to the thorough bass, one is set for six voices, and the last for nine, divided in a double chorus.

The first of these madrigals, *Ahi come a un vago sol*, is a magnificent testimonial to Monteverdi's ingenuity and originality. The basic structure he invented around 1600 anticipated a form which came into general use about half a century later. The madrigal is constructed as a rondo cantata, following the principle of the trio or trio sonata, which we have already discussed, and structural alternation is used to differentiate between soli and tutti. The structure of the work is worthy of a detailed description. Monteverdi treated the line "Ah che piaga d'amor non sana mai" as an organizing refrain. He inserted the refrain four times, each time presenting a textual variation, and rising to a climax. Thus at the third repetition the refrain gives first the whole line, then repeats the first half three times, and closes with the whole line. These insertions are in the manner of the rondo refrain, in which the musical material remains the same. In contrast to the intervening soloistic passages, the material of the refrain is characterized by the simplicity of its pure, chordal setting. The complex harmonies, note against note and syllable against syllable, suggest choral responses, if not in actual performance at least in the structural conception, which conforms to the alternation of soli and tutti. The first time the refrain appears, Monteverdi repeats the first part of the line: "Ah che piaga d'amor :|| non sana mai." The second time, the line is not repeated, but Monteverdi achieves an increase of tension by transposing the harmonies by a fifth. The third time, the refrain is sung in three parts, and then the repetition of the line employs all five parts for the first time. At the conclusion of the work, when the refrain appears for the last time, it is sung twice, both times by all five voices. Thus Monteverdi builds up his material to a climax at the end, merely by altering its structure. The three-part version of the refrain is also of stylistic interest, since it embodies the type of trio (trio sonata) that Monteverdi had used consistently in his previous madrigals: grouping an upper duet of two sopranos with a harmonic bass. This trio also has the accompaniment of a *basso continuo*, but—in contrast with the solo passages—the accompanying bass is merely a *basso seguente*, identical with the vocal bass. The refrain in the first version follows:

Ex. 81 v, 65

Such forms of the trio are innumerable. They are the predecessors of the soloistic duet with instrumental accompaniment, the genuine form of the trio cantata and sonata. This soloistic type of trio is consistently applied to the passages between the refrains, and the "responsorial" type to the refrain. Throughout the composition, the soloistic duet consists of two tenors which do not take part in the refrains, except for the phrases in five voices. The solo groups are also in sharp stylistic contrast to the tutti refrains, being highly ornamental and based on a virtuoso technique of singing which as *concertato* will more and more become the new vocal style. Sometimes the duet is linked by a parallelism in thirds which permeates the whole form of the trio sonata; sometimes the two voices are contrapuntally combined in a rapid imitation of short motifs, a method that will also be characteristic of the trio form:

Ex. 82 v, 62

In its embodiment of the contrast between virtuoso singing and instrumental accompaniment, this is an example of the fully developed *stile concertato*.

A further increase in virtuosity is shown in *Troppo ben può*, again a perfect example of the *stile concertato*, as in *E così a poco a poco*, the first madrigal for six voices and thorough-bass accompaniment. In both madrigals the long melismatic lines and the exuberance of the richly decorated melody are inspired by the connotations of individual words;

yet in the development of these motifs, the musical structure is the controlling factor. *Amor se giusto sei* and the strikingly beautiful *T'amo mia vita* have fascinating and unusual arrangements, combining solo declamation with the accompaniment of the *basso continuo*. The solo declamation is successively given to canto, basso, and tenore in *Amor se giusto sei*, each voice presenting alone with the thorough bass a long passage in noble, emphatic declamation or in elaborate virtuosity. Not until the line "non sostener Amor" does the simultaneous co-operation of all five parts begin. *T'amo mia vita* surpassed almost everything that Monteverdi had written and was a magnificent example of his skill as a dramatist. He singles out the direct expression of love, "T'amo mia vita," for the soloistic recitation, given to the canto alone. The narrative parts, "My dear love tells me most sweetly," are assigned to the three low voices in the style of choral recitation found in *Era l'anima mia*. Indeed, the situation is so vividly depicted that the imagination dramatizes the composition, with the choir in the role of the unemotional narrator, while the actor in the foreground bursts forth with the passionate exclamations "T'amo mia vita," until, toward the end, all share in the exclamation. This is drama on a small scale but of a profundity that no previous composer had expressed. Monteverdi has turned what was still called a "madrigal" into a short dramatic scene. This little composition can stand comparison with Monteverdi's most grandiose works, such as the *Amore* of his latest years. Artistically it was far more dramatic than anything the Florentines had developed on a more ambitious scale.

The fifth book closes with the madrigal *Questi vaghi* for nine voices and two instrumental sinfonie, a noble conclusion to a distinguished collection. It is striking not only because the double chorus—one for five voices, the other for four—breaks through the limitations of the madrigal, but also because of the new use of the orchestra, the sinfonie being written for five unnamed instruments. The two sinfonie use the same musical material, the *sinfonia seconda* being an abbreviation of the *sinfonia prima*.[23] The grouping of the voices in two antiphonal choirs derives directly from the madrigalesque dialogues of the sixteenth century which came into favor especially through Andrea Gabrieli. The dialogues had gone through a long development by the time Monteverdi took up the form. In this madrigal he used responses between the first and second choir but refined the technique so that it

[23] This observation has been made by Redlich, *op. cit.*, p. 121.

was more than the simple echo structure. At the beginning of the lines there is usually an immediate imitation of the initial chords, and for the most part the two choirs are closely worked into each other. A further novelty is the introduction of soloistic passages with thorough bass, separated from the choral section. Wherever the poem takes on a more personal and emotional tone, or where the poet speaks subjectively, Monteverdi turns toward the soloistic form, especially after the second sinfonia and the outburst "Deh, deh" in full chorus, in the phrase "se potessi anch'io." Double chorus, solo voices, *basso continuo*, and an orchestra with instrumental compositions that intervene in the course of the vocal work—these are the vast resources which can be drawn upon to shape the poem musically "upon the foundations of truth." It will be many years before Monteverdi returns to the full use of these artistic means, but the foundations of truth have justified his latest transformation of the madrigal and will justify the novelties of the future.

THE SCHERZI MUSICALI

In Monteverdi's progress toward transforming the madrigal and discovering a new basis of composition, one step followed the other, each seeming to issue logically from the preceding situation with extraordinary continuity. Up to the fifth book of madrigals this continuity was never disturbed. Then the *Scherzi Musicali* for three voices appeared in 1607. The scherzi resulted from a fresh contact with Italian native song, which once before had found artistic expression in the canzonetta when Monteverdi was searching for musical forces opposed to the elements of the Netherlandish style. The canzonetta was an effective medium to that end, and once it had been reached we might suppose that the native song had served Monteverdi's purpose. What could the composer expect from it, except a repetition? The phase of the five books of madrigals does not necessarily lead to the scherzi, which come somewhat as a surprise and must be taken as an artistic phenomenon that stands apart from the logic of the composer's development.

The *Scherzi* presented a new poet, Gabriello Chiabrera (1552–1638). With the exception of two poems by Ansaldo Cebá, *Deh chi tace* and *Dispiegate guance*, both set to music by Giulio Cesare Monteverdi, and one by Sannazaro, *La Pastorella mia spietata*, most of the texts were by him. Highly esteemed, Chiabrera had at one time been in touch with the Mantuan court, and Duke Vincenzo had accorded him many tokens of respect, which he was quick to record in his autobiography.[24] An ardent admirer of Greek poetry, to him the essence of all poetry, he seems to have followed Ronsard and the Pleiade, especially in his odes.[25] But his genuine love for Pindar's odes resulted only in a certain formalism, while his craving for startling novelties, typical of seventeenth-century art, made him rather the true contemporary of Marino. Light and spirited verses, Chiabrera's scherzi were written with musical composition in mind and have often been regarded as his best and most original writings.

Infractions of the rules of artistic composition are perhaps more frequent in the scherzi than in the canzonette. The parallelism in fifths and octaves, derisively used in such forms as the villanella, and the systematic use of the combination of three parts have their roots in the native song, as do certain rhythmic and melodic qualities. The vocal parts of the scherzi are for two sopranos and a bass, while the instrumental ritornelli have a corresponding combination of two violini da braccio and a bass instrument which also functions as *basso continuo*. Monteverdi suggested that the bass part be played by a chitarrone, a clavicembalo, or any other instrument on which the harmonies of the *basso continuo* can be realized. With the exception of the instrumental ritornelli, there seems to be no advance beyond Monteverdi's previous adaptation of the native song, yet the scherzi differ considerably from the canzonette.

In the first place, the trio combination is now strengthened as a result of Monteverdi's experiments with the five-part madrigals. The upper parts and the bass are separated from each other, and the two sopranos, or the two violins, form an inseparable entity as a duet, have their own motion, and completely absorb the melodic elements. The relation of the two upper parts is so close that neither can be taken by itself. They usually progress in parallel thirds, and only in or near the cadences are there deviations from this procedure. The voice-leading thus was of so great a simplicity that one cannot properly use the term, since it implies a certain contrapuntal independence of the parts, however slight. This coupling of two voices in parallel thirds is the product of harmonic thinking, in which the melody is not invented as a horizontal line, but is the direct result of the predominant verticalism of harmony. The

---

[24] See Achille Neri, "Gabriello Chiabrera e la Corte di Mantova," in *Giornale storico della letteratura italiana,* Vol. VII (1886).

[25] See Ferdinando Neri, *Il Chiabrera e la Pleiade Francese* (Turin, 1920), *passim.*

second soprano underlines the verticalism, for the parallel motion in thirds links it with the first soprano and at the same time produces the constituent tones of the chords. The duet is given a high range and keeps its distance from the bass so that the organic unity of the two upper voices is strengthened. The madrigals had used such combinations skillfully distributed over the composition as a whole, but never before had they occurred so consistently.

In the second place, the bass has been given a field of action all its own and never attempts to enter the sphere of the duet by swinging into the melodic motion of the upper parts or sharing their motifs, but is entirely absorbed in its harmonic functions. In previous works, especially in the canzonette, the bass would occasionally take part in the melodic motion of the upper voices, even though its predominant function was harmonic, and here and there motifs would also appear in the bass; but now the fundamental separation is complete. If the bass appears to be "melodious," such melodic parts, however brief, are formed independently or are a matter of its basic motion and have nothing to do with the motifs of the duet. But, in general, the bass does not strive to form melodic phrases, and its tones either skip from one root of the chord to the other or are diatonic passages through the scale. Whatever melodiousness may result, its phrases never fulfill the functions of a melody nor do they ever have the power of a motif. The bass is, however, divided into phrases of the same length as those of the upper duet and follows the verse lines. Though consisting of nothing but chordal tones, a phrase of the bass may be repeated in transposition, or a downward motion may be followed by a phrase in the opposite direction, or vice versa. These phrases are so shaped as to be "impersonal" and not characteristic in expression. This unexpressive behavior of the bass is related to Monteverdi's aspiration to work out a number of stereotyped patterns that can be used over and over again, and their similarity results from a tendency toward objective forms, from the limited range of chordal varieties, and from a relationship to dance basses, such as those of the passamezzo antico and moderno,[26] which we have previously noticed. The impersonal character of the bass is sometimes heightened by an unchanging rhythmic motion which makes the contrast between the bass and the duet more striking, especially when the two upper voices have brief melismata, or groups of tones set to a syllable. The bass maintains the basic rhythm in scherzi whose upper duet devi-

---

[26] See the excellent essay of O. Gombosi, "Italia: Patria del Basso Ostinato," in *RaM*, VII (1934), 14.

ates from the strictly syllabic form. Similarly, in the instrumental ritornelli, the bass ordinarily has a simpler, slower motion than the duet of the two violins.

In the third place, the systematically uniform rhythmic organization of the scherzi differs markedly from that of previous works, including the canzonette, and is primarily musical, as opposed to rhythms that are merely derived from the text. To be sure, the musical rhythm is by no means wholly separate from the verse rhythm, but many of the scherzi are not syllabic, and their musical rhythm obviously follows its own drive. In compositions whose organization is syllabic, the situation is less clear; the rhythms of the verse and of the music may coincide, and in works where great care has been taken with the accentuation a clear-cut decision is hardly possible. Yet the shift, for instance, from a triple to a duple rhythm, from 3/4 to 6/8, sometimes adopted for the whole composition and characteristic of a great many scherzi, is an eminently musical procedure. Such a shift is not necessarily produced by the verse, even if the verse has a comparable order, for it has a long musical past, independent of all texts. With composers such as Monteverdi, whose sensitivity reacted to the most subtle accentuations of the verse, a clear-cut decision is often impossible. Strangely enough, the scherzi actually fail to show Monteverdi's sensitivity at its best, for the musical accents are not always in full harmony with the textual accents. This may furnish a clue as to the priority of musical or textual rhythms. At all events, only the syllabic compositions pose the question, and in general Monteverdi's scherzi show that purely musical rhythm was usually the determining factor. This is proved by the handling of the rhythmic order, where each section which is of the same length as the verse line and is provided with a musical cadence tends to be repeated, so that the composition as a whole has a fixed pattern. Finally, the dance character of the scherzi is ultimate proof of the priority of musical rhythm.

The scherzi produced some new effects taken from the native song; these included the consistency of the dance rhythms, the sharp contrast between bass and upper duet, the rendering of the bass as *basso continuo*, and the peculiarity of the trio combination with its special style for the duet, not to mention the instrumental ritornello. In most of the scherzi Monteverdi drew together the material for both the instrumental and the vocal sections. The material used for the ritornello and the stanza, similar in melody, in rhythm, or merely in phrasing, had to be correlated, since the ritornello was to be played twice and then repeated after each stanza and too strong a contrast in the material would destroy the unity of a composition. The *Scherzi Musicali* constituted a transformation of the native song into the trio "cantata," a companion to the instrumental trio sonata. (The book concludes with two scherzi by Monteverdi's brother, Giulio Cesare, and a balletto in praise of beauty, *De la Bellezza le dovute lodi.* This last composition has been the subject of frequent discussion, because Monteverdi's authorship is by no means certain; indeed, stylistic evidence points to Giulio Cesare as the composer.[27])

[27] See Hugo Riemann, "Eine siebensätzige Tanzsuite von Monteverdi," in *SIMG*, XIV, 26. Riemann observes a debatable relationship between the seven sections of the balletto which he thinks have been worked out with the technique of variation. With good reason, Redlich, *op. cit.,* p. 132, doubts that there is such a technique in the work.

CHAPTER ELEVEN

The Mantuan Music Drama

ORFEO

THE YEAR 1607 brought great fame to Mantua and to Monteverdi. His first opera, the *Orfeo*, was produced in the spring at carnival time. It was also the first opera produced for the Mantuans, and though it was staged before the small group of members of the Accademia degl' Invaghiti, it was to be performed repeatedly at court. The libretto was by Alessandro Striggio, son of the famous madrigalist, a Mantuan nobleman and a court official. The book of the *Orfeo* was promptly issued by the printer of the Duke, *La Favola d'Orfeo rappresentata in musica il carnevale dell anno MDCVII nell' accademia degl' Invaghiti di Mantova*, in order "that every one of the spectators might be able to read the story while it was sung." Two years later the score of the *Orfeo* appeared in Venice, and it was reissued in 1615, a rare occurrence for an opera. Both Caccini's and Peri's versions of *Euridice* were published, but neither was reprinted. During the baroque age musical compositions, especially operas and cantatas, were inseparably linked to the occasions for which they were composed. This explains the incredible productivity of composers of operas and cantatas and is the reason why the medium of musical communication was the manuscript rather than the printed book. A baroque opera in print was very much the exception, and a reprint of an opera several years after its first performance was unheard of. But the *Orfeo* was in every respect a unique work, so far above anything that had been produced in the early days of opera that the genius of Monteverdi, "Musico ver del Paradiso," must have been apparent even to those who had previously shown reluctance to honor him. The Mantuans welcomed the *Orfeo* with great excitement, since they knew, as Carlo Magni recorded, that they were privileged to witness a unique event.[1] Vincenzo, who for many years had taken the keenest interest in that form in which "all actors shall speak musically" (Carlo Magni), could now give orders to recite (*fa recitare*) a music drama composed in his own city.

The legend of Orfeo was most appropriate for a performance at the Mantuan court. In one of the glorious frescoes of Andrea Mantegna, the *Camera degli Sposi*, completed in 1474, there can be seen, behind Cardinal Francesco Gonzaga, two men, one of whom is supposed to be Leon Battista Alberti and the other, Angelo Poliziano. Poliziano likewise may have reminded the Mantuans that his *Orfeo* was produced in Mantua for the first time upon the return of Cardinal Francesco in 1472. Even this early drama of the Italian Renaissance was performed in the manner, as the report goes, of a musical "recitation," and Baccio Ugolino, who played the part of Orfeo, "sang" his role to the accompaniment of the viol. This is only a matter of historical record, for the music itself has not come down to us. The legend of Orfeo had also been used in the early music dramas at Florence, and the collaboration of Striggio and Monteverdi may have been an artistic rivalry, undertaken in a desire to outdo the Florentines.

The production of *Orfeo* was under the auspices of the Duke, but his son and heir, Francesco, the recipient of the dedication, took the keenest interest in the work. The few reports we have of the performance are by Francesco, who seems to have followed every phase of the production. He was full of enthusiasm, especially over the feats of Giovanni Gualberto, the singer of the title role, who had been "loaned" to Mantua for the occasion by the Grand Duke of Florence. In a letter to his brother, Francesco says that his father not only attended the première before the elite of connoisseurs but also "numerous rehearsals," and immediately ordered another performance for the "ladies of the city." Monteverdi captivated the Mantuans with his new dramatic composition in which he gave the star singers many opportunities to show their skill. But it was the dramatic, emotional quality of the work and the unity of text and music that gained the praise of all true connoisseurs. Cherubino Ferrari, the theologian and poet from Milan, who

---

[1] Letter of Carlo Magni to his brother, the Mantuan ambassador in Rome, dated February 23, 1607, a day before the first performance at the court theater. See P. Canal, *Della musica in Mantova* (Venice, 1881), p. 101; see also Stefano Davari, "Notizie biografiche del distinto maestro di musica Claudio Monteverdi," in *Atti della R. Accademia Virgiliana*, p. 85; and Vogel, *op. cit.*, p. 343.

had added an encomiastic poem to Monteverdi's fifth book of madrigals, remarked of the *Orfeo* that "poet and composer have presented the affections in such an extraordinary manner that nothing remains to be criticized. The poetry is beautiful in the invention of the material, still more beautiful in its disposition, and most beautiful in its expression; it is, in short, as excellent as might be expected from a genius such as Signor Striggio. And finally, with regard to the music, one must confess that it is in no way inferior to the poetry; the music serves the poetry so fittingly that it cannot be replaced by any better composition."

The unity between drama and music, which Ferrari observed is, indeed, the great historic distinction of the *Orfeo*. At the dawn of operatic history, the music drama was created by Monteverdi alone, without any real precursor. For the Florentine music drama, even in the version of the gifted Peri, was artistically inferior to the *Orfeo*; it never attained the musical or dramatic quality of Monteverdi's work, and remained within the theoretical limitations established by the men around Bardi. Peri maintained that reason should be the principle governing every human action, and though he had a more musical disposition and greater spontaneity than his rival Caccini, the exclusively intellectual approach proved fatal to the Florentine music drama. Monteverdi was comparatively free from the burden of such theoretical considerations. He was, of course, an "intellectual" composer to an extraordinary degree, but in him the intellectual and the elemental musical powers were miraculously blended.

Monteverdi had transformed the musical vocabulary and laid the foundations for new stylistic idioms before he proceeded to the music drama, and this methodical work was an important factor in giving the *Orfeo* its superiority and lasting success. "Claudio Monteverdi came last and is first," as it was once said.[2] Monteverdi was also a born dramatist; whatever the medium, he brought to all his compositions a dramatic understanding of musical form. Technical, stylistic, and expressive preparations combined to make the *Orfeo* the first music drama in history.

Can it be said that Monteverdi was a disciple of the Florentines in the music drama? Only if the *stile recitativo* is understood in a very superficial way, and only in the sense that Monteverdi realized what

---

[2] "Claudio Monteverdi arriva ultimo ed è il primo." See Guido Pannain, "Claudio Monteverdi nell'opera in musica," in *Musica*, II (Sansoni-Florence, 1943), 36. Pannain's essay is a fine contribution to the study of Monteverdi's work.

the Florentines may have dreamed of but did not achieve. The dramatic perfection of the *stile recitativo* in the *Orfeo* is pre-eminently musical, and the relationship between word and tone is Monteverdi's own. "Truly every word is animated in the canto. It is a transfiguration, within pure sound, from speaking to melody, a re-creation of the life of the word through the sentiment which is enclosed in the word, and is not limited by verbal sonority and practical significance but reveals the possibility of going beyond the physical and reaching the roots of its spiritual essence."[3] Monteverdi adhered to the supreme law: "L'oratione sia padrona del armonia e non serva." He derived his musical form from the spiritual essence of the word, which is nothing other than the *affetto* Monteverdi and his contemporaries had in mind when speaking of the inner meaning of text and music. This responsiveness to the *affetto* results in the unique, tense, dramatic effect which gives the *Orfeo* its superior quality.

On a grandiose scale, the *Orfeo* demonstrated Monteverdi's conception of musical form. This not only implied a general expressiveness but was also meant to realize drama literally, not as something fixed and stable, but as an element continually progressing and changing, so that the musical form, in order to be dramatic, must exhibit a corresponding flexibility and variety. Monteverdi did not treat musical form as an unalterable preconceived scheme or pattern as did the later opera, where the *da capo* aria prevailed as a more or less fixed form. Such a conception of form occurs in very mature, even overripe, phases of historical development, and is the one usually adopted by a classic artist. The other and opposite conception occurs where the artist is not bound to an established scheme but creates a new form each time, according to the special conditions and by interpreting those conditions. All musicians who are born dramatists have taken form to be something flexible and responsive to the action of the drama. Gluck or Wagner may be mentioned here, but Monteverdi was the first in musical history to compose according to this totally new conception. This explains the great variety of forms in his music drama.

The *Orfeo* followed the traditional division of the drama into five acts. The prologue is sung by a personification of music, as befits the legendary Orfeo, whose powerful song charms man and beast, moves rock and tree. "La Musica" sings of her powers, which are the powers of Orfeo, in a strophic song introduced and concluded by an instrumental ritornello which reappears in the course of the drama. The

[3] *Ibid.*, p. 38.

prologue thus has an established form: the same material is used for all the stanzas and is composed on a bass which, except for its rhythm, remains the same throughout. Despite the stability, Monteverdi varied the line of the recitation in the individual stanzas according to the affection of the words and thus created a climactic centralization and a formal symmetry which the strophic song does not in itself possess. He places the double climax of expressive and formal concentration at the center of the song, in the third stanza. Music announces herself, "Io la musica son" (second stanza), and relates her power over man while singing to the accompaniment of a golden lyre (third stanza), "Io su cetera d'or cantando soglio." The recitation here deviates furthest from the melodic pattern of the stanza. Thus Monteverdi achieves a clear outline for the strophic song by creating a rise toward, and a decline from, the climax. The strophic song can only vary the melody from stanza to stanza and has no formal limits other than the number of stanzas in the poem, so that any symmetry or climax is an addition quite outside the nature of the form. Monteverdi nearly always gives the strophic song this additional form, thanks to his powers of organization and adaptation.

The *Orfeo* begins with exuberant rejoicing over the wedding of Orfeo and Euridice. All have the same desire—that the glorious day of joy may never end, that it may be the first of countless such days to come, that its happiness may last forever. The chorus sends its prayers to the gods that no misfortune may befall the lovers. (First act.) The festival joy is at its height, and Orfeo sings one of the powerful songs with which he charms the universe, at the end of which the Pastore exclaims that nature itself has become more beautiful. At the moment when the rejoicing reaches its climax and the Pastore utters once again his exclamation over the happy day, the Messaggiera suddenly breaks the news of the tragedy. Euridice, bitten by an envious serpent, has died: "La tua diletta sposa è morta." In keeping with the Greek thought that the gods envy men and strike because of jealousy, the chorus in the first act had prayed that the gods might not becloud the radiant day by any sinister deed. Now the chorus recognizes the bitter fate, the "caso acerbo," and draws the moral that mortal man should never trust the gods. (Second act.) In defiance of the gods, Orfeo is determined to break the law of mortality, to win his beloved Euridice back from the realm of Pluto. He approaches Hades, although immortal words should warn him: "Lasciate ogni speranza voi ch'entrate." Here **this** warning of Dante's *Inferno* appears. Caronte tries to hold Orfeo back from his blasphemous audacity. But now, once more, Orfeo must test the powers of his song, for it must charm Caronte into guiding him to Hades; and the power of his enchanting music achieves what never before has taken place—a mortal enters the realm of the dead. (Third act.) Pluto's wife, Proserpina, is the mediatrix for Euridice, who is to be permitted to return to the world of light. Pluto, a rather mortal captive of the beauties of his wife, yields to Proserpina's intercession. The triumphant Orfeo is overjoyed. Amid the exultation over his victory, he wonders whether Euridice is following him as had been promised. He gives in to his doubt and does what, according to Pluto's stipulation, he is forbidden to do: he turns around to look for Euridice. He loses his wife forever; Euridice must now return to Hades. Orfeo's lament is of no avail; there is no remedy for his fate; to him, the light of day is now forever odious, "l'odiosa luce." (Fourth act.) Wandering over the plains of Thrace, Orfeo gives himself to lamentation without hope. He is the great singer with a broken heart, who begs nature, trees, and rocks, to mourn with him in pity. The god Apollo descends from Heaven; Orfeo, his son, will be translated to divine immortality; risen to Heaven, he will enjoy the sight of Euridice in the stars: "Nel sole e nelle stelle vaghezzerai le sue sembianze belle." So Apollo and Orfeo rise to the stars, while the chorus joyfully sings that the happy Orfeo is to enjoy celestial honor: "Vanne felice a pieno, a goder celeste honore." In comformity with the idea of the dance of the spheres, the music drama concludes with a moresca, a dance of the heavenly ballet. (Fifth act.) This conclusion, the translation of Orfeo to the stars, brought about in all suddenness by Apollo and therefore always decried as an unsatisfactory *deus ex machina*, may not agree with our conceptions of a dramatic solution. Yet it has its peculiar historical significance; not the *deus ex machina*, but the act of transfiguration itself, symbolized in the dance, is the factor of importance.[4]

The dramatic turning points in the work exhibit the highest concentration of Monteverdi's artistic energy: Orfeo's praise of Amor, of undefiled joy and exuberant love, which he sings at the invitation of the Pastore and in which he is joined by Euridice; the first display of Orfeo's singing powers, which is interrupted by the messenger's news of the catastrophe; Orfeo's song testing the power of his music over

---

[4] A. Warburg's brilliant studies have shed a new light upon the relation of the ballet to the dance of the spheres. See especially his essay "I costumi teatrali per gli intermezzi del 1589," now in A. Warburg, *Gesammelte Schriften* (Leipzig), Vol. I, in *Veröffentlichungen der Bibliothek Warburg*, III.

Caronte; Orfeo's breach of promise and his final loss of Euridice; the
ascent of Apollo and Orfeo to Heaven—all are scenes of superior musical distinction. Only in the fifth act may we doubt whether the greater
artistic skill is shown in the moving scene of Orfeo's lament in the fields
of Thrace, rendered with great simplicity, or in the scene of Orfeo's
glorification, presented with brilliant display. Each of the principal
scenes, the musical and dramatic centers of gravity, is surrounded by
its antecedent and consequent, so to speak. The scene of greatest importance is not necessarily the one that employs the greatest profusion
of musical resources. The beginning and end of an act make a more
comprehensive use of all available means, and therefore the more impressive display, though this concentration of musical resources is not
necessarily evidence of dramatic and musical intensity. By strengthening the beginning and the end of each act, and by building up an
antecedent and a consequent to surround the dramatic core of a scene,
Monteverdi achieves a symmetrical organization, which gives balance
to the musical energies and a certain similarity to the acts. The climax
of an act comes in the scene which has the greatest dramatic concentration, though the act may proceed to a conclusion of far greater
brilliance. Only the fifth act fails to center on a dramatic core and
advances in one direction toward the end of the work. This straightforward movement is surely most appropriate for the ending of the
work, and makes it impossible to decide whether the greater artistic
concentration occurs in Orfeo's pitiful lament or his ascent with
Apollo. In his disposition of the material as a whole, Monteverdi manifests his powers of architectural thinking and his profound feeling for
dramatic presentation.

The central scenes, in which the musical and dramatic intensities
coincide, exhibit the individualism of his form at its best. In them,
flexibility of structure, based on the relation of tone and word, comes
into its own. When Orfeo sings his first song of joy, posing the chal-
lenging question whether there is anyone as happy as himself, the
melody is an organic mixture of recitation and arioso, with no clear
separation of one from the other. Certainly, an arioso seems to require
a melody, in contrast to the narration, and Caccini has described the
stile recitativo as something midway between a spoken recitation and
a full-fledged aria. Yet Monteverdi not only increases the melodiousness when embodying the arioso within the recitation, but often produces the arioso by a distinctive and sensitive reaction to the affection
of the word. Striking intervals, accidentals, or modulations may alter

the course of the recitation and give it a melodious character, though they are not introduced for the sake of melody, but in order to do justice to the text. More often, and by standards other than those of mere melodiousness, the arioso develops a structure appropriate to songlike melodies, which penetrates the recitative as an organizing factor. The recitation, of course, has no formal structure of its own. From the very beginning of the *stile recitativo* this was its most crucial problem, and one which the Florentines all too frequently tried to solve by providing the end of each line with a cadence. This, of course, had the effect of making each line a unit. But when such units occur as many times as the text has lines, there is still no formal organization. It is only fair to add that the Florentines occasionally discovered better solutions. Monteverdi begins the search for formal limits to the unlimited recitation by shaping the *basso continuo* according to a modulatory scheme with a strength and logic of its own in order to keep the cadences from coming to full rests. He also makes use of the fact that the phrases of the melodic recitation often have a certain correspondence with each other that closely approaches balance and symmetry and thus act as though they were constituent parts of a song. Orfeo's *Rosa del ciel*, and Euridice's brief response *Io non dirò*, which follows, are examples of this.

The most grandiose scene comes with the appearance of the messenger in the second act, and here Monteverdi draws upon all his resources. The structure is such that the dramatic music maintains a continuous flow. A ritornello in the form of a trio arrangement for two flutes and the thorough-bass instruments, two chitarroni and a cembalo, opens the scene, in which the chorus of the shepherds, written for five parts, requests Orfeo to fill the country with the charm of his song. A new ritornello, played by five viole da braccio, a contrabasso, two cembali, and three chitarroni, leads to Orfeo's song. The ritornello returns after each of the four stanzas with the exception of the last "Sol per te bella Euridice." The song is controlled by a rigid structure, without change in any of the stanzas. The melody, free from the element of recitation, has the quality of a simple aria, yet also the dignity which the chorus expected from Orfeo's song. The melody of Orfeo is at once taken up by the Pastore, who with utter joy finds that Orfeo's power has taken effect and that nature is beautified. This outburst of admiration and rejoicing is expressed by strengthening the character of an aria in the melody and by realizing a dancelike motion in the triple rhythm. At the very last line, with its renewed emphasis on the "happy day," the Messaggiera brings the news "Ahi caso acerbo." With the same suddenness with which the tragedy occurs, the character of the melody changes to a pathos befitting the catastrophe. In this scene Monteverdi attains an unmatched greatness, and what he achieves here is unique in the history of opera. He revived something of the Greek tragic sense, according to which extreme joy and serene happiness, to which only the immortals seem to have the right, are a challenge to Fate. This is accompanied by that utter unawareness of catastrophe which, in Greek tragedy, always has a terrifying effect. Orfeo alone is unapprehensive; the others have read the bitter tragedy in the face of the messenger, "in vista dolorosa," while Orfeo, ignorant of pain or harm, poses the question "D'onde vieni?" which Monteverdi was inspired to use as indicative of his terrible unawareness:

Ex. 83   x, 58

"To thee I come, Orfeo, an unhappy messenger of a still unhappier and more grievous accident; thy beautiful Euridice . . ."; it is only after this sentence, rendered in highly dramatic declamation, that Orfeo awakens to the threat of tragedy and interrupts the message with the exclamation "Ohimè che odo?" The Messaggiera concludes her mournful tidings with "Thy beloved wife is dead." Orfeo has but one exclamation: "Ohimè." The climax of the tragedy is thus anticipated, and then begins the lengthy report of the details of the accident. The recitation responds to the emotional quality of every word in a style that is not simply narrative, with a melody in which Monteverdi realizes characteristics that belong neither to an arioso nor to a recitative, yet which he always employs in a situation of the highest dramatic intensity, previously tried out in various madrigals. The Messaggiera's report about Euridice's death ends thus:

Ex. 84   xi, 61

Orfeo is silent throughout the report; it is the Pastori who first react to the "amara novella." This holding Orfeo back from any spontaneous reaction to the story makes the sudden shock convincing; he was totally unaware and is now stunned. It is as though he had not even heard what the Messaggiera recited at great length. For after the report has been sung and the two Pastori have expressed their reactions, Orfeo continues from the last words he heard, "La tua diletta sposa è morta," and begins with "Tu se' morta, se' morta mia vita," his final song of the act, in which he bids farewell to earth, sky, and sun, to join Euridice in death. This farewell song has the same melodic pathos as the Messaggiera's first uttering of the awful tidings. The act concludes with an elaborate concentration of chorus, soli, and orchestra, all in contemplation of the mournful event. The five-part chorus, *Ahi caso acerbo*, always inserting its impersonal pondering in the manner of a refrain, is set in contrast to the two tenors, two Pastori, who sing in trio fashion to the accompaniment of the regal and a chitarrone as thorough-bass instruments. The upper duet of the trio combination is in style and function the *concertino*, in opposition to the full chorus. This arrangement once again shows Monteverdi's sensitiveness to the dramatic implications of the text. The soli are an individual expression of pity for the sufferings of Euridice and Orfeo, one bitten by the serpent, the other pierced by grief: "Euridice e Orfeo, l'una punta da l'angue, l'altro dal duol trafitto"; while the impersonal chorus merely warns men not to trust the gods in view of this tragedy. Thus Monteverdi imparts a dramatic significance to the style of the *concertino*, of soli and contrasting tutti. But the climax is not shifted to the end of the act, which is contemplative, and the dramatic center remains in the scene of the Messaggiera.

The third act displays a new dramatic concentration, and beginning with the scene where Orfeo attempts by singing to persuade Caronte to grant access to Hades we again have a form of composition which grows and completes itself as it advances the drama. It is essentially a free form, uniquely adapted to the dramatic situation that gives rise to it. In this act the whole new art of soloistic singing is displayed. Orfeo's bold attempt at what might well be impossible for mortals, the supreme test of his gifts as a singer, would be a challenge to any composer. After the scene between Orfeo and Hope (Speranza), a dramatic recitative which culminates with the warning from Dante's *Commedia*, and an introductory sinfonia, Orfeo embarks on his aria *Possente spirto*, the most elaborate virtuoso aria of the opera. Its form is organized by the bass, which remains essentially the same in all but the fourth of the five stanzas. The continuity of the bass pattern for the stanzas does not apply to the rhythm, whose variation affords the solo voice a particular freedom. The frame of the melody is also retained for the solo part in the stanzas, but the deviations are so numerous as to make it impossible to decide which of the melodies of the stanzas is to be regarded as the basic form subject to variations. The fourth stanza, with its own bass, has its own melodic order: from the middle of the stanza to the end of the aria the alternative version of the solo part is broken off. In the earlier stanzas Monteverdi gave two versions of the melody: one a simple, unadorned form, the other provided with virtuoso ornamentation of dazzling brilliance. This presentation of a simple form and an ornate alternative which reflects the high standards of the art of solo singing in Monteverdi's period, is unique in seventeenth-century operatic literature. Apparently both versions have equal artistic value, since Monteverdi indicated in the score that, to the accompaniment of the regal and a chitarrone, Orfeo might sing one or the other. Did he intend the simple version for performances where no real star singers were available? For it would take a first-rate singer to render the ornate version adequately, and the simple form is suitable for singers of no particular training. Nevertheless, it is hard to believe that Monteverdi could even have imagined a production of a music drama apart from the cultivated entertainments at courts for which it was customary to hire great singers. From an aesthetic and dramatic point of view, the ornate version may be preferred. The fact that the ornamentation stops at a certain place not far from the end of the aria has, in all likelihood, a dramatic reason, and the degree of its virtuosity varies with the stanzas. Elaborate in the first stanza, the ornamentation is reduced in the second, greatly increased in the third, and after an elaborate beginning in the fourth, gradually decreases and stops at "O de le luci mie." The virtuosity seems to correspond to the intensity with which Orfeo makes his request of Caronte. When Orfeo first tries the effect of his brilliant skill, Monteverdi employs different instruments for the various stanzas and the ritornelli that separate the stanzas in order to heighten the effect. The accompanying instruments are two violins (first stanza), two cornetti (second stanza), two harps (third stanza), two violins and basso da braccio (fourth stanza), three viole da braccio and a contrabasso da viola (fifth stanza). When the vocal parts of the stanzas are characterized by virtuosity, the instrumental accompaniment and the ritornelli are equally brilliant, and as the virtuosity of the vocal parts decreases, so does that of the instruments. All end in simplicity, since the more intense Orfeo becomes, the more direct is his approach. After he has sung the moving "Sol tu nobile Dio" (fifth stanza) in an unembellished, bare form, Caronte confesses that he has been enchanted by Orfeo's song but still does not want to surrender to pity. Orfeo then presents his request in simple recitation with no instrumental accompaniment other than the thorough bass. The lines of the recitative are lowered by one tone through the scale, then followed, in chromatic rise, by the repeated, imploring phrase: "Rendete mi il mio ben, Tartarei Numi." Monteverdi uses such a structure in his later music dramas to produce the greatest intensity. Despite the rigidity of some of the structural elements, the whole scene presents a free evolution of form. In the aria the free variations of strophic order, built upon the same bass, attain an independent expression of great passion over a new form of the bass with a chromatic descent at the end of the fourth stanza. The simplicity of Orfeo's imploring (fifth stanza) is intensified in the *stile recitativo*, which is maintained for the rest of Orfeo's part in the act.

The act concludes with a madrigalesque chorus of the "Spirits," accompanied by a regal, an organo di legno, five tromboni, two bassi da gamba, and a contrabasso de viola, while a sinfonia for seven parts encloses the chorus.[5] Monteverdi has imparted new dramatic significance to the musical form by combining flexibility with a strictly disciplined structure. The *Orfeo* for the first time offers a musical, dramatic form that stands apart from all the traditional structures.

THE EVENTS OF 1608

In the year in which the *Orfeo* was produced, Monteverdi suffered the greatest personal loss in the death of his young wife Claudia at Cremona. He remained there for a time in the house of his father, who apparently gave him advice and consolation in his grief. But it was not long before he received an urgent letter from F. Follino, the chronicler of Mantuan court life under Vincenzo. In the letter, dated September 24, 1607,[6] Follino expressed the sympathy of the Duke and the court, but conveyed new and heavy demands on the creative work of the composer, for great preparations were in the making in Mantua. The wedding of Francesco, the heir apparent, with Margareta di Savoia was

---

[5] In two excellent studies the orchestra of Monteverdi has been discussed by J. A. Westrup, "Monteverdi and the Orchestra," in *M&L*, XXI (1940), 230ff. and by Paul Collaer, "L'orchestra di Claudio Monteverdi," in *Musica*, II (1943), 86ff.

[6] See Davari, *op. cit.*, p. 88.

planned for the spring of 1608, and the attendant festivities were to surpass any that the court at Mantua had ever undertaken. One of the chief events was to be a new music drama, and Follino summoned the composer to Mantua to begin his work. Dramatic music had already been recognized as a splendid medium for royal display, and Follino remarked that now was the moment for Monteverdi to reach the summit of fame that man can have on earth: "questo è il punto d'acquistarsi il sommo di quanta fama può avere un huomo in terra." Monteverdi quickly obeyed the summons to Mantua.

In consequence of the close communications he had maintained with the musical circles of the Florentine court, the Duke engaged Rinuccini to write the dramatic texts for the musical productions. In addition to the wedding festivities, Mantua was to celebrate the spring carnival, and to provide the carnival music Marco da Gagliano was called from Florence to Mantua in the fall of 1607 to produce the music to Rinuccini's *Dafne*, which was performed early in 1608. The elaborate preface which Marco wrote to his *Dafne*, an important source both for the nuptial festivities at Mantua and for Monteverdi's work,[7] is worth quoting: "Among the numerous admirable feasts that were ordered by His Highness upon the superb occasion of the wedding of Serenissimo Principe, his son, and Serenissima Infanta di Savoia, was the plan to represent a 'favola in musica.' This favola was *Arianna*, composed for the occasion by Signor Ottavio Rinuccini, whom the Duke had summoned to Mantua for that purpose. Signor Claudio Monteverdi, the most famous musician, head of the music at the court of His Highness, composed the arias in so exquisite a manner that we can affirm in all truth that the power of ancient music has been restored (*che si rinovasse il pregio dell' antica musica*) because they visibly moved the whole audience to tears."

Monteverdi is here praised as a most famous composer (*musico celebratissimo*) by a man who in connection with his Florentine activities was deeply involved in dramatic music, who contributed his *Dafne* to Mantua and witnessed the performance of *Arianna*. His praise was no empty compliment but a token of the reputation Monteverdi meanwhile had acquired among Italian musicians. Apparently it was also the first time that an outsider had compared Monteverdi's music to the music of ancient Greece. This reference was not to any

---

[7] I had the privilege to study the full score of Marco's *Dafne* in the copy of Dr. Alfred Einstein, for which I wish to express my gratitude. As is known, Eitner's publication of the *Dafne* is incomplete.

specific form or type of Greek music, but rather to the effect Greek music exercised upon man and the esteem in which music was held by the Greeks. It was the *pregio* (the value or the effect) of ancient music that had been restored, not any particular form of Greek music, as is sometimes mistakenly thought.

The composition of the *Arianna* was only one of the obligations the Mantuan wedding imposed on Monteverdi. Even at the time of the *Orfeo*, the demands made upon him by the court were extremely strenuous. In the *Dichiaratione* Giulio Cesare apologized for his brother's neglect of the dispute, saying that he was a very busy man who carried "not alone the burden of the church and court music, but in duty to the Duke also other extraordinary services, for the most part such as tournaments, balletti, comedies, various concerti, and lastly, the playing of the viola." Had Monteverdi composed music to "balletti, tournaments, dramas," previous to the *Orfeo* and the festivities of 1608? The remark of Giulio Cesare suggests such compositions. We know from a letter of Monteverdi's to Vincenzo from Cremona in December, 1604, that he had been occupied with the composition of music for a ballet based on the story of Endymion. Monteverdi acknowledged receipt of a letter in which the Duke demanded that he "should compose two entrate, one for the Stars that follow the Moon, the other for the Shepherds who follow Endymion; and also [that] he should compose two ballets, one for the Stars alone, the other for the Stars and the Shepherds together." Monteverdi suggested that for the first ballet he would compose an "aria allegra et corta" for all the instruments, to be danced to by all the Stars; that a different "aria" would follow, to be played by five viole da braccio and danced to by two Stars only, whereupon the first aria would be continued; and so the first and second arias would be further repeated, until the whole group of Stars, two by two, had performed the solo dance. Monteverdi added that he would await further instructions concerning the number of dancers which he needed in order to carry out the scheme of the ballet. Meanwhile he submitted to the Duke the second ballet for the Stars and the Shepherds, which he had already finished. There is no description of that part of the ballet, and its music is lost.[8] For what occasion the composition was intended we do not know, but such music may have been demanded as frequently as the remark of Giulio Cesare indicates.

At all events, music for intermezzi and balletti made up the additional

---

[8] See letter No. 3; ed. Malipiero, *Claudio Monteverdi*, pp. 131f.

commissions for the wedding of 1608. After the festivities were over, Monteverdi wrote that he had been requested to set fifteen hundred verses to music in short order.[9] The strain must have been taxing, for twenty years later he could think only with horror of the occasion and said that the speed with which he was expected to deliver large compositions had driven him almost to death.[10] Monteverdi also mentioned something about his ways of working—that he needed time for composition, to think through what he planned to compose. "I know one can compose fast, but fast and good do not go well together." The long process of thought that he needed is, indeed, recognizable in his works, which are notable for their discipline and logic, and their mastery of detail. He adds that hasty composition and performance can only produce "un mal recitar de versi, un mal concerto d'istromenti, et un mal portamento di armonie." The performance requires as much study and thoroughness as the composition; the *Arianna* "required five months of rehearsals in intensive work." [11] Monteverdi felt that the work of art placed great responsibilities upon the composer and refused commissions that did not allow him to do justice to those responsibilities. The artistic rewards, though not the material ones, were commensurate with his efforts.

With the exception of the *Lamento* and a few very brief and unrevealing excerpts given by Giovanni Battista Doni in his treatise on scenic music, the *Arianna* is lost. The reports we have concerning its origin, performance, and effect are, therefore, of particular importance. We know that Monteverdi worked closely with Rinuccini and that intrigues against the *Arianna* were started by the Florentine poet Cini and supported to some extent by Ferdinand of Gonzaga. Cini was anxious to replace the *Arianna* by his *Tetide*, with music by Peri. Nothing came of this intrigue, because Duke Vincenzo was determined to have Monteverdi's *Arianna* as the main drama. Another misfortune occurred during the period of preparation. In January, 1608, when Marco da Gagliano performed his *Dafne*, the star singer was the celebrated Caterina Martinelli, a pupil of Monteverdi, who had already been chosen for the role of Arianna. A few weeks later this brilliant artist died at the age of eighteen, and was commemorated by Monteverdi in a special composition. In her place, a singer from the famous troupe of artists, the Andreini, was engaged. Virginia, known as "La

[9] Letter No. 6, dated Cremona, December 2, 1608; *ibid.*, p. 138.

[10] Letter No. 89, dated Venice, May 1, 1627; recipient uncertain, possibly Alessandro Striggio; *ibid.*, p. 250.

[11] Letter No. 37, dated Venice, January 9, 1620; *ibid.*, p. 186.

Florinda," took over the part and performed to the admiration of the listeners.

In May, 1608, after their official wedding in Turin, the princely couple entered Mantua and the festivities began. On May 28, 1608, the *Arianna* was put on the stage. The luxury and brilliance of the production were so spectacular as to amaze all present. The crowd that attended the performance must have been enormous, for Follino says that six thousand persons were in the theater—a debatable figure that perhaps includes all the visitors. The Mantuans—that is, the nobility of Mantua—had to forego attendance at the theater in favor of the out-of-town guests. Follino reported that the captain of the ducal archers could hardly hold back the throng and keep the entrance free for the illustrious guests, anxious to display their wealth and luxury. "On account of the poetry alone and of the actors that took part, that opera—the *Arianna*—could well be classified as a beautiful work; but the opera became the subject of the greatest admiration in conjunction with the music of Claudio Monteverdi, a man whose great capacities are sufficiently known all over the world, but who on this occasion has surpassed his own faculty. The instruments, placed behind the scene, continually used for the accompaniment, were varied with any change in the character of the vocal music and were adapted to the brilliant voices of the singers, men and women. The lament of Arianna, abandoned by Theseus, was sung with so much warmth and feeling and represented in so moving a manner that all the listeners were most profoundly stirred and none of the ladies remained without tears." (This *Lamento* has been preserved.) The performance of the whole opera took about two and a half hours. In its musical-technical apparatus, the work was obviously as richly orchestrated and, with soloists and chorus, as elaborately constructed as the *Orfeo*.

A few days after the first performance of the *Arianna*, on June 2, Guarini presented his comedy *Idropica*. With various other Mantuan composers, Monteverdi was called upon to contribute to this production. According to custom, intermezzi were to be inserted between the acts of the comedy: a prologue, four intermezzi, and a licenza were needed. Gabrielo Chiabrera provided the poetry for all. The music of the prologue was composed by Monteverdi; Salomone Rossi composed the first intermezzo; Giovanni Giacomo Gastoldi, the second; a "messer Monco," the third; Giulio Cesare Monteverdi, the fourth; and Paolo Biat, the licenza. Monteverdi's music, as well as that of the other musicians, is lost. About the production Follino had this to say: "After the cardinals, princes, ambassadors and invited ladies had taken their seats, the customary signal of trumpets sounded from inside the stage (*si diede dalla parte di dentro del palco il solito segno del suono delle trombe*) and when the signal was given for the third time, the great curtain, very quickly, in the twinkling of an eye, disappeared. Three thick clouds could be seen, made so skillfully as to seem natural. Below the clouds, there were waves turning hither and thither, out of which there came gradually the head of a woman. This was Manto, the founder of Mantua. In well-measured movements she slowly rose to full sight, and by the time the trumpets ceased, she had reached the shores of a small island. There, standing amidst the reeds, she sang so delicately to the accompaniment of various instruments placed behind the scene that she enchanted all listeners."

Two days later, on June 4, another work of Monteverdi attracted the guests of the court. A mascherata, or balletto, was performed, the *Ballo dell' Ingrate*, composed *in genere rappresentativo*. Rinuccini and Monteverdi again worked together on this composition. Follino spares no praise, and, in pointing out the success of the ballo, he not only mentions its superior artistic quality, but stresses its effect on the audience. Monteverdi's music moved the listeners to tears, touched their hearts, and created a highly emotional state in the audience, as was his aim. The description of the emotional state into which his music transported audiences becomes more and more frequent. Coppini, whom we have already mentioned as the editor of Monteverdi's "spiritualized" madrigals, also attended the festivities in Mantua and witnessed the emotional reactions of the audience. "Claudio Monteverdi's music is of such excellence that those effects of music we read about to our great amazement in ancient sources should no longer appear strange. Of this, the *Arianna*, among many other compositions, gave clear evidence." Monteverdi showed himself "capable of forcefully making the famous audience weep thousands and thousands of tears." Indeed, the human element, as the basis of the affections, was the secret of Monteverdi's music and its spontaneous success. The theme was man, his passions and his experiences, and the artistic composition gave the theme universal validity.

The *Lamento d'Arianna* had an immediate success in Italy and was frequently imitated by Italian musicians. The composition was a favorite of Monteverdi's. He made an arrangement for five voices as a madrigal divided into four sections, which is included in the sixth book of madrigals, and at the end of his life, in the *Selva Morale e*

Spirituale (Venice, 1640–41), he presented a "spiritualized" version with the religious text "Jam moriar mi Filli." Entitled the *Pianto della Madonna*, it was the final work in the last collection published under his supervision. The full original version of the operatic *Lamento* is preserved in (among other sources) a Florentine manuscript. Its inclusion in this anthology of monodies was probably due to a performance of the *Arianna* given in Florence in 1614. Several other performances of the music drama are recorded, including one which Monteverdi saw at the end of his life, in Venice in 1640.

The composition of the *Ballo dell' Ingrate* apparently completed Monteverdi's creative share in the festival productions, although as maestro di cappella he was responsible for all musical performances, whether or not they included his own works. By June 10 the festivities of the wedding came to an end. From Follino's report we get the clear impression that Monteverdi was at the center of all artistic activities at the wedding. When Follino wrote the composer that this was an opportunity to acquire the greatest fame a man can earn, he was right. For after the events of 1608, Monteverdi became a European figure of such importance that he overshadowed not only his contemporaries, but also the great composers of the past.

Judging from the various arrangements made of it and its strong influence on the music of the time, the *Lamento d'Arianna* seems to have been the chief composition in the music drama. *Lasciate mi morire* is a purely monodic composition with *basso continuo*.[12] It is not a strophic song, for though the caesurae of the stanzas are maintained, the composition presents new material in every stanza. The form renews itself with every fresh subject, and consequently has the greatest individuality and adapts itself to each dramatic situation. The difficulty such a form imposes was in Monteverdi's mind many years later when in 1633 he wrote that he had to labor hard while composing the *Lamento d'Arianna*. No model, no book, had given him any aid.

He was struggling with the problem of imitation in art. What is imitation, and what should be imitated? These questions, always in his mind and ever present in his composition, involved the very existence of music as an art. For Monteverdi believed that imitation as a principle gives birth to any artistic work. Although absolutely certain of the principle, which he had taken from the Greek school of thought, and

[12] See Malipiero, *Opere*, XI, 161–167. Cf. Peter Epstein, "Dichtung und Musik in Monteverdis 'Lamento d'Arianna,'" in *ZfMW*, X (1927–1928), 216ff. See also J. A. Westrup, "Monteverdi's 'Lamento d'Arianna,'" in *MR*, I (1940), 144ff. Cf. Xavier de Courville, "L'Ariane de Monteverdi," in *RM*, III (1921), 23ff.

specifically from Plato, he was always searching for the object to be imitated in music. He had no doubt about it in general—the object was invariably the affection with its indispensable foundation in human existence and experience. The text established the affection, and Monteverdi always placed the human implications first and foremost. The difficulty was to apply the general principle to the specific case. Was it the general affection which the text as a whole indicated that should be imitated? If so, the text must be such that all the emotional qualities of the poem could be reduced to one predominant affection. At one time Monteverdi did say that this was the object of musical imitation. Or, were the affections, as they appeared sentence by sentence in the poem, the proper subjects for imitation? At another time Monteverdi indicated that this was so. Or should the affection of a single word be imitated? At one time Monteverdi objected to such a procedure, but in his works we find more than once that the individual affection of a single word is imitated. Each work involved him anew in the same problems and the same struggles; the musical form of each composition depended on his decision in this matter. It is clear that Monteverdi was constantly concerned with the problem of imitation, not as a technical device, but as the basic conception of artistic form.

The melody of the *Lamento d'Arianna* is built upon an understanding of the affections as they are formulated, line by line, sentence by sentence, and stanza by stanza. Moreover, at certain places in the text, at the imploring exclamation "Ah Teseo mio," for instance, or at the words "Invan piangendo, invan gridando aita la misera Arianna," the melodic line responds to the affection of even a single word. Such a form is so difficult to master that only a genius can handle it successfully. The danger is that the melodic pieces may never make a musical whole. But there are two devices that help to make an entity out of the individual melodic lines: first, the recurrence of predominant intervals used in conjunction with the general human situation of the *Lamento;* and second, the running of the melodic lines into one another in such a manner that each seems to result from the preceding one or to prepare for the next. With regard to the first device, the expressive intervals that are to prevail in the composition as a whole are presented in the first section of the *Lamento*. Monteverdi's use of poignant intervals here gives the basic affection of the *Lamento,* and the intervals recur throughout the composition where they maintain a more or less stable connotation. The second device may best be demonstrated by an illustration:

Ex. 85 XI, 165

Here each melodic line seems to grow out of another. The exclamation "Ah Teseo!" contains one of the prevailing intervals of the first section as does the phrase "lascerai tu morire," although it logically continues the exclamation. Even the chromatic rise, imitative of weeping and crying (*piangere, gridare*), comes naturally, without forcing; in fact, one almost expects the chromaticism after the chromatic interval on "morire." After being driven chromatically to the highest point, the melody drops down by way of a dissonant interval, directly expressive of the misery of Arianna, and the two concluding phrases are a logical continuation of the melody. Though responsive to every detail in the text, the melody proceeds according to its own logic, so that the procedure is entirely comprehensible on musical grounds.

The human qualities of Monteverdi's music defy abstract definition. Monteverdi himself said that the purpose of writing tones of such poignancy was to arouse sympathy with the suffering of a noble woman. His was an art of seeing, of knowing man and human nature, of setting music not so much to words as to the human accents with which the world resounds, of creating an artistic work expressive of human experience. Monteverdi's music is based on a sympathetic communication between the listener and the human force of the composition.

The *Ballo dell' Ingrate*, published thirty years later in the eighth book of madrigals, is equally a contribution to dramatic music. Monteverdi designated the work as a composition *in genere rappresentativo*, the term for theatrical music. Amor, Venus, Pluto, four Shadows of Hades, and eight Ungrateful Souls are named as the "Interlocutori," and the scenery is described as showing the entrance to the Inferno. There is some resemblance between the *Ballo* and the Hades scene in *Orfeo*, if merely on the basis of the characteristic subject. In both works, Pluto is implored to grant extraordinary requests. In the *Ballo dell' Ingrate* Amor beseeches his mother Venus to persuade Pluto to allow the Ungrateful Souls to come up from their abode of suffering and punishment. The Ungrateful Souls are those of women and girls who in their earthly lives foolishly refused the favors of Amor. Amor feels a nasty desire to see how they fared in Hell, where they are being punished for their insults to him. The *Ballo* begins with the scene in which Amor begs his mother to take on the role of an intermediary. Venus agrees, and with her all-powerful charm is successful in winning over Pluto. The Ungrateful Souls are permitted to come to the light of day. Clad in ashen gowns, with tears over their faces and clothes, and with mournful gestures, they step forth from the cave that leads to the Inferno, and the actual dance begins. This sight moves even Amor. Their joy at seeing the light of day is short-lived. Pluto asks the ladies of the audience to take the deplorable fate of these Ungrateful Souls to their hearts and give Amor what is Amor's due as long as they live. The Souls must return into darkness. The scene of their return to the Inferno is most moving; its human qualities rise far above the somewhat flippant character of the story. One of the Ungrateful Souls sings her farewell to light and air: "Aer sereno e puro Addio per sempre," and a group of four admonish the ladies: "Apprendete pietà Donne e Donzelle."

The text is far inferior to Rinuccini's *Arianna*. Though based on a dramatic theme, much of the poetry Rinuccini wrote for the *Ballo* has a narrative and descriptive character that does not lend itself too readily to Monteverdi's dramatic style, though the music raises the work beyond the quality of the poetry. The narrative caesurae, however, could not always be avoided, and the lines of the recitative follow rather closely the lines of the text. For the most part, Monteverdi must apply the style of the recitative to the narrative text, but as often as possible he approaches the arioso within the recitation. The sensitive reactions of the melodic line to all the emotional qualities of the text interrupt the simple recitation, and there are many passages for the solo voices that follow an independent melodic evolution. The part of Pluto often breaks away from the recitation into a freely developed arioso; and the long monologue of Venus, when she pleads with Pluto in favor of Amor, also displays the subtleties of a melody based directly on the connotations of the words. This is most strikingly apparent when, in imitation of the text, "invan gentil guerriero move in campo d'honor," the melody proceeds to a warlike theme in strict triple rhythm. Melodic passages such as those set to "fido Amante versar lagrime e sangue" also show the growth of the melody out of the affections.

The instrumental compositions have special significance and make up the largest part of the *Ballo*. Monteverdi prescribed five viole da braccio with harpsichord and chitarrone, and the number of instruments could be doubled if necessary on account of a larger hall. Three forms of instrumental composition are used: the sinfonia, the entrata, and the ritornello. The sinfonia, an independent composition, is skillfully inserted in order to give the illusion of a change of scene; it appears between the first dialogue, in which Amor presents his request to Venus, and the dialogue of Pluto and Venus, who intercedes in behalf of her son. The entrata is the ballet proper, played for the first time when the Ungrateful Souls appear from the Inferno, and repeated toward the end when they return after Pluto condemns them. While the Ingrate are taking their positions, the dance music is used as an *entrata* in the proper meaning of the word, and then serves for the dance itself. With the exception of a middle section, the same material is used for the entire ballo, but the basic rhythms, the steps and figures of the dance, change from section to section. The ritornello, true to its name, is a brief passage inserted after each stanza of Pluto's great recitative aria, *Dal tenebroso orror*, which comes directly after the dance.

A strong case has been made for the French characteristics of the *Ballo dell' Ingrate*. It is true that Rinuccini was considerably influenced by the French ballet de cour when he worked at the French court, with which he was connected as a natural result of the intermarriage of the royal house with the Medici. That the Italian had absorbed the French art of the courtly ballet is obvious, and when editing the poetry of his father, Rinuccini's son acknowledged his indebtedness to French models. The French influence on the *Ballo dell' Ingrate* makes itself felt in the general character and the structural outline of the text, but in Monteverdi's music no such influence can be detected, even in the entrata. The technique of rhythmically altering the same tonal material section by section had been practiced in Italian instrumental dances since the beginning of the sixteenth century, and the style of the instrumental forms and of all the vocal parts was very much Monteverdi's own.[13]

With the festivities of 1608, Monteverdi's activities in dramatic music came to an end, and his Mantuan period drew to its close. Immediately after the performances of the dramatic compositions that had brought him so much success and honor, Monteverdi found himself in the throes of a crisis. Despite honors and fame, despite recognition that Monteverdi was the rising star among all the Italian musicians, the Duke was reluctant to express his gratitude in material form. He gave generous remunerations to others, to outsiders such as Marco da Gagliano, who had contributed to the festivities of the marriage; but he did nothing in recognition of the work that had been artistically the most prominent. Completely exhausted, Monteverdi left Mantua, determined not to return, and went to his father in Cremona. He received an order to take up new work, through Annibal Chieppio, the counselor of the Duke. On December 8, 1608, Monteverdi, in a lengthy document, gave the reasons for his absence, for his irritation, and for his bitterness. But once again his father exerted a beneficial influence and persuaded him to put up with conditions at Mantua.[14]

---

[13] Prunières, *Claudio Monteverdi*, pp. 83ff.

[14] *RaM*, IX (Florence, 1936), 70, had the note "che nella Biblioteca Comunale di Mantova la signora Maddalena Pacifico ha ritrovato un codice autografo contenente il testo di tutti gli *Intermezzi e prologhi* musicati da Monteverdi." I investigated this manuscript at the Biblioteca Comunale in Mantua; it has the code H I 27 and the title *Rime diverse*. Although the manuscript is an important collection of texts of *Intermedii* with some interesting and detailed directions, it is not an autograph of Monteverdi; nor does it contain the texts of his works.

Fausto Torrefranca, "Il Lamento di Erminia di Claudio Monteverdi," in *Inedito, Quaderno Musicale*, II (Rome, 1944), 31–41 (the composition, *ibid.*, 1–8), has suggested that this *Lamento*, based on a passage from Tasso's *Gerusalemme liberata* (Canto XIX, stanzas 105–108) is a work of Monteverdi. He found the composition in a seventeenth-century collection of arias. The section of the manuscript where this *Lamento* appears has signed compositions of Ippolito Macchiavelli, Giuseppino (Giuseppe Cenci), Cesare Marotti, and, with the name of its author, the *Lamento di Arianna* by Monteverdi (No. 20). The *Lamento di Erminia*, "cantato dalla Saponara in casa Savelli" (No. 14), is anonymous, and its attribution to Monteverdi is purely hypothetical. Unfortunately, Torrefranca does not mention where he found the manuscript; nor does he refer to its present owner. The bibliographical evidence in support of Monteverdi's authorship is unconvincing; the arguments brought up in favor of 1610 (the year when Monteverdi was in Rome), as the date of composition, and of 1611, as the date of performance, are very strained; and the method of the stylistic discussion is not historical. Unless more solid evidence turns up, the attribution to Monteverdi appears unacceptable.

CHAPTER TWELVE

Sacred Music in Mantua

WHEN the position of maestro di cappella, which Benedetto Pallavicino had occupied, became vacant in November, 1601, Monteverdi sent Duke Vincenzo a formal letter of application for the post, asking that he be allowed to conduct the musical affairs of both court and church.[1] The answer was favorable, and from 1602 on, Monteverdi seems to have been responsible for all the musical activities at the Mantuan court. That same year he and his family acquired Mantuan citizenship, granted as a favor by the Duke.

The position of maestro di cappella at the court church of Santa Barbara imposed new duties on Monteverdi. In this capacity he had to supervise and also to provide the music for the services or for special occasions of a religious character. It must have been the ambition of an artist that made him so anxious to re-establish the personal union of the two positions, maestro di cappella della camera and maestro di cappella della chiesa, which had existed under Giaches de Wert. It is hardly conceivable that he felt an impulse to devote himself to religious music, for he did not compose any religious music until it was demanded of him by the position he occupied in Mantua, and it was twenty-eight years before he decided to publish any new sacred compositions. In 1610 he published a selection of religious works under the title: *Sanctissimae Virgini Missa senis vocibus Ad Ecclesiarum Choros Ac Vespere pluribus decantandae cum nonnullis sacris concentibus.* For nearly a decade Monteverdi had composed religious works whenever called upon to do so, but he obviously did not feel it necessary to publish these

---

[1] See letter No. 1, dated November 28, 1601; ed. Malipiero, *Claudio Monteverdi,* pp. 127f.

compositions. This is in sharp contrast with his attitude toward his secular music, for his collections of madrigals appeared regularly, as though he were anxious to make each artistic phase known in its turn. But when he finally made a selection of his religious music, his reasons for doing so had no concern with any artistic program, but were purely personal.

Monteverdi did not enjoy the economic security to which his fame, the volume of his work, and his leading position in Mantua entitled him. Financial pressure, which did not cease until he left Mantua for Venice, made the care of his family difficult, and he frequently alluded in his letters to the poverty of his two sons. In order to improve his financial situation, he decided to enter Francesco, his oldest son, in the Roman seminary, and in the hope of securing a grant for him, he planned a special journey to Rome. Furnished with powerful letters of recommendation, he had good reason to anticipate success, especially since he could count on the good services of Cardinal Ferdinand Gonzaga. The Cardinals Montalto and Borghese had the final word in the matter, and Monteverdi's letters of recommendation were addressed to both. So in the fall of 1610 he made the trip to Rome, and on his way south called upon Caccini in Florence. In a letter he mentioned that he had heard the daughter of Caccini, a singer of great fame, and although he found that she sang well and played well on the lute (*chitaronato*) and harpsichord, he preferred Signora Adriana, of Mantua, who sang, played, and spoke, all in the best manner.[2] Both in Florence and Rome, he was eager to meet new singers, who might be available for engagements at Mantua.

Before setting out on the journey to Rome, Monteverdi prepared himself artistically, hoping that his work might further the purpose of his trip. In the spring of 1610 he had begun the composition of a Mass which he intended to submit and dedicate to Pope Paul V, of the Borghese family. Paul V sought to establish the ideals of the Counter Reformation as set forth by the Council of Trent, and passionately insisted upon the privileges of the papacy, thinking to invest it with new powers over worldly rulers. It was during his pontificate that the famous struggle about the prerogatives of church and state broke out between Venice and Rome.

The relation of Paul's policy to the ideals of the Counter Reformation was not without its influence on Monteverdi. In order that his work

---

[2] Letter No. 10; *ibid.*, p. 146.

might be favorably received, he composed the Mass in the conservative Northern style, which the Papal Chapel was known to have accepted for liturgical music. It would be a complete misunderstanding of Monteverdi and of the principles of his work, were we to regard this choice as opportunism or expediency. The style of the past was to him an exclusively artistic problem and a very complicated one, fraught with difficulties both technical and religious. He knew from the *Prima Prattica* that religious intensity could be given only by Netherlandish polyphony, and selected from the vast output of the Northerners not what was nearest to him in time but what he thought to be the most genuine manifestation of the style. His choice is evidence both of his discrimination and of his considerable knowledge. He selected the motet *In illo tempore* by Gombert as the model for his Mass for six voices, with the number of voices raised to seven for the last Agnus Dei. Such a choice was no accident. According to the *Dichiaratione*, Monteverdi traced the derivation of the *Prima Prattica* properly from Ockeghem, at a time when this ancestor of all Netherlandish musicians was forgotten, and here again his stylistic insight led him to a composition of Gombert.

Monteverdi's Mass has, in its published form, an additional *basso continuo* to be used for the organ accompaniment, the *continuo* being merely a *basso seguente*. It has, therefore, neither the function nor the characteristics of the more modern thorough bass and could well be discarded. Monteverdi apparently yielded to the demands of his publisher that he present the work nominally, if not factually, in accordance with modern tendencies. Such demands were frequent at that time, and composers met them by merely adding a duplication of the vocal bass. That Monteverdi composed the Mass for a choir only is indicated in the work itself.

Monteverdi began to compose the Mass half a year before he went on the trip to Rome, since he was no longer accustomed to writing in the manner of the past and needed extensive studies in order to render the composition appropriately. When he composed his *Sacrae Cantiunculae*, he had found himself at variance with the Northern style, but now that his technical skill had grown immensely, we should expect him to have mastered it. We find, however, that his nature was still opposed to the style and he was not at ease when writing in a manner that he himself had made obsolete. As evidence of this, we have a letter written by Bernardo Casola on July 16, 1610, commenting on Monteverdi's labors, in which he calls this Mass for six voices a composition of study and great toil: "una missa a sei voci, di studio e fatica grande." [3]

His extensive studies and general artistic maturity did, however, enable Monteverdi to write a faultless composition in the old idiom and to imitate the past with an uncommonly pure feeling for the style. Many other contemporary musicians wrote in the polyphonic style of the sixteenth century; the Roman school especially was full of such composers: Giovanelli, Nanini, Lodovico da Vittoria, the Spaniard, to name only a few. But their work was a direct outgrowth of the style of Palestrina; there had been no break in their development and no lack of uniformity in their work. To them, choral polyphony was still a living style which they believed in as long as they composed. Monteverdi was the first to make use of the style as one who knew he was dealing with a historical subject. During the seventeenth and part of the eighteenth centuries, composers consciously imitated Palestrina's style, as Monteverdi imitated Gombert, but none of them, not even the most gifted, like Alessandro Scarlatti, could keep the style of his day from leaving its traces in the Masses à la Palestrina; none of them could produce the purity of style we find in Monteverdi's Gombert Mass. Monteverdi used all the complicated devices the Netherlandish composers had developed in treating a structure based on a *cantus firmus*. Augmentation and diminution of the *cantus firmus* play a role in his work equal to their role in the Northern style. Canonic and fugal devices are as faithfully handled as in the compositions of Gombert, who was a master of canonic structures. In his treatment of the extensive melismata and by his avoidance of caesurae and cadences, Monteverdi proved that he had full control over the very essentials of the Netherlandish style. A retrospective evaluation, therefore, shows that the earlier *Sacrae Cantiunculae* were much farther removed from Northern art than was the Mass of 1610. When Monteverdi composed his Mass, time had considerably widened the gap that separated him from the sixteenth-century musicians, so that his effort to force himself into the spirit of their style was all the more laborious. A total renunciation of his musical nature, the Mass is unquestionably the purest imitation of the sixteenth-century style; yet there are brief passages in which the grouping of rhythms and the handling of melodic sequences betray the fact that Monteverdi was a composer of the seventeenth century.

The rest of the works in the publication of 1610 differ widely from the Mass. The letter of Casola suggests that not only the Mass but also

[3] See Davari, *op. cit.*, p. 99.

the compositions for the vespers were the work of the early summer of 1610, but it is possible that Monteverdi merely selected compositions from his previous output of religious music, which must have grown impressively in the course of a decade. The title of the collection of 1610 is astonishing enough, not with regard to the Mass, which is said to have been written for the use of church choirs, but with regard to the vespers and some additional sacred compositions, which are designated as having been written for use in the chapels or palaces (literally: "rooms") of the princes: "Ad Sacella sive Principum Cubicula accommodata." If these compositions had only a general religious character, and were not committed to a specific liturgy, we could understand their use in church and palace alike. But the compositions are liturgical in the strictest sense and definitely related to specific services which could never take place in profane surroundings. If the reference to a performance in the palace has any meaning at all, it must mean that the compositions were subject to a purely artistic and aesthetic understanding. This would be comprehensible only if the principles of art were given precedence over those of the liturgy, a supposition which is confirmed to some extent by the style of the compositions.

In view of Monteverdi's artistic style, his treatment of the liturgy was more conservative than one might expect. It has generally been overlooked that Monteverdi selected his compositions for one and the same liturgy, and was following the order required by the officium of the first vespers "In Festis Beatae Mariae Virginis." All but two of the fourteen works can be assigned their proper liturgical place. It was the proprium of the ecclesiastical hour that Monteverdi intended to represent. Were it not for *Duo Seraphim*, the only composition that disturbs the order of the specific liturgy, all the works could be taken as making up one liturgical entity.[4] In speaking of these compositions, Casola also indicates that they were for only one service of the vespers.

The order Monteverdi gave to his compositions is that of the liturgy. The group begins with *Domine ad adiuvandum*, the initial part of the

---

[4] While *Audi Coelum*, though not prescribed liturgically, is related to the veneration of St. Mary, the composition *Duo Seraphim* seriously disturbs the liturgical unity. For *Duo Seraphim*, with the verse "Tres sunt qui testimonium dant" does not belong to the liturgy of the vespers. It is a responsorial chant and, in accordance with all responsories, follows a lesson. Its liturgical place is in the third nocturn of the matin, to be sung after the eighth lesson on Sundays in the period from the third Sunday after Pentecost to Advent. Hence only when a Feast of St. Mary falls on a Sunday within that period, will *Duo Seraphim* be the responsory in the third nocturn of the matin. It never can be part of the vespers. Yet Monteverdi united *Duo Seraphim* and the three other soloistic compositions under the aspect of a common style.

ordinary of the ecclesiastical hours, not "an Introit based on the Doxology 'Domine ad adiuvandum.'"[5] Psalm 69, *Deus in adiutorium*, is used only for the antiphon of the Introit of the Mass on the twelfth Sunday after Pentecost, but no Introit has an antiphonal style that resembles the *cantus firmus* of Monteverdi's work. At the beginning of any of the ecclesiastical hours—"in principio omnium horarum"—the *Pater noster* and *Ave Maria* are to be said, and *Deus in adiutorium* to be chanted, to which *Domine ad adiuvandum* is, of course, the response, to be followed immediately by the doxology *Gloria Patri*. Monteverdi placed the tonus of the recitation in the cantus, but disregarded the flexions at the end of the verse lines:

Ex. 86 XIV, 123

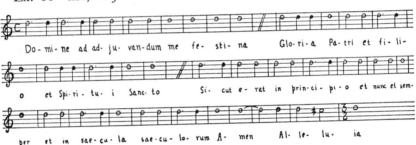

(The repetitions of the *Alleluja* which follow have not the quotation of the chant.)

The second composition, *Dixit Dominus Domino Meo*, opens the *Commune per annum*, the specific liturgy of the vespers "In Festis B. Mariae Virginis." The liturgy requires the singing of five psalms with their antiphons, a hymn, and the Magnificat with its antiphon. The required antiphons and psalms are the following: 1. Antiphon *Dum esset rex* with Psalm 109, *Dixit Dominus*; 2. Antiphon *Laeva ejus* with Psalm 112, *Laudate pueri*; 3. Antiphon *Nigra sum* with Psalm 121, *Laetatus sum*; 4. Antiphon *Jam hiems transiit* with Psalm 126, *Nisi Dominus*; 5. Antiphon *Speciosa facta es* with Psalm 147, *Lauda Jerusalem*. The hymn of the day is *Ave maris stella*, and the Magnificat has the antiphon *Sancta Maria succurre miseris, juva pusillanimes, refove flebiles: ora pro populo*.

[5] See Hans F. Redlich, "Monteverdi's Religious Music," in *M&L*, XXVII (London, 1946), 209. This essay is a review of Malipiero's volumes of Monteverdi's religious music—a review in which Redlich shows his comprehensive knowledge of Monteverdi's work. As competent as his musical interpretation is, his attributions of the compositions to the liturgical services are somewhat too generous.

Monteverdi faithfully followed the order, and the five psalms are those prescribed for the feast. Artistically, these psalm compositions are uniform in style, being written for large groups of instruments and voices, in the *stile concertato* or in polychoral form. Monteverdi has initial compositions that precede the last four psalms, 112, 121, 126, and 147; they are: *Nigra sum, Pulchra es, Duo Seraphim,* and *Audi Coelum.* Like the psalm compositions they have stylistic unity—all are composed for from one to three solo voices, with accompaniment of the *basso continuo.* Whereas all the psalm compositions are based on the psalm tone, which is artistically rendered in various ways, the four initial compositions do not have the *cantus firmus.* Are they all antiphons? Only *Nigra sum sed formosa* is the proper antiphon for the third psalm. In addition to *Nigra sum,* Monteverdi's *Pulchra es, amica mea* is based on a text of the Song of Solomon, as are all five of the proper liturgical antiphons. *Pulchra es, et decora* is the antiphon of the fifth psalm in the lauds of the Feast of Assumption of St. Mary (August 15). That Monteverdi intended the four compositions to function in the place of the proper antiphons we have no doubt, for the liturgy of the day is observed in the rest of the collection. Included is the hymn *Ave maris stella,* set for a double choir of eight voices, which is the hymn prescribed for the liturgy. The *cantus firmus* of the hymn is placed in the uppermost part. The collection concludes with two compositions of the Magnificat, both using the customary psalm tone. The antiphon to the Magnificat has been omitted, and no composition has been put in its place. We are unable to give any reason for the inclusion of two renderings of the Magnificat, one more elaborate than the other; but both are written in the same "mode." If a strict adherence to the mode can be claimed for these works, the first mode undoubtedly prevails. Finally, there is the *Sonata sopra Sancta Maria ora pro nobis,* which Monteverdi placed between the fifth psalm and the hymn. The formula of the litany, "Sancta Maria, ora pro nobis"—there is but one exclamation repeated eleven times in the composition—is not prescribed for the officium of the vespers and seems to be an artistic addition made by Monteverdi on his own initiative.[6] Although a proper liturgical place cannot be assigned to this work, its religious connotation fits the general content of the collection, so that even liturgically it does not disturb the unity as much as, for instance, *Duo Seraphim.* Despite minor changes, the collection as a whole observes the liturgical order.

---

[6] Attention may be called to the text of the antiphon of the Magnificat which contains the words: "*Sancta Maria* succurre miseris, . . . : *ora pro populo.*"

How far do the works preserve a liturgical quality? The only consistent liturgical procedure seems to be the *cantus firmus*, which is maintained in the psalm compositions and the Magnificat, as well as in the hymn and the sonata upon the litany. The use of the complete psalm, as the rite prescribes, and the regular inclusion of the doxology at the end of the psalm may also reflect a faithfulness to the liturgy, but the overpowering impression made by the vespers is of their artistic quality. Is this not a serious contradiction? We have assumed that the Mass has a liturgical, religious character, though there can be no denying that it also embodies artistic principles. But it is clear that in the vespers Monteverdi has made a bold advance toward a modern style in religious music. Something of an artistic radicalism, generally so foreign to Monteverdi's temper, breaks through. He is moving religious music away from its sixteenth-century basis and for the first time making a determined attempt to modernize sacred music by giving secular and sacred forms the common denominator of a unified style. It is a systematic plan, because he submits all the works of the collection, except the Mass, to a radical modernization; it is a comprehensive plan, because he uses all shades and varieties of the modern, secular style; it is a radical plan, because he adopts all the elements of the style without exception and without hesitation. There is no precedent in musical literature for this systematic, comprehensive, and radical procedure, but only isolated examples, which may themselves be the result of Monteverdi's advance. Taken together, the vespers and the Mass bring out the irreconcilable conflict in religious music, which has already been discussed. The appearance of this conflict in the artistic work itself, and not merely in a theoretical dispute, shows the extent of the cleavage. Monteverdi had gained such mastery of profane forms that the expansion of their idiom into all other forms became a necessity. The tendency to expand is inherent in any style that has on its side the strength, the artistic program, and the aspirations of the time. Such expansions occur repeatedly in musical history, especially at turning points where new styles have their beginning. When he carried over the profane vocabulary into sacred music, Monteverdi was only recognizing its inherent force. The religious compositions have now lost their artistic independence and originality and take second place in the stylistic order of music.

In accordance with this modernization, the vespers exhibit nearly all varieties of the *stile concertato*, though the use of the monodic *stile recitativo* is limited. The principles of the *concertato* are worked out chiefly as contrasts of various media, opposed to each other and vying one with another. The contrast between solo voice and instrumental accompaniment is, of course, the simplest and most direct manifestation. Similarly the soloistic voices can be grouped together as a duet or trio in opposition to the accompaniment. In both cases, the accompaniment is performed by the instrument which has the part of the *basso continuo*, which in the vespers is the organ. This is the arrangement of the *concertato* in *Nigra sum*, *Pulchra es*, *Duo Seraphim*, and *Audi Coelum*, and in sections of the two Magnificat compositions. A solo voice can also be set over against a large body of instrumental accompaniment, as is the case in sections of the Magnificat I and, on a large scale, throughout the *Sonata sopra Sancta Maria ora pro nobis*, whose accompaniment requires, besides the organ, a large orchestra consisting of two violini da braccio, two cornetti, two tromboni (or one trombone and one viola da braccio), one viola da braccio (or a duet, in case one trombone is replaced by another viola), and one trombone doppio.

In regard to the choral combinations, the principles of the concerted style allowed numerous variations. There can be a pure contrast of two choral groups accompanied by the organ, illustrated in the psalm composition *Nisi Dominus* for ten voices divided in two equal choirs, or a large choral group may be contrasted with a large orchestra in a simultaneous accompaniment of contrasting nature, as in *Domine ad adiuvandum*. The concerted style may also be presented by voices in the style of soli contrasting with a large chorus, as in the psalm *Laudate pueri*. There may also be the free alternation of soloistic and choral passages that is to be seen in various other compositions. Again, the *concertato* may be expressed by setting formal vocal and instrumental sections against each other, as in the orchestral ritornello, which occurs in the hymn *Ave maris stella* or in the psalm *Dixit Dominus*. Thus the composer may use the *stile concertato* in ever changing combinations. Monteverdi gave each composition its own special medium, so that the collection does not repeat any one treatment and represents a comprehensive cross section of the fascinating changes of the style.

In contrast to the antiphons of the liturgy, *Nigra sum* and *Pulchra es*, Monteverdi's compositions use a more extended text. His selection from the *Canticum Canticorum* has, for instance, these lines: "Nigra sum sed formosa filiae Jerusalem, Ideo dilexit me rex et introduxit me cubiculum et dixit mihi: surge, amica mea et veni iam hiems transiit umber abiit et recessit flores apparuerunt in terra nostra tempus putationis advenit." The third antiphon of the liturgy has only the first part of

Nigra sum, and the text *Jam hiems* is used for a fourth, separate antiphon, but Monteverdi combines them in one work.

Nigra sum reveals its relation to the principle of the *concertato* only in the contrast of the solo voice and the *basso continuo*. The melodic style is marked by elements of a recitative, like that which Monteverdi had used in parts of his last madrigals and especially in his dramatic work. The declamatory character of *Nigra sum* comes closest to the style of some of the solo parts in the *Orfeo*. The freedom from any preconceived pattern results in that improvisation which becomes more and more characteristic of Monteverdi's declamatory melodies. Monteverdi conveys a feeling of freedom and spontaneity, despite the fact that he organizes and balances the phrases with care and uses repetition of phrases, literal or varied, as an organizing factor. That improvisation does not imply formlessness can be seen in the over-all structure of *Nigra sum*: the whole second part, *Surge amica mea*, is literally and completely repeated in the fashion of an aria structure.

This declamatory recitative, taken over from madrigalesque and operatic surroundings, recurs with stylistic purity only once in the rest of the vespers, in the first section of *Audi Coelum*, which is written for a solo voice, while the second section, *Omnes hanc ergo sequamur*, continues in choral style for six voices. The operatic origin of the recitative is here emphatically brought out. The endings of the melodic phrases are often provided with elaborate coloraturas, such as the *Orfeo* had in greater abundance; and these endings are repeated in the manner of an echo, actually prescribed: "gaudio, *adio;* benedicam, *dicam,*" and so forth. The Florentine composers were especially fond of such echo effects in their dramatic compositions. With the inclusion of *Omnes hanc ergo* as a chorus structurally joined to the first section, the whole composition, *Audi Coelum*, solo and chorus, has the makings of an operatic scene, so far as structure is concerned. In its combination of two different media, each worked out in its own style, and in its artistic entity, *Audi Coelum* is a complete cantata in the seventeenth-century baroque style and as such, one of the first of its kind. The appearance of a sacred text is merely accidental and is certainly not reflected in the style of the music.

The two other soloistic compositions of the group, with their contrast between solo and accompaniment, treat the *stile concertato* in a more exhaustive manner. They embody the style, not only as to the medium, but in all their structural elements, and predominantly in their melody. *Pulchra es* once again lengthens the text, as Monteverdi uses the two verses of the *Canticum* (II, I, 6; 3 and 4) in full. This composition written for two soprani works out the trio combination with the soloistic duet and the *basso continuo*, and to a certain extent *Duo Seraphim* also maintains the combination at least for its first section; when, in the second half, the text proceeds to "Tres sunt qui testimonium dant," a third voice is added to the previous duet—a characteristic realism in which the word "three" is taken literally. The typical features of the trio, however, are best shown in the special handling of the vocal duet. In sharp contrast to the "improvised" melody of the recitative, the melodic motion of the concerted style is regulated schematically. The phrases are patterns, as concise in motif as in rhythm, which are used to create uniform analogies and correspondence. Repetition and the use of stereotyped materials predominate. It is astonishing how far Monteverdi has advanced in constructing melodic formulas of a typical character. The combination of the solo duet, furthermore, produces a parallelism of voices, largely in thirds, which is a basic texture of the trio style; even when the voices enter successively and suggest a contrapuntal imitation, the parallelism links them harmonically. In addition to an effect of stylistic purity, the mannerisms themselves have acquired almost the smoothness of a routine.

Duo Seraphim, in many passages the more artistically valuable work of the two, experiments with a fantastically elaborate ornamentation of the solo voices. The melody is studded with ornaments, arranged in imitation of successive parts or in parallelism of thirds. This arrangement practically redoubles the virtuosity used to express the jubilation of the text "Plena est omnis terra gloria est" and "Sanctus, sanctus, sanctus, Deus Sabaoth," as even the simple form is intended to convey symbolically what the text implies. The words "et hi tres unum sunt" are given in simple triads, and on the word "unum" the three voices sing in unison:

Ex. 87 XIV, 194

et   hi   tres   u -   num sunt   et   hi   tres   u -   num sunt

Despite their interesting treatment of the concerted style and their use of secular idioms, the soloistic compositions do not equal the art of their profane models.

The psalm compositions, however, the sonata, and the Magnificat convey artistic impressions not fully realized in previous secular forms.

The use of the *concertato* to provide a contrast of profuse media and large sonorities had only occasionally been attempted by Monteverdi in his madrigals. The fifth book contained *E così a poco a poco*, which applied the concerted style to six voices, but only the final composition of the book, *Questi vaghi*, with its double chorus and orchestra for the sinfonia, anticipated the magnificent exploitation of tone color and volume that the psalm compositions systematically exhibit.

Although Monteverdi had given the madrigal a variety of colorful effects and could have pointed to his own achievements in exploring powerful sonorities, his psalm compositions undoubtedly originated under the direct influence of both Giaches de Wert, his predecessor in Mantua, and Giovanni Gabrieli, whose polychoral work had made a deep impression on many contemporary musicians. On festival occasions Giaches de Wert presented even the Mass with solemn sonorities of large choral and instrumental groups. He probably was influenced by the older members of the Venetian school, such as Andrea Gabrieli. In 1597, Giovanni Gabrieli had brought out his *Sacrae Symphoniae*, a collection of motets which became one of the most influential publications in Italy and south Germany, and for more than forty years the Venetian school had devoted itself to exploiting the ever changing possibilities of polychoral composition, especially in relation to the psalms for the vespers of the ecclesiastical hours. Thanks to the achievements of the school, it had become a tradition to employ several choirs for compositions to be sung during the vespers. Andrea Gabrieli, whose work was more original than is now generally assumed and who was, in the estimation of the sixteenth century, of a higher rank than composers now unjustly more praised, extended the use of a combination of vocal and instrumental groups which rivaled or supplemented each other in producing an extraordinary display of colorful sonorities. His nephew Giovanni, a devoted pupil of Andrea, went a step further along the same path without making essential changes.

Monteverdi started from the last phase of the Venetian polychoral style. Aside from the use of the *cantus firmus*, in the treatment of which he displayed an ingenuity all his own, the psalms *Nisi Dominus* and *Lauda Jerusalem* are closest to the Venetian model; but he adopted the general arrangement rather than the stylistic organization of individual elements, such as melody and rhythm. In the astoundingly beautiful *Nisi Dominus* he set long contrapuntal lines against the psalm tone, which stands out remarkably with its emphatic, prolonged values, sung in unison by the two tenors in each of the two choirs. The contrapuntal lines, brisk in motion, sharply set off in phrasing caesurae, rapidly repeated by sequential techniques, have almost the swinging effect of a dance; their motion becomes immensely intricate through the syncopations in various parts:

Ex. 88   XIV, 198

Such counterpoints are in sharp contrast to the psalmodizing *cantus firmus* and make its long-drawn-out values all the more perceptible. The doxology uses the music of the first verse of *Nisi Dominus*. In the rest of the verses Monteverdi alternates the choirs, and while retaining the psalm tone as *cantus firmus* in the tenor he imitates its monotony in the other parts.

Ex. 89   XIV, 203

In *Lauda Jerusalem* he uses the same even, monotonous recitation of the psalm tone in all the parts except the voice which carries the *cantus firmus*.

The astonishing variety of Monteverdi's inventions for the *cantus firmus* is outstanding. In the rest of the polychoral works, where the stylistic influence of Venetian music is largely confined to the orchestration and the grouping of parts in choirs of instruments and voices, the treatment of the *cantus firmus* changes with every composition, and even with every section of a work. The psalm tones do not vary much and—with the exception of typical formulas for beginning, middle, and end—have the characteristic recitation on one tone, called *tenor* or *tuba*. The psalm tone is not a melody and, because of the extended repetition of one tone, does not lend itself easily to a *cantus firmus* treatment, so that it is difficult to produce any variety at all. Whatever variety exists is structural and not simply the result of a change of orchestration or grouping. To show Monteverdi's ingenuity, a few examples may be given.

In *Domine ad adiuvandum*, based on the recitation of the psalm tone, all six vocal parts are pulled together; they recite the whole text on one chord (D) in the manner of the psalmodic "faburden," and only at the end does the "Alleluja" break the monotony of the repeated D chord. But while the voices have immovable material, the groups of instruments, composing an orchestra of cornetti, viols in various sizes, and tromboni, present a sharp contrast. Their material has fast, precise rhythms, and schematic motifs which are not varied much because they have to fit the one harmony of D. The contrast, therefore, comes in the attack of the rhythms.

The psalm *Dixit Dominus* has a variety of structural interpretations of the psalm tone as *cantus firmus*. It is composed for six voices and an equal number of instruments, with ritornelli that can be played *ad libitum*. At first Monteverdi handles the psalm tone as though it were a melodic *cantus firmus:* he takes it as a fugal subject, introduced by successive imitation in the various voices and with a counterpoint set against it. Then he presents the psalmodic recitation as a faburden, with the chord repeated as many times as the text has syllables: "Done ponam inimicos"—"scabellum pedum"—"Tecum principium in die" —"In splendoribus." This is the type of harmonic recitation which Monteverdi had previously used in some of his madrigals. The verses that have pure psalmodic recitation in faburden end in elaborate passages, to which, on the last word or even only on the last syllables, an extended conclusion in concerted style is added, containing material which, profane in origin, anticipates the following ritornello. Since the vocal conclusion already contains the material of the instrumental ritornelli, they could be omitted without substantial loss.

An extraordinarily ingenious treatment of the psalm tone as *cantus firmus* is carried out by means of a trio structure, in which the vocal duet is based on independent melodic material linked together in typical fashion. Since the psalm tone has the repetition of the reciting tone, it can better be used as a harmonic basis than as a melodic interpretation. This is exactly what takes place: The monotonous *cantus firmus* forms the bass for the free vocal duet above. It occurs in the verse "Virgam virtutis tuae." Later the *cantus firmus* is presented in a liberal interpretation of the faburden, in which three voices are combined in a simple and rigid recitation in chords, while the rest of the voices are given a lively rhythmic figuration, as in the verse "Judicabit in nationibus." Finally, the doxology has its own climactic rendering of the *cantus firmus*, in which the chanting begins in the tenor with "Gloria Patri," without any accompaniment except the *basso continuo*, and proceeds in the bass on "Sicut erat," while the whole chorus sets its contrapuntal arrangement against it. In the last part of the doxology, in "et in saecula saeculorum Amen," the chanting is doubled: singing in octaves, bass and soprano make the chant most prominent while the previous contrapuntal structure is continued in the four middle parts. This one work presents an amazing variety in the structural use of the *cantus firmus*, which reaches far beyond the scope of sixteenth-century music, including the Venetian school, where the exclusive interpretation of the *cantus firmus* as melodic subject undoubtedly prevailed. It may be said that Monteverdi has dramatized the use of the psalmodic *cantus firmus*.

The most striking use of the *cantus firmus*, however, appears in the famous sonata for eight instruments, against which one voice, a soprano, sings in solemn tones "Sancta Maria, ora pro nobis" on the formula of the chant. The rhythmic form of this orison changes with every repetition, and there are eleven such repetitions without any alteration in tonal pattern. This unchanging repetition suggests the monotony of a litany, whose nature implies an increase of intensity at every chanting of the orison. Monteverdi could not have rendered the character of a litany in a more artistically convincing or dramatically effective manner.

Since the repeated prayers represent the stable element contributing to the effect of monotony, the accompaniment of the colorful orchestra might be expected to offer greater variety, but Monteverdi stresses the repetitive nature of a litany even in the accompaniment. At first there is a sharp contrast between the solemn motif of the chant and the material of the orchestra, and thereafter the same or similar material is maintained in the instrumental accompaniment, though rhythmic variations are offered with every prayer. The sonata as a whole is organized in three structural sections, the last being a repetition of the first. The larger middle section has its own material which is submitted to rhythmic variations as the prayers proceed. All the motifs are shaped with a view to their repetition, in which the sequential technique is the main device. Manifold as are the rhythmic variations, there is little change in melody, motif, or tonal material. The whole structure grows out of the repetition which, though perhaps stimulated by the repetitive element of the litany, is nonetheless the general structural force of the modern baroque style.

It has often been said that this sonata shows Venetian influence, and in the orchestration and the grouping of the instruments the influence is obvious. The whole structure, however, the form of the motifs, the stereotyped figuration, the repetitive, nonmelodic bass with harmonic tones or passages through the scale, and the full exploitation of the organizing element of persistent repetition—all these show Monteverdi as the creator of seventeenth-century idioms. The leading of the bass and the figurative motifs of the upper parts, in particular, will recur throughout the baroque age and recur in exactly the same form in Bach and in Handel.

The sonata is proof that in religious compositions also Monteverdi followed the rule that the word and its connotations must govern the concept of composition. The *Sancta Maria, ora pro nobis* is, indeed, dramatically conceived. Intent upon the meaning of the prayer, the composer derives the form from the artistic possibilities of the element of repetition. The chant retains its objective religious quality, but his method of making the structure expressive of the text is an artistic approach of secular origin, an individualistic interpretation of the traditional values inherent in the chants. The *cantus firmi* are no longer taken to be the objective elements of an artistic structure, as in Monteverdi's Mass on the motet of Gombert, but are now tested with regard to the textual connotations. Despite the maintenance of the chants, despite the observation of the liturgical order, the vespers are a highly individualistic reinterpretation of a religious heritage, an expression of personal devotion and piety. The vespers of Monteverdi, therefore, have a double significance: they testify to the secularization and to the individualization of sacred music.

PART FOUR

The Years of Fulfillment

CHAPTER
THIRTEEN

Venice

WHEN Monteverdi arrived in Rome near the end of 1610, he was received by the Cardinals Montalto and Borghese, the latter writing that he had become attached to the composer because of his extraordinary gifts. Monteverdi submitted his religious compositions to Pope Paul V, but was not successful in obtaining a grant for his son and returned to Mantua to pursue his official duties at the court and in the chapel. Vincenzo's tireless efforts to engage Adriana Basile as his star singer had finally been crowned with success. She made her appearance at the regular evenings on Friday in the Sala degli Specchi and captivated her audiences. Monteverdi considered her voice and technique as unsurpassed examples of vocal art, and many of his works must have been sung by her.

Though Monteverdi's fame had risen to great heights, he was apparently still subjected to hostile criticism, and in his dedication to Paul V he had expressed a hope that these evil tongues might be silenced. The Mantuans were well aware of his unique capacities, but the treatment Monteverdi received from the Duke was exasperating in its shabbiness. Vincenzo continued to slight the composer and to hold back monetary rewards that were long overdue. This behavior was all the more painful to Monteverdi, since Vincenzo constantly overpaid his singers and other favorite artists.

Mantua, meanwhile, was moving with alarming rapidity closer to its final decline. Two events occurred, disastrous in their consequences for the illustrious house of Gonzaga, the glories of the court, and the welfare of the city itself. Early in 1612 Vincenzo died, the victim perhaps of his "lascivious dissipations." His wife, Eleonora de'

Medici, had died a few months previously, and as though a curse were hanging over the family, death struck the infant son of Francesco, Vincenzo's son and heir, and later that year Duke Francesco himself. The house of Gonzaga was dying out, and the duchy of Mantua and Monferrato was soon to become the object of diplomatic intrigues on a European scale involving Spain, France, the Duc de Nevers, the Emperor, and Carlo Emmanuele, Duke of Savoy, to say nothing of the other branches of the Gonzaga family. The Mantuan ruling house was to pay a heavy price for having become involved, by intermarriage, in the politics of powerful princes. The end was to be the war of the Mantuan succession and the sack of Mantua, which shocked even those who were responsible for the war.

It was natural that long before the final disasters a decline in the artistic life of the court should set in. It began, in fact, immediately after the deaths of Vincenzo and Francesco. The brilliance of Mantua's musical culture at the beginning of the seventeenth century was never to return. Monteverdi only anticipated the course of the decline when he submitted his resignation after Vincenzo's death. Although Francesco inherited an interest in the new music from his father, he accepted the resignation, apparently with bad grace and bad manners. Some years later, in 1615, the thought of the end of his work at Mantua was still exceedingly painful to Monteverdi. "I departed from that court so disgracefully that, by Jove, I took with me no more than twenty-five scudi after twenty-one years," he wrote to Alessandro Striggio. The bitterness of Monteverdi's feelings after years of devoted service is comprehensible, and there may have been court intrigues to influence the administration against him.

An experience Monteverdi had in Milan seems to prove the existence of some hostility toward him. After his resignation he went to Cremona, and later in the year traveled to Milan. The purpose of this trip is not known though he may have planned to seek a position there. The unpleasant incident started in Mantua, for as soon as he appeared in Milan, some unnamed people at the Mantuan court spread the rumor "that Sigr. Claudio Monteverdi for some days had been in Milan intent upon getting the position of the Maestro di Cappella at the cathedral, and that one morning when practicing in that capacity, the performance of the music became so disorganized that he was incapable of restoring order, and consequently he returned to Cremona with very little honor." The Duke, suspicious that the rumor might have been started by persons with no good will toward Monteverdi, requested Francesco

Campagnolo to write Alessandro Striggio, at that time the Mantuan ambassador in Milan, to investigate the matter.[1] On October 10, 1612, Striggio replied: "Far from the truth is the rumor that Monteverdi had departed from this city with little to his credit; on the contrary, he had been greatly honored, well liked, and courted by noblemen and artists as well. His works are sung here with great applause at the most notable gatherings. It is not true that he took it upon himself to conduct the music in the capacity of a Maestro di Cappella in this cathedral, which position Monteverdi did not desire, or to do harm to the person who occupies it." [2] No more is known about the affair, but it may shed some light on the conditions under which Monteverdi worked in Mantua. In this case, the Duke obviously was quick to get at the truth of the matter, but we can imagine that in the past both he and his father may have given ear to malicious intrigues.

Fortunately it was not long before Monteverdi received a post that was worthy of his great merits. On August 19, 1613, Federico Contarini, Nicolo Sagredo, Zuanne Cornaro, and Antonio Landi, the Venetian procurators, named Monteverdi maestro di cappella of St. Mark's. The description of the appointment is of interest, for it shows the thoroughness of their search and the completeness of their satisfaction. "Intent upon the election of a Maestro di Cappella at the cathedral of St. Mark in place of the late Rev. Padre Giulio Cesare Marrinengo, the Most Illustrious Procurators have, in accordance with the rules of the Most Serene Republic, written to the Most Illustrious Ambassador in Rome, also to all the chargés d'affaires of the Terra Firma as well as those resident in the Most Serene Signoria in Milan and Mantua to obtain information on persons qualified, in this profession, for the said service. They received answer that the person of Sig. Claudio Monteverdi, previous Maestro di Cappella of the Most Serene Duke Vincenzo and Duke Francesco of Mantua, is most eminently recommended. Concerning his faculty and character their opinion has most thoroughly been confirmed, in view of his compositions that are published, in view also of those works which today, in the cathedral of St. Mark, performed by the musicians of the Cappella, the Most Illustrious Procuratia has heard to its fullest satisfaction: therefore the Most Illustrious Procurators unanimously voted by ballot that said Sig. Claudio Monteverdi be elected the Maestro di Cappella at the cathedral of St. Mark with an annual salary of three hundred ducats, and with the normal

[1] Vogel, VfMW, III, document No. 9, p. 430.
[2] Davari, op. cit., p. 28.

and customary regalia; he shall have, in the Canonry, an apartment which will be properly accommodated, with all necessary refitting done as soon as possible; he, furthermore, shall be given an additional fifty ducats to reimburse the expenses of his journey and the time spent in this City upon request of the Most Serene Republic." [3]

Thus Monteverdi was appointed to a position that for its international renown must have been the ultimate ambition of every famous musician. If the size of his salary is any indication, Monteverdi was esteemed above his predecessors at St. Mark's, for at the time of his appointment the yearly stipend was raised from two hundred ducats to three hundred, and three years later was again raised to four hundred. The four procurators, the lay overseers of St. Mark's, had always been most careful in selecting the maestro di cappella to survey all possible candidates, and thanks to the widely ramified political channels of the republic, when a candidate was presented on the recommendation of the Venetian agents, the procurators could feel assured that they had made the proper choice.

Venice opened new vistas and wider horizons, for Monteverdi came to a city that had grown enormously in size and in its taste for luxury. Its magnificent public spectacles had been, from ancient times, the business of all the republic. In contrast, life at the court of Mantua had a certain narrowness for those who, by birth and occupation, were excluded from participation in affairs except by way of professional service. Monteverdi had friends among the noblemen and high officials of the Mantuan court, but his social position was merely that of an artist. As an employee of the court he was not allowed to work for other people or on occasions unrelated to the courtly interests. A prince who hired artists, singers, and musicians seldom permitted them to appear at a court other than his own, and then only as a loan, with plenty of stipulations and often for the sake of a special favor in political business. No such limitations existed in Venice, and Monteverdi was free to work for any of the Venetian nobilities. He was even permitted to accept commissions from outside Venice, so that many of his activities in dramatic music were for patrons in Mantua and Parma. His social rank also was higher. In classifying the governmental representatives Francesco Sansovino, the sixteenth-century Venetian historian, lists the maestro di cappella directly after the procuratori di San Marco, and the same rank is shown in pictures of solemn processions that included the doge and the whole government of the republic. If salary is an in-

---

[3] Vogel, *op. cit.*, document No. 11, pp. 431f.

dication of the social importance of his position, Monteverdi's post
ranked high indeed, for even the counselor of state received less than
the composer. In sharp contrast to the custom at some courts, where
high salaries were paid to artists as "stars," the maestro di cappella of
St. Mark's received his large remuneration because of the social distinction connected with his office. In general, officials of the Venetian state
were well paid, for the government wisely realized that low pay opened
the way to bribery and corruption.

Venice thus gave Monteverdi new social distinction and artistic independence. But what probably counted most was the extraordinary
liberty that Venice granted its citizens and its visitors of station high
and low, as long as they were prudent enough not to mingle in the
political business of the republic. Venetian liberty or liberalism had
become proverbial. To say "We are in Venice," meant "We are in a
place of liberty"; this *Siamo à Venezia* often "is the sole response of
some to a charge of dishonesty, and of others who are taxed with insolence and are frequently wanting in respect for those to whom
respect is due, even if they are not Venetian nobles." Venice resounds
with this word "liberty"; "it is on the lips of everyone from the last of
the people to the first of the Senators." [4] This liberty was not the result
of the elimination of class hierarchy or the abolishment of authority,
but it was rather an indefinable "laissez faire" in the conduct of life. "I
would be embarrassed were I asked to define the liberty of Venice,"
said Alexandre Toussaint de Limojon, when he was in Venice at the
time when Count d'Avaux was French ambassador. He found that this
liberty gave "all the subjects of the Republic and especially the people
of Venice the freedom to pursue, with impunity, all that contributed to their pleasures, as long as the public interest was not involved;
but the very same liberty also included a total exemption from all the
deference the inferiors owe to their superiors, as long as the government
is not offended; thus I find that the liberty of Venice is, properly
speaking, a political, free and easy manner (*libertinage*), advantageous
to the Republic, suitable to the Nobility, and agreeable to the people."
This liberty is, more than anything else, "a manner of living"; it gives
assurance that "everyone can live according to his own ways" (*un-
chacun peut s'y conduire à sa mode*).

Venice had often given refuge and protection to those who suffered

---

[4] Alexandre Toussaint de Limojon, Sieur de Saint Disdier, *Description de la Ville
et la Republique de Venise* (Amsterdam, 1697), p. 350. (Alexandre Toussaint was in
Venice in 1672.)

from a lack of tolerance and freedom elsewhere. When Monteverdi came to Venice, the city still echoed with the sharp contest the republic had gallantly and successfully fought against an attempt to limit its freedom. Venice had come to grips with the papal court, and Paul V, the Pope to whom Monteverdi dedicated his religious works of 1610, had become its bitterest foe. Driven by passion and stubbornness, the Pope was determined to force a decision even at the cost of war. The conflict, which had broken out when Venice insisted on the right of jurisdiction in criminal matters over lay and clergy alike, grew in importance and became in fact a struggle between church and state. For a time, Venice was excommunicated, though this was without any lasting effect or practical consequences. The state protected the clergy who, in defiance of the excommunication, continued to discharge their duties in the churches of Venice. The republic succeeded in enlisting one of its greatest patriots as spokesman of the Venetian cause: the brilliant and learned Fra Paolo Sarpi. Almost alone, but under the circumspect protection of the state, he fought the literary war against the papal lawyers and theologians. A man of incredible mental gifts, frail in body but strong in mind, insensitive to luxuries and incorruptible by any material benefit, hated by Rome and loved by Venice, he became the foremost defender of political independence. All Europe listened to him with more than theoretical interest. As theological adviser of the republic and later as sole counselor of state, his political influence extended to the channels of international diplomacy all over Europe. As much as anything he wrote, his letters show the acuteness of his mind, his admirable learning, the vast ramifications of his political interests, his never ceasing love of freedom, and his upright character. His enemies made several attempts on his life, one of which was almost successful. In its anxiety for the life of the state's most beloved son, the Council of Ten increased his protection and offered him a haven in the canonry of St. Mark's; but Sarpi refused and continued to lead a simple life among his brethren, the friars of the order of the Servites. When he died in 1623, with his last prayer for Venice, "Esto perpetua," on his lips, the republic lost its greatest patriot and the most ardent defender of its independence.

There is a touch of irony about this brilliant championship of independence. Though Venice was successful in the immediate contest —the papal court revoked the interdict without the customary publicity—its actual political power was steadily on the decline. While Venice was fighting its most vigorous battle for independence, declining wealth and the gradual loss of its political and military strength were making the republic more and more dependent on powerful neighboring states. At a moment when the republic's resources were being drained and its vital energies sapped, and when dependence on others was becoming inevitable, Venice arose as a champion of independence.

The surface of things in seventeenth-century Venice was indeed deceptive. The luxuries, the licentiousness, the pomp, the free and easy manners, the colorful displays that were as dazzling as ever—all gave an impression of power, wealth, and brilliance, but the impression was illusory. The Council of Ten, responsible for the fortunes of the state, even encouraged an increase in extravagant festivities, and licentiousness grew in inverse proportion to the decline of power. The council conducted the affairs of the state in the utmost secrecy. Complete freedom in the conduct of daily life was granted the Venetians on condition that they should never meddle in political matters, and those who interfered paid promptly and dearly for their audacity. Thus the subjects of Venice were even prodded by the state to indulge in diversions and entertainments of all kinds and lived wholly unaware of the actual conditions, which called rather for Spartan simplicities and ascetic restrictions than for license and diversion.

Monteverdi entered Venice in time to witness the struggle for independence, and for ten years he was able to watch the work of Fra Paolo Sarpi. He may never have met the secretive counselor of state personally, though they had common interests in experimental scientific studies, and the composer must surely have read some of Sarpi's numerous pamphlets in defense of the Venetian liberty, just as he also witnessed the unbounded display of luxurious entertainments. Certainly, because of its social character, the art of music must have benefited from this passion for distractions and amusements. It is significant that such arts as painting and sculpture, which lack the social potentialities of music, were already declining from the height they had reached in sixteenth-century Venice. The rise of Venetian baroque music was certainly due in part to the increase in social entertainments that placed new demands upon Venetian musicianship.

While music benefited from the luxurious pastimes of the festivals, the morals and energies of the people, especially of the nobility, were undoubtedly undermined by indulgence in unnerving luxuries. If we read accounts of the festivities, particularly those held in the season of the carnival, written by the Venetians themselves or by the princely visitors who flocked to the city at that season to enjoy liberties granted nowhere else, we see that no one respected any limitations. The princely visitors were among the first to cast away restraint and customarily rented palaces where they could enjoy an endless sequence of feasts, balls, intimate dances, musical performances, comedies, intermezzi, banquets, and games. The dissipations of Duke Vincenzo Gonzaga, which prudent men looked upon with eyes of reproach and dismay, were commonplace in Venice, and forgetting the dignity and rank of a sovereign prince, he (incognito) indulged recklessly in amusements. The greatest spendthrifts may well have been the Dukes of Brunswick, who made a regular appearance in Venice for the whole winter season. Within fifteen or sixteen carnival seasons they are said to have spent twelve million thaler on operas and courtesans, and when reduced to the bottom of their fortunes, they sold their own subjects as military conscripts. The council of the republic probably favored such expenditures by the visitors, for they helped to stop the drain on the treasury, so sadly depleted by the decline of Venetian political and commercial power.

The noble families of Venice had their own share in the luxuries and dissipations. Alexandre Toussaint de Limojon held the peculiar education of the young nobility responsible for the decadence of Venice. He found that they lived for amusement and were brought up to think that they were superior to any prince. Their insolence at times appeared unbearable, and only those noblemen who had traveled retained any sense of proportion. This judgment may be the hasty and distorted generalization of an outsider. Yet, when we read Venetian chronicles, whose authors describe not only the political history but the customs and intimate life of the city, we have the impression that amusement, making love, gambling, and attending performances of music, comedies, and operas were the chief occupations of these noblemen.

The rage for entertainments, whether enjoyed in the privacy of the palace salon or in public with the participation of all, gave an abundance of opportunities for musical activities. The splendid gatherings in the palaces of the individual families at least had a certain refinement and culture. Such soirees, arranged not for the celebration of any special occasion but largely for the sake of musical performances, provided musical composition with its most artistic setting. It was for such gatherings that most of the madrigals and cantatas by Monteverdi and the other musicians of his time were composed. The Contarini, Grimani, Foscarini, Giustiniani, and Mocenighi were among those who at various times and in varying degrees opened their palaces to musical culture. Whenever the elite were brought together by special celebrations in one or other of the families, madrigals and cantatas had their share in the festivities, and there were also works of a more representative and festival nature, such as the ballo in *genere rappresentativo*, that is, in actual production as a ballet on the stage. Scenic cantatas of a dramatic character were also dedicated to such purposes, and Monteverdi contributed to various occasions of that kind. Until Venice had its own public theaters, dramatic performances were restricted to the palaces of the nobility in the city, or their summer residences along the Brenta.

A special characteristic of the exorbitant freedom of Venice was the entertainment offered in the convents or nunneries. The chronicles record stories of sheer license and outrageous depravity, many of which must be taken with a grain of salt. The relatively frequent pictures of social gatherings in the parlors of the convents are similar to those of life in the salons of the noble families, totally profane, to be sure, but nevertheless in the fashionable style of refined entertainment. Most historians who speak of this shockingly worldly behavior overlook the fact that those convents of whose profane conduct we have pictorial and verbal records did not come under the strict rules of monastic life. There were more than thirty convents in seventeenth-century Venice, and only half of them were bound to observe strict monastic rules. The other half were permitted to maintain relations with the world outside the convent, and the nunneries, in particular, enjoyed extraordinary privileges. About half a dozen were reserved for noble ladies exclusively, and the ladies obviously took more than their share. There can be no doubt that in the open convents there was a laxity of morals that did away with any excuse for their existence. Regular receptions were held in them, concerts given, singers introduced, comedies produced, masquerades held, buffooneries presented; and, particularly in the carnival season, attending the masquerades in the convents was a favorite pastime of the Venetians. Many of the cantatas, madrigals, balletti, and mascherate were certainly performed at receptions in the convents given over to musical entertainment.

Balls were arranged for innumerable occasions, most frequently of course during the carnival. They were private and exclusive occasions for the nobility, and orchestras of good size were engaged for such dances. On a much simpler scale, the so-called "little balls" at carnival time gave the lower classes frequent opportunities to have their own amusements. A manager was in charge of these affairs, a violinist and a harpsichordist were engaged, and the people danced the dances of their class and sometimes imitated the dances of the nobility. Such was the people's "Festina," of which there were many in the season, and often the noblemen used them as hunting grounds. All these balls were part of the picturesque musical entertainments, but Monteverdi contributed nothing to them, since at no time in his artistic career did he take an interest in purely instrumental music. The ballo, based on poetry and plot, interested him for its higher artistic implications.

The great Venetian feast was, of course, the Marriage of Venice to the Sea, celebrated on the Feast of Ascension. The doge, the procurators, and the whole government, went out to sea on the *Bucintoro*, the doge's large and stately boat, which was surrounded by an innumerable flock of gondolas, large and small. The whole city was afloat, and visitors came from far and wide to watch the unique spectacle. When the doge's party reached the open sea, motets were sung to celebrate the occasion. Motets had been composed and performed for the great feasts of the Venetian state early in the fifteenth century, and motets were still in use during the seventeenth century at this specifically Venetian feast. Although none of the motets which Monteverdi composed in his Venetian period can be associated with the Feast of the Marriage of Venice to the Sea, as maestro di cappella of St. Mark's he must have performed this honorable duty. As a matter of fact, he once mentioned in a letter that he had to provide the composition for the occasion. "According to order I shall have to compose a certain cantata in praise of the Doge (*una certa cantata in lode di sua Serenità*) which is sung every year on the *Bucintoro* while the whole Signoria goes out to the Wedding with the Sea on the day of Ascension." [5] Unfortunately, his compositions dedicated to this feast are lost. Yet it is intriguing to imagine that the French philosopher René Descartes, when he admired the famous ceremony in Venice on Ascension Day, May 16, 1624, might have heard a festival composition of Monteverdi. The musicians, instrumentalists and vocalists, were placed at the bow of the *Bucintoro*, where they performed their music. The climax of the ceremony was the recitation of the ancient formula: *Desponsamus te mare nostrum in signum veri perpetuique domini*. To conclude the wedding, an abundance of flowers was thrown upon the water. In the evening a gala banquet was given by the Doge in his palace, with musical entertainments, which included the performance of madrigals

---

[5] Letter No. 30, dated April 21, 1618; ed. Malipiero, *Claudio Monteverdi*, p. 177.

or arias sung by the best singers available. Equally festive were the official celebrations in the doge's palace on the feasts of such saints, dear to the Venetians, as St. Stephen, St. Vido, and above all, St. Mark.

Naturally, on the occasion of special visits of important dignitaries or princes, the doge and the procurators arranged entertainments to honor the guests of the state. In 1628, when the Grand Duke Ferdinando of Tuscany and his brother Carlo de' Medici visited Venice, the republic gave a feast, "Real Convito," in the arsenal. For that occasion Monteverdi produced a cycle of madrigals to *I cinque Fratelli*, sonnets by Giulio Strozzi; however the music is lost.

If we take into account the special feasts of favorite churches in Venice, especially the Chiesa di Salute, whither people flocked to hear amazing performances of music that became more and more secular and profane, we can picture Venetian musical culture in the richest imaginable colors. The vast scope of entertainment was a never ceasing challenge to the composer who made his art part of the musical life in the city. "There is not a nobleman who would not hold me in esteem and honor, and whenever I perform my music, either profane or sacred, I can assure you that the whole city flocks together; *il servitio poi è dolcissimo* (the service is the sweetest)": [6] thus, for once enthusiastic, Monteverdi could write in 1620 of his work in Venice.

---

[6] Letter No. 46, to Alessandro Striggio, dated Venice, March 13, 1620; *ibid.*, p. 199.

The New Art of Madrigals

MONTEVERDI had last presented to the public a selection of his madrigals in 1605, but though preoccupied with the composition of his first dramatic works and religious music, he had continued to compose madrigals that exhibited new achievements in craftsmanship and in expressive power. In 1609 he had completed the madrigal *Una donna fra l'altre*, a composition for five voices with additional *basso continuo*, set as "Concertato nel Clavicembalo." The work was circulated among his fellow musicians and friends, and a loyal admirer, Aquilino Coppini, who persistently sought out his latest compositions, obtained a copy and published it in his third selection of Monteverdi's works, *Il terzo libro della musica di Claudio Monteverdi*. Coppini provided, as before, a new Latin text, *Una es*, and this spiritualized version appeared five years before Monteverdi published the original text.

The *Arianna* had been so enthusiastically received that demands for its most famous song, the *Lament*, or for the whole were urgently expressed. In 1613, after the composer had left Mantua, Francesco de' Medici wrote the Duke of Mantua an imploring letter: "Since I have the most ardent desire to possess Claudio Monteverdi's music to Ottavio Rinuccini's *Arianna*, I beg you most urgently to do me the favor of sending me the score." [1] In response to the demands of his admirers —Giovanni Battista Doni in his *Trattato della Musica Scenica* tells us that the request was made by a Venetian—Monteverdi recomposed the *Lamento d'Arianna* as a madrigal for five voices. As can be seen from its place in a cyclic composition, there were other artistic reasons that

---

[1] See the letter in Davari, *op. cit.*, p. 47.

impelled him to recast the *Lamento*. It was not long after the feasts of 1608, when the *Arianna* was produced as a musical drama, that he decided to make this rearrangement. Monteverdi was working at it in 1610, as we learn from a letter from Casola to Cardinal Gonzaga in July of that year, which says that he was occupied with the composition of a group of madrigals for five voices, consisting of three laments: "He also is preparing a set of madrigals for five voices which will consist of three Lamenti or Pianti: that of Arianna with the well-known text; the *Lamento* of Leandro and Hereo by Marini; the third, given him by His Highness, is that of the Pastore on the death of his Ninfa, whose text, by the son [Scipione] of Signor Conte Lepido Agnelli, is on the death of Signora Romanina." [2] It was in memory of Caterina Martinelli, called "Romanina," that Monteverdi in 1610 composed the *Sestina*, the *Lagrime d'Amante al Sepoloro dell'Amata*. Both the *Lament of Arianna* and the *Sestina* were published in 1614, but we do not know about the other lament in the group, on the text of Marini. Since Casola is accurate in his information about the rest of the works, all of which were completed including the Mass and the vespers, it is probable that the *Lamento* of Leandro and Hereo was completed but lost.

The professional world of musicians did not wholly approve of the transformation of the monodic *Lamento* into a polyphonic madrigal. Giovanni Battista Doni, generally a sincere admirer of Monteverdi, criticized the work, though thought most highly of *Arianna* as a drama and called it "così bella composizione." He praises the lament as a model of dramatic music in monodic style, which has the singing quality and the beautifully handled motion of an aria, but finds that these qualities are lost in the process of transferring the composition to another medium. "In the concerto for several voices, however [he calls the madrigal a "concerto"], one very often feels that certain passages have little grace and appropriateness in relation to the text, as the passage at the beginning of the bass shows," and he quotes the initial phrase of the bass part to *Lasciate mi morire*. Doni even tried to apologize for Monteverdi: it was not his fault that the lament was transformed into a madrigal; he had done it "in order to please others rather than himself, as he himself admitted in one of his letters." But this seems unlikely, since he would hardly have composed a whole set of *Lamenti* in the same medium or selected this composition for publication, had he not been convinced of the artistic value of the madrigal. In still another passage

---

[2] Vogel, *op. cit.*, document No. 8, p. 430.

of his treatise, in the chapter "On Choral Music," Doni referred for the third time to the madrigalesque *Lamento*, again criticizing the initial phrase of the bass and suggesting that, instead of asking for a vocal version of five voices, the Venetian nobleman would have done better to request the composition of four instrumental parts to be used as an accompaniment of the most beautiful monodic aria.

Immediately upon assuming his new position in Venice, Monteverdi prepared for publication his sixth book of madrigals, which appeared in 1614 and represented a survey of some five or six years' work in madrigalesque composition. We believe that these publications are, more and more, selections of what Monteverdi regarded as worthy of publication and do not necessarily comprise all that he composed.

The sixth book contains eighteen madrigals, ten of which belong to the two cyclic laments. The reappearance of Petrarch with two poems, *Zefiro torna e'l bel tempo rimena* and *Ohimè il bel viso*, repeats the surprising anachronism we have met before, which seems to have extended to the compositions themselves. In the sixth book a new poet, Giambattista Marino, comes to the fore. More than any other poet, Marino set the tone for poetry in the seventeenth century. Monteverdi's choice of poems, or rather his interpretation of the chosen poems, was always made on human grounds, but first he searched for design, observed the rhythmic intricacies, the subtly tonal motion of the verse, and strove to discern what we would call the musical constituent of poetry. As his artistic sense became keener with advancing age, he responded to the inherent musical qualities in poetry, and it was on this basis that he made new discoveries in Marino.

"E del poeta il fin la meraviglia"—Marino thus defined the goal of the poet as the marvelous, the startling effect. This goal Marino reached by the use of precious artistry, fanciful sophistication, and a lascivious sensuality that was obscene but hidden. Marino's artistic philosophy is naturalistic: it proclaims the apotheosis of the senses. Yet nature is no longer an inexhaustible mine of unspoiled riches where man can find the laws of his vitality, and the senses are no longer the unpolluted faculties of man's physical nature. Sensuality becomes a voluptuousness that must be veiled and skillfully contrived to please an age whose morals have been perverted. For pleasure dictates that art must be conquered by nature; and Marino meant to place the surfeited senses in command. He considered Caravaggio his equal and companion, and thought him greater as a creator than as a painter (*Mentre che Creator più de Pittore*), because he made "the lie more beautiful than truth"

(*Per cui del ver più bella è la menzogna*), for the beauty of art is above that of nature. Perhaps Caravaggio's *Venus and Adonis*, or even more his lascivious *Bacchus*, is next of kin to Marino's *Adone*. Both are glutted with sensuality repulsive in its implications; yet both have an infectious fascination that emanates from brilliant intellectuality, from an abundance of refined designs and disguises, from uncanny facilities. The enormous success of Marino's poetry is doubtless based on this opalescent effect of an intellectuality that is used to veil sensuality. This mixture produced the style of ornate and figurative profusion that was so much admired by the age. Marino's followers felt that he had attained the true florid elegance that was the ideal of the epoch. They appreciated the exquisite clarity of Marino's descriptive details, even where he carefully elaborates accessories that distract from the main action and harm the unity of an epic. For only the minutest detail and the precious elaboration of particulars afford the sensual experience that results from making "pleasure" the end of poetry. Grandiloquence of ornamentation goes hand in hand with perspicuity of style. It may lead to redundancy, to exaggeration, to the grotesque as an end, but even that is part of the ideal. Nothing less than the extravagant, the excess of artistry, can excite astonishment. Therefore, Marino's verse abounds with repetitions which lose contact with the imagery the further they are drawn out; it is deprived of substance by its prolixity. Intense emotion is often present in such verse; indeed, rhetorical repetition, inversion, figurative antithesis, and the presentation of the same verbiage in artfully changed phrases often succeed in conveying the fluctuations of emotion and can be called realistic, because they reflect the vacillating nature of emotion.

Wherever uncertainties of feeling torment man's soul and body, there Marino's success with his orgy of parallels and antitheses is greatest:

> Ardo, lassa, o non ardo! ahì qual io sento
> Stranio nel cor non conosciuto affetto!
> E forse ardore? ardor non è, chè spento
> L'avrei col pianto; è ben d'ardo sospetto!
> Sospetto no, piuttosto egli è tormento.
> Come tormento fia, se dà diletto?

It was the nature and structure of this verse that attracted Monteverdi to Marino's poetry. Whether its sensuality and frivolous conceptions exercised an equal fascination on him, we do not know. It is difficult to imagine Monteverdi becoming involved in riotous frivolities, since he was always upset when anything interfered with his artistic work. Outside his compositions, he always expressed himself in an unvarnished manner, as plain as it was earnest, and, especially in the latter part of his life, he lived in stern and almost monastic seclusion. If any interpretation of a man's features is at all permissible, the troubled gravity of Monteverdi's face speaks of tragedy and grief, rather than of frivolity; it speaks of the implacable seriousness of purpose that marked every one of his artistic efforts. There is not one passage in his compositions that can be read as the artistic product of frivolous voluptuousness, though there is strong sensuousness in his tonal world. As many of his letters show, Monteverdi, like most of his contemporaries in art, was troubled by the relation between nature and art. To him, nature did not mean an apotheosis of the senses, but rather a well of resources which provided the original, elemental powers of rhythm, melody, and harmony, and gave vitality and balance to the powers of intellect. Monteverdi's art is by no means identical with Marino's sensuality.

It was the verse technique and, above all, the artistic devices in Marino's poetry that fascinated Monteverdi. For he, too, was concerned with constructing new figurative rhetorics in music. What could be more suggestive than the poetic devices of antithesis, inversion, and repetition? Such structures lent themselves at once to musical interpretation. Monteverdi was already on his way toward new musical rhetorics before he adopted the poetry of Marino, and his artistic process was probably accelerated by the stimulus of setting Marino's verse to music.

The madrigals based on Marino's poems are the most modern in the collection. All of them are designated as compositions in the concerted style, and some of them can well be placed at the side of compositions in the seventh and eighth books. Since one of the madrigals, *Una donna fra l'altre*, described as a "Concerto nel Clavicembalo," dates back to 1609, that is evidently the time at which Monteverdi became more and more confident that the *concertato* was the modern idiom of the madrigal.

At first sight, the two large cycles of *lamento* character, and especially Petrarch's *Zefiro torna*, seem to grow out of the older forms of madrigalesque composition. The larger part of that composition is in a triple rhythm whose dancelike character was perhaps prompted by such phrases as "Ridono i prati e'l ciel si rasserena" or "E cantar augelletti." At all events, the declamatory unit has a relatively large value: the half note (minim). In older madrigals the half, or quarter, note was indeed the smallest unit used for the declamation, which had a correspondingly slow tempo. Monteverdi, and for that matter all composers throughout most of the seventeenth century, retained the large value for all sections written in triple rhythm and even used the old forms of sixteenth-century notation. However, the tempo in the sections with triple rhythm is actually faster than in those with duple rhythm, where the declamatory unit is ordinarily the eighth note and the notation is usually modern.

Other features are equally suggestive of older stylistic manners— for example, the imitative entrances of the voices at the beginning of the verses. These initial imitations, however, do not fulfill their promise; they begin as though an elaborate counterpoint were to follow, yet nothing of the sort happens. The second or third entrance of a theme brings a harmonically controlled parallelism of voices in thirds or sixths—a device Monteverdi had used in previous madrigals to produce a new form of polyphony. The result is that a predominant duet and a harmonic bass still are the main constituents of the composition. "Polyphony" loosens the solid body of the voices but is not allowed to disrupt the control exercised by those elements, so that the counterpoint of *Zefiro torna* behaves according to the modern manner. The structure as a whole is influenced by the dance song; the rhythmic order, whose steady triple pattern is the unmistakable product of the dance, and the repetitive arrangement of sections are both derived from various types of songs. The music of the initial section is repeated like the couplets of the villanella. The elaborate, slower middle section (in C), however, shows no influence of the dance; its independent material has a strongly contrasting character, which provides the element of conflict within the structure as a whole. The contrasting section responds to characteristic changes in the text. The first section, in narrative style, is the objective part of the poem. The second section presents direct speech and expresses the personal feeling of the lover in the scene: "Ma per me lasso tornano i più gravi sospiri." The change from the objective to the subjective brings a difference in atmosphere: nature is gay, but the lover is unhappy. The last section returns to the personal utterance of the lover, "sono un deserto," and again the music reflects the change. This last part, though in less sharp contrast than the middle section, is set off by its own rhythmic differentiation (in C). The structure of the composition as a whole is responsive to the succession of scenic description and personal expression in the poem. Such differentiation is, of course, not entirely new. What is new, however, and ingenious is the arrangement of the groups in an over-all plan of repetitive song structure. Two different conceptions of musical form meet here, and Monteverdi achieves a unity of what appear to be irreconcilable elements by subordinating a flexible dramatic form to a preconceived structure. While *Zefiro torna* is in some stylistic details not the most modern work of the collection, its form is the outgrowth of Monteverdi's modern principles. The madrigal is dramatized. The sections of the form are not musically independent, they are not music for its own sake; even where the sections follow a pre-established song structure, they are fulfilling a dramatic function.

The two cyclic laments also combine dramatic content and musical form. The dramatic aspect had, of course, been anticipated in the monodic version of the *Lamento d'Arianna*, and even the *Sestina* approaches an imaginary monodic prototype so closely that the reconstruction of a monodic version would be easy. Casola reported of the laments that Monteverdi composed "una muta di Madrigali a Cinque voci"—a group of madrigals for five voices in succession. Since the monody of Arianna's *Lament* existed first, its style was imposed on the whole group. The transference of an actual monodic model into the madrigalesque medium involved more than just a harmonization of the solo part by means of the *basso continuo* of the original, and what Monteverdi accomplished was a transformation rather than a mere transcription. This fusion of madrigalesque style with monody is also evident in the *Sestina*, for which there is no monodic predecessor, but which is guided by monodic principles in large sections of the extensive cycle.[3] Although the various groupings of voices in both the *Lamento d'Arianna* and the *Sestina* at times obscure the leading position of the "monodic" voice, there is an unmistakable concentration on an upper part that has the lead and a lower part that provides the support. This arrangement, frequently encountered in previous madrigals, results more directly from the typical trio combination than from the monodic *Lamento* of the opera. Groups of trios in various forms are used throughout the two cycles and demonstrate again their organizing functions. The monodic conception helped to clarify the distribution

---

[3] In view of this inherent monodic element, Prunières suggested that the tenor might well represent the soloistic vocal part, while the rest can be played on instruments; cf. his *Claudio Monteverdi*, pp. 145f.

of the leading forces over the uppermost and lowest parts, but did not actually produce it.

Monteverdi accepts the dramatic idea of musical form more resolutely in these two cycles than in *Zefiro torna*, and a still more subtle sensitivity to the connotations of the text makes the musical form develop from the changing affections. Repetitive arrangements and the stressing of individual phrases or sections are frequent, and nearly always have an expressive, as well as a formal, function. The dramatic intentions are often revealed in details as well as in the comprehensive structure. The expressiveness of the interval plays an important role: dissonances and chromatic progressions had long proved their expressive potentialities and are now used with masterly assurance, especially in the *Arianna* cycle, to bring out the *lamento* character. Though dissonance is still used for an isolated word of grief, the effect is that of a broader, dissonant "situation," which transmits a more general affection, an atmosphere, and is not confined to an individual word. Monteverdi has thus succeeded in making the listener recognize unremitting tragedy and poignant melancholy as ever-present overtones in the composition as a whole. This effect raises his use of dissonance far above a madrigalesque mannerism. Other intervals also acquire connotations of plaintive anguish and tribulation; fourths and sixths are associated with the expression of melancholy, and the harmonic combination of these intervals, affecting the harmonies of the fauxbourdon, is identified with ideas of sorrow and lament. A more or less extended succession of descending chords in the fauxbourdon combination of fourths and sixths is found in *O chiome d'or*, the *quinta parte* of the *Sestina*:

Ex. 90   VI, 64

In *Ma te raccoglie*, the *quarta parte* of the *Sestina*, Monteverdi develops a brief passage of such chords with the most subtle artistry in order to present a poignant melancholy. On the text, "e su la tomba cantano i pregi de l'amato seno," there is first a simple succession of chords:

Ex. 91   VI, 59

Then the descending line is used as the bass, above which a duet sings the motif to "Cantano i pregi de l'amato seno":

Ex. 92   VI, 59

In the repetitions that follow, both the motif of the bass and that of the duet are kept together as though one were the counterpoint of the other. First the phrase is repeated in a different combination of voices; then the motif of the bass is used for successive imitations to frame the duet in the middle; then two motifs of the bass and the duet are inverted and presented in successive imitation; and finally all the voices "cantano i pregi de l'amato seno." This is an entirely new polyphony. Strikingly ingenious as the devices undoubtedly are, they are only instrumental and subsidiary to the primary task of expression. The artistic device organizes the sequence of tones and is itself humanized. A similar stroke of genius is found in *Darà la notte il sol*, the *terza parte* of the *Sestina*, at the words "prima che Glauco di bacciar," where an almost identical polyphonic device is used with the utmost subtlety and emotional profundity.

The group of the *concertato* madrigals, almost all based on texts of Marino, advance farthest in style. The *stile concertato* applies not only to the contrast between the group of voices that are shaped mostly in a soloistic style and the instrumental accompaniment of the *basso continuo*, but also to the contrasting sections of the individual composition, so that the madrigal has an entirely new aspect. In previous madrigals all five voices were not occupied throughout the composition and smaller groups used varying combinations of voices, but these groups continually co-operated in the organic development of the composition. This is no longer the case in the *concertato* madrigal, where the individual voice is given a section of its own set off as a structural entity against the group of all five voices. Thus the greater part of the madrigal may be carried by one voice only, so that passages for all five parts produce the effect of subsidiary responses. *A Dio Florida bella* is an example of such an organization. The text presents a farewell scene of two lovers. With his unmatched ability to derive the formal organization from the dramatic realities of the text Monteverdi renders this madrigal as a dramatic dialogue. For the text of the lament between two lovers who must part, the style of the soloistic monody is employed; for the text of a more contemplative passage— in the middle and at the end with the farewell "A Dio"—the five-part chorus is used. Floro, the lover, first utters his plaintive monody, which is followed by that of Florida. After these two extensive monodies, the full madrigalesque chorus inserts its narration, which ends musically with a complete cadence. As though it were a second part, the lovers again present their dialogue, this time, however, in a simultaneous duet, and the madrigalesque chorus concludes the composition with the mutual farewell, "A Dio Floro—A Dio Florida."

A similar organization is found in the *concertato, Misero Alceo*. The long monologue "Ecco Lidia ti lascio" has the appropriate form of the monody, which is clearly identified with the individual persons, or "actors," in all these *concertato* madrigals. The chorus is reserved for the narrative, contemplative, or generally descriptive parts, whereas the solo represents the active element that displays human individuality. Thus passivity and activity as elementary contrasts become the dramatic constituents of the musical form. Not every poem clearly suggests monody by an actual monologue or dialogue, but wherever the poet peoples the scene, wherever the human factor enters, the musical form responds. No longer is there an attempt to interlace the sections at the points of juncture; the madrigal ceases to be one uniform organism, and becomes a sectional composition. Yet the repetition of sections for the sake of organization may still reveal the presence of an over-all conception. *Qui risi Tirsi*, whose solo sections have a virtuosity of figuration, each being a variation of the florid melody, introduces contrastingly simple choral material three times in the course of the composition. This material recurs unaltered in text and music and functions as a structural refrain, so that the form of this madrigal is actually that of the baroque refrain cantata, created by Monteverdi long before Lodovico Rossi or Carissimi. Cantata-like also is the last composition of the collection, *Presso un fiume tranquillo*, with a text by Marino, the only work for seven voices. Monteverdi calls it a *dialogo concertato*, although its structural organization, based on the alternations of the dialogue, is not much different from that of the other *concertato* madrigals. In quiet, unpretentious chords, sung by a chorus of five parts, the madrigal first sets the scene: "Presso un fiume tranquillo Disse a Filena Eurillo." The speech of Eurillo follows as monody. The narration continues, "Filena with all her love responds to Eurillo," and is presented in a choral version, whereas the actual reply of Filena appears as a solo melody. Thus, soli and chorus follow each other, until at the end all seven voices are combined on the "guerra" motif, of which Monteverdi gives two versions: one for the two soloists, highly figurative, in sharp rhythms; the other for the choral parts, in equally sharp accentuation, but in rapid syllabic declamation. It is the rhythms of the "guerra" motif that are to play the most distinguished role in the *Madrigali Guerrieri*. The starting point for this novelty is even here the five-part madrigal, but in this *dialogo* the soloists join the chorus as additional voices, while in the preceding madrigals the soloists are taken from the five-part chorus. Even in its *concertato* version it is still the five-part madrigal that explains the transformations of structure. Monteverdi's tenacity in adhering to this medium for more than twenty-five years is proof of the importance the composer attributed to it. He needed these years of logical concentration and systematic work to free the style from the given category and to wed it to a new medium. The *concertato* madrigals of the sixth book, despite their superior artistic quality, show that the composer can no longer make full and harmonious use of all the elements of the medium, for throughout large sections decisive forces lie idle. Eloquent as the structures and new formal conceptions are, the five-part madrigal is no longer an artistic necessity. The ideas of form inherent in the *concertato* madrigals reach forward into the sphere within which the compositions of the seventh book originate. The balance between category, medium, and style is restored in the works of the new collection, which characteristically carries the new programmatic title *Concerto*.

On December 13, 1619, Monteverdi signed the dedication of his seventh book of madrigals to Catarina Medici-Gonzaga, Duchess of Mantua, and on the same day he dispatched a letter to the Mantuan secretary, Alessandro Striggio, who had become his intimate friend, in which he mentioned that the book was off the press. In a letter of February 1, 1620, he indicated his plan to go to Mantua in order to submit the work to the Duchess. A few days later, on February 8, 1620, he requested Alessandro Striggio to do him the favor of presenting the book to the Duchess in his name, as he was prevented by necessary duties from doing so himself. In the dedication he expressed his loyalty to the house of Gonzaga. "These my compositions, whatever else they are, will be a public and authentic testimonial of my devoted affection for the august house of Gonzaga, which I have served with all loyalty for many a decade." According to these letters, Monteverdi hoped to receive a pension which had been promised him upon departure from Mantua, but which he had never obtained. If so, he must have been disappointed; for, instead of the overdue pension, he received a golden necklace.

In his choice of texts, Monteverdi had reached a final stage. Marino had marked the last phase and, together with Guarini and Chiabrera, he reappeared in the seventh book. From the poetry of these men whose work he had distinguished with his music he selected those poems that stirred his imagination with their emotional intensities, passionate scenes, and especially with such formal arrangements as suggested dramatic structures in musical composition. Monteverdi had reached the phase of assurance which comes with full maturity and the achievement of a lifetime. The compositions are all the works of a master, without any trace of experiment, and with the finality of perfection in style, technique, and expression. They formulated a musical language which would be used for more than a century.

The seventh book presents an extraordinary variety of media. Since the five-part madrigal has been superseded, the choice of medium is freely made, either in relation to the text or because of artistic interest in some specific combination of voices. Monteverdi used many combinations of solo voices; duets are most frequent, for two soprani, two tenors, bass and tenor; but there are trios, quartets, even a sextet, in addition to compositions for the solo voice. All have an instrumental accompaniment, either in the simple form of the *basso continuo*, or with an additional small orchestra of two violins and two flutes, as in the sextet *A quest' olmo*, or even with a large orchestra of three instrumental choirs, as in *Con che soavità*. These varieties, indeed, give proof of the complete freedom the composer had gained. The style is the governing factor and no longer depends on a special medium; and the form has been stabilized in relation to style and text.

The first madrigal of the volume is again intended to reveal the stylistic program. Even the text, *Tempro la cetra*, ingeniously chosen from Marino, is a prelude that alludes to the content of the whole work. It introduces the singer-poet as though he were the composer himself who seizes the lyre to sing of the heroism of Mars, but "it seems impossible to him that the lyre will resound with anything but love." Love is the theme throughout, and, in contrast to the texts of his previous madrigals, the tragic note, so characteristic of his frame of mind, is less frequent. There are tones of sweet melancholy, especially in Guarini's texts, but for the most part the madrigals are free from poignant grief, even if the poet, in *O come sei gentile*, envious of the bird that lives while singing, dies: "vivi cantando et io cantando moro." The tones of gaiety in love are more frequent, as are those of sultry sensuality, particularly in Marino's erotic lyrics. One loses track of all the "baci" that are liberally given and taken. Marino's rather violent *Eccomi pronta ai baci* makes a strange appearance in the tonal disguise by which Monteverdi covers violence with grace.

Although the madrigals of the seventh book have scarcely one stylistic element that is completely novel, there is a new systematic uniformity. All that Monteverdi had previously accomplished in building up the structures and vocabularies of modern musical expression, all that he had worked out before, in detail or in isolation, is here brought together with a climactic effect. In so far as the stylistic expressions of the past are unmistakably modern and appropriate to the new style, they are employed as models, to be expanded, or simply repeated if their former rendition seemed adequate.

Thus, the first madrigal, *Tempro la cetra*, recalls a model that Monteverdi had used twelve years earlier with great effect—Orfeo's bravura aria, *Possente spirto*. The strophic structure is used in both works, the new composition adding clarity to the organization. In *Tempro la cetra* Monteverdi drew further consequences from the strophic structure on a fixed bass: he carried the principle of variation into the melody; and though the melodies of the solo voice in the four strophes are never the same, the idea of varying a melodic substance exists. Indications of this principle are found in Orfeo's aria; but the madrigal further clarifies it. Except for the elaborate coloratura that reappears in the madrigal (though to a considerably lesser degree than

6 Cantoria of St. Mark's

7 Chapter-House of St. Mark's

8 Venice, from an Engraving by Giuseppe Heintz, Showing the Ceremony of the Marriage of Venice to the Sea

in Orfeo's *Possente spirto*), the melody departs much further from the dramatic and expressive *stile recitativo*. The elements of arioso and recitative have been so completely worked into each other that it is hard to determine where one begins and the other ends. Yet in *Tempro la cetra* the arioso, which has also simplified the rhythmic order of the melody, prevails over the recitative. The instrumental ritornello, played between the strophes, is as much of an organizing element as it had been in *Orfeo*. Part of the introductory sinfonia incorporates the ritornello, which also serves as the beginning and the end of the final sinfonia. Hence, the new madrigal, which embodies contrasts of structure through contrasts of medium on the firm basis of an unaltered, unifying element, proves to be a sectional composition similar to the cantata.

The seventh book contains only three more works for the solo voice: *Con che soavità*, with orchestral accompaniment and unique in most of its aspects, and the two *Lettere amorose*, in monodic form with simple *continuo* accompaniment. *Se i languidi miei sguardi* is the *Lettera amorosa* most frequently referred to; *Se pur destina*, though also called *Lettera amorosa* in the edition of 1623, is better known under the title *Partenza amorosa* of the original edition. Both letters belong to the *genere rappresentativo* and are to be sung *senza battuta* (without strict rhythmic beat), according to Monteverdi's own instruction. Doni discussed these compositions, both of which he referred to as *Lettere amorose*. He criticized Monteverdi's composing them— at least *Se i languidi*—for a soprano, when the text required a man's voice; but that is an irrelevant criticism. Doni remarks that the works are on the whole more "capricious" than "reasonable," but admits that all in all they can be prescribed "as models of the *stile recitativo* proper." He differentiates the *stile recitativo* from the *stile rappresentativo*, and it is interesting to examine this differentiation. He defines the various types of the recitative style. First, it includes a melody sung gracefully by a solo voice in such a manner that the text can be comprehended; this type may appear in compositions for the theater or the church, in the oratorio, or for private use. Then there is a type of music, soloistic with instrumental accompaniment, in which the melody approaches ordinary speech, but is very effective. Figurative material, runs, and elaborate ornamentation are usually added to this style of melody. Not that Doni approves of these extraneous ornamentations; he thinks them void of any capacity to express affections, and believes that they were brought in to please people of little understanding and taste and were used by singers to display their expertness and technical skill. In keeping with the peculiarities of the Italian language, the style allows a great many repetitions, though not as many as are customary in madrigals and motets. Doni defines the *stile rappresentativo* as any kind of melody to be sung with scenery—that is, any music composed for dramatic action.[4] Doni, therefore, understands the *stile recitativo* as a melody midway between spoken declamation and formal song, which may also appear in scenic music. The ornamentation of this reciting melody may either be written out by the composer or inserted by the singer in the form of an improvisation.

These characteristics hold true in almost every detail for Monteverdi's two extensive monodic *lettere*. These compositions have a melodic motion that approaches the characteristic declamation; they also have the element of repetition in certain phrases, though they do not have the elaborate ornamentation which Doni thinks typical of the style, unless we count the final, somewhat florid, passage of the *Partenza*. It is possible, and quite in keeping with the vocal customs of the time, that in actual performance the singer would add ornamental coloraturas, in which case Doni's requirement would be met. Monteverdi was always careful to indicate wherever he desired the florid style of the vocal art, and since he made no such indications, it is safe to assume that he did not regard the coloratura as appropriate to his *lettere*, irrespective of what the singer might do. Despite some discrepancy in regard to ornamentation, it seems obvious that Doni abstracted his ideas of the *stile recitativo* from the *lettere*, all the more so as he referred to them in his definitions. The rhythmic freedom (*senza battuta*), which Monteverdi prescribed to avoid rigidity in the manner of singing, increased the effect of recitation, and was essential to convey the impression of "improvisation" which is so characteristic of his recitation. Monteverdi ordinarily used *genere rappresentativo* to refer to music that was actually presented on the stage, as did Doni, but the two *lettere amorose* are not scenic compositions. Hence, Monteverdi for once must have understood *genere rappresentativo* to be identical with Doni's later definition of the *stile recitativo*.

Although these works have often been the subject of scholarly discussion, their full meaning remains to be explained. Were they really composed as late as their publication in the seventh book suggests?

---

[4] G. B. Doni, *De Musica scenica*, *Opera*, II, 28ff. (Chapter: "In che differisca lo stile Recitativo dal Rappresentativo.")

There are various features that do not fit easily into the picture of Monteverdi's logical development. We find stylistic elements that are astonishingly close to the type of monody produced by the academic Florentines at the turn of the century—a type that was already twenty years old and rather generally disapproved of by composers. Moreover, Monteverdi had intentionally by-passed the somewhat sterile Florentine monody in his earlier dramatic works. The monodic *Lamento d'Arianna*, for instance, had little in common with the style of the Florentine Camerata, and only a limited similarity to the two *lettere*. These compositions scarcely belong in their stylistic environment; they are definitely obsolete by 1619 and have no forerunners in Monteverdi's own work. It has been suggested that he wanted for once to realize the very principles and "radical prescriptions of those famous prefaces and treatises with which Caccini, Peri, Bardi, and V. Galilei shocked and delighted the artistic world a quarter of a century before." [5] Such a deliberate imitation is not impossible in Monteverdi's work, as has been shown in other cases. If he imitated, he certainly improved upon the Florentines, and Doni was correct in citing the compositions as a model of the style.

Another madrigal of the seventh book that has also been related to the monodic style of the Florentines is the duet for two tenors, *Interrotte speranze*.[6] Such an attribution is not justified, however, and it would be hard to find any comparable composition among the Florentines. Only the use of sharp caesurae, which set off the melodic lines for both voices simultaneously line by line, resembles the phrasing of monodic music; but it is not necessarily derived from monody, since ordinarily Monteverdi takes the setting of caesurae with full cadences from the native song. With the voices tightly locked together, Monteverdi carries the declamatory phrases, one by one, upward to a dramatic climax, over the unaltered "organ point" of the bass, and then reverses the procedure, leading the phrases downward, and concludes the composition with rising phrases built with the precision of song motifs, which start with a canonic imitation. There is nothing of Florentine monody in this ingenious structure, but much of what Monteverdi had previously exploited in dramatizing the musical form. He often arranged the phrasing of his late madrigals according to the verse lines,

[5] Redlich, *Claudio Monteverdi*, p. 167.
[6] E. Schmitz, "Zur Geschichte des italienischen Continuo-Madrigals in 17. Jahrhundert," in *SIMG*, XI (1910), 513.

with unconcealed caesurae and cadences in all parts. This procedure is followed chiefly in melodies that unmistakably follow the outlines of the canzonetta. *Eccomi pronta* is so organized.

Most of the madrigals have a combination of two voices either of equal or different timbre, for Monteverdi cultivated the solo duet with particular care and provided for it the first truly classical solution, in which the harmonic counterpoint adds a flexibility and variety unexpected in such a restricted medium. The long and repeated series of parallel voices are, however, his favorite form of voice leading, and have a strikingly sensuous sonority. They embody a realism that is the basis of all baroque artistic forms, no matter how much ornamentation and rhetoric may embroider and veil the realistic core of sensuality. In addition to their profound intellectual and human qualities, these tonal effects exercise a powerful impact upon the senses. In this alluring sensuality Monteverdi speaks the language of his time; but with him, it is the basis upon which the work is built and not an end in itself. It is not only the amount of sensuality, but its use as an end or as a means that separates the chaff from the wheat among baroque musicians. There are forms in Monteverdi's compositions in which sensuousness is the prevailing feature—as for example, the long sequence of parallel voices with its remarkable harmonic effects. Was not the prevalence of harmonic conceptions in the new counterpoint also an indication of the new importance of sensuous impression in his approach to the artistic work? In the duet combination of the madrigals Monteverdi skillfully used contrapuntal devices, many of which produce harmonic effects, and the form of the melodic motifs points altogether in that direction. The devices employed in the treatment of motifs vary from madrigal to madrigal; a particularly effective one is the dramatic or expressive rendering of contrapuntal imitation of motifs, as in *S'el vostro cor Madonna,* for tenor and bass. First, the motif is presented by each voice alone, in successive imitation, and each time the motif is raised in the manner by which Monteverdi so often gave the simplest device an expressiveness of great intensity. The motif rises in imitation until the voices unite, whereupon an imitative procedure locks the motifs more tightly together. The procedure works with hints and allusions, as it were, rather than with a systematic directness. This type of contrapuntal device has decidedly the character of improvisation, and spontaneity seems to be its main force; but in the end the composition has unfolded itself as a series of steps, well considered and even calculated. This technique of imitation is found in all the duets and trios of the collection. The type of the motif, however, changes melodically, and each has its own stylistic background. First, there is the motif in the manner of recitation, mostly very simple, sometimes even monotonous. Monteverdi uses this largely in passages of intense melancholy; but it is least frequent in these madrigals. It has its origin in those monotonous recitations of madrigalesque works in which Monteverdi approached the character of a litany or of psalmodic reciting. The second form of motif, represented in almost every madrigal, and used either throughout the composition or in parts of it, is derived from the canzonetta. It has a rapid syllabic declamation and a parlando effect if the declamatory line is extended:

Ex. 93   VII, 59

Che va·ga e vo·la e non si può te· ne· re   non si può te· ne·re non si può non si può

This canzonetta type, reduced to a brief motif, has a remarkable precision:

Ex. 94   VII

E un spi· ri· tel· lo   Ec· co· mi pron· ta

The type branches out to include general characteristics of the native songs and forms the basis for either an arioso (in duple rhythm) or a dance melody (in triple rhythm):

Ex. 95   VII

Sa· ran no i tro·fei vostri el ro·go mi·   o   Sa· ran no i trofei vo·str el ro·go mi· o

O· lu· ci bel· le   Deh sia· te si ru· bel· le   di lu· me

There is also a third form of the motif, with melismatic groups and often profuse figuration of a stereotyped nature, a form that had been developed in previous madrigals:

Ex. 96 VII

It is this style of melody which Monteverdi worked out within the *stile concertato*, and he uses it chiefly in connection with suggestive words. A special form of this type serves the purpose of expressing excitement and stirring passion; its characteristics are an unusually wide range and large intervals, in addition to the figuration:

Ex. 97 VII

And there is finally that extraordinary motif, specifically Monteverdian, which is dramatic not only in direct expressiveness, but also in origin, since Monteverdi used it in his dramatic music. It is, therefore, related to the monodic recitation, but also has the wide range and the exclamatory intervals:

Ex. 98 VII

All these forms of motifs, which, of course, have their bearing upon his conceptions of melody in general, are stylistically differentiated, completely clarified, and used with an artistic subtlety and assurance of purpose which show that Monteverdi has reached the last phase of his maturity.

The madrigals of the seventh book also clarify the structure of the bass. We have seen in previous madrigals that Monteverdi, bent upon discovering a uniform structure for the composition, frequently worked with stereotyped basses, which were for the most part basses of dances or their derivatives. In the seventh book this principle reached a new maturity. The most famous example is the *Romanesca*, for two soprani, which is, with its four sections, the most extended cantata of the volume. In all four parts, the bass, which has the *Romanesca* melody, remains the same.[7] While Monteverdi had previously endeavored to formulate the *basso ostinato* or its likeness, even as early as in the first book of his madrigals, it is here that full mastery of that structure is achieved. For along with a bass melody that remains the same throughout the sections goes the art of variation in the soloistic duet. Also in the upper parts the substance of the material remains the same; the technique of variation is an outstanding example of Monteverdi's structural ingenuity. As a matter of fact, the "Ohimè" motif, for which he had invented some typical formulas, determines the course of the whole *prima parte*, and since the three following sections vary the material of the *prima parte*, the "Ohimè" motif governs the whole cantata.

Next to the *Romanesca*, the madrigal *Con che soavità*, for solo soprano with orchestral accompaniment, represents his highest artistic achievement. Here Monteverdi combines many styles of melody to make a new entity: There is a simple, haunting melodiousness at the beginning with the symmetry of a song; there are vivid motifs of the *concertato* style and an intensive declamation with little variety of tonal range; and all these are used in conjunction with an orchestra which in three *continuo* groups is divided according to the tone color of the instrument. The sonata on the litany of 1610 has a similar imposing largeness in its formal idea, but Guarini's *Con che soavità* has a profundity which puts it beyond its own age and makes it valid for all time.

---

[7] Concerning such basses and their relation to dances, see O. Gombosi in *RaM*, VII (1934), 14ff.

CHAPTER FIFTEEN

The Art of Representation: Ballo, Scenic Cantata, Drama

TIRSI E CLORI

THE madrigals of the seventh book are the classic formulation of Monteverdi's madrigalesque art and set the standards of the musical culture that Monteverdi brought to Venice. They were the music through which the aristocratic circles and the connoisseurs learned the nature and artistic greatness of the new style, which had now attained a form that endured through the century. Monteverdi's art became the guide for musicians near and far, as his madrigals spread throughout Italy and into foreign countries. In Padua, Bologna, Florence, Milan, Rome, Mantua, his madrigals took first place in the repertory of the time.

Many of his works went immediately to Mantua, where his previous madrigals and other compositions were apparently still performed on the regular concert evenings in the ducal palace. Communications between Monteverdi and the Mantuans remained lively. Especially in the earlier years of his Venetian period, his letters to Mantua—that is, to his friend, the ducal counselor Alessandro Striggio—were numerous; five or six letters went to Mantua almost every year, and for the year 1620 we have no less than twenty-three. It is from these letters that we know many of the artistic plans considered by Monteverdi and learn of works now lost. In them Monteverdi often discussed basic ideas of his art and principles of composition, and these discussions reveal important secrets of his music.

Although Monteverdi was bound by his engagement at St. Mark's and had to secure permission for outside activities from the procurators of the cathedral, he apparently had no difficulty in obtaining it. The Mantuan court continued to call for his works, even immediately after he accepted the position in Venice. At the end of 1615 he was commissioned to write the music for a ballo scheduled for performance at the Mantuan court. Duke Ferdinand, anxious to preserve the magnificence of the artistic court life of Vincenzo's time, still needed the contribution of his former maestro di cappella. What the occasion for the ballo was, we do not know; possibly it was to be part of the festivities for a wedding which Ferdinand planned.[1] He had cast his eyes upon a young maid of honor, the beautiful Camilla Faà di Bruni, who, though noble and the daughter of Count Ardizzino, was yet of inferior rank. Ferdinand seems to have married her secretly, but in view of the scandal and his family's indignation he soon afterward annulled the marriage and disposed of the unhappy girl by putting her into a nunnery for the rest of her life, separated from her son Giacinto. It may also be—and this is perhaps more probable—that the ballo was performed on the occasion of Ferdinand's coronation on January 5, 1616.

Whatever the occasion, Monteverdi responded promptly and dispatched the work, *Tirsi e Clori*, to Mantua in November, 1615. He included the ballo in the publication of his seventh book of madrigals four years later as *Ballo Concertato con voci et instrumenti à 5*. In his letter to Alessandro Striggio, dated November 21, 1615, he gave interesting instructions for the performance. He suggested that the performers stand in a half circle, like a half-moon, and that at each corner of the half circle there should be placed a chitarrone and a clavicembalo as *continuo* instruments in the orchestral groups, one for Clori, the other for Tirsi. Clori and Tirsi themselves should have chitarroni in their hands, and play and sing together with the two orchestral *continuo* instruments; or it might be still better if Clori could have a harp instead of a chitarrone. After the dialogue they would join in the ballo, for which an orchestra of eight viole da braccio, a contrabasso, a spinet, and two small lutes was recommended, and the ballo should be danced in the measure appropriate to the nature of the arias.[2]

The dialogue between Tirsi and Clori is composed in sections suitable to a cantata. Tirsi has a dance song, in triple rhythm, and in structure like the balletto, while Clori's part follows an arioso style, in duple rhythm, but free from any dance pattern, melodic or rhythmic. The

---

[1] This is suggested by Domenico de' Paoli, *Claudio Monteverdi* (Milan, 1945), p. 203.
[2] Letter No. 19; ed. Malipiero, *Claudio Monteverdi*, pp. 161ff.

dance song of Tirsi is used for the first and third strophes, the arioso of Clori for the second and fourth, each with slight variation. For the fifth strophe, however, which ends with the request to dance, "Balliamo," Tirsi and Clori unite in a duet that has the same material as Tirsi's dance song. The ballo itself, sung by a chorus of five parts and accompanied by an orchestra, which is specified in the letter but not in the score, is sectionally arranged; the sections are all repeated and have the structure of dance songs. While the first half of the ballo is governed by the triple rhythm, the second half varies the dance patterns in three groups: ♩♩♩|♩♩♩|| ♪♪♪|♪♪♪||♩♪♪♪♪♪♩| ♩♪♪♪♪♩||

In comparison with the *Ballo dell' Ingrate*, *Tirsi e Clori* has no dramatic implications and concentrates on the pure characteristics of the formal dance.

IL COMBATTIMENTO DI TANCREDI E CLORINDA

The *Ballo* of 1615 was composed for the Mantuan court, but it must be assumed that this work was also used for festival purposes in the circles of the Venetian nobility, where Monteverdi soon acquired many friends and admirers. The inclusion of the *Ballo* in the seventh book of madrigals would seem to indicate this. Among the Venetians who were devoted to Monteverdi's art was Girolamo Mocenigo, a member of one of the oldest families, who also had a genuine interest in the dramatic implications of the new music. He was apparently the first among the Venetians to recognize the representational nature of music produced on the stage, and he made every provision for the theatrical performance of dramatic music. Early in the twenties the music drama was already a part of the festival representations in the palaces of the Venetian aristocracy, and this would probably have led to stage productions in the palaces and perhaps to the foundation of an operatic theater, except for a disaster that befell Venice in 1630. In a little over a year, forty-six thousand Venetians were reported to have died from the plague, and the city of pleasure became a city of death.

The first dramatic composition of Monteverdi that is related to Venice was produced in the palace of Girolamo Mocenigo and originated a style which Monteverdi called the *stile concitato*. When he introduced it in 1624, he explained it as a novelty, although we have seen that it had long been in preparation in his work. In his elaborate preface to the eighth book of madrigals, the *Madrigali Guerrieri et Amorosi* of 1638, he gives an account of the origin and character of the *stile concitato*.

"I have recognized that among our passions or affections (*affettioni del animo*) there are three principal ones: wrath (*Ira*), temperance (*Temperanza*), and humility or prayer (*Humiltà* or *supplicatione*), as our best philosophers affirm and even the very nature of our voice with its high, middle, and low range verifies; and the art of music substantiates them as well, in the terms *concitato*, the excited, *molle*, the soft, and *temperato*, the temperate. In all the works of composers of the past I could not find an example of the excited genre, though of the soft and the temperate, there were many. Yet Plato has described this type in the third book of the *Republic* in these words: 'Take that harmony which in tone and accent imitates those men who bravely go to battle.' Since I was aware that it is contrasts more than anything else that move our souls, and that the end of all good music is to affect the soul, as Boethius affirmed when he said that music, naturally inborn in our being, ennobles man or depraves his morals, therefore with no little study and endeavor I set about the rediscovery of this music. I took into consideration that, according to all the best philosophers, it was the fast pyrrhic meter that was used for bellicose and excited dances, while the slow spondaic meter served for the opposite expression; consequently I began to see that one semibreve (full note) in its full value corresponded to one spondaic beat, that, however, the semibreve divided into sixteen successive semicromes (sixteenth notes), beaten one after the other, and connected with a text that contained wrath and indignation, could well resemble the affection of which I was in search, although the text might not be able to follow the fast tempo of the instruments. In order to give a major example, I took the divine Tasso, the poet who expresses all the passions he sets out to describe in his poetry, with all propriety and naturalness. I found his description of the combat between Tancred and Clorinda; for I had here contrasting passions to be set to music: war, prayer, and even death. In 1624, in the presence of the Venetian nobility, I had the music performed in the house of the Illustrious and Most Excellent Gerolamo Mozzenigo, princely cavalier, and a leading governmental dignitary of the Most Serene Republic, my particular patron and protector. The music was received with great applause and praise. After I had once made a successful beginning of the imitation of wrath, I continued to investigate the style further through more studies and composed sundry works for church and court; and this style was so much appreciated by composers that they not only praised it orally, but also wrote imitations, much to my pleasure and honor. Yet it seems to me appropriate to make known that I am the author of the first investigation and of the first proof of this style so necessary in music, without which music can reasonably be called imperfect, since it had only two styles, the soft and the temperate. At first, musicians, especially those who had to play the *basso continuo*, thought the playing of a note sixteen times to the measure was more ridiculous than praiseworthy; hence they played the tone only once to the measure and thereby reduced the pyrrhic meter to the spondaic; thus, they abolished any resemblance to the excited text. Hence I recommend that the *basso continuo* with its accompaniment be played exactly in manner and form as written. In this style we likewise find that all the other elements must be observed as in other compositions of other styles; for in music there are three such elements: text, harmony, and rhythm. The style of warlike expression which I discovered made me write some madrigals to which I gave the title *Madrigali Guerrieri*. Since the music of great princes is used at their courts in three ways to their delight—in the theater, in the court hall, and for balls—I have, therefore, in my present work alluded to the three kinds in the titles *Guerriera*, *Amorosa*, and *Rappresentativa* [*Musica*]. I know that the work is imperfect, for my capacities are generally limited, especially in this new style of martial expression. Since 'all beginning is feeble, *omne principium est debile*,' I beg the benevolent reader to take pleasure at least in my good intention; I shall expect greater perfection in the nature of this style to come from his pen; for 'it is easy to add to the discovery, *Inventis facile est addere*,' and—*viva felice*." [3]

Each composition was for Monteverdi another attack on the total problem of art, and he gave eloquent evidence that his stylistic achievements resulted from thorough investigations which he thought indispensable to the purpose of his music—the expression of human passions. Monteverdi frankly admitted that he was searching for an adequate musical expression of extreme passion and excitement. If music is to reflect the human passions, all the passions must be conquered and embodied in the artist's work. Music which is limited by dealing with a few selected passions is but a torso of art and a fragment of life. Monteverdi explored the capacities of music and, through antiquity, became the discoverer of the *stile concitato* as the medium for extreme passions.

The *Combattimento di Tancredi e Clorinda* is based on the text of Torquato Tasso's *Gerusalemme liberata*, from which Monteverdi

[3] Preface in Malipiero, *Opere*, VIII; reprinted in Malipiero, *Claudio Monteverdi*, pp. 89ff.

chose sixteen stanzas of the twelfth canto (52–68; stanza 63 is omitted). It is a theatrical composition—in Monteverdi's words, a work *in genere rappresentativo*—and has the makings of scenic music, except that it is limited in size. Even the season at which it was first produced was appropriate for dramatic music. Monteverdi reported in the score that the *Combattimento* was performed in the carnival season as an entertainment at a soiree: "per passatempo di veglia." He also added other valuable information. If the work is performed as a stage production, it has its greatest effect after various other madrigals have been sung *senza gesto* (without theatrical presentation). These madrigals "without gesture"—those that were published in previous books, especially in the sixth and seventh books—were evidently in the repertory of the Venetian soirees. Monteverdi gave further scenic instructions. From that side of the hall where the musicians are placed, suddenly (*alla sprovista*) Clorinda shall appear fully armed but on foot, while Tancred, also armed, shall appear on a horse. The Testo (narrator) immediately begins his part. All the actors express the meaning of the text in steps and gestures, in strict observance of tempo, beat, and step (*tempi, colpi, passi*); and the instrumentalists accurately distinguish between the parts that are *concitati et molli* (excited and soft). The Testo recites rhythmically (*a tempo*) and in such a manner that all three acting parts [4] are united in one. Clorinda speaks when her turn comes, and the Testo is silent, as is Tancred. The orchestra consists of four viole de braccio—soprano, alto, tenore, and basso—and a contrabasso da gamba that goes with the clavicembalo. The instrumentalists must play their parts in imitation of the affections inherent in the text (*ad imitatione delle passioni dell'oratione*). The Testo, in a position somewhat removed from the orchestra, must sing his part with clear, firm voice and good pronunciation in order to make the text comprehensible. He must not insert coloraturas and trills, except in the song for the stanza that begins with "Notte" (54). For the rest, his pronunciation should observe the imitation of the passions in the text (*similitudine delle passioni dell'oratione*).

What type of composition is the *Combattimento*, this work that moved all listeners "to the affection of compassion" and to tears, that was praised because nothing like it had ever been seen or heard? For Monteverdi not only presented a new style, he created a completely new

---

[4] These instructions are reprinted in *Opere*, VIII, 132f. Malipiero has: "che le creationi venghino ad incontrarsi in una imitatione unita." This, of course, does not make sense. The original has correctly: "che le tre ationi," etc.

category which can be clearly defined on the basis of Monteverdi's own reasoning. If the previous madrigals were *senza gesto*, this is a madrigal *con gesto*, and the *Combattimento* can best be defined as a scenic madrigal or, in harmony with baroque conceptions, a scenic cantata. Monteverdi had worked for years to find a structural organization that would differentiate between the narrative section and the direct speech or dialogue, so that, in every respect except that of actual stage production, the composition became a dramatic madrigal. Carrying the differentiation a step further toward the reality of stage production, the dialogue could easily be personified and assigned to actors. The narrative portion of the poem, however, posed some difficulties. Monteverdi had two possible solutions. He could give the narrative in choral form, in contrast to the acting parts. But this solution would too closely resemble the dramatic madrigal *senza gesto*, where he had often given the individual, spoken parts to solo voices and assigned the narrative or contemplative sections to the chorus. The other solution, which Monteverdi actually chose, was to personify the narration in the poem; thus it is that the narrator, or *testo*, enters the madrigal.

The *testo* part retains in its melody the narrative characteristics of its origin. For large sections the range is rather narrow, in order to maintain the monotony of the reciting character. Yet this effect is counterbalanced by a strict rhythmic regulation that proceeds in precise patterns of passionate rhythms. Extensive portions of the *testo* are accompanied, simultaneously or in alternation, by the orchestra, in the form known as the *recitativo accompagnato*. In all these sections, the *testo* has a rhythmic regularity derived from the accompaniment; the melodic expressiveness is that of a simple recitation within a narrow range. All expressiveness, even the exploitation of pictorial effects, is given to the accompaniment. Where the *testo* part, however, has merely the accompaniment of the *continuo* instrument, the melody becomes freer, wider in range, and more dramatic in expression; it approaches the style of monody Monteverdi had previously used for dramatic subjects. This style is used for parts of Tancred and Clorinda, regardless of the accompaniment. It seems that Monteverdi did not intend to exploit fully the resources of melody and harmony. To express extreme passions, he apparently concentrated on the powers of rhythmic motifs, in other words, on the *stile concitato*. There are moving melodic phrases, boldly expressive harmonies; there are techniques which unite separate sections by the strength of a stereotyped harmonic bass. Nevertheless, the rhythm, for once, appears to be the most powerful element. It is presented even in abstract patterns, as it were; the hammering of the rhythm on one tone also occurs in other patterns than the rapid repetition of sixteenth notes. Simultaneously, rhythm and orchestral accompaniment serve the realism which Monteverdi thought necessary for rendering human passions convincingly. In his zeal to exploit his discovery, he may have overworked this powerful realism; at least, he never again presented the style in such a radical fashion.

THE MUSIC DRAMA: PLANS AND COMMISSIONS

The ballo *Tirsi e Clori* showed that the Mantuan court still relied on Monteverdi's contributions to its festival occasions. Soon after Ferdinand, under the pressure of his family, had cleared himself of the disgrace of his secret marriage, plans were made to find a nobler spouse, his engagement to Catarina de' Medici was officially announced, and the wedding was set for February, 1617. The event called for elaborate and careful preparations, and the Mantuans again turned to Monteverdi for the festival music drama. They submitted a text, *La Favola di Peleo e di Teti*, by Count Scipione Agnelli, and in a letter of December 9, 1616, Monteverdi acknowledged the receipt of the commission and of the libretto.[5]

This letter is an artistic document of the first importance, in which Monteverdi sets forth the principles of his approach to a text. The *Favola* had impressed the Mantuans—apparently a reading had tested its effectiveness—and they had great hopes for it; but Monteverdi was not at all impressed, and rejected the composition. His reasons are those of a modern dramatist. Monteverdi assured the Mantuans most politely that he had no desire but to serve the Duke of Mantua, that he was always ready "to obey the orders of His Highness with every respect and promptness." He did not know the poet of the libretto, and, as he said, poetry was not his profession; but he had serious reservations to make, as a musician, in view of the maritime subject upon which the libretto was based. Playing with words, he remarked that first of all music "wants to be mistress over the 'air' and not exclusively over the water." This means "in my language, that the *concerti* described in the text are altogether too base and terrestrial." He noted an extraordinary lack of opportunities to employ beautiful harmonies. He referred

---

[5] Letter No. 22, to Alessandro Striggio; ed. Malipiero, *Claudio Monteverdi*, pp. 165ff. Prunières, *Claudio Monteverdi*, p. 132, states that Monteverdi was not asked to contribute to the marriage, which he dates 1616. The marriage was set for 1617; and in the above letter Monteverdi expressly refers to the service which he was requested to render "nelle future nozze di S.A.S."

to the prescribed noisy wind machines on the stage that would make necessary the doubling of the instrumentation, not for musical reasons, but merely to stand up against the noise. Three chitarroni would be necessary instead of one, three harps instead of one; and even then the voice of the singer would have to be forced. Furthermore, in order to carry out the imitation of the text properly (*la imitatione propria del parlare*), he would have to use more wind instruments than delicate strings. For, in his opinion, the harmonies set for the Tritons and the other marine creatures ought to have trombones and cornets, and not the cetra, clavicembalo, or harp. The whole action takes place out of doors; and did not Plato teach that "cithara debere esse in civitate, et tibia in agris"? Thus, if the harmonies are delicate, they will be inappropriate, and if they are appropriate, they will not be delicate. Then, in looking through the list of actors, one finds that they are all winds, "Amoretti, Zeffiretti, et Sirene"; they all require the range of soprani, and these Zeffiri and Boreali must sing. "How, dear sir, shall I be able to imitate the speaking of winds that do not speak; and how shall I be able to move the affections by such means? Arianna was moving, because she was a woman, and likewise Orfeo was moving, because he was a man, and not a wind. . . . The harmonies imitate human beings, not the noise of winds, the bleating of sheep, the neighing of horses." The imitation of the speech of winds is utterly impossible. The text as a whole appears to him full of ignorance; there is not a scene (*ponto*) that would move the composer, or only with great difficulty, if he wanted to be moved; also, the ending did not affect him. Again he returned to the human aspect—that is all-important. "Arianna moves me to a real lament, and Orfeo to a genuine prayer, but this story—I do not know whither it carries me," wrote Monteverdi. "And I should compose such a text?" he asked his friend Striggio.

Apparently strong pressure was brought to bear on Monteverdi, for in his next letter three weeks later he seems to have given in to the strict "command" of the Duke. He made sure, however, to refer to his heavy duties and wrote that he would do what he could. He does not appear to have started actual composition at once. Meanwhile, Striggio tried to change the Duke's mind. In a letter to the Duke, he mentioned that Count Agnelli was working on another text, *La Congiunta d'Alceste et d'Admeto*, which when completed should immediately be dispatched to Monteverdi. On the other side, he tried to assure the composer that *Le Nozze di Peleo e Tetide* was not really a music drama, such as *Ari-*

anna or *Orfeo;* the work was intended to be performed in single scenes or acts as intermezzi to the "great comedy." Under these circumstances, which eliminated the dramatic and human problems, Monteverdi accepted, and proceeded with the composition.

There must have been a good deal of confusion in the preparation of the Mantuan festivities, which were to be on a large scale. No less than five music dramas or similar scores were in the making. The *Nozze di Peleo e Tetide* of Monteverdi was planned as a group of intermezzi. The *Alceste* had been suggested by Striggio, who had already informed Monteverdi to prepare himself for its composition. The comedy *Galatea*—another watery affair—by Chiabrera was in the hands of Sante Orlandi, the successor of Monteverdi at the Mantuan court. *La Favola di Ati e Cibele* had as its composer Francesco Rasi, the famous singer who played a leading role in the operatic annals of Mantua. *La Favola di Endimione,* written by the Duke himself, was also planned as a music drama. All these simultaneous projects were bound to get in each other's way. The first work that was dropped by order of the Duke was *Le Nozze di Peleo e Tetide!* And in the end the *Galatea* alone was performed—a poor result after such profuse preparations.[6] Monteverdi, whose work on the *Nozze* was called off, was naturally disappointed and indignant, since he had completed all the monologues. Moreover, he had been invited by Ottavio Rinuccini to attend the wedding of Duke Ferdinand with Catarina de' Medici in Florence, where all the nobility and the Grand Duke himself were anxious to see him, and had rejected this invitation to keep himself free for the composition of the *Alceste,* the order for which he was waiting in vain.

In spite of this shabby treatment, Monteverdi continued to give his art to the Mantuan court. That same year he composed his share of a co-operative work, the "Sacra Rappresentazione" *La Maddalena,* the text being written by the famous leader of the troupe of comedians, Giovanni Battista Andreini, with whom Monteverdi had an acquaintance of long standing. The composers of this sacred play were Muzio Efrem, Alessandro Giuvizzani, and Salomone Rossi. Monteverdi wrote the instrumental ritornello for five parts and the prologue sung by "Favor divino." Both compositions are very short and artistically insignificant. All the music to *La Maddalena* was published by Andreini in 1617: *Musiche de alcuni eccellentissimi musici composte per la*

---

[6] See Achille Neri, in *Giornale Storico della letteratura italiana,* VII, 327.

Maddalena, Sacra Rappresentazione di Gio. Battista Andreini Fiorentino.[7]

Monteverdi was even encouraged to write dramatic works for Mantua, and always answered promptly with a disarming willingness to serve the house of Gonzaga. In 1618 a request came from Vincenzo, the brother of Ferdinand and the heir apparent, who wanted to have a libretto of Ercole Marigliani set to music. Monteverdi accepted and may have started composition immediately. But was his heart really in the work, or did he merely accept because it was a commission from a Gonzaga? At all events, the work took a long time. Monteverdi frequently apologized, when he was reminded of his delay by Alessandro Striggio, referring to the burdensome demands upon him whenever great religious feasts called for special compositions. Nevertheless, he kept on working at the score and inquired about one or another aspect of the composition. By the spring of 1619 he does not seem to have accomplished much, and at the end of the year, when further complaints were accompanied by a sudden demand that the work be completed for the carnival in 1620, he was quite upset and wished Marigliani to be informed that he could not possibly compose at such speed. Even if he could finish the music, there would be no time for the rehearsals, which he considered essential. Monteverdi was asked to come to Mantua to take charge of the performance, but he declined, and the work was undoubtedly never completed. Whatever the reason, in this case the Gonzagas can hardly be blamed for the failure.

From the correspondence with Striggio on Marigliani's *Andromeda*, we learn that Monteverdi had composed a ballo and a text by Striggio, an "egloga," as he called the *Apollo*, apparently in the nature of a scenic cantata, *con gesto*. This piece was produced several times in Venice at the house of a certain Signor Benbi for an audience of noble ladies and gentlemen. The *Lamento d'Apollo*, especially, had a great effect, for the audience was pleased with the plot, the verses, and the music as well.[8] In view of its success, Monteverdi thought the *Apollo* might well be performed in Mantua, perhaps in place of the *Andromeda*, but nothing came of it. Since the music is lost, the suggestion that it may belong to the new category of scenic cantatas is, of course, hypothetical.

The year 1620, in which there was a lively correspondence between Monteverdi and Mantua, brought the composer face to face with an important decision. First, Duke Ferdinand, a man of impulsive action,

---

[7] See the two compositions of Monteverdi in Malipiero, *Opere*, XI, 170f.

[8] Letter No. 39, dated February 1, 1620; ed. Malipiero, *Claudio Monteverdi*, p. 188.

made an urgent request that Monteverdi's *Arianna* be performed again in the Mantuan theater. The composer quickly responded by sending off his score with some changes and improvements inserted on the spur of the moment. The performance was canceled as suddenly as Ferdinand had conceived the idea. The death of Sante Orlandi now created a vacancy in the office of maestro di cappella in Mantua. Through a special agent and by letter the Duke offered the position to Monteverdi in consideration of his previous service and continued loyalty to the Gonzagas, in view of their uninterrupted communications, especially in regard to dramatic work, and, naturally, because of the unrivaled reputation of the composer. In a long reply, dated March 13, 1620, Monteverdi rejected the offer. As politeness dictated, he begins by expressing his gratitude for the great honor and by remarking that the years of his youth in Mantua had left an indelible impression on his heart. That was undoubtedly true and helps to explain Monteverdi's astonishing loyalty. But he measures his position at St. Mark's against the offer. He speaks of his present authority, of the general respect that has been shown him, of the generosity with which the procurators have responded to his work, of honors granted him and of enthusiasm over his music; all Venice flocks to hear it. Indeed, it is the "sweetest service." Mantua, however, had no sweetness in the service. Then all the bitterness and anger that had accumulated over the years breaks through. He had not been treated with due respect; minor talents had received greater favor than he; and humiliating treatment was always accorded him when he begged for his due. "I did not suffer any greater mental humiliation than at those times when I had to wait in the antechamber to obtain what was due to me." It was a frank letter, and Monteverdi apologized for its frankness. It was a document that reflected no particular honor on the court administration, and, because of it, the court did not pursue negotiations further.[9]

In connection with the education of his son Francesco, who was studying law at Bologna, Monteverdi went to that city in 1620. Among his many friends and ardent admirers, there was the composer Adriano Banchieri, whose works occupy a distinguished place in the history of music. Banchieri had previously expressed his adherence to the new music of Monteverdi, and apparently it was he who prepared a festival that took place at a meeting of the Accademia Florida, called together for the occasion in the monastery of St. Michele in Bosco on June 13, 1620. Girolamo Giacobbi and others of the best musicians of Bologna

---

[9] Letter No. 46; *ibid.*, pp. 198ff.

were present; speeches were given and concerti played in honor of the eminent guest.[10]

Requests for compositions of dramatic music continued to challenge Monteverdi's creative powers. He accepted the commissions readily, because the *genere rappresentativo* was his chief interest; in fact, he now thought that any other form of music distracted him from his true tasks. Most of the dramatic compositions were still connected with the Mantuan court. In the spring of 1621, Ercole Marigliani, the secretary of the Duke and the poet of the ill-fated *Andromeda*, commissioned Monteverdi to compose the music for three "Intermedii," apparently by Marigliani himself. No specific festivity was mentioned as the occasion for these intermezzi. The composition took Monteverdi more than half a year, and in November, 1621, he wrote the Duchess that the intermezzi had been sent to Marigliani. There is no record of any performance and no trace of the music.

The Mantuans were not the only ones who were anxious to obtain dramatic compositions from the famous composer. Many Venetian noble families were eager to introduce the music drama into their palaces, and Monteverdi must have been asked to write, if not elaborate dramas, at least such scenic cantatas as he presented with his *Combattimento*. Giustiniano, a member of one of the twelve families of the highest Venetian aristocracy—the Mocenighi were one of the thirty families next in rank—was apparently among those who favored the composer with such theatrical plans. At one time, he even sought the good services of Monteverdi to persuade the Duke of Mantua to permit the famous troupe of the Andreini to "come to Venice to recite comedies." Monteverdi sent off his letter of intervention in behalf of "Giustiniano Gentilhomo di molta autorità in questa Ser.ma Republica." [11] Other princes also approached Monteverdi to produce dramatic compositions: in a letter dated March 15, 1625, he mentions that he has been very busy with compositions "in chiesa et alla camera," for "quest' Altezza di Pollonia." [12] This commission has been taken to indicate the vast range of Monteverdi's fame, extending even to Poland, but it is more likely that this Highness was one of the numerous princes who regularly came to Venice to seek pleasure incognito, who rented a palace and held court as custom prescribed. They not only had soirees

---

[10] Vogel, *op. cit.*, document No. 14, pp. 433f.

[11] Letter No. 69, to Alessandro Striggio; ed. Malipiero, *Claudio Monteverdi*, p. 226.

[12] Letter No. 79, to Ercole Marigliani; *ibid.*, p. 239. Monteverdi mentions the "prencipe di Pollonia" as his patron once more in letter No. 102, September 10, 1627; *ibid.*, p. 269.

with elaborate musical entertainments, but also made arrangements for special church services, often with stupendous musical performances, not so much to atone for their all-too-worldly pleasures as to enjoy the opportunity of meeting the ladies in church. Among the commissions Monteverdi received from the Prince of Poland may well have been one or more compositions of a dramatic nature.

In 1626 Duke Ferdinand died without an heir, and was succeeded by his brother, Vincenzo II, a sick man. Vincenzo had always had a great admiration for Monteverdi and attempted to call the composer back to Mantua with the same result as before and the same excuses for rejecting the offer being given. Possibly in connection with Vincenzo's coronation, an important operatic work originated. We hear about it for the first time in a letter of 1627 (from that year no less than twenty-five letters are preserved). On May 1 Monteverdi wrote: "I have composed many stanzas of Tasso, beginning with Armida's 'O tu che porte,' and followed by the whole lament and burst of wrath, together with the replies of Ruggiero [*read:* Rinaldo] which will probably not displease." This composition is not preserved, but Monteverdi had once before, in madrigals of the third book, treated parts of this *Armida* scene. Then he continued: "I have composed the *Combattimento di Tancredi con Clorinda,* and have now thoroughly thought over a little work (*operina*) of Giulio Strozzi, a very beautiful and curious one; it comprises about 400 verses and has the title *Licori finta pazza inamorata d'Aminta;* there are a thousand ridiculous ideas, ending with the marriage, done with a beautiful art of intrigue, very appropriate for episodes." Monteverdi thinks of contrasts and complications that would lend themselves to his style of music.[13] He succeeded in whetting Striggio's appetite; for a few days later he sent the libretto upon request and added that the text was not yet set to music, neither had it ever been printed or performed on stage, for the author had brought the libretto directly to him as soon as it was finished.

Never before had Monteverdi shown such enthusiasm; he went on to praise the qualities of the text for which he would compose music if the Duke gave an order: The libretto has highly emotional parts (*amoratissimi componimenti*), and is distinguished by the beauty of its verse and by the invention and the development as well. "It is true the part of Licori is very varied and must be given only to a singer who would be able to act now as man, now as woman, with lively gestures and extreme passions; for the imitation of feigned madness must always

---

[13] Letter No. 89, *ibid.*, p. 250.

involve a momentary situation only, not one in the past or in the future. The imitation must rest upon the single word, not upon the meaning of the whole sentence; if the text mentions 'war,' it must be imitated; if 'peace,' the imitation must be applied to it; if 'death,' it has to be imitated and so forth; and since the transformations and imitations follow one another with great rapidity and have the main share in arousing the comic effect and sympathy, it will be necessary for the singer to omit any imitation other than the momentary one which the word suggests. I believe that Signorina Margherita [Basile] will be most excellent. But I know for certain that the work will cost me great pains to bring out with greater effect my inner feelings (*per mostrar di più effetto del mio interno affetto*)."

Monteverdi goes on to speak of a libretto by Rinuccini, the *Narciso*, which he has sent to Striggio to get his friend's opinion on it. He had received the libretto from Rinuccini himself, when he was still alive, and the poet had been very anxious to see his *Narciso* composed by Monteverdi. Yet he has been thinking about it, and, in his opinion, the *Narciso* does not have the power which he could wish. There are also too many soprani for the nymphs and too many tenors for the shepherds, so that there would be too little variety, and the end is too tragic and gloomy.[14] Here again Monteverdi demonstrates the keen judgment with which he considers texts. It may be added that the *Narciso* was not composed.

The enthusiastic judgment on *La finta pazza Licori*, on the other hand, caused Monteverdi to make a remarkable statement, which reveals his depth of feeling. He speaks of the inner affection that enters into his musical composition. The human passions, the affections which he characterizes in his work, are always those of all men. In his work he measures the depth and essence of these passions, of his own human capacities, of his experience and affection; these capacities enable him to respond to the nature of human passions where others hear nothing or remain insensitive. He speaks of the thorough mental preparation (*assai digesto in mente*) that precedes composition and involves the object and method of imitation, whereby he sounds out both the objective passion and himself, in order to discover the appropriate form with which to respond to the object.

Monteverdi's mind was occupied for a long time with this mental exploration of the material of *La finta pazza Licori*. All the letters of May, June, and July discussed the subject from various angles, and he

[14] Letter No. 90, *ibid.*, pp. 252f.

was always concerned with the problems of imitation. He got the author, Strozzi, to come to Venice to go over with him certain changes which he thought necessary. He requested an arrangement of five acts instead of the original three, and he was very pleased with Strozzi's graciousness in following all his ideas. At last he was able to send the first act to Striggio in Mantua on July 10, 1627, pointing out that in every act there would be a ballo, each different from the other, and that they would be bizarre.[15] On September 10, 1627, he finally dispatched the remainder of the score to Mantua. And that is the end of the story! We hear nothing of a performance, and the music is lost. Many of Monteverdi's dramatic works were lost, but this is the most to be regretted, for *La finta pazza Licori* was his only comic opera and the first in the history of music.

When he wrote Striggio that the score of *La finta pazza Licori* was on its way to Mantua, Monteverdi mentioned that he had started new compositions in dramatic music. The Marchese Bentivoglio had asked him to compose the music for the festivities at the wedding of Odoardo Farnese of Parma and Margherita de' Medici, which was arranged for 1628. Monteverdi agreed, and Bentivoglio enthusiastically reported to the Duchess of Parma that his delight at the commission was indescribable; for Monteverdi was "the most affable gentleman and the greatest artist in his profession whom we now have." [16] Luigi Inghirami, who was to report on these festivities, praised Monteverdi in equal terms, saying that he was "today the greatest musician in Italy."

The commission involved full responsibility for all the musical performances as well as the composition of various large works. One of the intermezzi that Monteverdi composed for the occasion, *Gli Amori di Diana et d'Endimione*, is specifically mentioned in a letter dated unmistakably September 10, 1617. Because of the date, this intermezzo, which was described as divided into four scenes, has been related to contacts Monteverdi is supposed to have made with Parma before the marriage. But the date of the letter was changed to 1627 by Malipiero, and undoubtedly the emendation is correct.[17] According to Monteverdi's own description the subject of *Gli Amori di Diana e di Endimione* was the wrath and discord between Venus and Diana, the re-

---

[15] Letter No. 97, *ibid.*, p. 263.

[16] Vogel, *op. cit.*, p. 385, n. 4.

[17] See Frank Walker, "Verdi & Francesco Florimo: Some Unpublished Letters," in *M&L*, Vol. 26 (1945), pp. 201ff. (Walker here accepts the date 1617 as authentic.) Walker now agrees with Malipiero on 1627; see F. Walker, "Correspondence concerning a Monteverdi Letter," in *M&L*, Vol. 29 (1948), p. 433.

establishment of order and calm by Pluton, and the love affair between Diana and Endimione. Monteverdi was interested in the subject because of the contrasts of affections. The composition involved five intermezzi on texts by Ascanio Pii, the "comedy" being the *Aminta* of Torquato Tasso.

In October, 1627, Monteverdi went to Parma to begin the composition and study of the works, though the wedding was not celebrated until the following October. We have only two descriptions of the wedding festivities, one by Marcello Buttigli and one an unofficial report by Luigi Inghirami.[18] The intermezzi were performed as late as December 13, 1628, and Inghirami described the subjects and scenes but had little more to say of the music than that the compositions were "marvelous," "divine," and "of heavenly voices and instruments," though he adds that "the music was the spirit and soul of the whole." Many musicians came to the wedding: instrumentalists from Piacenza and singers from Rome and Modena, among whom was the celebrated Loreto Vittori.

A second major work by Monteverdi was performed a week later in the beautiful Teatro Farnese. This was the torneo, *Mercurio e Marte*, by Claudio Achillini, a lengthy work of more than a thousand verses. The torneo gave Monteverdi trouble, as was always the case where a text did not present contrasting, well-defined affections. The text of the torneo was "far removed from music," it had no "variations of the affections"; so Monteverdi brought some variety into the music and hoped for the best.[19] The part of Aurora, as sung by Settimia Caccini, aroused great enthusiasm in the audience.

In a letter of December, 1627. and again in one of February, 1628, Monteverdi mentions his *Armida* as a work that has been completed. It was urgently requested by Duke Vincenzo II, who might have heard it before, since the composition was much to his liking. Monteverdi ordered the work to be copied and then apparently forgot about it, for when he was in Parma, he had to write Striggio that the *Armida* was in the hands of Count Mocenigo. What *Armida* did Monteverdi have in mind? Does he refer to the composition on Tasso's lines, "O tu che

---

[18] See Marcello Buttigli, *Descrittione dell'apparato fatto per honorare la prima, e solenne entrata in Parma della Serenissima Prencipessa Margherita di Toscana, Duchessa di Parma, Piacenza* (Parma, 1629). Cf. P. Minucci del Rossi, "Le Nozze di Margherita de' Medici con Odoardo Farnese, Duca di Parma e Piacenza," in *Rassegna Nazionale*, VII (Florence, 1885; issues February, April, May).

[19] Letter No. 114, dated Parma, February 4, 1628; ed. Malipiero, *Claudio Monteverdi*, p. 287.

porte," that he composed in 1627 at the time he started *La finta pazza Licori*? We are convinced it is this scene to which Monteverdi refers in his letter.

Ill fate attended these dramatic works of Monteverdi. All are lost, and nothing remains from all these festivities except some scanty reports. There is one more severe loss to record. In 1630 the two families whose special friendship and admiration he enjoyed, the Mocenighi and Giustiniani, intermarried. The wedding of Giustiniana Mocenigo and Lorenzo Giustiniani took place in the palace of Count Girolamo Mocenigo, where six years before the *Combattimento* had been produced. The author of *La finta pazza Licori*, Giulio Strozzi, was invited to write the text which was entitled *Proserpina Rapita, Anatopismo del Sig. Giulio Strozzi, honorato di musica dal Sig. Claudio Monteverde.* The performance of this music drama equaled in splendor those of the reigning princes for whom Monteverdi had worked. The ballet master was Girolamo Scolari, and the chief engineer, the "ingegnoso signore Giuseppe Schioppi." The Venetian nobility presented the music drama in its entirety long before the first public opera house was opened, but Monteverdi's share in this achievement can only be gleaned from fragmentary records.

CHAPTER
SIXTEEN

The Composer at St. Mark's

A S MAESTRO di cappella of St. Mark's, Monteverdi was in a
position of absolute musical authority over about thirty singers
and twenty instrumentalists, and though they were occasionally un-
ruly, and the maestro had to intervene as a peacemaker, the relations
between the musicians and Monteverdi were generally of the best.
They admired him as a great artist, and a good many of them became
his disciples. Since the rehearsals and technical preparations of the
performances were duties of the vice maestro, the chief function of
the maestro was to compose music for the services. Monteverdi published a selection of these sacred compositions in his *Selva Morale e
Spirituale*, with a dedication to "Sacra Cesarea Maesta dell'Imperatrice
Eleonora Gonzaga," dated May 1, 1641. After the composer's death,
Alessandro Vincenti made a selection which he published in 1650
under the title *Messa a quattro Voci et Salmi*, and some twenty additional religious compositions appeared in anthologies for which Monteverdi was not responsible. In the *Selva Morale*, there are twenty-nine
compositions, besides the parody *Pianto della Madonna*, a complete
Mass with three substitute compositions, and a Gloria. In the collection
of 1650 there are fourteen compositions and a complete Mass. Altogether, two complete Masses and a Gloria, and sixty-four compositions
of varied religious character represent Monteverdi's creative contributions to the music of the service. Spread over a period of thirty years,
this output is not voluminous, though we must take it for granted that
many works are lost. Of the loss of at least three major cycles, we have
definite knowledge, in addition to the loss of all the motets or cantatas
that were written for the religious ceremony of the Wedding of Venice

to the Sea on the Feast of Ascension. When we consider that the composition of sacred music was an inescapable obligation on which the composer's position depended, we must find the volume of his sacred work relatively small. He was not required, of course, to provide original compositions for all the liturgies of the year for which music was used. As was the custom, he augmented the musical repertory with works of other composers. Especially in the less solemn liturgies, the church was beginning to use works of the sixteenth century; and Venetian musicians who held secondary positions at St. Mark's also contributed music for the services. Even so, it is surprising that Monteverdi did not produce far more liturgical music than is preserved.

For the high feasts of the year, special solemnities were prescribed, and the demands on the composer were particularly great. Christmas, Holy Week, Easter, the Feast of St. Mark, Pentecost, the Feasts of the Holy Cross and the Ascension—all were occasions on which the maestro di cappella was expected to devote himself to the services. Special feasts of saints favored by the Venetians were celebrated in their favorite churches, and these also called for occasional contributions by Monteverdi. These were not obligatory, but his reputation was so great that his compositions were much in demand. We know of at least two contributions he made to music in churches other than St. Mark's: one to San Salvatore in 1620, the other for the nuns of S. Lorenzo. The latter was not necessarily a liturgical composition, although Monteverdi referred to it as "certa musica ecclesiastica." The religious compositions he offered to the Mantuan court, one for the Duchess and one for the Duke, were in all likelihood works that had been composed for Venetian services. In 1621 Monteverdi offered a Mass, which he was sure would delight the Duchess; and in 1627 he inquired whether the Duke would like to have a Mass and vespers. These works probably had already been performed in Venice, and Monteverdi wanted to make further use of them.

Monteverdi's attitude toward his sacred music was rather peculiar. References to religious music are not infrequent in his letters, especially when the pressure of his duties was heavy on the great feasts of the year, but while in discussions of his profane compositions he is often expansive, interested in details of form and expression, and wholly absorbed by the project at hand, his religious music is mentioned only to indicate the business (the *affari*) that went with his position: "We have just had Holy Week, and I have been terribly busy"; "Easter is approaching, and that means much business"; "Dur-

ing the Christmas holy days I am wholly occupied," and so on. Not
once is there a reference to the stylistic character of a work or to his
artistic intentions, nor even an expression of interest in a composition.
His letter of April 21, 1618, to Alessandro Striggio, is almost entirely
an apology for not having sent the music to *Andromeda* because of
his duties: first there were the "giorni santi" (Holy Week) and Easter;
then the Feast of the Holy Cross was approaching, when "the Most
Holy Blood will be displayed and it will be my duty to prepare a Mass
concertato and motets for the whole day, since all day long the Most
Holy Blood will be shown on an altar in the middle of St. Mark's."
This time Monteverdi mentions that it will be a Mass in the *stile concertato*, but his description shows more interest in the display than in
the music; he adds that he has to arrange for the solemn Mass and vespers on the Day of Ascension, always sung on that day in St. Mark's.[1]

Monteverdi is sometimes even more outspoken in his attitude, as
where he says he would proceed faster with his profane music if he
did not have to compose ecclesiastic music, or applies the phrase "servitio de la musica" to religious music, implying that it was merely a
burden (1627), or refers to his labors at St. Mark's (1620). In January,
1620, he writes that "my ecclesiastical service has removed me somewhat from the species of theatrical music," and in a similar mood he
says, "The service at St. Mark's has distracted me"—distracted him, of
course, from his dramatic profane music. Monteverdi leaves no doubt
that he means "servitio" to be taken literally as a duty and a burden.
This is the more surprising, since he is genuinely appreciative of the
advantages and honors he received for his "servitio." It would be totally
erroneous were we to conclude that he was indifferent to religion or,
indeed, to conclude anything about his religion at all. So far as we
know, he was unquestionably a religious man, and this conflict between profane and sacred music was not a religious problem, but exclusively an artistic one. His true task—his mission as an artist—was
in the sphere of profane and dramatic music, and anything outside that
was an interference. Whatever did not serve his profane art was a dis-
traction, an obstacle, and he looked upon it with dismay. His church
music was written to fulfill the duties of his official position; his secular
music was an inner, artistic necessity.[2]

---

[1] Letter No. 30; ed. Malipiero, *Claudio Monteverdi*, p. 177.

[2] This aspect of Monteverdi's religious music and of the related passages in his
letters has been entirely overlooked. Even the detailed investigation of Bettina Lupo
does not discuss the matter; see her essay "Sacre monodie monteverdiane," in *Musica*,
II (Florence, 1943), 51ff.

Monteverdi's religious work at Venice includes the ordinary of the Mass and, in the form of motets, mostly psalm compositions, the Magnificat, a few antiphons, a litany, and a small set of hymns. Most of these works belong to a certain part of the officium, to a limited section of the services. His musical activities were severely restricted in the liturgy. Only on prominent feast days, when the church calendar prescribed solemnity for the Mass and vespers, could elaborate artistic compositions be justified. The Mass on Sundays did not admit the full employment of his artistic resources. This long-established practice did not result from any opposition to the use of art in the liturgy, but rather from a certain neglect or indifference. Monteverdi had singled out the Mass and vespers for his province, even during his Mantuan period, and his choice remained the same in Venice. In his letters Monteverdi mentions his work in sacred music only in connection with the high feasts, never in relation to the regular Sunday services. Obviously he was not expected to provide new compositions for them; had this been the case, he would have had reason to complain of his "servitio" more frequently! The music for the Sunday services was of a simple character, without full instrumental apparatus, a purely choral, a cappella performance. For the a cappella form, the composer naturally chose a choral polyphony in harmony with the sixteenth-century style; in such works, the otherwise abandoned, antiquated contrapuntal polyphony made its reappearance. Even the inclusion of instruments in a religious composition did not necessarily imply the use of all the available apparatus. The combination of a few instruments with a few soloistic voices was thought to be sufficiently expressive of solemnity, as we know from descriptions of musical performances at the services of special feasts. Monteverdi occasionally mentioned soloistic singers whom he tested for St. Mark's. They would be used in works written in the modern idiom, and thus, the modern style was also associated with some degree of liturgical solemnity.

Monteverdi's religious work was in three distinct styles: the a cappella composition with the organ as basso continuo, the monody with characteristics of the stile recitativo, and the stile concertato in all its numerous varieties. The monody in stile recitativo was not favored, and was hardly ever presented in its pure form. The Pianto della Madonna is the best example of a dramatic monody in religious music; but the Pianto is a parody. Through its new Latin text, dedicated to St. Mary, it takes on a religious connotation, but there is no place in the liturgies of the St. Mary feasts to which one would dare assign it.

There is one other composition in which Monteverdi approached the recitation of the monody, a *Salve regina a voce sola*, composed in 1620, or shortly thereafter, since it made its first and only appearance in the anthology of religious music which Simonetti published in 1625.[3] As an antiphon, its place is in the liturgy of the compline, and it must have been used in that service. Stylistically, it does not present monody in its pure form. Its beginning is clearly that of an arioso with a typical melodic phrasing. When the actual prayers start "Ad te clamamus" with increased emotional intensity, the *stile recitativo* is used, in keeping with the dramatic, passionate connotations of that style. The exclamatory phrase at "Ad te clamamus" is derived from a passage of chant melody which Hermannus Contractus composed; there are a few additional melodic lines that sound as if Monteverdi had the chant in mind and could not entirely free himself from it. Also characteristic of the dramatic monody is the emotional exploitation of certain technical devices. For the plaintive words of man's misery on his earthly journey, "Ad te suspiramus, gementes et flentes in hac lacrimarum valle," Monteverdi uses a chromatically descending bass, which draws the voice into its descent. This had been his way of expressing dramatic passages whose content was one of sorrow, pain, and lamentation, and the musical device had thereby obtained a distinct affection. The coloratura is also used in association with the affection: the trill expressive of the sighs of lament, "suspiramus," and the imploration, "O Regina." [4]

There are but two complete Masses, both composed in the old *a cappella* style, one published in the *Selva Morale e Spirituale* of 1640–41, the other posthumously in the collection, *Messa a quattro voci et Salmi*, of 1650.[5] The time at which they were composed cannot be established, since this style is no longer chronologically fixed. Are these two Masses the works Monteverdi mentioned in his letters? Three times he referred to definite Mass compositions, two of them apparently completed works, the third a composition that was still to be written for a definite occasion, the Feast of the Holy Cross, in 1618. Since Monteverdi speaks of the "coming Thursday"—the letter is dated April 21—it must be the Feast of the Inventio S. Crucis, May 3.

---

[3] Malipiero, *Opere*, XVI, 475ff.

[4] Monteverdi uses "O Regina" in place of "exsules, filii Hevae." With the exception of repetitions and a different position of "Ostende," there is no further change of the text.

[5] Malipiero, *Opere*, XV, 59ff. and XVI, 1ff.; the latter also edited with an excellent introduction by Charles van den Borren.

According to him, the feast required a "messa concertata," but these two Masses are not in the *stile concertato*. He designated as "una messa solenne in musica" a Mass composition that he offered in 1621 to the Duchess of Mantua. If the *a cappella* Mass was indeed exclusively used for services without any particular liturgical solemnity, the solemn Mass of 1621 must have been in the modern concerted style. And when writing in 1627 to Mantua (probably to Alessandro Striggio) to inquire whether the Duke had any need for the vespers and a Mass, Monteverdi expressly pointed out that he had compositions in the taste of the Duke, without naming the style. But we can surmise that the "gusto" of the Duke was closer to the modern style than to the old polyphony. Thus, none of the Masses Monteverdi mentions in his letters can actually be linked to the two works that exist.

There are other unanswerable problems of general interest in this connection. If the *a cappella* Mass was used for ordinary Sundays, why did Monteverdi select this work for publication in full and choose only a fragment of the solemn Mass? For the selection of 1650 he is, of course, not responsible; yet the choice is surprising when we consider that the Venetians were enthusiastic over works that were written for solemn occasions in the profuse, luxurious modern style. Were the two Masses used for solemn occasions? That is possible, but not conclusive, and we shall point to a unique feature in the Mass of 1641 in support of its "solemnity."

In a totally different style is the *Gloria a 7 voci concertata con due violini et quattro viole da brazzo overo 4 Tromboni*, in which, according to instructions, the trombones can be left out if circumstances do not allow their use.[6] The dating of this work involves difficulties of a different kind. In the first place, this Gloria can be part of any of the Masses Monteverdi speaks about in 1618, 1621, and 1627. But there is another occasion for which an extraordinary solemnity of the Mass is recorded. In 1630 Venice was afflicted by the plague, whose horrors lasted till late in 1631. Since the epidemic wrought great havoc among the Venetians, it is understandable that the Doge, Francesco Erizzo, ordered a general thanksgiving in St. Mark's when it was over, and on November 28, 1631, this service took place. It has been described by Antonius de Episcopis, who also wrote some laudatory poems in dedication to Monteverdi: "There was sung the most solemn Mass, composed by Claudio Monteverdi, the Maestro di Cappella, the glory of our century; in Gloria and Credo the voices were joined by trombones

---

[6] *Selva Morale, ibid.,* XV, 117.

which produced an exquisite and marvelous harmony." [7] This description exactly fits the Gloria which Monteverdi selected for his *Selva Morale*, and since it has the beauty and maturity of stylistic technique that distinguish the late compositions of Monteverdi, we may believe that it belongs to the Mass he composed for the thanksgiving of 1631.

Of a similar composition that stirred its hearers there is only a record, but its importance calls for a discussion. In 1621, on the death of Cosimo II de' Medici, the Grand Duke of Tuscany, the colony of Florentines residing in Venice, desirous of an appropriate and most solemn commemoration, charged Monteverdi to write a Requiem. It was sung in SS. Giovanni e Paolo on May 25, 1621, and its performance was vividly reported by Giulio Strozzi, with whom Monteverdi collaborated.[8] "The music of the Mass and the responsories [apparently the responsory *Libera me*, to be sung after the Mass] have been composed and performed for the occasion by Claudio Monteverdi, whose famous name makes the quality of the work best understandable; in these compositions he has devotedly expressed a particular affection, which carrying away our princes with enthusiasm made them honor him for his genius. The ceremonies began with a plaintive instrumental sinfonia which moved the listeners to tears; it imitated the ancient mixolydian mode which Sappho discovered. After the sinfonia, Don Francesco Monteverdi, son of Claudio, sang most delicately these words of sorrow: 'O vos omnes attendite et videte dolorem nostrum . . . Requiem aeternam.' The Introit [*Requiem aeternam dona eis*], frequently interrupted by the sinfonia, was most attentively listened to by the assembly, . . . it made a deep impression upon them. The Kyrie was composed by Gio. Battista Grillo, the organist at St. Mark's, while the Gradual and Tractus were by D. Francesco Usper. The *Dies irae* and the delicate *De profundis* were again compositions by Claudio; the latter, as it were, a dialogue between souls in purgatory and visiting angels; they were profoundly admired for their novelty and exquisiteness." *Domine Jesu*, the offertory, was composed by Grillo, whereas the responsories after the Mass were by Monteverdi. The loss of the extraordinary music of this Requiem Mass is deeply regrettable. We can imagine how Monteverdi, the great dramatist in music, would have responded to such stirring subjects as *De profundis*, *Libera me, Domine*, and above all, the *Dies irae*.

[7] Vogel, *VfMW*, III, p. 393, n. 3.

[8] *Esequie fatte in Venetia dalla Natione Fiorentina al Ser.mo D. Cosimo II. Quarto Gran Duca di Tocana, il dì 25 di Maggio 1621* (Venice, 1621). Vogel, *op. cit.*, pp. 376f.

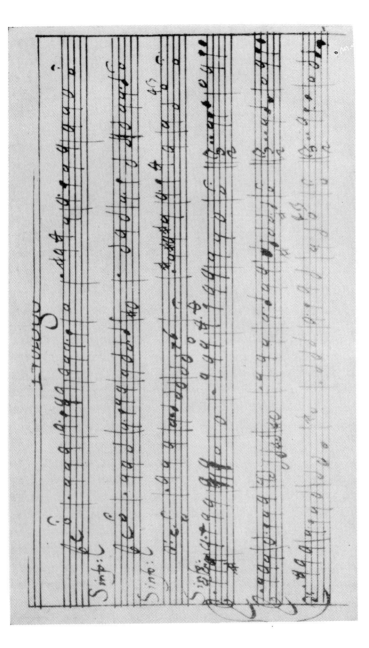

9 *L'Incoronazione di Poppea*, the Sinfonia of the Prologue

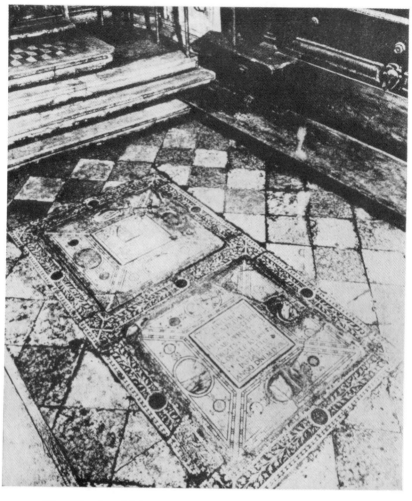

10 The Tomb of Monteverdi, Santa Maria dei Frari, Venice

The *a cappella* style in the two Masses testifies to Monteverdi's thorough knowledge of the old art of polyphony. Compared with his other works, however, this art is impersonal, with nothing of the powerful individualistic expression which Monteverdi made the basis of his modern music. That he handled the style as a contrapuntist of the first order is a sign of personal mastery, and the complete change from one style to the other, with full perfection in each, is a startling achievement. The Mass of 1641 presents a unique arrangement of the Credo. For three of the verses Monteverdi provided substitute compositions in a wholly different style; the verses are "Crucifixus etiam pro nobis," "Et resurrexit tertia die," and "Et iterum venturus est." These verses, and the verse "Homo factus est," had in the past challenged the skill of many musicians. Monteverdi singled them out and wrote special compositions in *stile concertato* to replace the versions in *a cappella* style. The modern idiom is employed to give the verses fresh distinction and express their meaning in a new individualistic form. "Crucifixus," for four solo voices, is based on a motif in chromatic descent that Monteverdi used as a symbolic expression of pain; "Et resurrexit," for two soprani and two violins with *basso continuo*, is in the typical style of a trio cantata; "Et iterum" for two contralti and bass is in the highly figurative concerted style, with an accompaniment of four trombones, or viole da braccio, surely to indicate the instruments that shall sound on the day of the Last Judgment.[9]

Although Monteverdi designated several other compositions as *a cappella*, they are not all in the old style. Nearest to it is the *Magnificat in genere da Cappella*, for four voices,[10] and Psalm 115, *Credidi propter quod locutus sum*, for eight voices in double chorus.[11] The latter has a purely chordal structure, the unit of recitation being the half note. Its structure and style are not too far removed from the sixteenth-century form. The psalm composition belongs liturgically to the vespers of the *feria secunda*, doubtless written for a feast that fell on a Monday. Also for the vespers (*feria quarta*, Wednesday) is *Memento Domine David*, with a double chorus of eight voices.[12] Although it has a chordal faburden for many voices, the unit of recitation is here the quarter note. This acceleration brings the style closer to the *concertato*, which, with its typical figurative material, is actually used in some

---

9 Malipiero, *Opere*, XV, 178, 182, 187.
10 *Ibid.*, XV, 703.
11 *Ibid.*, XV, 544.
12 *Ibid.*, XV, 567. The verse of the psalm in the edition of Malipiero should be corrected.

verses. Two more vespers compositions may be grouped in the *a cappella* section: *Domine ne in furore* (Psalm 6), sung in the compline (*feria secunda*), of which there are only three verses in the publication of motets which Bianchi brought out in 1620; and Psalm 112, *Laudate pueri*, for the Sunday vespers.

Bianchi's selections pose an interesting question. They are *Christe adoramus te*, for five, and *Adoramus*, for six voices.[13] The first is the responsorium breve *Adoramus te Christe* which is sung in the sext of the Feast in Inventione Sanctae Crucis. Monteverdi's *Adoramus* has the same text as the responsory, except that "Quia per sanguinem tuum pretiosum redemisti mundum" stands in place of "Quia per Sanctam Crucem tuam redemisti mundum." Monteverdi wrote in the letter from which we have quoted that, besides the "messa concertata," he had to compose motets for the whole day of the feast "Santa Croce" on the "coming Thursday when the Most Holy Blood was displayed." Since ordinarily he did not compose for any liturgies other than those of the vespers, since he made the responsory of the sext a motet, and since he said he had to have compositions for the whole day, it seems certain that both *Christe adoramus te* and *Adoramus* were composed in 1618. A further interesting thesis is at least worthy of mention. With a motif in rising chromaticism on "per Sanctam Crucem," the *Christe adoramus te* is in style and form comparable to the substitute *Crucifixus*. If this thesis is correct, the *Crucifixus* in concerted style would also belong to 1618, and that date could then hold for the whole Mass. The *concertato* in *Crucifixus* would therefore have a particular link to the Feast of the Invention of the Holy Cross; because of the solemnity of the feast the two other substitute sections were offered, and the whole Mass might still be the "messa concertata" mentioned in the letter.

In the sacred works Monteverdi composed for Venice the *stile concertato* prevailed; in fact, all the remaining compositions are examples of it. The forms are truly comprehensive, as if Monteverdi tried to show every possible variety of the style in sacred music. It is nearly always the same subject that appears in so many different lights, for Monteverdi chose the same set of psalms of the vespers. There are the Psalm 109, *Dixit Dominus*, Psalm 110, *Confitebor tibi*, Psalm 111, *Beatus vir*, Psalm 112, *Laudate pueri*, all for the vespers on Sunday; furthermore Psalm 121, *Laetatus sum*, Psalm 126, *Nisi Dominus*, Psalm 97, *Cantate Domino*, Psalm 116, *Laudate Dominum*, Psalm 147, *Lauda Jerusalem*; and there is the St. Mary antiphon of the compline *Salve*

---

13 *Ibid.*, XVI, 428, 439.

regina. Those are the texts that recur continually in two or more renderings, each in *stile concertato.* In addition, there are a few single compositions, such as *Ego flos campi, O quam pulchra, Ego dormio,* based on passages of the Song of Solomon, and *O beatae viae,* a motet for St. Rochus, a favorite saint of the Venetians, in whose honor a special church had been built. Although there is only one version of these motets, each is organized according to the *stile concertato.* Great variety results from the varied make-up of the medium. There is a large choral group with soloistic participation, with or without orchestral accompaniment, yet always provided with the *basso continuo* and always with the concerted conception of melody and rhythm. There are, furthermore, the pure solo compositions, for one voice only or for as many as six; all are soloistic, and all of them maintain the *concertato* principle by contrasting the leading voice and the accompaniment, for which the *basso continuo* and an orchestral group are used.

Compared with the religious works Monteverdi published in 1610, the Venetian compositions show a more determined trend toward secularizing sacred music. Actually, he no longer recognized any limitations other than those of pure art. He treated religious texts exactly as he treated the texts for his profane music; in both spheres he was the same ardent interpreter of the affections conveyed by the text. In 1610 he was still working with the objectivity of liturgical music, and used such fixed factors as the *cantus firmus* or the psalm tone as a counterweight to prevent the artistic imagination from straying into complete individualism, but the new sacred works in the *stile concertato* dispense with such a balance and avoid the conflict between individualism and liturgical tradition in music. The *cantus firmus* has disappeared from the compositions except for the *a cappella* Masses; where the chant is still allowed to influence the artistic procedure, it occurs only as a vague impression upon the melody. Also the psalm tone has lost out to the passion of artistic interpretation, though it has not been entirely discarded. There are some psalm compositions, such as Psalm 109, *Dixit Dominus* (the second),[14] or Psalm 147, *Lauda Jerusalem,*[15] which give a place to the psalm tone in some of the verses. But an enormous change has taken place, which must certainly be regarded as the most important stylistic aspect of the compositions. In the first place, no more is left of the psalm tone than the maintenance of the reciting tone for a phrase or two. While Monte-

---

[14] *Ibid.,* XV, 246ff.
[15] *Ibid.,* XVI, 358ff.

verdi in the works of 1610 faithfully adhered to the psalm tone as though it were a *cantus firmus*, the monotony typical of the recitation of psalms is now nothing but a rapid repetition of one tone to a line. More important, however, is a discovery that psalmody lends itself perfectly to the *stile concitato*. He applied to psalm composition the style he had developed in his madrigals and employed in the *Combattimento* in a programmatic manner. The recitation was based on the rhythmic unit of the eighth note, sometimes even of the sixteenth note. The result was an extraordinary rapidity of declamation, which conforms to certain qualities of the *stile concitato*. Even in phrases where there is a recitation on one tone, the impression is never one of monotony, but of agitation. This is no longer an unemotional recitation; it is passionate, declamatory language, which possesses the "excitement" of the *stile concitato*. When, for instance, Monteverdi in the doxology of his second *Laudate Dominum omnes gentes* presents vehement rhythms in the declamation of "Gloria, gloria, gloria, gloria, gloria Patri, gloria Patri," he gives the *stile concitato* in its purest form.[16] In the first version of the same psalm, when he suddenly interrupts the rapid, excited declamation in order to conform to "misericordia eius" with a slowly descending chromatic line, he is dramatizing the psalmody to a greater degree than ever before. The composition of *Beatus vir* (Psalm 111), especially in its first version, unmistakably shows that Monteverdi has turned the psalmodic recitation into the motifs of the *stile concitato*. The *Gloria concertata* is also for the most part governed by the excited, forceful rhythms and melodies of the *stile concitato;* here again, the agitation is interrupted to give the meaning of "Pax," and once more to express thanksgiving, "Gratias agimus tibi." In this work Monteverdi truly exhausted every stylistic possibility to achieve an appropriate, but highly individualistic interpretation of the text. In it he presented the drama of affections through contrasts and ever changing tone colors, and most ingeniously held together the fluctuating variations by a firm bass that has the persistency of a *basso ostinato*. It is probably the greatest composition of the kind that the seventeenth century produced.

Monteverdi also radically applied to sacred music structural techniques developed in secular music. The stereotyped basses occur invariably, often in a repetitive manner, so that the numerous varieties of textual interpretations in the extensive psalm compositions are unified by the stability of the bass. Types of the *basso ostinato* are

---

[16] *Ibid.*, XV, 510ff.

therefore not infrequent; but none is as rigid and powerful as the *basso ostinato* of the tones G-g-c-d used, with a deviation in a small passage, throughout the lengthy psalm composition *Laetatus sum.*[17] This bass is comparable to the rigid *basso ostinato* structure which is used for more than a hundred measures in the *Zefiro torna* of the *Scherzi Musicali.* In every respect, Monteverdi secularized religious composition: he applied repetitive structures of sectional songs even to the psalm; he took the "echo" aria from the drama for use in his *Audi Coelum;*[18] he simplified the concerted style through songlike characteristics in the solo duet, as in another *Salve regina;*[19] he even used the secular material of his madrigal *Chiome d'oro*, published in 1619, for the first version of the psalm *Beatus vir.* A highly interesting secularization can be seen in the small group of hymns. Monteverdi changed the strophic hymn to a strophic song of secular origin. He drops the chant melody here, too, and writes a simple aria with an accompaniment of two violins, which also play their ritornelli between the strophes. He assigns all the other hymns in the same meter to the same model. In addition, he gives the solo duet form with ritornelli as the most modern aspect of such an adaptation. The influence of the *Scherzi musicali* (1607) suggests itself.[20]

Is this secularization of sacred music by way of a profane style, this unlimited individualism, the end of religious music? In terms of the liturgical tradition, such is undoubtedly the case. On the other hand, Monteverdi—for the first time in modern history—made an individual interpretation of religious texts possible; in other words, he established the exegesis of the traditional texts as an individual experience in terms of art. Schütz and Bach were Monteverdi's heirs. Through the functions of interpretation, the musical form can have incomparable profundities of religious expression. But Monteverdi, who was first and last an artist, started thereby a new struggle between art and liturgy.

---

[17] *Ibid.*, XVI, 231ff.
[18] *Ibid.*, XV, 724ff.
[19] *Ibid.*, XV, 736ff.
[20] *Ibid.*, XV, 622ff.

Fulfillment of Madrigalesque Composition

T HE madrigalesque work of Monteverdi's old age is chiefly contained in three collections: the *Scherzi*, and the eighth and the
posthumous ninth books of madrigals. The *Scherzi Musicali Cioè Arie,
& Madrigali in stile recitativo, con una Ciaccona A 1. e 2. voci* were
edited by Bartholomeo Magni and published in Venice in 1632. Just
as he had entrusted the previous collection of scherzi to his brother
Giulio Cesare, so Monteverdi took no part in the editing of this new
volume. On the title page he is called "Reverendo," indicating that he
must have become an ecclesiastic and had probably been ordained at
the time when Magni published the new collection. It has been suggested that there was a connection between the events of the plague
and Monteverdi's decision to take orders.[1] Whatever the significance
of this decision, it had no apparent influence on his art. In 1638 he published his eighth book of madrigals, the *Madrigali Guerrieri, Et
Amorosi Con alcuni opuscoli in genere rappresentativo, che saranno
per brevi Episodii frà i canti senza gesto*. The last work that Monteverdi edited was the *Selva Morale e Spirituale* of 1640–41, the first part
of which contained "spiritualized" madrigals, which may be included
among his madrigalesque work. After Monteverdi's death Alessandro
Vincenti published the ninth book in 1651, the *Madrigali e Canzonette
a due, e tre, voci.*

This is not the first time that Magni appears in Monteverdi's career.
He was a great admirer of the composer and spoke for many in his
dedicatory letter to the *Scherzi*, when he exclaimed that the century
was fortunate to have been so favored by Heaven as to be able to

---

[1] Vogel, *VfMW*, III, 393.

enjoy the genius of such a man. Magni's selection gives the impression of a rather disorderly gathering of works that were to be published merely because they bore the name of the famous composer. In view of the methodical way in which Monteverdi arranged his own publications, we can take for granted that he was in no way responsible for this little anthology. Of actual scherzi there are only two strophic songs, with simple melodies, a *basso continuo* and a straightforward organization, comparable to the scherzi of 1607, except that these two, *Maledetto sia l'aspetto* and *Eri già tutta mia*,[2] have no instrumental ritornelli. These two little songs are surely odd remnants from an earlier period. From 1607 on, the scherzi had exercised an influence on contemporary musicians, among whom was Claudio Saracini, an especially close follower, who dedicated a lament *Udite lagrimose spirti* to Monteverdi.[3] Stylistically these two scherzi have nothing to do with the problems of composition which Monteverdi was trying to solve around 1630. Equally disorganized in its combination of various styles and phases of composition, the posthumous collection of 1651 also contains some remainders from the scherzi period, such as the canzonetta *Quando dentro al tuo seno*.[4] There must have been quite a few such little dance songs of native character which circulated among musicians but which Monteverdi did not regard as worthy of special publication. This seems to be proved by the inclusion of *La mia Turca*, or *Si dolce e' il tormento*, in Milanuzzi's anthology of 1624.[5]

Another type of composition in the *Scherzi* is the strophic song, which uses the same bass in all the strophes but with a varied melody above. *Quel sguardo sdegnosetto* best represents this type, which, in Monteverdi's work, goes back to the first decade of the century. He presented it in *Orfeo*, and often used the structure with artistic license. The principle of varying the melody in the strophes, or using fresh material for each, allowed the melody to respond to the changing affections of the text; and we have seen that Monteverdi always preferred a structure that permitted a continual renewal of musical material in relation to the text. Thus he transformed the melodies for the second and third strophes of *Quel sguardo* according to the needs of the text. It is, therefore, not so much a technique of melodic variation as one in which the affections produce a variety of melodies. In *Quel sguardo* Monte-

---

[2] Malipiero, *Opere*, X, 76, 80.
[3] See also his *Lamento della Madonna*. Cf. A. W. Ambros–H. Leichtentritt, *Geschichte der Musik*, IV (Leipzig, 1909), 816ff. Redlich, *Claudio Monteverdi*, p. 193.
[4] *Opere*, IX, 56.
[5] *Ibid.*, IX, 117ff.

verdi created the melody for each strophe on the basis, of symmetry, and the phrases establish correspondences among themselves. Such a melodic style had long before been achieved by him, and melodically the composition might be dated around 1620. There is, however, a more modern aspect to the rhythm, for which Monteverdi used the triple meter alla breve, making the half note the metrical unit; yet by itself this is not a safe criterion for dating the piece.

Ecco di dolci raggi is also a strophic song. Magni's version of the song, which Malipiero reproduced in his edition, is incomplete,[6] another sign that the *Scherzi* are a haphazard collection. *Ecco di dolci raggi* actually has five strophes, the fifth of which, *Io che armato sin hor*, Magni-Malipiero give as a separate composition.[7] G. B. Camarella, a Venetian musician who worked under Monteverdi, published this work in its proper form about 1633, in his *Madrigali et Arie*. The first four strophes are based on the same material, while the final strophe, *Io che armato*, has fresh material of its own. Such an arrangement is not extraordinary in a composition derived from the native song, which often responds to the text by presenting fresh material in one or more strophes. Though the structure is not unusual, Monteverdi gave it an interesting variation, which shows the degree to which his mind was intent on artistic problems even in forms of minor importance. *Ecco di dolci raggi* is one of the best examples of a composition in which Monteverdi combined two entirely different types of declamation. Both types are rapid and syllabic, the declamatory unit being the eighth note; one type is derived from the canzonetta and incorporates a songlike melody; the other comes from the *stile recitativo*. The first four strophes have the canzonetta declamation and end with an arioso melody; the first part of the last strophe, however, has the *stile recitativo*, which swings directly into the canzonetta style, ending with the refrain that is common to all the strophes. This composition also has no stylistic peculiarities that would necessarily date the work around 1630. There is one strophic composition, however, *Et è pur dunque vero*, which has the structural maturity of compositions of 1630. It is an extensive work that carries the strophic structure to cantata-like proportions, employing contrasts of instrument and voice.[8]

---

[6] *Ibid.*, X, 81.

[7] *Ibid.*, X, 91f.

[8] *Ibid.*, X, 82ff. It has seven strophes, not six as Prunières, *Claudio Monteverdi*, p. 154, maintains.

The most important works in this somewhat confused collection are *Zefiro torna* (Rinuccini) and *Armato il cor*, both for two tenors with *basso continuo*.[9] *Armato il cor* reappears in the eighth book, which Monteverdi himself prepared, and Vincenti, the editor of the ninth book, also chose it for his collection. *Zefiro torna*, on the other hand, was never published by Monteverdi himself, though it reappears after his death in the ninth book. Apparently these two works had special success; at all events, it is in them that the two great musical minds of the century—Monteverdi and Schütz—met. Schütz imitated both works, but it is not known whether he found them in the *Scherzi*, sent to him after his return to Dresden, or saw them in manuscript while he was in Venice in 1628, in which case, they must have been completed by that date.

Heinrich Schütz shared the same artistic ideas as Monteverdi, not so much because the younger German imitated the older Italian as because the two came from the same spiritual stock. From the early twenties, Schütz grew more and more restless in his position in Dresden. He had already been in Venice to study under Giovanni Gabrieli, and now he learned that since his departure decisive musical events had taken place there and that it was a different Venice from the one he had known—the Venice of Monteverdi. He implored his prince to release him from his duties in Dresden, that he might see and hear for himself the novelties with which the musical world resounded, and he commissioned agents, ambassadors, and merchants who went to Italy to bring back examples of the new music. At last, in 1628, he got his leave and went to Venice to see Monteverdi. It is unfortunate that no document survives to picture the meeting of the two most extraordinary musicians of the century. Both had the same cast of mind, the same power of understanding all matter of music, the same passion as interpreters of the word in their compositions; and both had a profundity that awes those who respond to their works. We do not know that the two actually met, but Heinrich Schütz was aware of Monteverdi's ingenuity, his sagacity, his keenly penetrating mind. Schütz studied Monteverdi's compositions thoroughly, and must have heard many of them in 1628 and 1629, both at St. Mark's and in the palaces of the Venetian patricians. At that time he may have learned of Monteverdi's seventh book of madrigals, from which he chose *Chiome d'oro* for adaptation; and it was either then or on his return after the publi-

[9] *Opere*, IX, 9, 27.

cation of the *Scherzi*, that he chose *Zefiro torna* and *Armato il cor* for similar adaptations.

Based on Rinuccini's poem, not on Petrarch's which Monteverdi had previously used, *Zefiro torna* has fascinated historians as it attracted Monteverdi's contemporaries. It is a brilliant work, less deep and moving than most of the compositions of Monteverdi's last years, largely because the poem, for the most part, has a light, charming lyricism inspired by nature and expressed in scenic images. At the beginning of the poet's, or the lover's, speech, however, tone and affection change, and with them the musical form and expression. It was its brilliant musical structure that gained the work so much praise. A bass motif, two measures in length, is repeated fifty-six times in succession, and five more times toward the end. *Zefiro torna* is thus a ciacona, and is so designated on the title page of the *Scherzi*. The over-all rhythm, persistent and sweeping, is governed by a dance pattern inspired by the passage, "fa danzar al bel suon." In the composition as a whole, the melodic motifs are suggested by the motifs of the text, yet the melody moves in free evolution over the steadily repeated bass, for Monteverdi develops the individual phrases so that one seems to grow organically out of the other with the continuity of a logical process. The distribution of the melody between two tenors stresses this continuity by a technique in which the melodic material is exchanged phrase by phrase. The most astonishing achievement is, however, the ingenious combination of a comprehensive musical logic with the interpretation of the text. Throughout the composition, and almost word by word, the melodic phrases reflect the connotations of the text. "L'aer," "l'onde," "mormorando," "notte," "da monti e da valle," "ime e profonde," "raddoppian l'armonia"—the melodic motifs for all those words are the most realistic imaginable. One might expect that such a procedure would seriously disturb the formal unity of the melody, and preclude any logical musical development. The logic is there, however, and every musical phrase can be explained without regard to the text. At his maturest and best, Monteverdi was always able to achieve this enigmatic unity.

The sectional grouping of the ciacona is also influenced by the text. With the expression of personal emotion, "Sol io per selve abbandonate e sole" (I alone in the lonesome desert), Monteverdi breaks off the *basso ostinato* and, with a sudden harmonic shift (from G to E major), begins a new section in *stile recitativo*, most appropriate to the personal effusion of the lover. Here, in response to the affection of suffering, the expressiveness of the dissonance is exploited to give the effect of the lover's weeping. With these dissonances Monteverdi startled his contemporaries, and though they were sometimes criticized, it was through them that he revealed the depth of his humanity.

On the surface, his use of dissonances for expressive purposes seems radical and relentless, and at times, it is. This technique owes something to the baroque desire to startle with the marvelous and extraordinary. "Si vis me flere, plorandum est" (If you wish me to weep with you, you must lament)—this verse of Horace was of central importance in the theories of baroque art, and had obtained a new interpretation: if ordinary means do not stir the listener, the extraordinary and startling must be employed. But no matter how startling Monteverdi's dissonances are, they follow a musical logic. The way in which he introduces dissonances is remarkable; and that it is a deliberate method is proved by the frequent occurrence of the same technique. The dissonance appears so often with the effect of surprise that it seems wanting in preparation; and preparation is, indeed, lacking, if we are thinking in terms of harmony or chords. In many cases, Monteverdi does not produce dissonance as the result of harmonic developments; a seventh, ninth, diminished, or otherwise dissonant "chord" is not the result of a succession of preceding "chords." Only in its effect is the dissonance harmonic; its cause is melodic. The melodic lines, often running close together, are led in such a way that at a certain anticipated point of juncture they must form a dissonance, sometimes only one dissonance, at other times, several in succession; and since the lines are so close together, the dissonance sounds all the more harsh or startling. The procedure is this: the composer takes two or three melodic phrases, each of which is regarded as a complete entity; to convey this completeness, each phrase is provided with a melodic cadence, so that in its advance toward the cadence the phrase follows its own logic. Combined simultaneously according to their inherent logic, the phrases must produce the dissonance within the cadences. *Zefiro torna* offers a good example of this procedure; it is not Monteverdi's boldest or harshest, but it is instructive for its clarity. The melodic phrase "Come vuol mia ventura hor piango" is first brought in successively by the two voices, one tenor follows the other with the phrase, which is raised with each repetition, and where one phrase ends and the other begins, a dissonant juncture appears. Then the two tenors sing the phrase simultaneously, and in the melodic cadence the voices meet in a dissonance:

Ex. 99 IX, 19

Co- me vuol mia ventura hor pian- : - - go

This technique is an example of the kind of unity that Monteverdi established between a purely musical, but technical, device and the expressive purpose. For it is always in conjunction with tension, passion, suffering, melancholy and death that this poignant dissonance is used.

Armato il cor, also for two tenors, is a brilliant example of the *stile concitato* whose gradual and systematic development Monteverdi began in the early twenties. While this style is associated with all the passions, it is most used with martial expressions in the war of arms and of love. Monteverdi used it during the twenties with various affections, all of which had in common the highest degree of excitement. In the *stile concitato* he was working in two directions: toward formulating the motif as adequately as possible, and toward exploiting the structural elements to express passionate excitement. In formulating the motif, Monteverdi used melodic types with only chordal tones in a fanfare-like arrangement; the motifs are all short and precise, and the effect is strengthened by the sharp rhythms that accompany them. The exploitation of the structural function of the style was more complicated. Again and again Monteverdi showed that a technical device in the musical structure, though it has a purely musical nature, can and must serve expressive purposes. He achieves such an effect in *Armato il cor* by extensive exploitation of the devices of sequence and imitation. After having stated the melodic motifs of martial character—"armato" and "militar"—the composition turns to the warrior in the realm of love who will struggle with Heaven and with Fate and battle with Death: "Contrasterò col Ciel e con la sorte, pugnerò con la morte." Through a whole section of the work, the theme of the text, distributed between the two voices and provided with excited, sharp motifs, is repeated and imitated in the succession of the voices and in the rising and falling of sequences; as a third constituent, the *basso continuo* takes part in imitation and sequences. The result is a direct transmission of the excitement suggested by such struggles: [10]

[10] *Ibid.*, IX, 28ff.

Ex. 100   IX, 28

This arrangement succeeds in arousing tension and excitement by the use of accumulative devices. Such an accumulative expedient as imitation is not used merely for the sake of polyphonic structure, but in order that the structure of the *stile concitato* may serve the text. This passage from *Armato il cor* also contains material that is to become part of the standard vocabulary of the baroque musician; it can be heard in countless compositions, including some by Handel and Bach.

In the posthumous ninth book, too, compositions of various styles and dates are combined. *Armato il cor* reappears in it, showing that the collection includes compositions that are previous to the eighth book. *Se vittorie si belle*, a companion piece of *Armato il cor*,[11] must have been composed at the same time, that is, before 1632. The style of these works goes back to the early twenties, to the time of the seventh book, in which we find some anticipations of it. Such a work as *O come vaghi*, for two tenors with *basso continuo*, already published in 1624 in the collection of Anselmi, resembles compositions of the ninth book, especially in the expressive exploitation of accumulative devices. Even so mature a composition as the wonderful duet, *Ardo*, and its stylistic companion piece, *O sia tranquillo il mare*, are explainable as works that

---

[11] *Ibid.*, IX, 21ff.

originated around 1630. Whereas the "modern" compositions of the thirties form a recognizable group, a disturbing factor in the ninth book is the incorporation of works patterned after such dance songs as the balletto and also after the canzonetta. All of them have the simple structures of their prototypes, and all are strophic songs, some with refrains. It is difficult to establish definite dates for them. They could be very early compositions, although the elaborate canzonetta structure of *Si Si ch'io v'amo* never occurred during the period at which Monteverdi occupied himself systematically with native songs. An interesting experiment appears in *O mio bene*,[12] where the *stile concitato* is used in conjunction with the form of the native song. In its second section, the words "non più guerra d'amore" suggest that style, and, indeed, in the *basso continuo* we have the rapidly hammering repetitions of one tone which Monteverdi described in the style of the *Combattimento*. However, it is doubtful whether the experiment can be regarded as a success. To impose the weighty and significant technique of the *stile concitato* on the small and unpretentious song structure is to overload a vehicle incapable of carrying such a weight.

THE EIGHTH BOOK AND THE SELVA MORALE

The madrigalesque composition of Monteverdi is crowned by the eighth book which was published in 1638 as *Madrigali Guerrieri et Amorosi* and dedicated to Emperor Ferdinand III, himself a musician and composer. Monteverdi had previously offered to dedicate the collection to the emperor's father, Ferdinand II, who was married to Eleonora Gonzaga. Since Ferdinand II died in February, 1637, the eighth book of madrigals must have been ready for publication in 1636. Monteverdi's preface gives this volume a special distinction; for, as has been mentioned, it sets forth his doctrine of the musical composition as a work of art founded on imitation: every artistic work is achieved by imitation, not as a special technique, but as a principle that gives birth to art. Throughout Monteverdi's creative life this was the productive principle that created the complexities of his style. In a letter of October 22, 1633, to an unknown Roman, possibly Doni, he says his work is a lifelong demonstration of what he has understood imitation to be. He declares that the nature of music must justify any particular form of imitation, that the imitation of a certain affection is as much artistic as it is human, but that since human affection is the subject of all musical composition, the imitation of the nature of music

---

[12] *Ibid.*, IX, 95ff.

must conform to the imitation of human passions. The eighth book is the fulfillment, the final answer to the constant search which gave meaning to his artistic life. When he chose the texts for his last compositions, the poet, his personal characteristics and his poetical form, no longer counted. The poems of Rinuccini, Guarini, Marino, were chosen, not because they were favorites of Monteverdi and his contemporaries, but because of the human passions they embodied. As a presentation of human passions and an example of the humanization of music, the eighth book sums up Monteverdi's art. We have lost all his music dramas except the first and the last, but the madrigals that embrace the whole of the Venetian period make up a human drama in their own right. Whatever the music dramas may have presented in the way of human passions, they cannot have differed greatly from the human tones of the madrigalesque drama. From 1619 to 1638 Monteverdi's language is uniform in purpose and in style, it has an unbroken line of achievement in its clarity and directness.

At the side of the madrigals of the eighth book stand the five moral madrigals which open the *Selva Morale e Spirituale*. This last collection was dedicated to Eleonora Gonzaga, the wife of the late Emperor Ferdinand II. Thus even the dedications reinforce the idea that the eighth book and the *Selva Morale* are companion collections—one summarizing the aspects of Monteverdi's profane art, the other presenting his sacred music. The religious compositions are preceded by five secular works of a moral character, which set a tone that seems to sound through all the last years of Monteverdi—the tone of melancholy resignation. They sing of the futility of life and human endeavor; they sing of men who are blinded by wealth, power, and treasure, and put their hope in mortal affairs (*O ciechi ciechi*); they sing of the errors of youth, of the days when the pains, sighs, and hopes of love were thought to be all that mattered: "You have listened to my rhymes that resounded with those sighs with which I nourished my heart in my first juvenile error when I was another man than I am now"—now "I hope to find piety" (*Voi ch'ascoltate* by Petrarch); they sing of life that is brief as a flash of lightning: "The past is dead, the future not born, and the present lost" (*È questa vita un lampo*); they sing of beauty that does not last, and warn that none is safe from Heaven's wrath (*Spontava il dì*); and they sing of the futility of love: "Today we laugh, tomorrow we weep; now we are light, now shadow; today life, tomorrow death" (*Chi vol che m'innamori*). There is undeniably a personal note in the selection of these five poems for the moral madrigals. The placing of these works ahead of the other compositions would seem to give them the character of a personal "confession." We have no letters from the last decade of Monteverdi's life; the latest is dated 1634; only the compositions reveal the composer's mind at the close of his life. After the plague in Venice, the increasing melancholy gravity of his nature seems to have made a retreat into contemplation appear to be the most desirable way of coping with the hazards of life. Monteverdi became a priest and made a vow to go on a pilgrimage to Loreto as a thanksgiving for surviving the ordeals of the plague. He also occupied himself—as early as the twenties—with studies in natural science, with odd experiments in alchemy, that were not entirely out of keeping with the prevalent interest in experimental science. One of the obituary poems was to praise him as a learned man, a "professor" of science, and something of this preoccupation with the nature of truth manifests itself artistically in the moral madrigals.

The comprehensiveness of the eighth book with its great variety of media presents, in a sort of summary, the development of the madrigal. One set of madrigals realizes voluminous sonorities, using a large chorus combined with a group of soloists, varying in number, accompanied by an orchestra and a *basso continuo*. The orchestra, usually small, may consist of only two violin parts, and at its greatest expansion comprises four viole da braccio and two violins, as in the initial composition, *Altri canti d'Amor*. This large medium, vocal and instrumental, is used in seven works of the eighth book and in two of the *Selva Morale*, if we include the "second parts" of all madrigals as separate compositions. But the madrigals for soloistic voices in the *stile concertato* are still in the majority. Though many combinations of the voices are present, the solo duet of two tenors is again the medium for which Monteverdi shows a special liking. Tenors and bass; alto, tenor, and bass; or one solo voice are other groupings, and the solo trio is employed in the moral madrigals. The old favorite, the five-part madrigal recurs in *E questa vita un lampo*. The technically mature form of the *basso continuo* and the structure as a whole suggest that this work may have been composed at the same time as the madrigals of the eighth book. Two other five-part madrigals that make their first appearance in this collection have been discussed previously: *Dolcissimo uscignolo* and *Chi vol haver felice*, to be sung *alla francese*. They are earlier compositions and appear here in order that the book may present a "summary" of artistic efforts. That they were patterned "on the model of the airs de cour" is impossible to believe, and it is only because the manner of performance was French that this impossible thesis has been advanced: [18] "Monteverdi was himself so completely persuaded of the decrepitude of a genre [the madrigal] from which he had extracted everything it could give that he again turned to France for ideals through which to rejuvenate it." There is nothing in these two madrigals to rejuvenate the category, and they were chosen to illustrate artistic problems that Monteverdi had solved in the past, as were a number of other compositions which belong to earlier periods.

The collection is divided into two sections: the first contains the "canti guerrieri" and opens with a composition dedicated to the Emperor Ferdinand; the second contains the "canti amorosi" and opens with *Altri canti di Marte*, in which the theme is: "I sing of love" (*Io canto amor*). Each section concludes with compositions that are examples of a category, of some special style, or of the solution to a particular artistic problem. In the first section, after the latest madrigals, comes the *Combattimento di Tancredi e Clorinda*, a prototype of the warlike *stile concitato*, followed by a ballo, apparently a late composition, which must have been written for the accession of Ferdinand III in 1637. The introduction welcomes "il Re novo del Romano Impero," and expresses the hope that under his reign "a century of peace" may dawn; and the ballo ends with an apotheosis of Ferdinand.

The second section has a greater variety in its concluding group of compositions. It begins with two madrigals *alla francese* and two modern compositions, the first of which is important for its artistic quality and because it belongs to the *genere rappresentativo*. Monteverdi calls it a "canto rappresentativo"; in other words, it is a madrigal *con gesto*, a scenic cantata in three sections, the long middle part being the *Lamento della Ninfa*. The modern madrigal *Perchè t'en fuggi o Fillide*, which combines recitation with contrasting, dancelike arioso sections, may represent a type of the late twenties. Two simple strophic dance songs follow; and the book ends with the *Ballo dell' Ingrate*, which Monteverdi had composed in 1608. As a survey of the madrigal, the eighth book shows careful organization.

The opening composition, *Altri canti d'Amor*, draws upon a large orchestra and a chorus of six parts and solo voice to produce the brilliant effects expected in a piece dedicated to an emperor. An instrumental sinfonia, for two violins and one viola da braccio with *basso continuo*, serves as prelude to the composition. The short stereotyped, repetitive bass anticipates the structural behavior of the bass in the vocal part—a

---

[18] Prunières, *Claudio Monteverdi*, p. 158.

frequent procedure with Monteverdi. The organization of the vocal work in sections, dictated by the contrasts of affections, lifts the madrigal out of the limitations of its category and turns the composition into a cantata. The sharpest contrast naturally is between the god of love, Amor, the "tender archer" (*tenero arciero*), and the fierce god of war, Mars (*Marte furibondo e fiero*). The first part, in the dancelike style of the amorous section, has a soft and elastic melody carried along by the consistent dance rhythms. The dance character is stressed by the structurally forceful bass, which has a descending motif that is repeated in an approach to the *basso ostinato*. Only the vocal trio is used for it. The martial section breaks in suddenly. The motif for the phrase "Di Marte furibondo e fiero" has the rapid declamation, which Monteverdi used in the *Combattimento* as the musical equivalent of the excited pyrrhic meter, and exploits the same hammering on one tone, with the sixteenth note as the unit and with the *basso continuo* sharing in the explosive repetitions. The rest of the section, always responsive to the connotations of the text, is wholly given over to stark realism. Thus, at the phrase "hard encounters and bold battles," the motifs run in contrary motion; with sabers flashing and the guns firing, a noisy tumult of whizzing runs and cracking motifs portray the battle; yet despite this seeming turmoil, the work is in fact very well organized by means of strict contrapuntal form.

The apotheosis of Ferdinand makes up the second major section, which is organized as a bass solo with chorus. The bass anticipates what the full chorus carries to a climax by repeating the same material. The bass renders homage to Ferdinand with a degree of melodic intensity comparable to the solo in *Con che soavità* of the seventh book. A six-part string orchestra and a harpsichord accompany the bass solo, and the string instruments are advised to play with the bow in "long and suave" tones. Here, too, the motifs are derived from the text: "war" has a fanfare-like theme, "proud chorus" a dancelike stride, "singing" a figurative coloratura. After the solo has introduced these motifs, they are polyphonically worked out by the full chorus and orchestra in a climactic conclusion. Such relentless realism may now be regarded as a deficiency, but it is presented with taste, skill, and musical integrity. It has rightly been said that Monteverdi introduced forms of an illustrative power that are still valid, and that it is only because some of them have been worn out by all-too-frequent handling in later periods that they now appear as trivialities, even in the work of their creator. Certainly Monteverdi gave the baroque age the musical vocabulary to express martial excitement and passion. And the lucid structure retains musical values aside from its descriptive relation to the text.

The opening composition of the second part with the "canti amorosi" follows the style and concept of the martial madrigal. That it appears artistically superior, though no less realistic may be due to the greater poetical value of the text, *Altri canti di Marte*, by Giambattista Marino. The work is distinguished by the transparency of Monteverdi's new, completely free, unsystematic counterpoint. The repetitive motifs, the sequences, the descending lines, and the steadfast motion of the bass are the most powerful structural elements. The repetitive nature of the bass motif approaches the *basso ostinato*, as is shown in the second part of this madrigal, *Due belli occhi*, where, as the upper parts grow more excited and disjointed, the bass becomes steadier. These two madrigals resemble the two initial moral madrigals, *O ciechi ciechi* and *Voi ch'ascoltate;* the latter especially has striking similarities with *Altri canti di Marte*.[14] The subtlety with which the volume of sound is increased or reduced in careful gradations reveals the maturity of a master.

But of all the madrigals in a large medium, *Hor ch'el Ciel e la Terra* and its second part, *Così sol d'una chiara fonte*, are artistically the most perfect.[15] The sonnet of Petrarch has been given the most ingenious translation possible into music. Monteverdi seized upon the contrasting imagery for its expressive potentialities, and it offered him not only a definite formal outline, but also the inspiration to create a correspondingly forceful musical imagery. The first part gives three affections which Monteverdi exploited structurally: calm, restlessness and suffering, and war. The poet is kept awake by the torments of his love in the midst of the calm night. A deathlike silence lies upon heaven and earth; even the ocean does not stir; sleep holds in silence beast and bird alike; but "I am awake, I think, burn, weep" (*Vegghio* [*sic*], *penso, ardo, piango*); "War, that is my state, full of ire and pain" (*Guerra è 'l mio stato d'ira e di duol piena*); the thought of the beloved alone brings peace. These sharp contrasts within a few lines lend themselves to Monteverdi's style. The image of deadly silence is portrayed in dark, midnight colors of deep chords: there is a harmonic declamation on one low chord. In abrupt contrast, the chorus and the orchestra then present the ecstatic outcries: "veglio [*sic*], penso, ardo, piango"; with a truly inspired device, Monteverdi has the two tenors continue the verse in rapid declamation while the rest of the chorus interjects at intervals the

14 *Opere*, XV, 1ff., 15ff.
15 *Ibid.*, VIII, 39ff.

painful outbursts of the poet. "War" (*guerra*) provides the motif for the new section, which is wholly in the *stile concitato*, and the violent repetitions increase the excitement. But this martial style is balanced by the musical motif set to "peace," which is rendered in slow, quiet, full chords of bold, striking harmonies. Once more the contrast of war and peace is given in the repetition and expansion of the martial idea. This is no longer realism, a merely pictorial presentation of the subject. Thanks to the power of a dramatist to make actions felt and feelings audible, the musical form becomes a drama whose concreteness and energy seem beyond the nature of music. Monteverdi was first to discover these potentialities, without which we are now unable to imagine that artistic music could exist.

In contrast to these rich and voluminous madrigals are several for soloists with *basso continuo* accompaniment, of which three may be singled out: Guarini's *Mentre vaga Angioletta*, the cycle *Ogni Amante è Guerrier*, and the *Lamento della Ninfa*. Guarini's poem is in praise of the characteristics of music, and we give a translation: [16]

> While the angelic voice
> singing makes every gentle soul rejoice,
> my heart throbs
> at the sound of her melodious song.
> Choosing only notes
> resonant and pure, the Music-Genius feigns
> and fashions novelty
> of fluent and skillful harmony;
> tempers the shrillness of the flexible voice,
> and bends it or constrains
> so with the windings, twists and broken accents
> that now it slows to a poise,
> now hastens, terminating
> in low and lively tones. Then alternating
> flights and rests and peaceful moments,
> he holds it now in balance,
> now up, now down, now uttering no sound.
> Here it darts off and vibrates,
> there it whirls around,
> one moment trembling, another rebounding,
> then strongly resounding.

---

[16] The translation was provided by the late Professor Angelo Lipari (Yale University) for the concert given at Yale University in commemoration of the three hundredth anniversary of the death of Claudio Monteverdi, in 1943.

Thus singing, and repeating, by his art
Love transforms the heart
into a nightingale,
which takes its flight, not to remain in sadness.

It is understandable that a musician should be attracted by such a poem, although its numerous suggestive images might easily call forth a composition full of pictorial realisms likely to impair the unity of structure and form. At best, the progress from one word to the next by pictorial presentation increases the difficulty of finding an over-all form, and Monteverdi's composition, written for two tenors and *basso continuo*,[17] does not entirely escape this danger. Only by a strong grasp of style and by emphasis on a stable element unaffected by the constant changes does Monteverdi achieve a synthesis. The concerted style embodies the contrast between the solo voice and accompaniment, giving each distinct features, and the bass has a stabilizing function. With one exception, in the passage "pieghevol voce," where it is led in a chromatic descent through a full octave, the bass holds its own against the solo duet throughout the composition because of the stereotyped, "impersonal" character of the motifs, which are continually repeated, either literally or in variation. While the bass proceeds with regularity, in quarters and in halfs, the duet builds up its own peculiarities through the contrasts of the *concertato*. Since the text enumerates all the virtues of music, they are reflected in the melody. Both the principle of the *concertato* and the imitation of the meaning of the words lead to the unfolding of vocal virtuosities which are, indeed, not far from the graces of a nightingale.

An equally brilliant example of the *stile concertato* is the cycle *Ogni amante è guerrier*, in four parts—*Riedi*, though published separately, being the fourth part. Each part has a different medium: two tenors, bass solo, tenor solo, and all three voices in *Riedi*.[18] The cycle offers a program of the musical content of the volume; in the nature of their affection, love and war are alike. "Therefore, mendacious tongues, refrain henceforth from calling love mere wantonness and sloth; love is the impulse of the warrior's heart." The "martial verse, breathing soft love, with clash of arms resounding, clearly has shown that love and warlike spirit alike are but one impulse of the hero's heart." The composition has special significance because of the frequent changes of the rhythmic order in response to the changes of affection.

---

[17] *Ibid.*, VIII, 246ff.
[18] *Ibid.*, VIII, 88ff.

All these changes of rhythm produce special forms of melody, so that the melodic forms that Monteverdi had explored appear in this cycle. A dancelike melody in triple rhythm is used for an arioso or aria with balanced and proportionate phrases; recitative is extensively used, especially in the two sections for bass and tenor; rapid declamation, mostly on one tone, but also with thrusts of passionate exclamation, represents the *stile concitato;* a richly figurative melody, melismatic and in concise, stereotyped groups and patterns, used for realistic expressions such as "cantare" or "riedi," is typical of the *stile concertato*. Still another form that occurs in this cycle of madrigals is marked by great simplicity. A clear rhythm controls its motion, not organized by any repetitive pattern, but almost always in metrical groups of 4/4. The melody has sensuously drawn lines, and the phrasing avoids complications in order to achieve clarity and simplicity. Always very melodious and effective as an arioso, this type seems to be the final result of Monteverdi's occupation with the native songs. It has none of the stylistic marks of the canzonetta or the villanella or any other specific native song, but has acquired a personal style and often serves to express feelings of great intensity and intimacy. The large cycle—a sestina—*Gira il nemico insidioso* [19] has this form here and there; it occurs in sections of the soloistic works and sporadically in the large madrigals of the eighth book; and it appears prominently in the moral madrigals.

Scenic music is extensively represented in the eighth book; we have already listed the works of that category. The *Combattimento*, which we take to be a scenic cantata, and the two balli clearly reveal their association with the *genere rappresentativo* in form, style, and general make-up, but the *Lamento della Ninfa* and its two surrounding compositions are not so easy to classify. Had Monteverdi not specifically indicated that the work belonged to the *genere rappresentativo*, we would have no idea that it did. In what way and setting the composition is "representative" is never clarified, and there is no description of the scene or surroundings in which the singers are to appear. Monteverdi's introductory explanation is short: "The way to produce the following song: The three parts which are sung before the *Lament of the Nymph* are separated [that is, printed in part books], because they are to be sung in the tempo of the beat (*al tempo de la mano*); the other three parts, however, which sing with soft voice in pity over the Nymph, are set in score so that they can follow the *Lament*, which must be sung in the tempo of the affection (*a tempo dell'affetto del animo*) and not

---

[19] *Ibid.*, VIII, 75ff.

in tempo of the beat (*non a quella de la mano*)." [20] The short composition after the lament is also in separate parts for the three male voices, two tenors and a bass. Both the initial and final compositions are, therefore, in the strict, regular rhythm that the beat of the hand indicates, while the *Lamento* takes its rhythmic motion from the affection of the Nymph, and it is to this affection that the three accompanying voices must submit themselves. This implies liberties and irregularities in singing of a kind not customary in ordinary rhythmic performance. It is noteworthy that the *Lamento* has more of an irresistible, constant rhythmic motion, patterned on dance rhythm, than the two compositions that surround it.[21] Nevertheless, Monteverdi apparently allowed some flexibility in the singing in order to present the affection appropriately, although he did not single out any particular passage where he expected the "tempo del'affetto del animo." The initial *Non haveo Febo ancora* is in a simple structure and contains some features characteristic of the melodies of Monteverdi's late style: they are simple, direct, balanced, in quiet motion, and have a careful declamation. The melody seems to be placed in the middle part (second), and also in the brief conclusion, *Si tra sdegnosi*, which unpretentiously, in twelve measures of narration, brings the cycle to an end.

The *Lamento*, famous for its structure of a strict *basso ostinato* with the descending motif through a fourth, has the unusual arrangement of a solo voice, the Nymph, over a group of three male voices as an accompaniment. Abandoned by her lover, the Nymph sings her melodious lament in pitiful, appealing tones, while the three other parts, singly or together, interject their expressions of sympathy and pity, "miserella, ah più no no." The bass repeats its four descending tones throughout the composition. The *lamento* character is identified with the structure of the descending *ostinato* motif, and later composers have taken it as a model for works of that nature. The structure and the technique are but the servants whose purpose is to express the human affections. Monteverdi's contemporaries understood at once that the technique was subservient to the affection. It was a stroke of genius to have a group of voices accompany the Nymph with a dimness of sound expressive of pity. It is a simple device, but one that could be invented only by a genius, and a man who had grown in knowledge of human affections.

---

[20] *Ibid.*, VIII, 286.
[21] The basic rhythm of the *Lamento* is in 6/1; in older terminology the rhythm has *tempus imperfectum* and *prolatio major*, that is, two triplets to the measure.

There are few compositions that have this human directness—unadorned, utterly simple, and perhaps for that reason unmistakable. Is it this "affetto del animo," this humanization of the music, that places the *Lamento* in the sphere of dramatic, representative music? Is it representative because the human affection becomes a *dramatis persona* and makes his appearance in the madrigal? Human affection is the substance of the music drama that Monteverdi created. The cantata, the madrigal, or indeed any of the musical forms is no less than a human drama if the musical interpretation of the affection is grounded in human nature.

CHAPTER
EIGHTEEN

The Final Drama

M ONTEVERDI had never interrupted his dramatic work since
he left Mantua. Because his *Orfeo* and *Arianna* were recognized
as the outstanding music dramas of the age, he was constantly requested
to write operas for the nobility. He complied with the requests, not
only from ambition, but also from his own natural impulse, which
was so strong that all his compositions were dramatic in the last analysis,
whether they were madrigals, operas, or even religious music in the
modern form. Except for the two last dramas, all the dramatic compositions of Monteverdi's Venetian period are irretrievably lost, but the
guiding principle that gave all his compositions a dramatic character
can help the imagination to reconstruct the style of these lost dramas,
and the few extant scenic compositions, including the ballo, offer further assistance. At all events, these, and the dramatized madrigals with
or without gesture (*con e senza gesto*), serve to refute the assumption
that there was an irregular or inconsistent development in Monteverdi's
dramatic style. It has often been said that between the *Orfeo* and the last
dramas there is so complete a break that Monteverdi must have become
estranged from the conceptions of his *Orfeo*. The contrary is true.
Monteverdi composed his madrigals with such unswerving logic that
the works in the sixth, seventh, and eighth books are the inevitable
result of those that preceded. Just as the *Orfeo*, though a music drama,
was prepared for by the madrigals, so there is nothing in the two last
dramas that was not anticipated in Monteverdi's madrigalesque composition. It is true that the madrigals before the *Orfeo* had more of a
preparatory function, irrespective of their completeness as art works,
and that once full adequacy of form and artistic intention had been

reached, Monteverdi's efforts were no longer preparatory but were concentrated on intensifying the dramatic expression and sharpening the stylistic tools, so that the madrigal after *Orfeo* was, in every respect, an end in itself.

The music drama had been, and still was, the chief artistic form for representations at the courts on state occasions. Monteverdi composed his dramas for the courts of Mantua and Parma, and his minor scenic works, as well as one full drama, for the patricians of Venice. In Venice, during the twenties, certain patrician families, such as the Giustiniani and the Grimani, took a great interest in dramatic compositions, and had it not been for the plague, this interest would have had earlier and more tangible results. The festivities in the noble palaces of Venice had been in no way inferior to those at princely courts, but the Venetian state could hardly allow any one family to monopolize such a concentration of splendor and power, and it is probably for this reason that public performances of music dramas were begun and the first "public" theater in Venice opened. Public it was, though owned and fully controlled by the Venetian nobility, but to differentiate between a "democratic" opera of Venice and an "aristocratic" opera of the courts is absurd in view of the city's social structure and the legal ownership of the Venetian theaters.

After the wounds of the plague had healed, there was a wave of interest in the musical forms of dramatic entertainment. In 1637, a memorable year, the first theater, the Teatro S. Cassiano, was opened in Venice, by the noble family of the Tron. The music drama presented at the opening was the *Andromeda*, by F. Manelli and B. Ferrari, the latter a follower of Monteverdi, from whose hands he said he received the achievements of the new art. The patricians now began to compete with one another in founding theaters, which were built not because the people clamored for more shows, but because of the rivalry of the leading families. By 1641 Venice had four operatic theaters, and at the end of the century, there were sixteen, all owned by noble families, who leased boxes for the season to the other nobles of Venice. A theatrical group was hired for the carnival season at which the operas were performed.

Monteverdi had no part in the opening of the Teatro S. Cassiano, but when in 1639 the family of the Grimani erected the Teatro SS. Giovanni e Paolo, a work by Monteverdi was commissioned—*Adone*,[1]

---

[1] Livio Nisco Galvani, *I teatri musicali di Venezia nel secolo XVII* (Milan, 1879), p. 30.

a "tragedia musicale." Its librettist, Paolo Vendramin, came from a noble family which in the same year opened a theater of their own, the Teatro S. Moisè. Only the libretto of the *Adone* is preserved, and Monteverdi's authorship of the music is not entirely certain. Since the days of Marino, the *Adone* had been a favorite subject, and it had been used by Cicognini for a music drama reported to have been set to music by Jacopo Peri. When the Vendramins opened their Teatro S. Moisè, they presented Monteverdi's famous *Arianna*, which the composer had improved for Mantua some twenty years before; it is to be assumed that this corrected version, if not one with still further changes, was given on the Venetian stage in 1639, where it ran for a full year.

The year 1641 was a great one for Monteverdi. The Teatro SS. Giovanni e Paolo presented *Le Nozze d'Enea con Lavinia*, by Giacomo Badoaro, a patrician of Venice, and though the music is lost, the libretto contains Badoaro's brief remarks about Monteverdi's composition. In the same year, the oldest theater—S. Cassiano—produced a drama *Il Ritorno d'Ulisse in patria*, with a libretto by Badoaro and music by Monteverdi. Finally in 1642, one year before his death, Monteverdi's last work was presented in the theater of the Grimani, SS. Giovanni e Paolo. This was *L'Incoronazione di Poppea*, with a libretto by Francesco Busenello.

From Monteverdi's correspondence concerning *La finta pazza Licori*, we know that he exerted a strong influence on the form and character of the text, that he persuaded the poet to add scenes and characters, to divide the work into five acts instead of three, and particularly to give a proper presentation of the affections. A similar influence is recorded by Badoaro in connection with *Le Nozze d'Enea con Lavinia*. The *Argomento*, in which poets usually discussed the content and character of the libretto and their ideas of drama, gave Badoaro an opportunity to speak of his collaboration with Monteverdi, whom he praises in extraordinary terms as a composer who has brought music in general and dramatic music in particular to perfection, as an artist whose name is known in all countries where music is cultivated, as a musician whose art is immortal. Badoaro adds: "I avoided all farfetched thoughts and conceptions and paid more attention to the affections as Monteverdi wished to have them; to his satisfaction I also changed and left out many of those materials that I first had used." This was indeed Monteverdian; the stressing of the human affections was a basic tenet of his musical art, whose subject was always man. Abstract ideas, purely mythological figures, inanimate matter did not interest him; he rejected them just as in the past he had rejected a proposal to write about winds instead of human beings. By his concentration on the affections, he brought music and man together, and certainly in the drama such a concentration was indispensable.

Badoaro and Busenello are part of a movement in the Italian drama that had gradually turned from the pastoral or purely mythological to historical subjects. At the same time different factions affirmed or questioned the Aristotelian unities of time, place, and action. The dispute was as much concerned with approval or disapproval of the rules of Aristotle as with the desire of the poets that the spirit of the time should prevail over tradition. Were the "modern rules of caprice and of passion" superior to "the good rules" of the old masters? Badoaro, by no means anti-Aristotelian, wisely assumes that rules are formulated according to the prevailing temper of a period and that had Aristotle lived in the seventh century he would have formulated rules in harmony with the aspirations of that age. It is the aspiration of the seventeenth century to speak of the passions of men, above all of the passion of heroism. Thus it is the heroic figures of history and those mythological figures who have heroic character that attract the dramatic poets, and not the lyricism of the pastoral. It is also the "capriccio" of the time to understand art as something that is above the ordinary and the common and that is superior to natural simplicity. Just as the prince is above the common people, and the hero above the ordinary man, so complication is above simplicity, art above nature. Complications are proof of the degree of art. Hence, in opposition to the Aristotelian unity of action, the seventeenth-century "capriccio," sometimes even called the "capriccio bizzarro," develops unexpected turns in the plot or brings in secondary plots that parallel or even interfere with the main action. The dramatist appeals to the studious connoisseur who is capable of unraveling complicated plots and is best pleased when the actions of men are out of the ordinary.

Did Badoaro at first follow the "capriccio bizzarro"? Monteverdi, he admitted, had insisted on omitting the farfetched conceptions. The composer was probably more inclined to preserve unity, to avoid the distractions of too many secondary lines, and to think that the variety of affections, essential to the dramatic interpretation of music, did not necessitate the devious contrivances of the "capriccio bizzarro." In one respect, however, the general trend of the drama agreed with his art: the heroic passions, as shown in history and legend, lent themselves to his concepts of dramatic interpretation. The presentation of heroic passions in music drama, on a scale as grandiose and exemplary as a story of heroic man, becomes the "decoro di Personaggi grandi." The ordinary affairs of life must be enlarged to remarkable proportions so that the great passion of the historical hero can be made to harmonize with the baroque passion for the great personality. Monteverdi's *Il Ritorno d'Ulisse in patria* is something of a hybrid—half mythological, half historical—but *L'Incoronazione di Poppea* is the first great historical music drama and will beget a long line of opere serie dealing with the heroic figures of history.

Whether Monteverdi was the composer of *Il Ritorno d'Ulisse in patria* has been a subject of dispute for many years. The majority of Monteverdi students accept the authenticity of the work, though Giacomo Benvenuti, an expert on the music of that period, has recently denied that Monteverdi was the composer. The reasons for doubt, expressed for the first time by Emil Vogel,[2] are based on the considerable discrepancies between Badoaro's libretto, which has five acts, and the anonymous score, which has only three acts.[3] Since the disputes have not been fruitful, we shall not reproduce them here. It is sufficient to say that the link between the opera and his madrigalesque composition is convincing proof of Monteverdi's authorship. To complicate matters, the existence of another *Ulisse* attributed to Monteverdi was brought into the discussion by Giordani in 1855, when he reported the publication of *Le glorie della Musica e della Poesia rappresentandosi in Bologna la Delia e l'Ulisse nel teatro degli illustrissimi Guastavillani. Bologna 1630, in 4, musica di Claudio Monteverdi e di Francesco Manelli.*[4] This pamphlet has never been seen by anyone but Giordani, and while a *Delia* by Francesco Manelli is recorded elsewhere, no other reference to an *Ulisse* by Monteverdi has ever been discovered. We may add that the existence of an *Ulisse* of 1630 is very doubtful, because at that time Monteverdi was a fairly active correspondent, and except for the church music he wrote for the nuns of S. Lorenzo, he makes no mention of any work in that year.

Badoaro's libretto *Il Ritorno d'Ulisse in patria*, extant only in manuscript in the Marciana in Venice, expressly names Claudio Monteverdi

---

[2] Vogel, *VfMW*, III, 403f.

[3] This is so in manuscript 18763, preserved in the National Library in Vienna, which is the basis for the editions. See Malipiero, *Opere*, XII, and *DTOe*, Vol. 57 (Vienna, 1922; ed. Robert Haas). Discussions of the authenticity of the work: Hugo Goldschmidt, "Claudio Monteverdis Oper Il ritorno d'Ulisse," in *SIMG*, IV and IX; Robert Haas, "Zur Neuausgabe von Monteverdis Il Ritorno," in *StzMW*, IX (1922).

[4] See Gaetano Giordani, *Intorno al Gran Teatro del Commune e ad altri minori in Bologna* (Bologna, 1855), p. 62.

as the composer. In the *Nozze d'Enea con Lavinia* of that same year Badoaro had stated that upon the advice of Monteverdi he omitted several parts criticized by the composer. Is it not possible that Monteverdi also suggested alterations for *Il Ritorno d'Ulisse in patria*, which were not worked into the manuscript libretto but account for the discrepancies with the Viennese score? [5]

Badoaro's libretto is based on the last books of Homer's epic. After his endless wanderings, Ulisse is finally allowed to return to Ithaca, the goddess Minerva having overcome the intrigues of Nettuno. Disguised as an old beggar, Ulisse goes to the herdsman Eumete without being recognized. Minerva, the protectress of Ulisse, brings his son Telemaco home from Sparta to be welcomed by the overjoyed Eumete. Penelope, beset by suitors greedy for the royal riches of Ulisse's wife, has been waiting for her husband in unswerving loyalty. The suitors dissipate Ulisse's wealth and make themselves the impudent masters of his palace. A last attempt by the suitors to persuade Penelope to choose one of them in marriage is met by Penelope herself who says she will marry the one who bends Ulisse's bow. None succeeds until Ulisse, who has been watching the impertinence of the suitors, bends his own weapon and, aided by Minerva and his son, kills the suitors. For a while Penelope hesitates, doubting whether he is really her Ulisse, but a final scene of recognition and rejoicing concludes the "drama in musica," as Badoaro calls this work.

It opens with the customary prologue with characteristic allegorical figures: Human Fragility, Time, Fortune, Love, in Monteverdi's score; Fate, Prudence, Fortitude, in Badoaro's libretto. In its balanced proportions the prologue exemplifies Monteverdi's structural organization. The part of L'Humana Fragilità is handled as a musical-refrain form, with a slight variation each time the refrain occurs. Each of the allegoric figures has its own melodic style: L'Humana Fragilità, an arioso which comes closest to the song with its proportionate lines and corresponding phrases; Fortuna, the melody of a favorite dance rhythm, which exploits the sequential technique and in so doing heightens the irresistible sweep of a dance song; Tempo, a melodic motion charac-

---

[5] Cf. Guido Pannain, *Musica*, II, 42ff. When in a production at the *Maggio musicale* in Florence (1942) the *Ulisse* was revived, the response was divided, and there arose the old argument that the *Ulisse* could not be by Monteverdi because it was aesthetically less satisfactory than, for instance, the *Incoronazione*—a rather dubious argument. Guido Pannain at last raised an overdue question which we believe strikes at the core of the matter: Is it really true that the *Ulisse* is an inferior, artistically unsatisfactory work? Pannain vindicated the artistic quality of the opera.

teristic of the *stile concitato;* and Amore, a mixture of the balanced arioso of L'Humana Fragilità and the dancelike motion of Fortuna. With the exception of L'Humana Fragilità, the allegoric figures at the end make up a trio which has the transparent structure realized by Monteverdi in his later years when he made use of the canzonetta.

Using the same sinfonia that served as introduction to the prologue, the first act opens in the royal palace where Penelope is attended by Ericlea, the nurse of Ulisse. It is one of the greatest scenes in dramatic literature, and any doubt as to Monteverdi's authorship is incomprehensible. Penelope's lament in which she bemoans her loneliness and endless waiting for Ulisse has its direct ancestor in *Orfeo* and *Arianna.* The musical diction has grown maturer, the human intensity profounder, and yet the essentials of the *stile recitativo* in the early dramas have been retained. The formal design of the scene reveals Monteverdi's inexhaustible ingenuity in the invention of expressive structures. Divided strophically into three sections, twice interrupted by Ericlea's brief interjections, which appear as contemplative refrains on the helpless misery of Penelope, the structure reinforces the increase of affection. Each section ends with the thought of Ulisse's return. The first is a lament that Ulisse alone of all the Greek warriors has not been allowed to return home, expressed in a typically Monteverdian rise of chromatic melody. The other two sections end with the same imploration of Penelope, "Torna, torna, deh torna Ulisse," melodically a refrain whose poignant chromaticism expresses the affection, the last time ingeniously preceded by the repetition of "Tu sol del tuo tornar." In the third stanza there is a further structural rise to a climactic tension, as Penelope implores the elements, wind and water, to make possible Ulisse's return. She begins with a songlike melody whose simple, balanced style resembles the intensive melodies of Monteverdi's latest madrigals. The combination of the *stile concitato* with the declamatory line of the recitative produces that mixture of styles which Monteverdi cultivated in the dramatic recitations of his madrigals.

No less grandiose in its proportions is the monologue of Ulisse when, cast on the shores of Ithaca, he awakens not yet knowing where he is. As he sees the shores and breathes the air after the ordeal of the storm, he does not trust his senses and fears he is deceived by a dream, the brother of death. These uncertainties are expressed at the beginning of the monologue in striking harmonies, whose bold shifts express fear, distrust, and the dread of awakening to new torments, if and when the dream ends. Although this monologue is not as rigidly controlled by a premeditated structure as Penelope's, and although the melody proceeds with the continuous renewal of phrases for every line which is typical of the *stile recitativo*, Monteverdi holds the form together by the strength of a repeated phrase in the *basso continuo*. When Ulisse blames the Phaeacians, his companions, for betraying and abandoning him, when he sings "mi lasciaste in questa riva aperta . . . misero abbandonato," the passage is an exact duplicate of the lamenting phrase of Arianna abandoned by Theseus.

The long scene (8) that follows Ulisse's monologue, in which Minerva appears in the disguise of a little shepherd to aid Ulisse, is a brilliant demonstration of unity of style and dramatic purpose. All the artistic experiences of his madrigals are used by Monteverdi to supply a variety of styles responsive to his expressive intentions. First there is a light, unpretentious canzonetta melody, the idiom of Minerva, the little shepherd; then the enchanted Ulisse follows with his pastorela. In the course of the scene, the style changes rapidly as recognition and revelation develop, and all the styles are directed toward the climactic joy of Ulisse's home-coming to Penelope. There is a concerted form with the running bass; a section in triple rhythm with the florid melody which Monteverdi used in sections of his madrigals and in his latest ballo *Movete al mio bel suon* (1637); there is an acceleration of changes in rhythm, meter, and style, all paralleling the increasing tensions of the situation and culminating in Ulisse's joy over Minerva's determination to lead him back to his throne. At the moment when Minerva sings of her vengeful destruction of Troja, the martial *stile concitato* of the eighth book of madrigals appears. Her triumphant outburst takes the form of a virtuoso coloratura which Orfeo had used and which recurred in Marino's *Tempro la cetra*, and the final duet is a repetition of similar passages from the madrigalesque compositions. In fact, the madrigalesque achievements are found throughout the first act. Thus, in Ulisse's strophic aria *O fortunato Ulisse*, Monteverdi appears to be quoting his own madrigalesque work, and the passage Melanto sings (scene 10), "Un bel viso fa guerra, il guerriero," is a literal quotation from the eighth book. Moreover, the love duet between Melanto and Eurimaco (scene 2), *Dei nostri amor*, is a companion of duets in the seventh book. Of particular interest and equally Monteverdian is the "psalmodic" recitation previously used in the madrigal for purposes of special expressiveness, which appears here as the climactic confession of love. In every detail of all its sections, this second scene could well function as one of the amorous madrigals that Monteverdi expanded

and transformed into cantatas for a solo duet with the sectional groupings of the *stile concertato*.

The *concertato* combined with the canzonetta is also exploited for
comic purposes, as in the brief scene (12) between Iro, the parasite and
court fool, and Eumete, the herdsman. Monteverdi also revived the
French manner of performing solo and chorus: the solo starts out, and
when the chorus follows, the solo appears as the upper part of the
choral group. Such is the arrangement of the chorus of the Phaeacians,
In questo basso mondo (scene 6). Penelope's *Amor, Amor*, especially
the passage "in constanza, in constanza e rigore," with the sequential
structure between voice and *basso continuo*, is directly modeled on
passages in such madrigals as *Mentre vaga Angioletta* ("hor la preme,
hor la rompe") or better still *Armato il cor* ("contrasterò col ciel").

The second act also abounds with reminiscences of madrigalesque
compositions. Whole scenes are modeled on a certain late type of
madrigal. Especially suggestive was the madrigal *Mentre vaga Angioletta*, with its sectional groups and its profusion of contrasts in affection. The outline of a madrigal like *Ogni amante è guerrier* also inspired direct imitations. The strophic *Ohimè ch'io cado*, the melodic
and rhythmic ductus and structure of *Alle danze, alle danze*, and the
magnificent *Ardo*, all provided models with which Monteverdi worked
in the drama.[6] The second scene, with Eumete, Ulisse, and Telemaco
is largely madrigalesque. It begins with Eumete's *O gran figlio d'Ulisse;*
and the duet of Eumete and Ulisse, *Dolce speme i cor lusinga*, is, in
regard to rhythm, melody, and especially the *basso ostinato* with its
motif of four descending tones, an imitation of the *Lamento della Ninfa*
in *genere rappresentativo* from the eighth book. One of the great
scenes, a duet between Ulisse and Telemaco, in which the two rejoice
in their mutual love—"Oh Padre sospirato—Oh figlio desiato"—has
from a formalistic point of view been anticipated by such madrigals as
S'el vostro cor Madonna, in the seventh book. The duet ends with
Ulisse's request to his son to go to Penelope, "Vanne alla madre," in
that rhythm of 6/1 which Monteverdi favored in his late work to express affections of urgency and tension.

Two scenes stand out in the second act: the first (scene 5) which
shows Penelope surrounded by her imploring suitors, and the extensive
finale (scene 12) which ends with the victory of Ulisse over the suitors.
Monteverdi organizes both as musical entities with structural balance
and dramatic expressiveness. This fusion of structure and expression

---

[6] Malipiero, *Opere*, IX, i, pp. 68 and 32, respectively.

is as characteristic of his art and aesthetic sense as it is of his dramatic and human strength. He thinks of the scene as an organism whose continuous growth must follow a preconceived form and direction, and carefully avoids an arbitrary succession of parts strung together without structural logic. To this end, he constructs his scenes and, musically speaking, operates with repetitive forms, with refrains, soloistic, choral, or instrumental. The repetition, in particular, allows us to recognize the factors that organize the whole. In this respect, Monteverdi could, and did, draw upon achievements in his madrigalesque work.

In the scene (5) with Penelope and the suitors, the organization is established by a rondo form with a double refrain. The chorus of three lovers, *Ama dunque*, imploring Penelope to return their love is one refrain. When the lovers join in a new, but similar trio, *All'allegrezze dunque al ballo*, at the end of the scene, they introduce the concluding "ballo greco." Performed by eight "Mori," this dance, of which only the text has been preserved, recalls the ending of the *Orfeo*. The arioso strophe of Penelope, *Non voglio amar*, the denial to the suitors, is the second refrain. These two refrains present the dramatic situation in essence, and aided by their strength the composer gives to all other parts of the scene a logical and balanced order. Each suitor presents his plea in a different melodic style. Antinoo begins with a bass recitative in the style which Monteverdi used for the first time in the Plutone part of his *Ballo dell'Ingrate*. To add strength to his plea, the trio *Ama dunque* follows, and Penelope's denial presents the answer to the plea. Then the order is reversed. The trio begins, Penelope answers, and the suitors Pisandro, Anfinomo, and Antinoo again make their individual pleas, in three strophes and three different styles: the late song style, the ballo style with a following canzonetta, and the concerted style. The trio and the response of Penelope appear again as refrains. The new trio and the ballo terminate the scene. As a whole, the organization of this scene resembles that of the rondo cantata, which was soon to come into use. Since the dramatic situation—that is, the affection of the scene—is stable and consists largely of a mutual imploring and denial, a uniform, organic structure could be directly derived from this effect.

The last scene of the second act, which handles a variety of affections, requires an entirely different organization, since it has a forward thrust toward a dramatic climax, the victory of Ulisse. There are, in fact, two actions, two fights and two victories; the first fight is the wrestling between Iro and Ulisse. These actions directed toward similar goals could hardly be fitted into a repetitive structure, and the continuity of action requires the *stile recitativo* for the dialogue, which has no particular form of its own. Monteverdi uses different musical forms for the two actions, but gives them a similar ending in the martial *stile concitato*. The first action, in pure dialogue, begins with Antinoo's mockery of the old, shabby beggar, who should consort with Eumete's hogs rather than remain in sight of the nobles in the palace. The stuttering fool Iro joins in, and for his impertinence is challenged by Ulisse to a wrestling match. The suitors, anticipating great fun, ask Penelope's permission, which is granted, and the match takes place and Ulisse is victorious. The continuity of the dialogue and its more or less narrative character, void of any particular affection, did not allow the musical form to be regulated by a series of passions. Monteverdi put the dialogue in the *stile recitativo*, but attempted to link together the beginnings of the melodic phrases in the alternations of the dialogue: the result is a sequence of unsystematic but easily detected correspondences. The consistent characterization of the comical stutterer Iro helps further to balance the dialogue recitatives against each other. The part of Ulisse is a mixture of the *stile recitativo* and the *stile concitato*, and all the parts converge on the *stile concitato* at the mention of "guerriero," "combattitor," and "lotta," which is accompanied by an instrumental sinfonia. The second action, which follows immediately, lends itself to a more disciplined organization. Here, also, two situations of different emotional content challenged the structural sense of the composer. The suitors, one by one, present royal gifts to Penelope, who responds to each. When the last has offered his present, she decides that she will no longer deny their petition; she will be the prize of the suitor who bends Ulisse's bow. Hardly has she spoken her decision than she regrets it, but the suitors express their joy in a regular madrigal, *Lieta gloria*. The succession of the suitors with their gifts is musically characterized by a gradual increase of the song-like factors in the melody of the recitative, which is most marked in Antinoo's presentation, a genuine arioso throughout. Penelope's responses remain constant, but rise to an ornamental style and to the *concitato* in the section where she makes her promise. The competition itself brings once more the succession of the suitors. Here the martial competitive affection is prevalent and the *stile concitato* is the over-all stylistic form. The appearance of one suitor after the other also suggested a certain structural arrangement: the instrumental sinfonia is used as a refrain that introduces each of the competitors. Since each suitor prays to a different god—Pisandro to Amor, Anfinomo to Mars, but Antinoo to Beauty, to Penelope herself—Monteverdi differentiates their strophic melodies. All end with the admission of failure, and this ending is rendered in a uniform way as a kind of refrain. Penelope assumes the *stile concitato* at the moment when she allows Ulisse to try his strength at the bow. With the *Sinfonia da Guerra*, and the victory of Ulisse, aided by Minerva, the *stile concitato* comes to a most appropriate climax. The musical organization of this complicated scene, responsive to every characteristic of the text, required, indeed, the hand of a genius.

The third act is dramatically the weakest. The final outcome is twice delayed, once by the Council of the Gods, where Minerva prays to Giuno, Giuno to Giove, Giove to Nettuno, to forgive Ulisse, and again by Penelope's slowness in recognizing her husband. Though dramatically weak, the act displays extraordinary musical qualities particularly in the initial Iro scene, in the two scenes of the gods with the concluding "Coro in Cielo," in Ericlea's soliloquy (scene 8) and in the final scene of recognition. The first scene with Iro's solo has special interest, for Iro's aria is marked as a "parte ridicola." It is an irregular refrain aria, in which Iro bemoans his terrible misfortune in being deprived of food and drink from the tables of the suitors who have all been killed. To make this lament ridiculous, Monteverdi parodies every feature of his noble madrigalesque style; he even uses the ciacona bass of his own madrigal *Zefiro torna*. The beginning "Oh dolor, oh martir" stretches the "Oh" over eight long measures, and the style of profound expression is increasingly exaggerated, until Iro decides that instead of running around with an empty stomach he will commit suicide on the spot: "Voglio uccider me stesso." It is the first aria in which exaggeration of the new distinguished, serious style is used for comic effect. The scenes with the gods are particularly brilliant: the highly florid coloraturas over the *stile recitativo* of the Minerva part, the virtuoso *stile concertato* of Nettuno's part, the madrigalesque *concertato* of Giuno. Ericlea's solo is artistically notable, for it is a refrain aria, expanded to make up a whole scene for the first time in Monteverdi's work. The refrain is actually twofold, in the strophic form, three times recurring at the end of the strophe, and the ritornello between the strophes. In the final recognition scene Monteverdi prescribes an orchestral accompaniment for Penelope's *Illustratevi o Cieli*, and this aria has particular structural significance: the melodic phrases for the lines of the strophe are repeated in alternation, while the orchestral accompaniment functions as a ritornello between the lines and not simultaneously. The final duet of Ulisse and Penelope, *Sospirato mio sole*, is modeled on the madrigalesque duets of the seventh book.

There can be no doubt that *Il Ritorno d'Ulisse in patria* is Monteverdi's work, or that from a musical and aesthetic point of view it has great value. Monteverdi here carried over into the opera all the dramatized styles of the madrigal, and in so doing raised the art of dramatic characterization far above his early works. Monteverdi is at his greatest as an artistic interpreter of situations; but the situations must be human and passionate, not objective, inanimate, or purely narrative. The *Ritorno d'Ulisse* does not abound with human conflicts and affections, but wherever the drama gives an opportunity for the presentation of human passion and suffering, Monteverdi at once realizes that musical language of human pathos that is entirely his own. Even when the drama fails to formulate the full tones of affections in conflicts and humanized tensions, Monteverdi demonstrates his superiority as a master of form, style, and artistic organization. His transference of the style of the dramatized madrigal to the opera is not merely a shift of style, for the *Ritorno d'Ulisse* gives renewed evidence that techniques and devices are justified only if they cease to exist for themselves and are fully identified with expressive intentions. As a drama, the *Ritorno d'Ulisse* is a hybrid and does not completely achieve the realism that the seventeenth century was beginning to favor.

The final step toward that realism was taken in Busenello's *Incoronazione di Poppea*. The human reality of passions in conflict was one of the articles of Monteverdi's artistic faith, and on this ground Busenello's text must have inspired the composer considerably more than Badoaro's work. Francesco Busenello, a Venetian lawyer, was for some time ambassador at the court of Mantua and became a leading librettist. His dramatic work had brought him into contact with Monteverdi's pupil and successor, Cavalli, who was beginning to make a name for himself as an operatic composer. At the age of seventy-five, Monteverdi composed the *Incoronazione*, which was first performed in Venice in 1642, with great success. The *Incoronazione* was repeated for several years after Monteverdi's death and has been regarded as the supreme music drama of the epoch. At all events, it has proved its artistic greatness in modern revivals. What Monteverdi presumably set out to accomplish, he realized: the synthesis of his art, of the art of his time, and, prophetically, of the art of the seventeenth century. There were operas that in many ways were the equals of his, but of genuine music dramas there was none. His dramatic work was so complete a synthesis that "reforms" were necessary to bring opera back to the basic dramatic conceptions of his work. Gluck's reform, for instance, was actually a return to the principles of Monteverdi.

The *Incoronazione* is preceded by a prologue which anticipates the theme of the drama—all-powerful love. The allegoric figures Fortuna, Virtù, Amore, dispute as to the degree of power they hold in the world of man; the dispute leaves Amor victorious; he is the ruler over men.

The drama is built upon principles that began to become "modern" with the generation of Busenello, though it still falls short of the over-complicated stories of intrigue that fill the librettos of the second half of the century. Secondary situations, contrasting actions, even some roles that are quite apart from the main theme, contribute to the dramatic conflicts and add to the variety of affections. The secondary actions, however, do not confound the spectator with a continual shifting of the dramatic accents, but converge, in a contributory manner, upon the main theme of the drama: the love of Nero and Poppea which, despite all hindrances, comes to its fulfillment with Poppea's coronation. The chief conflict springs from the situation in which the two lovers find themselves at the very beginning: Poppea is married to Ottone, Nero to Ottavia. A further conflict and hindrance to the desires of the lovers is caused by Seneca, the Emperor's wise counselor and the guardian of the law, who thinks that renouncing all private desires, the princes of the world should exhibit their pomp and ceremony to the world but never reveal their inner suffering. Since he is against all lawlessness, especially among kings, he opposes the plans of Nero and Poppea.

The story of the opera is as follows. In order to satisfy his ardent love of Poppea, Nero had dispatched Ottone on state business into remote regions from which he unexpectedly returns. The opera opens with Ottone's return home, where he has unsuspectingly prepared to serenade his Poppea, in typically Italian fashion, "Apri un balcon Poppea." He discovers Nero's guard, the soldiers fast asleep in front of Poppea's room, and knows that Poppea has been disloyal in his absence: "Ah, perfida Poppea." His outburst of painful wrath awakens the soldiers whose conversation further reveals the calamitous tidings to the hidden Ottone. The morning dawns, and Nero and Poppea say farewell in a love duet, secretly witnessed by Ottone. After these three scenes, skillfully drawn, the drama is ready to develop. Warnings, counterplots, and intrigues are contrived to restrain the lovers. The first warning comes from Arnalta, Poppea's old nurse, and in this scene Monteverdi shows great skill in exploiting the contrast of affections for the sake of the musical structure: Arnalta's warning to Poppea to beware of Ottavia's jealousy is contrasted with Poppea's defiant and triumphant love. With subtle feeling for dramatic contrast, there follows immediately a companion scene: Ottavia with her nurse. Arnalta's warning is justified; Ottavia laments her fate, the fate of all helpless womanhood; she pictures Nero in Poppea's embrace, and swears vengeance. Thus the plot takes shape.

Ottavia goes to Seneca for advice; but his advice is that of philosophical wisdom—to maintain imperial dignity and to follow virtue. This is no balm for the burning wounds of her jealousy, and she rejects the advice, her young page (*valletto*) taking her side. Disappointed, Ottavia leaves Seneca, and Pallas Athene appears to warn him that death will come to him on that very day; the warning anticipates the intrigue of Poppea and Nero against him; yet Seneca welcomes death: "Venga, venga la morte." As though to strengthen the warning, Nero immediately appears, though not yet set upon an evil plan. In a violent dispute, presented in a musically outstanding, rapid dialogue, Nero reveals his intention to dispose of Ottavia in order that he may marry Poppea. In fulfillment of his intention, Nero goes to Poppea, Ottone being a secret witness of their meeting. In the midst of this love scene, Poppea, in her ardent ambition to become empress, uses her seductive charms to persuade Nero to have Seneca killed; Nero gives his promise: "in questa sera ei mora." In the seventh scene, Ottone and Poppea at last meet, with the nurse Arnalta as an eavesdropper. Poppea recognizes Ottone's undiminished love, but Fortuna has decided, and she is determined that her ambition shall know no hindrance: "e così l'ambitione sovra ogni vitio tien la monarchia." Ottone, left alone, is deeply wounded by Poppea's cold calculations and despises womanhood, "that imperfect sex that has nothing human but the body." He is joined by Drusilla, a young lady from Poppea's court, who is in love with him. Taking advantage of her feelings, Ottone plans to kill Poppea with her aid.

The second act begins with a scene in the house of Seneca, who is once more forewarned of his approaching death, this time by Mercurio. His answer remains the same: "O me felice." His servants vainly implore him not to go to his death. In sharp contrast, the fifth scene, which is fragmentary in the extant version of the score, is an intermezzo of a comic character, made up entirely of songs presented by the page and a young girl (*valletto* and *damigella*). The sixth scene shows Nero in wild exuberance over Seneca's death, which seems to give his love a free course—and of his love he will sing: "Hor che Seneca è morto cantiam amorose canzoni." Ottone's important monologue (scene 8) centers on his plan to murder Poppea. When he is joined by Ottavia, who also demands Poppea's death, Ottone becomes her agent as well. He persuades Drusilla to lend him her dresses that he may have easy access to Poppea's room. But Poppea is under the special protection of Amor, who watches over her while she sleeps (scene 13). Ottone enters in disguise, and when he advances to murder his wife, he is barred by Amor. Poppea awakens and Amor triumphant sings his song: "I have defended you, Poppea, for I wish to make you empress."

In the third act disaster befalls those who have plotted against the Emperor. Drusilla is arrested and brought before Nero, who by all manner of tortures extorts her confession. Rather than accuse her beloved Ottone, she declares herself guilty of the murder, but Ottone assures Nero of her innocence; in noble rivalry each wants to save the other; and Ottavia is finally accused. Drusilla and Ottone, united, are sent into exile, and Ottavia is condemned to be put out to sea alone in a boat. Ottavia sings her moving farewell: *A Dio Roma, a Dio patria.* The drama concludes with the public coronation of Poppea, the victory of Love, and the duet of Nero and Poppea, *Pur ti miro, pur ti godo.*

In this last work Monteverdi adapted the musical form to the dramatic situation and to the nature and action of the characters more than ever before. The result was a wealth of forms, structures, styles, that served the purpose of dramatic characterization. No longer did he need to invent each form to express each dramatic situation, although the work contains many novelties that testify to his ever-creative mind, but for the most part, he was able to draw upon his previous work. His own madrigal reaches its greatest triumph in the music drama, and, in this respect, the *Incoronazione di Poppea* rises above *Il Ritorno d'Ulisse in patria.* Not only the duet forms, but many of the solos are unthinkable without the madrigal. It is the variety of affections that are musically interpreted, rather than the variety of characters. The madrigal had served to present specific, single, and limited affections, and now, in this work it provides formal and structural inspiration as well as musically defined affections.

The soliloquies, some of which have extraordinary scope, test the composer's capacity for uniting the dramatic and the musically comprehensive form. Although it was the tradition to present the monologue largely in the *stile recitativo,* whose structure must always be invented anew, Monteverdi never used the pure *stile recitativo* throughout extended monologues. In the *Incoronazione,* the monologues of Ottone and Ottavia, which are not only very long but also of the greatest dramatic intensity, are almost always divided into well-defined parts, so that the recitative never serves a purely narrative purpose but is always reserved for dramatic passages. The first monologue of Ottone illustrates this technique. Seven strophic entities are to be distinguished within the musical form. Twice the aria, and twice the recitative organize the whole complex, in perfect proportions. A short aria on a repetitive bass figure with ritornello opens the monologue, and the first passage of heightened emotion, "O dearest home, the dwelling of my life and love," is given in a short recitative. There follows a long serenade-like strophic aria, three strophes on the same bass with ritornelli, and the last strophe passes directly to an equally lengthy recitative with a brief arioso ending. The recitative is inserted at the dramatically decisive place: "Alas, what do I see," when Ottone is faced with the proof of Poppea's betrayal. Even long recitatives such as this one are not without subtle symmetries, almost imperceptibly introduced, which give further articulation.

In most soliloquies, just as in the first scene, the use of the full aria makes for a symmetrical arrangement of the recitative. Shorter monologues may also use the aria, but in a different way, since the full aria would curb the recitative. Ottone's monologue in which he decides to punish Poppea's perfidy is another example of the coincidence of musical structure and human affection; the affection of the monologue is pain and vengeance, and the division is made accordingly. Monteverdi used the aria phrase "Otton, mio cor, torna in te stesso" as a refrain, repeated three times on the same bass between the lines of the recitative. When Ottone resolves to murder Poppea, at this decisive moment the monologue is given wholly in recitative, which has an eminently dramatic function.

Ottavia has two monologues of the highest rank in operatic literature: *Disprezzata Regina* in the first act and *A Dio Roma* in the last act. Both have such a continuity of affection that a division into parts cannot easily be made; nevertheless, Monteverdi imposes a musical organization upon the recitative. To the passage in the middle of the first monologue, "In braccio di Poppea tu dimori felice e godi," he applies the aria style, on account of the words "godere, lieto, felice," using the aria rhythm which he designated 3, that is 6/1. By thus rendering a central passage in typical aria style, he gives the recitative symmetrical form without depriving the *stile recitativo* of its poignant tones. The monologue in which Ottavia bids farewell to Rome, to her country, and to her friends, exhibits Monteverdi's ability to express the pathos of human tragedy at its height. Such compositions as this farewell go far to explain the emotional reactions ascribed to Monteverdi's audiences. The monologue seems to have the freely handled structure of a song, for the latter part has reminiscences of the beginning, thus indicating a bisectional arrangement. Its melody is in the style of Monteverdi's most dramatic recitative, that indefinable mixture of recitation, arioso, and *concitato*, that can hardly be separated into its elements.

Still another form of the monologue occurs when Seneca speaks to the unhappy Ottavia of the duties of royalty and of the bliss of faith. The beginning and the end convey the dominant affections: a dignity befitting the empress' high position and a constant faith. Both are presented in *stile recitativo*, while the long middle section is governed by melodic styles of madrigalesque origin, so that the style changes three times in accordance with the change of affections. A unique arrangement of a solo part occurs in the scene (II, 13) in which Amor watches over the sleeping Poppea. Appropriately given in recitative is a short passage in which Amor expresses his fear that Poppea is sleeping without caution, for human beings, living always in darkness, are wont to think themselves secure from evil when they close their eyes. At the line, "O sciocchi o frali sense mortali," the solo continues with a large strophic song of four stanzas with ritornello. The beginning of this strophic structure in the Venetian manuscript is marked "Aria"—the only appearance of this term in Monteverdi's dramatic scores.

In the monologues, or solo scenes, of the *Incoronazione*, Monteverdi's creative inventiveness came into full play. There is not a single repetition of the same formal arrangement in any of the monologues; each is new and unique. For the general ductus of the melodic motion Monteverdi could make use of his earlier achievements, but for the structure of the *stile recitativo* in the monologue, he had no models, because the dramatic situations were never identical.

In the case of the duets, the texts to which they are set have a character that is more lyrical than dramatic, and since they dwell on one affection, the madrigals could be used more freely as models. Ordinarily the duet does not work with the pure *stile recitativo*, and even where it occurs, it is fully absorbed by other elements of the madrigal. We must also differentiate between the true duet form and that of the dialogue. In dialogue, as in the monologue, the *stile recitativo* may be used for the purpose of expressing a climactic affection. The meeting of Ottone and Poppea (I, 11) has a musical structure that organizes the whole scene on a grandiose scale. It is a double strophic aria in alternation on two bass melodies and with two ritornelli, all doubled in order to give the dialogue an alternating form and also a superior, uniting organization; and it ends at the emotional climax with a recitative melody in alternation.

The *stile recitativo* is also employed in the scene of Drusilla's examination before Nero, where it seems an appropriate medium for the quick, excited questioning of the suspected culprit. Here the aria style also gives a pattern to the line of the dialogue; for instance, when Nero orders Drusilla tortured, the martial *stile concitato* provides the form. In this scene, however, the recitative is characteristically transformed by the mixture of two styles, emotional excitement being expressed by the *stile concitato* and great intensity by Monteverdi's late arioso style of utter simplicity, which is used when Drusilla admits that in her soul love and innocence are struggling fiercely with each other. Whenever the discourse proceeds with a rapid alternation of the speakers, the dialogues can use the medium of the recitative without encountering complicated problems of organization, and in such passages Monteverdi establishes the logical continuity of the phrases without forcing them into any predetermined structure. Such dialogues use the *stile recitativo* when the affection is the direct result of the specific dramatic situation, and the arioso melody when the affection is more general and not closely linked with a tragic moment. It is in such subtle procedures that Monteverdi reveals himself as a genius who weighs one form against another in such a way as to make the dramatic development serve the logical process of the music.

The duets proper, which are considerably less frequent than the dialogue in either arioso or recitative, follow closely the structural ideas which arose within the madrigalesque style, and would not be out of place in the seventh and eighth books of madrigals. In respect to these structures Monteverdi became the teacher for more than one generation of musicians. They were repeated and imitated so many times that in later periods they often verged on the commonplace, especially when handled by those who were incapable of unifying the affection and the structure.

It is interesting to note that most of the structures adopted by Monteverdi's contemporaries and successors were related to repetitive arrangements of the bass, for the late music drama, like the madrigals, demonstrates that the bass is the all-powerful element in baroque music. In innumerable passages of arias and recitatives, in solos and dialogues, in instrumental sinfonie and ritornelli, in fact in every single composition of the music drama, the bass plays its decisive role, operating with stereotyped material in two principal forms. One of these has only harmonic tones with which the bass at once circumscribes, or fixes, the harmonic design for the whole passage. Such a bass is not melodious, though it has the full length of a melody. This bass "motif" may be repeated unchanged, if the harmonic scheme is to remain the same, or transposed, if harmonic variations are intended; or merely its rhythmic pattern may be repeated, or any other variation imposed on it; repetition is, at all events, not an indispensable feature of this bass motif. The other form is an offspring of the *stile concertato*, in which the bass is as active and lively in motion as the upper parts but equally stereotyped, for it consists mainly of figurative material. It lends itself to a contrapuntal relationship to the other parts, and the short imitations between the bass and upper parts often achieve the intricacies of contrapuntal writing. Both these forms of the bass may underlie the structures of arias or duets or dialogues. The duets, however, impose a further strictness upon the bass by adding a repetition that is in the nature not only of the strophic aria but of the more rigid type of the *basso ostinato*. Strophic repetition is found in the only trio of the *Incoronazione*, *Questa vita è dolce troppo,* sung by the "Famigliari," the servants of Seneca, while in the preceding *Non morir, Seneca,* an *ostinato*-like repetition of a chromatically rising motif is used.

The role that the strict types of repetitive bass structures are to play in the duets of the drama is anticipated in the duet of Fortuna and Virtù in the prologue: *Human non è, non è celeste core.* The bass here proceeds in equal tones (half notes) and in diatonic descent through the whole octave: g-G. This motif is repeated as an *ostinato,* but each repetition lowers the descending scale by a tone: g-G; f-F♯; e-E; d-G. The fourth repetition, incomplete, has an additional, different ending. It is also of structural interest that the lowering of the scale passes through the range of a fourth: g, f♯, e, d. This is exactly the motif of the *basso ostinato* for the finale: the duet of Poppea and Nerone after the coronation. *Human non è* has the duet in strict canon during the first two repetitions of the bass; during the last two, however, the two upper voices are more loosely linked by free imitation and parallelism. The melodic style follows closely the figurative *concertato*, which is particularly appropriate because of the mention of the rivalry with the powers of Amor, and the restless duet contrasts sharply with the calm, even persistent bass.

The duet between Nerone and his companion Lucano has a structure of equal importance and, since it occupies a full scene (II, 6), of particular complexity. Sectionally organized and stylistically differentiated, the scene with all its variety resembles a cantata and belongs with Monteverdi's last madrigals. The text, which is lyrically descriptive of Poppea's feminine charms, is complete in itself, since it plays no part in the dramatic development, and the scene would have the character of an intermezzo, were it not for a highly dramatic, repeated exclamation, drawn out and emphatic, Nero's "Ahi, Ahi destin." With characteristic ingenuity, Monteverdi used this exclamation to relate this scene to the drama as a whole, and by an extraordinary device he conveys this link in purely musical terms. The profoundly intellectual disposition of Monteverdi's art is revealed in this scene, whose music we are familiar with in all its details from his madrigals. He has made the scene dramatic by eliminating the large banquet scene which would tend to give the section the character of an intermezzo.

The scene is divided into four parts, the third of which, "Idolo mio cebrarti io vorrei," is a short recitative by Nero that is followed by his ritornello aria *Son rubin amorosi*, both ritornello and aria having similar basses. The first two sections of the scene are given over to a duet, whose elaborate concerted style and figurative ornamentation require a good deal of vocal virtuosity. Words such as "cantiamo amorose canzoni," "ridente," and "glorie" have here called forth a florid style modeled on the madrigal. Structurally the section is handled as a free refrain, with a musical recurrence of the bass and the florid upper parts on "cantiamo." The second section, though directly connected with the first, is set off by a new rhythmic meter. Lucano gives an extended aria in praise of feminine charms, while Nero, with Poppea and his love (that is, his destiny) in mind, interjects his passionate exclamation, "Ahi destin." This whole dramatic duet aria is based on a *basso ostinato* which makes a diatonic descent through a fourth: g, f♯, e, d, in long, even, rhythmic values. In the prologue, Fortuna and Virtù declared Amor the victor—Amor the lord over man's fate—and that theme finds musical expression in both the form and its symbolic connotations.

Here at the close Poppea is the incarnation of love, and love Nero's destiny; the theme again finds the same musical expression, with the same symbolism of affection in the musical structure; the last duet links the end to the beginning.

There is yet another type of duet form, whose organization depends on the bass, but in a different manner. This is a free *ostinato* structure whose motif forms itself in the course of the composition and is repeated in the customary *ostinato* fashion; at the same time there takes place a concentration of affection. This type occurs in the meeting of Poppea and Nero shortly before the coronation (III, 5). Both are jubilant that the day has finally come on which their new life begins. After a long dialogue in *stile recitativo* as well as aria form, the two join in the duet, joyfully singing that no further delay will interfere with their desires. Together with an increase of affection, with the statement in the text that one has stolen the heart from the other, musically the bass congeals, as it were, into a motif and moves on as a *basso ostinato*. The motif is not the "symbol of love," but has a certain resemblance because of the passage through a fourth (e, f♯, g♯, a/a, g, f, e); it recurs as an *ostinato* in the second part of the duet, again with a renewed concentration of affection, and from then on to the end of the scene, there is a gradual growth of intensity in the expression of mutual love —"I shall be lost in thee"—and a second *ostinato* is formed, repeating the same octave in descent (a-A). The diatonic descent through the octave and the fourth are the bass motifs which Monteverdi prefers for *ostinato* structures and are always symbolic of affections at their height.

The last duet of Poppea and Nero, *Pur ti miro, pur ti godo,* is an ecstatic outburst of love heightened by the fulfillment of all aspiration. It has often been praised for its exemplary structure, tonal beauty, and sweeping affection.[7] If this is the last composition Monteverdi wrote, it is a noble ending to his noble efforts and sets the pattern for operatic compositions of the whole baroque era, so that its full importance can only be felt in the arias of operas after Monteverdi's death. The structure of the duet is that of a fully developed *da capo* aria (*ab:ba*). The roots of its form lie in the duet of Fortuna and Virtù in the prologue. In view of this intimate relationship, one can assume that Monteverdi composed the prologue after the drama had been completed—a pro-

---

[7] There is no need to mention all the quotations of this duet in the secondary literature Special attention may, however, be called to the essay of Egon Wellecz, who discusses the significance of the *basso ostinato;* see his "Cavalli und der Stil der venetianischen Oper," in *StzMW*, I (1913), 40ff.

cedure in keeping with the habits of the time. The duet in the prologue does not have the *da capo* structure, but the form of the first part of *Pur ti miro, pur ti godo*, whose two sections are repeated in reversed order, is structurally identical with the duet *Human non è*. The *ostinato* motif is the basis of the structure; and the motif of the *ostinato* in the finale is the symbolic theme g, f♯, e, d. The *ostinato* underlies the first section (*a*), but a new bass formula is used for the second section (*b*). Thus, the finale is expanded beyond the concentrated form of the prologue, though the organization of the upper voices is often the same. Similarly, in the finale the canon links the upper parts together, and is also extended into the second section. The strictness of structure seems again to coincide with the highest form of affection, as though an outburst of such proportions demanded the artistic control of the greatest discipline. At the same time, the flow of melody is restrained by an unerring sense of symmetrical balance. The voices in the duet move within so close a range that the phrase of one voice seems to be the logical and commensurate response to the phrase of the other—a style Monteverdi had studiously refined in his madrigalesque duets. The melody has an almost intoxicating sensuousness and euphony that was the consequence of Monteverdi's growing simplicity and directness. This unity between a vital sensuousness and the rational control of carefully balanced symmetries in the melody, between climactic affection and a disciplined structure, has a classic perfection only achieved when an artist has analyzed his medium and discovered by experience, by learning, or by inborn wisdom, the secret essence of his art. Monteverdi's last work, the *Incoronazione di Poppea*, is a classic achievement of complete equilibrium of all the forces active in an artistic form. In this last work Monteverdi attained the perfection he had been striving for from the beginning, in which art fulfills its nature, and form and expression are one.

With the *Incoronazione di Poppea* Monteverdi's work was finished, and his life, too, was near its end. He was almost seventy-six, and these last years had been most fruitful. The *Madrigali Guerrieri*, the *Selva Morale*, four music dramas, and several additional compositions that appeared after his death were composed within four or five years, and the composer felt his age and the strain of his efforts. Early in 1643 Monteverdi submitted a request for leave to the procurators of St. Mark's. He wanted to visit once again the scenes of his youth, of his first successes, of his rise to fame. Though frail and declining, he set out on his journey to Cremona and Mantua. He became a witness to his own renown and the deep admiration felt by lovers of his art. Many receptions were held in his honor as tokens of devotion, too many, in fact, for a man of his age. His strength began to fail, and he felt that the end was near. "Like a swan that, feeling the fatal hour near, approaches the water and, in it, a 'Musico gentile,' passes on to another life singing, with suaver harmony than ever, the sweeter tones, so Claudio in great haste returned—to Venice, the Queen of all waters." [8] Upon his arrival in Venice, Monteverdi fell ill, and a few days later died on November 29, 1643. By order of the procurators, the most solemn funeral service was performed at St. Mark's as a tribute of the state of Venice. Giovanni Rovetta, Monteverdi's pupil and successor, conducted the music, and all Venice attended, mourning. Monteverdi was buried in the Cappella di S. Ambrogio of the church of S. Maria dei Frari. A few days later the Venetians again gathered in the church of S. Maria dei Frari to honor again the great musician with a commemoration which Matteo Caberloti has described in *Laconismo delle alte qualità di Claudio Monteverde*. "With truly royal pomp a catafalque was erected in the Chiesa de Padri Minori de Frari, surrounded by so many candles that the church looked like a night sky luminous with stars." All the singers of Venice took part. Monteverdi's old friend and companion from the days of Mantua, Giovanni Battista Marinoni, now maestro di cappella at the cathedral of Padua, was in charge of the solemn music.

The fame of Monteverdi was unsurpassed. When he was called the "most celebrated composer of the century," or "the greatest musician of Europe," such praise was not mere politeness or flattery in the language of the day; it was an acknowledgment of reality. Upon receiving the news of Monteverdi's death, the ambassadors at Venice hastened to inform their home governments. Even compositions were named after him. He could not have asked for greater success, for greater admiration and approval of his work.

When a few months after Monteverdi's death Marinoni published the *Fiori Poetici Raccolti nel Funerale del Molto Illustre, E Molto Reverendo Signor Claudio Monteverde* (1644), he paid tribute in the manner of the time. Some fifty poems and a necrology by Caberloti were dedicated to the sovereign in the realm of music, of which he

---

[8] Matteo Caberloti, *Laconismo delle alte qualità di Claudio Monteverde* (in Marinoni, *Fiori Poetici*, 1644), p. 11. We have no doubt that the "Musico gentile," with reference to the swan and thereby to Monteverdi, is actually a citation of Tasso, *Gerusalemme Liberata*, XVI, 42, "Qual musico gentil."

knew all, the natural, the human, and the artistic: "La Musica reggava Claudio in Terra, Naturale, et humana, L'artificiale ancor, che non è strana." Although the effusion of such eulogies was the custom of the time, most of these poems, in spite of their poetical mediocrity, testified to Monteverdi's effect on his contemporaries and to his greatness, to the human aspects of his work. When they praised the eminence of his art, they spoke of the human affections and of the incredible power of his music over men's minds and emotions. From the *Orfeo* on, Monteverdi's music, with its human qualities, had exercised the most powerful influence on the feelings of his audience; his listeners were unanimous as to this. Johann Albert Bannius, a friend of Descartes', a thorough connoisseur and a most intelligent student of Monteverdi's music, wrote William Boswell that the Italian madrigals and French airs de cour deserve little praise since they merely attempt to realize the indispensable relationship between word and tone. In this respect the French are even a bit better than the Italians, but though this music may be delightful, it does not move the human soul. Monteverdi alone is capable of speaking in musical terms of pathos; only his music has the "zinroerende kracht" (the power to move the human mind).[9] Music must be expressive of affections and must move the affections of man—that is the force which Monteverdi's contemporaries felt in all the elements of his composition. A rather singular poem concludes the *Fiori Poetici*. It is a *Sonetto Musicale*, by Padre Maestro Paolo Piazza, in which he relates the rhythmic values to the specific individual affections which he lists, and speaks of affections in the "counterpoint of human actions" (*Il contrapunto delle humane attioni*). Monteverdi himself had taught that musical rhythm is bound up with human affections.

Caberloti brought the eulogy of his *Laconismo* to its climax when he praised Monteverdi as the molder of affections which are the essence of all his music. "Claudio alone possessed the total comprehension of the affections; at his will he engendered the affectionate dispositions in the human minds and moved the senses to that climactic delight which he conveyed to them," especially in his dramatic music, where "the affections varied from moment to moment." Thus Monteverdi enslaved man to the human dispositions of his music; he guided his listener through the labyrinth of affections and in so doing unfolded human nature. The experience of his music is an experience of humanity.

Caberloti gave Monteverdi's music this distinction on the basis of a

---

[9] See W. J. A. Jonckbloet and J. P. N. Land, *Correspondance et oeuvre musicales de Const. Huygens* (Leyde, 1882), pp. LXIIIf., CXXVIIIff.

comparison of the affections of his compositions with those of Greek music, as they were related to the Dorian, Phrygian, Aeolian, and Lydian harmonies. Whether he was right or wrong about Greek music and this particular ancient doctrine, he is comparing Monteverdi's music with the general effects of Greek music rather than with its particular forms, and finds that Monteverdi has become the equal of the ancients; the power of music over man has been reborn in him. When Monteverdi introduced a new style for an affection he felt he had neglected, he himself believed that he had discovered a new power in the wealth of antiquity and that he had become the equal of the Greek musicians. Caberloti even thought Monteverdi surpassed them, for never had the human affections been expressed so comprehensively in the work of one artist.

It was the conquest of human affections that gave Monteverdi his triumph over antiquity. In his embodiment of human passions, he is the prophet of modern music. He created forms that musicianship has cultivated ever since, and laid the foundation of the principal concepts of melody, harmony, style, and structure. He made his artistic work the medium of a message concerning man and human nature in which the work of art is inseparable from human existence. Monteverdi created his work on the foundation of the basic truths of human nature. He was the "Oracolo della Musica."

BIBLIOGRAPHY

THIS BIBLIOGRAPHY is selective; it has been limited strictly to the literature on Monteverdi. All general histories of music and monographs on subjects of the music of the sixteenth and seventeenth centuries have been omitted even if they contain chapters on, or special references to, Monteverdi. There are enough satisfactory and comprehensive bibliographies on baroque music available. Two admirable works, however, have been listed for the benefit of the reader: that of Carl von Winterfeld, and the new standard history of the madrigal by Alfred Einstein. None of the small, but rather general, articles which appeared in newspapers have been included here; they are particularly numerous whenever works of Monteverdi, such as his operas, were revived in modern performances. In view of the enormous vastness, the literature of general culture, on subjects of literature, poetry, art, artistic theories, philosophy, religion, etc., though used, had to be omitted completely; even Molmenti's classic study on private life in Venice could not be listed. For any selection from that vast literature would have been questionable, no matter how carefully selective the list might have been.

ADEMOLLO, ALESSANDRO. *La bell' Adriana ed altre virtuose del suo tempo alla corte di Mantova* (Città di Castello, 1888).
———. "I Basile alla corte di Mantova [1603–1628]," *Giornale Ligustico,* XI (Genoa, 1885).
Anonymous. "Preziose scoperte di autografi di Claudio Monteverdi," *La Bibliofilia,* Vol. 38 (Florence, 1937), pp. 69–70.
Arkwright, G. E. P. "An English Pupil of Monteverdi," *The Musical Antiquary,* IV (1912–1913), 236–257.
Artusi, G. M. *L'Artusi ovvero delle imperfettioni della moderna musica* (Venice, 1600 [?]; 2nd edition, 1603).
[Artusi, Giovanni Maria]. *Discorso secondo mvsicale di Antonio Braccino da Todi. Per la Dichiaratione della lettera porta ne' Scherzi musicali del Sig. Claudio Monteverde* (Venice, G. Vincenti, 1608). *Collezione di trattati e musiche antiche edite in fac-simile. Bollettino bibliografico musicale* (Milan, 1934).

BENVENUTI, GIACOMO. "Il manoscritto della' Incoronazione di Poppea," *RMI,* Vol. 41 (1937), pp. 176–184.
———. " 'Il Ritorno d'Ulisse in Patria' non è di Monteverdi," *Il Gazzettino* (Venice, May 17, 1942).
Bertolotti, A. *Musici alla Corte dei Gonzaga in Mantova dal secolo XV al XVIII* (Milan, 1891).
Borren, Charles van den. *Messa a 4,* edited by A. Tirabassi (Brussels, 1914), Preface.

Borren, Charles van den. " 'Il ritorno d'Ulisse in Patria' de Claudio Monteverdi," *Extrait de la Revue de l'Université de Bruxelles*, No. 3 (Brussels, 1925).

CAFFI, FRANCESCO. *Storia della musica sacra nella già cappella ducale di San Marco in Venezia dal 1318 al 1797*, 2 vols. (Venice, 1858).

Canal, Pietro. "Della Musica in Mantova," *Memorie del R. Instituto Veneto di Scienze, Lettere ed Arti* (Venice, 1858).

———. *Della musica in Mantova, notizie tratte principalmente dall' archivio Gonzaga* (Venice, 1881).

Carse, Adam. "Monteverde and the Orchestra," *The Sackbut*, Vol. 2, No. 1 (London, 1921), pp. 12–17.

Castéra, R. de. "L'Orfeo de Monteverdi," *Guide musical*, Vol. 50, No. 13 (Brussels, 1904), pp. 286–288.

Cesari, Gaetano. "Die Entwicklung der Monteverdischen Kammermusik," *III. Kongress der IMG, Haydn—Zentenarfeier* (Leipzig-Vienna, 1909), pp. 152–156.

———. "L' 'Orfeo' di Claudio Monteverdi all' 'Associazione di Amici della Musica' di Milano," *RMI*, XVII (1910), 132–178.

Cimbro, Attilio. "I Madrigali di Claudio Monteverdi," *Musica*, II (Florence, 1943), 3–34.

Collaer, Paul. "L'orchestra di Claudio Monteverdi," *Musica*, II (Florence, 1943), 86–104.

———. "La Représentation du *Corps et de l'Âme*, de Cavalieri—Le *Ballet des Ingrats*, de Monteverde," *Le Monde Musicale*, XLVII (Paris, 1936), 108–109.

Courville, Xavier de. "L'Ariane de Monteverdi," *RM*, An. 3, No. 1 (1921-22), pp. 23–37.

DALLAPICCOLA, LUIGI. "Per una rappresentazione de 'Il ritorno di Ulisse in patria' di Claudio Monteverdi," *Musica*, II (Florence, 1943), 121–136.

Damerini, Gino. "Venezia al tempo di Monteverdi," *Musica*, II (Florence, 1943), 105–120.

Davari, Stefano. "La Musica a Mantova. Notizie biografiche di maestri di musica, cantori e suonatori presso la Corte di Mantova nei secoli XV, XVI, XVII, tratte dai documenti dell' Archivio storico Gonzaga," *Estratto della Rivista Storica Mantovana*, Vol. I, Fasc. 1–2 (Mantua, 1884).

———. *Notizie biografiche del distinto maestro di musica Claudio Monteverdi* (Mantua, 1884).

Dufflocq, Enrico Magné. "L'Orfeo di Claudio Monteverdi. Commento di Enrico Magné Dufflocq," *Edizioni sonore Musiche Italiane Antiche*. [Contains also reprint of the libretto].

EINSTEIN, ALFRED. *The Italian Madrigal*, translated by Alexander H. Krappe, Roger H. Sessions, and Oliver Strunk; 3 vols. (Princeton, Princeton University Press, 1949).

Epstein, Peter. "Zur Rhythmisierung eines Ritornells von Monteverdi," *AfMW*, VIII (1926), 416–419.

———. "Monteverdi in unserer Zeit," *Die Musik*, XXII (Berlin, 1929-30), 86–88.

FERRARI, PAOLO EMILIO. *Spettacoli drammatico-musicali e coreografici in Parma dall'anno 1628 all' anno 1883* (Parma, 1884).

Fischer, Rudolf von. "Claudio Monteverdi," *Neues Musikblatt*, Vol. XVI, No. 32, pp. 7–9.

GALVANI, LIVIO NISO. (*See* Salvioli, Giovanni.)

GOLDSCHMIDT, HUGO. *Studien zur Geschichte der italienischen Oper*, 2 vols. (Leipzig, 1901–4).

———. "Monteverdi's Ritorno d'Ulisse," *SIMG*, IV (1902–3), 671–676.

———. "Claudio Monteverdi's Oper: Il ritorno d'Ulisse in patria," *SIMG*, IX (1907–8), 570–592.

HAAS, ROBERT. "Zur Neuausgabe von Claudio Monteverdis 'Il Ritorno d'Ulisse in Patria,'" *StzMW*, IX (Vienna, 1922), 3–42.

Heuss, Alfred. "Die Instrumental-Stücke des 'Orfeo,'" *SIMG*, IV (1902–3), 175–224.

———. "Ein Beitrag zu dem Thema: Monteverdi als Charakteristiker in seinen Madrigalen," *Festschrift zum 90. Geburtstage Sr. Excellenz des Wirklichen Geheimen Rates Rochus Freiherrn von Liliencron überreicht von Vertretern deutscher Musikwissenschaft* (Leipzig, 1910), pp. 93–109.

Howes, Frank. "Notes on Monteverde's Orfeo," *Musical Times*, Vol. 65 (London, 1924), pp. 509–511.

Hughes, Charles W. "Porter, Pupil of Monteverdi," *MQ*, XX (New York, 1934), 278–288.

KINKELDEY, OTTO. "Luzzasco Luzzaschi's Solo-Madrigale mit Klavierbegleitung," *SIMG*, IX (1907–8), 538–565.

Kreidler, Walter. *Heinrich Schütz und der Stile Concitato von Claudio Monteverdi*, dissertation, University of Bern (Stuttgart, 1934).

Křenek, Ernst. "Meine Textbearbeitung von Monteverdis 'Poppea,'" *Anbruch*, XVIII (Vienna, 1936), 106–108.

———. "Zur musikalischen Bearbeitung von Monteverdis 'Poppea,'" *Schweizerische Musikzeitung*, LXXVI (Zurich, 1936), 545–555.

———. "Zur dramaturgischen Bearbeitung von Monteverdis 'Poppea,'" *23, eine Wiener Musikzeitschrift*, Nos. 31–33 (Vienna, 1937), pp. 22–30.

Kretzschmar, Hermann. "Die Venezianische Oper und die Werke Cavalli's und Cesti's," *VfMW*, VIII (1892), 1–76.

———. "Monteverdi's 'Incoronazione di Poppea,'" *VfMW*, X (1894), 483–530.

LALOY, LOUIS. "La musique. Un précurseur du drame lyrique: Claudio Monteverdi," *Revue de Paris*, An. 28, Vol. V (Paris, 1921), pp. 653–664.

Leichtentritt, Hugo. "Claudio Monteverdi als Madrigalkomponist," *SIMG*, XI (1909–10), 255–291.

Lupo, Bettina. "Sacre monodie Monteverdiane," *Musica*, II (Florence, 1943), 51–85.

MALIPIERO, G. FRANCESCO. "Claudio Monteverdi da Cremona," *RaM*, II (1929), 453–458.

MALIPIERO, G. FRANCESCO. *Claudio Monteverdi* (Milan, 1930).

——. "Claudio Monteverdi da Cremona," *Illustrazione* (1937).

——. "Claudio Monteverdi," *Musica*, II (Florence, 1943), 1–3.

Marinoni, Giovanni Battista. *Fiori poetici raccolti nel funerale del' signor Clavdio Monteverde maestro di cappella della ducale di S. Marco. Consecrati da d. Gio: Battista Marinoni, detto Gioue . . . all' illvstrssimi [sic] & ecceilentissimi [sic]sig. procvratori di chiesa di S. Marco* (Venice, 1644).

Mitjana, Rafaelo C. *Claudio Monteverdi y los origines de la ópera italiana* (Málaga, 1911).

——. "Claudio Monteverde och det lyriska dramats uppkomst," *Ord och Bild*, Vol. 20 (Stockholm, 1911), 337–351.

Müller, Karl Friedrich. *Die Technik der Ausdrucksdarstellung in Monteverdis monodischen Frühwerken*, dissertation, University of Berlin (Berlin [1931 ?]).

ORTOLANI, GIUSEPPE. "Venezia al tempo di Monteverdi," *RaM*, II (1929), 469–482.

PANNAIN, GUIDO. "Claudio Monteverdi nell'opera in musica," *Musica*, II (Florence, 1943), 35–50.

Paoli, Domenico de. "Claudio Monteverdi," *Bollettino bibliografico musicale*, An. 4, No. 2 (Milan, 1929), pp. 1–16.

——. " 'Orfeo' and 'Pelléas,' " *ML*, XX (1939), 381–398.

——. "A few remarks on 'Orfeo' by Claudio Monteverdi," *The Chesterian*, Vol. XX, No. 143 (1939), pp. 61–67.

——. *Claudio Monteverdi*, con 12 illustrazioni fuori testo e 3 ariette inedite (Milan, 1945).

Parry, Sir C. Hubert H. "The significance of Monteverde," *PMA*, Session 42 (London, 1916), pp. 51–67.

Pereyra, M. L. *Explication de la lettre qui est imprimée dans le cinquième livre de Madrigaux de Monteverdi* (Paris [Schola Cantorum], 1911).

Picenardi, Guido Sommi. "D'alcuni documenti concernenti Claudio Monteverde," *Archivio Storico Lombardo*, Serie terza, Vol. IV, Anno XXII (Milan, 1895), pp. 154–162.

——. *Claudio Monteverdi a Cremona* (Milan, 1895).

Prunières, Henry. Review of L. Schneider, "Cl. Monteverdi," *RM*, Vol. II, No. 4 (February, 1921), pp. 178–179.

——. "Monteverdi and French Music," *The Sackbut*, Vol. III, No. 4 (November, 1922), pp. 98–110.

——. "L'Orfeo de Monteverdi," *RM*, IV (August, 1923), 20–34.

——. *La vie e l'oeuvre de C. Monteverdi* (Paris, 1924 [1931]; English translation, London and New York, 1926).

——. "Monteverdi à la chapelle de Saint-Marc," *RM*, VII (1926), 260–278.

——. "Monteverdi e la Musica francese del suo tempo," *RaM*, II (1929), 483–493.

Pulver, Jeffrey. "Claudio Monteverdi," *The Strad,* Vol. 25, No. 297 (1915), p. 297; Vol. 26, No. 309 (1916), p. 271.

REDLICH, HANS FERDINAND. "Monteverdi-Gesamtausgabe," *Anbruch,* Vol. X, No. 6 (1928), pp. 207–211.

———. *Claudio Monteverdi. Ein formgeschichtlicher Versuch. Band I: Das Madrigalwerk,* dissertation, University of Frankfurt, 1931 (Berlin, 1932).

———. "Sull' edizione moderna delle opere di Claudio Monteverdi," *RaM,* VIII (1935), 23–41.

———. "Monteverdi-Renaissance," *Atlantis,* VIII (Leipzig, 1936), 768.

———. "Zur Bearbeitung von Monteverdis 'Orfeo,'" *Schweizerische Musikzeitung,* LXXVI (Zurich, 1936), 37–42, 74–80.

———. "Das Orchester Claudio Monteverdi's. I. Instrumentalpraxis in Monteverdis Madrigalwerk," *Musica Viva,* I (Brussels, London, Rome, 1936), 55–64.

———. "Monteverdis 'Incoronazione di Poppea,'" *Schweizerische Musikzeitung,* Vol. 77, No. 23 (December, 1937), pp. 617–626.

———. "Notationsprobleme in Claudio Monteverdis 'Incoronazione di Poppea,'" *AM,* X (1938), 129–132.

———. "Monteverdi's Religious Music," *ML,* XXVII (1946), 208–215.

———. *Claudio Monteverdi. Leben und Werk. Musikerreihe.* In auserlesenen Einzeldarstellungen herausgegeben von Paul Schaller Basel. Band VI. Olten (Switzerland, 1949).

Riemann, Hugo. "Eine siebensätzige Tanzsuite von Monteverdi v. J. 1607," *SIMG,* XIV (1912–13), 26–33.

Ronga, Luigi. "Tasso e Monteverdi," *Poesia,* Vol. I (Rome, 1945).

Ruthers, Herman. "Oud italiaansche opera's," *Caecilia en De Muziek,* XCIII (X), (Bussum, 1936), 300–305.

[SALVIOLI, GIOVANNI.] *I teatri musicali di Venezia nel secolo XVII (1637–1700). Memorie storiche e bibliografiche raccolte ed ordinate da Livio Niso Galvani* (Milan [1878]).

Schmitz, Eugen. "Zur Geschichte des italienischen Continuo-Madrigals im 17. Jahrhundert," *SIMG* (1909–10), pp. 509–528.

Schneider, Louis. *Un précurseur de la musique italienne aux XVIe et XVIIe siècles. Claudio Monteverdi. L'Homme et son temps. Le Musicien* (Paris, 1921).

Schwartz, Rudolf. "Zu den Texten der ersten fünf Bücher der Madrigale Monteverdis," *Festschrift* (Leipzig, 1918), pp. 147–148.

Solerti, Angelo. *Le origini del melodramma* (Turin, 1903).

———. "Un balletto musicato da Claudio Monteverde sconosciuto a' suoi biografi," *RMI,* VII (1904), 24–34.

———. *Gli albori del melodramma,* 3 vols. (Milan, 1905).

Striggio, Alessandro. *L'Orfeo di Monteverdi* (Bologna, 1928). [Reprint of the libretto.]

Stuart, Robert Louis. "Busenello's L'Incoronazione di Poppea," *Musical Opinion,* Vol. 51, pp. 379–380.

TESSIER, ANDRÉ. "Les deux styles de Monteverde," *RM*, An. 3, No. 8 (June, 1922), pp. 223–254.

———. "Monteverdi e la filosofia dell'arte," *RaM*, II (1929), 459–468.

Tiby, Ottavio. "L'Incoronazione di Poppea di Claudio Monteverdi e Gian Francesco Busenello," *Maggio Musicale Fiorentine: 27 aprile–9 giugno 1937—XV* (Florence, 1937).

———. *Claudio Monteverdi. Collezione I Maestri della Musica*, No. 30 (Turin, 1944 [?]).

Tiersot, J. "L'Orfeo de Monteverde," *Le Ménestrel*, Vol. 70, No. 10 (Paris, 1904), pp. 75–77.

VOGEL, EMIL. "Claudio Monteverdi," *VfMW*, III (1887), 315–450.

WESTRUP, JACK ALLAN. "Monteverde's Orfeo," *Musical Times*, Vol. 66 (1925), pp. 1096–1100.

———. "Monteverde's 'Il ritorno d'Ulisse in patria,'" *Monthly musical record*, Vol. 58 (1928), pp. 106–107.

———. "The originality of Monteverde," *PMA*, Session 60 (1934), pp. 1–25.

———. "Monteverdi and the Orchestra," *ML*, XXI (1940), 230–245.

———. "Monteverdi's 'Lamento d'Arianna,'" *The Music Review*, I (1940), 144–154.

Winterfeld, Carl von. *Johannes Gabrieli und sein Zeitalter*, 2 vols. (Berlin, 1834).

EDITIONS

ONLY CRITICAL, historical editions have been listed. All arrangements of separate compositions or complete works such as the operas, i.e., the editions by Vincent d'Indy, Křenek, Redlich, Westrup, and others have been omitted since each would require more or less elaborate comments.

L'incoronazione di Poppea, facsimile del manoscritto It. Cl. 4. N. 439 della Biblioteca nazionale di S. Marco in Venezia. Introduzione di Giacomo Benvenuti. Milan (Fratelli Bocca), 1938.

L'Orfeo, favola pastorale in un prologo e cinque atti di Alessandro Striggio figlio. Realizzazione della partitura del 1609 e riduzione per canto e pianoforte a cura di Giacomo Benvenuti. I Classici musicali italiani, Vol. 9, Milan, 1942.

Messa a 4. Selva morale, 1641. Ed., A. Tirabassi. Preface by Charles van den Borren. Brussels, 1914.

[L'incoronazione di Poppea] Berceuse d'Arnalta, air inédit de l'Incoronazione di Poppea (1642), (Acte II, sc. 12) de Claudio Monteverdi. Réalisation de la bass continue et traduction de Ch. van den Borren, *RM*, An. 3, No. 9, Suppl. musical, July 1, 1922.

Salmo, per sei voci, coro, organo ed orchestra. Elaborazione di Alfredo Casella, Musiche vocali e strumentali, rari e profane sec. XVII, XVIII, a cura di Bonaventura Somma, fasc. VI, Rome, 1943.

La musica in Cremona nella seconda metà del secolo XVI e i primordi dell'arte monteverdiana: Madrigali a 4 e a 5 voci di M. A. Ingegneri, Sacrae cantiunculae e Canzonette di C. Monteverdi, a cura di Gaetano Cesari. Con prefazione di Guido Pannain su appunti di G. Cesari, Istituzioni e monumenti dell'arte musicale italiano, Vol. VI, Milan, 1939.

L'Orfeo, favola in musica da Claudio Monteverdi; Die Oper von ihren ersten Anfängen bis zur Mitte des 18. Jahrhunderts, I, 121–229; Publikationen aelterer praktischer und theoretischer Musikwerke, hsg. von der Gesellschaft für Musikforschung (Robert Eitner), 1910.

L'incoronazione di Poppea; Hugo Goldschmidt, Studien zur Geschichte der italienischen Oper im 17. Jahrhundert, Leipzig, 1901–1904, Vol. II.

Il ritorno d'Ulisse in patria. Die Heimkehr ᵈes Odysseus. Mit deutscher Übersetzung und ausgesetztem basso continuo bearbeitet von Robert Haas, Denkmäler der Tonkunst in Österreich, XXIX. Jahrgang, Vol. 57, Vienna, 1922.

Tutte le opere di Claudio Monteverdi . . . nuovamente date in luce de G. Francesco Malipiero, 16 vols. in 17. Asolo, 1926–1942.

Monteverdis Orfeo, Faksimile des Erstdrucks der Musik, eingeleitet und herausgegeben von Adolf Sandberger, Augsburg, 1927.

Torchi, Luigi. L'arte musicale in Italia; Vol. 4, 39–72: Cruda Amarilli, O Mirtillo, Sonata sopra 'Sancta Maria'; Vol. 6, 197–239; Il ballo delle ingrate; Vol. 6, 135–195: Il combattimento di Tancredi e Clorinda.

INDEX

CITY COLLEGE LIBRARY
1825 MAY ST.
BROWNSVILLE, TEXAS 78520

ML   Schrade
410   Monteverdi
.M77
S35
1979

LEARNING RESOURCE CENTER
1825 May St. Ft. Brown
Brownsville, Texas   78520

BROWNSVILLE PUBLIC
CAMERON COUNTY
PAN AMERICAN UNIVERSITY BROWNSVILLE
TEXAS SOUTHMOST COLLEGE